THE ADELPHI
PAST AND PRESENT
A History and a Guide

CH00434446

THE ADELPHI
PAST AND PRESENT
A History and a Guide

By

David G C Allan

To
Ronald Gerard OBE FRSA

Whose initial benefaction made possible
the publication of this book

and with thanks for generous
financial support to:

James Harrison FRSA
and
The Hon Simon Stuart

Copyright © David G C Allan 2001

ISBN 0 9541275 0 1

Published by
Calder Walker Associates
PO Box 60
London SW15 5WS

Designed by Louise Millar

Printed by The Basingstoke Press
Basingstoke, England

Cover illustrations:
Front: The Adelphi late Durham Yard by B Pastorini, 1771
Back: The Adelphi looking towards Westminster, 1791. From the engraving by Benjamin Green

Contents

Illustrations

MAPS

Acknowledgements

The invaluable assistance of Mrs Susan Bennett, former Curator of the Royal Society for the encouragement of Arts, Manufactures and Commerce, deserves pride of place in this list. The RSA's permission to reproduce items from its historic collections and archives is also gratefully acknowledged.

Thanks are also due to the staffs of the following institutions which have generously responded to recurrent visits and repeated requests: The Bishopsgate Institute, The Institute of Historical Research, The Green Room Club, The Guildhall Library, The Sir John Soane Museum, The Savage Club, The Society of Antiquaries, The Richmond and Twickenham Libraries, The Westminster Archive Centre and the Victoria & Albert Museum.

Various Adelphi residents and institutions have given helpful advice, notably Mr James Minter, Mr Edward Baldwin and Mr Thomas Carter of A H Baldwin & Sons Ltd, Mr Barry Mather of the Chartered Institute of Public Finance and Accounting, the late Pierre Corneille of the Green Room Club and Mr Bill Aldridge of the Little Adelphi.

Mr J P Bond, whose survey of the street directories is printed in the appendix, an amazing labour of love, has made helpful criticisms of the main text. He wants particularly to acknowledge the help given to him by Mrs Llinos Thomas and Ms Praha Shah in tracing street name changes. Mr Ron Sandford has kindly given permission for his drawing of John Adam Street to be reproduced. Mrs Corrie Lamberth's historical reconstructions and modern photography also deserve gratitude as does the encouragement and assistance given by numerous individuals notably Mrs James Barrie, Dr Simon Bradley, Dr Glen Cavaliero, Dr Heather Creaton, Miss Alison Kenny, Mr Edmund Keohane, Mr Peter Longley, Lady Joan Reid, Mr Brian Louis Pearce, Dr Ann Saunders, and Mr Graham Twemlow.

Finally, particular thanks are due to Alan Gordon Walker, publisher of the book and to Louise Millar, its designer.

The article from the 'Adelphi Idler' series, and its accompanying illustration, is reproduced by kind permission of the Editor of the *RSA Journal* and Mr Quentin Blake.

Introduction

The area between the Strand and the River Thames, bordered on the east by Shell-Mex House and the Savoy and on the west by Charing Cross Railway Station and Craven St, is rich in historical associations and surviving specimens of domestic and public architecture. In the Middle Ages the Bishops of Durham built a riverside palace which still gives its name to parts of the area. Many of the dramatic conflicts in Church and State during Tudor and Stuart times took place within its walls: as the names of such sometime residents as Catherine of Aragon, Thomas Wolsey, Lady Jane Grey and Sir Walter Raleigh, and its use by Spanish and French Ambassadors suggest.

The name 'Adelphi' was chosen by the Adam brothers to commemorate their development of the area and although their riverside terrace was demolished in 1936 amidst a national outcry much of the periphery of their estate remains, notably the Royal Society for the encouragement of Arts, Manufactures and Commerce (RSA) in John Adam St which is the earliest example of a purpose built headquarters for a learned society in the country. The former 'Lancet' building which with the adjacent sometime home of Sir Richard Arkwright is now called 'Adam House' has survived and is used as a centre for executive offices. The western side of Robert St where Robert Adam himself resided and where in modern times Kingsley Martin strove to maintain the literary character of the district once associated with Thomas Hardy, J M Barrie, Richard D'Oyly Carte and George Bernard Shaw is now maintained by the Chartered Institute of Public Finance and Accounting.

Within the walls of the RSA James Barry painted his masterpieces and the idea of the Great Exhibition was conceived. Charles Dickens who served on its Council had once worked in the hated blacking factory at Hungerford Stairs, and wandered in his misery through the Adelphi arches and vaults, where to this day the Green Room Club maintains 'Fagin's Kitchen'. He had also lodged in Buckingham St where Pepys had once lived and whose name recalls the great George Villiers, Lord High Admiral, as the surviving Watergate and many fine 17th century houses remind us. At 21 John Adam St (once 4 Duke St) the Business Exchange preserves a splendid Charles II interior.

Victorian ebullience led to the creation of the Embankment gardens and the building of the Hotel Cecil and the Savoy Hotel. The Cecil gave way to Shell-Mex House which inspired the development of the new Adelphi. Bomb damage in the Second World War is illustrated by Ronald Fuller's remarkable drawings preserved by the RSA.

The concluding section of the book describes the area as it is today with Hamp's great office building embellished, the 17th and 18th century buildings restored and some post-modern structures, notably Heron House on the north-west corner of Adam Street, built in sympathy with their scale. John P Bond has supplied an introduction to go with his survey of the street directories, as well as some invaluable notes. An examination of the names and addresses – with their rich variety of occupations, which he has extracted from the early directories, will make an interesting accompaniment to the walk outlined at the end of Chapter 12.

CHAPTER ONE

A Note on the Topographical Setting

Flowing down stream from Brentford to Wandsworth the river Thames begins a northward course to Westminster and Whitehall. It then curves quite sharply into a long easterly stretch which takes it to London Bridge and the Tower. It is at this curve and on the north bank that our area is centred and the river provides the key to its history. The walled city of Roman and post-Roman times defined the spot which would become, as William Fitzstephen called it in 1183, the 'seat of the monarchy of England' spreading 'its fame wider' sending 'its wealth further' and 'lifting its head higher than all the others'.[1] The height of the city is indeed literal and begins to rise steeply from the river bank in the area we are considering. Evelyn, writing in the Restoration period, noted that London 'is built upon a sweet and most agreeable Eminence of the Ground, at the north side of a goodly and well conducted river'.[2] As for its being the seat of the monarchy, this was not strictly the case since the sovereigns often resided in the Tower at the eastern edge of the City and it was on the westerly island of Thorney that Edward the Confessor built his Abbey and palace of Westminster, and in the course of the centuries this became a centre of the law and a place for the King's Great Council and Parliament to meet.

The acquisition of the adjoining palace of Whitehall by Henry VIII emphasised the political significance of these western approaches which both the River, and the bankside artery called 'The Strand', linked to the great wealth and commercial power of the city. The journey by water made use of numerous wharves and stairs, of which the Watergate at the bottom of Buckingham Street is a magnificent surviving example, but between Whitehall and Somerset House there were at least five other landing places. The Strand ended at the hamlet of Charing, the name being said to be derived from the old English word *cerran*, to turn. In 1290 Edward I put up the last of the twelve crosses which commemorated the resting places of his widow Queen Eleanor's funeral cortege, on its long journey from Nottinghamshire to Westminster. The rebel parliament had the cross pulled down in 1647 and, after the Restoration, the statue of King Charles I was erected on its site and stands there to this day. A replica of the Cross, put up in 1865, can be seen in the forecourt of Charing Cross station.

CHAPTER TWO
Medieval Splendour

The occupants of the See of Durham ranked second only to the Primate in the province of York and were held in high esteem by the Archbishop of Canterbury and the Popes themselves. As 'Counts Palatine' they wielded secular as well as ecclesiastical sway and like other great dignitaries of the Church, they played an important part in state affairs and found it convenient to build a house or 'Inn' on the banks of the Thames in London. As early as 1099 there is a record of Bishop Flambard, Lord Chancellor to William Rufus, being kidnapped from 'his house on the Thames'.[1] In 1238 when Bishop Le Poore died, Durham House was considered sufficiently fine to be lent to Cardinal Otto, the Papal Legate, and nine years later one hundred bishops and abbots assembled at its gate to join King Henry III when he came in procession from St Paul's Cathedral carrying the sacred blood of Our Saviour to be deposited in Westminster Abbey. In 1258 Bishop Kirkham allowed Simon de Montfort to stay in what was now called 'The Noble Pile' of Durham House and when during a storm on the Thames, King Henry's boatman wished to land their royal master at Durham steps, the King told the Earl he feared him more than thunder or lightning.[2]

The building or more probably the re-building at Durham House has been attributed to two later prelates: Anthony Beck (Bishop 1284-1311) and Thomas Hatfield (Bishop 1345-1381). From a grant made by Bishop Hatfield to some of his followers we learn that the House contained extensive gardens with walls, a gate house on the Strand side with houses for the Keeper and his servants, and a chapel with a 'vaulted chamber' below and a solar by the chapel entrance and a vestibule with two other chambers. On the east side of the Strand gateway was the hospicium where guests of the Bishop could be lodged. The great hall, used in the 15th century for trials at law and royal entertainments, was described at the end of the 16th century as 'stately and high, supported with lofty marble pillars. It standeth upon the Thames very pleasantly'.[3] A screen passage opening in the hall could be reached from the river through a waterside gallery which had a gate with steps leading down to the shore. The roof of the great hall was crenellated and it had five bays divided by buttresses each with large gothic windows. Its lofty interior has been compared to that of the royal castle at Winchester.

12

The chapel was in a similar architectural style and there were rectangular towers to the east and the west and a turret commanding views to both the City and Westminster. The landward approach was through a series of courts and gardens so that the overall effect would be similar to that of one of the great Oxford or Cambridge Colleges or the Archbishop of Canterbury's palace at Lambeth.[4]

1. Durham House in the 16th century. From a reconstruction by Corrie Lamberth based on the 1544 panorama by A. van den Wyngarde, the 1626 plan in the State Papers Domestic and Hollar's view (No.3)

Thomas Langley, Bishop from 1406 to 1437 had owed his preferment to Henry Bolingbroke. An executor of John of Gaunt his fortunes were identified with those of the House of Lancaster. He served as Lord Chancellor in 1406 when he opened Parliament with a text from Scripture which compared King Henry IV to Ahasuerus 'who asked advice from the wise': and it is no surprise to find that when Prince Henry – the future Henry V – came to London in 1412 he 'lay at the Bishop's inn of Durham'. The Bishop, who had been created a cardinal in 1409, also served as Chancellor to Henry V and Henry VI. His successor Robert Nevill, Bishop 1438-1457, was related to the Kingmaker. Lawrence Booth, who followed Nevill, was Chancellor to Queen Margaret.[5] The fifteenth century closes with the episcopate of Richard Fox (Bishop 1494-1501), Henry Tudor's indispensable minister and diplomat,[6] whose involvement in the King's complicated marriage negotiations on behalf of his sons and himself helped to bring about the crises in state relations which would dominate the succeeding century.

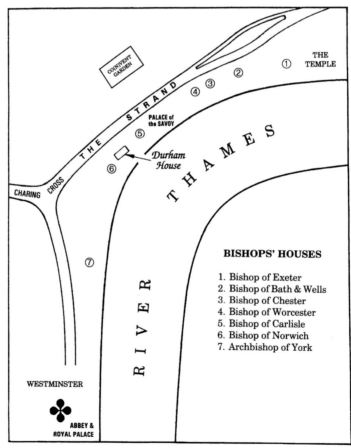

Map a) North bank of the Thames between Westminster and the City at the end of the Middle Ages.

CHAPTER THREE

Politics and Religion in the 16th and 17th Centuries

The Tudors

The event which more than anything presaged the great conflicts in church and state during Tudor and Stuart times was the coming to England of Princess Catherine of Aragon in 1501. She was married first to King Henry VII's eldest son Arthur but he died in April 1502, and the seventeen year old widow took up residence in Durham House, attended by a retinue of fifty Spaniards. Her late husband had been only fourteen and there was much private discussion as to whether she was still a virgin. One of her ladies at Durham House, Donna Elvira, seems to have known the truth, but none could be sure. It was a nagging doubt in this matter which would cause her second husband, the future Henry VIII, to divorce her after twenty four years of marriage and to separate the Church of England from Papal Suzerainty.

The chief actor in the opening stages of this drama was Cardinal Wolsey, Archbishop of York, Papal Legate and Lord Chancellor of England. His friend and supporter was Thomas Ruthall, Bishop of Durham since 1509 and Keeper of the Privy Seal since 1516. Wolsey often stayed with him at Durham House. Indeed in 1516 and 1517 during the completion of the work on his great palace later to be known as Whitehall he was a frequent visitor. On 24 March 1518, it was recorded that 'on Saturday last the King and my Lord Cardinal, with others of the Council, dined with my Lord of Durham'. The Bishop seems to have lived in surroundings of considerable magnificence. The walls of the Durham House were adorned with fine tapestries depicting scenes from classical mythology and history. There were also rich hangings, which, with the tapestries, were later acquired by the greedy Cardinal who, on the Bishop's death in 1523, not only purchased them from his executors, but obtained the See of Durham itself to hold *in commendam* with his many other preferments. Durham House was now his to use as his pleased.[1]

In 1525/6 the Cardinal accommodated the household of the King's six year old illegitimate son, Henry Fitzroy, Duke of Richmond and Somerset in Durham House. He moved in extra

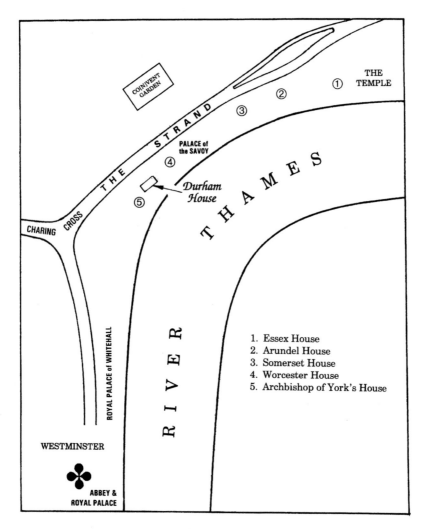

Map b) North bank of the Thames between Westminster and the City in the later 16th century.

furnishings from York Place (Whitehall) and Hampton Court in 1528, possibly to accommodate Sir Thomas Boleyn, father of the Lady Anne whose star was now in the ascendant. In May of that year Dr Edward Fox found Wolsey in bed at Durham House when he arrived late at night after travelling from Rome with a commission from the Pope to the judges in the King's divorce suit. In the summer of 1529 Cranmer stayed there as the Cardinal's guest so that he might have quietude to write his opinions 'concerning the King's question', that is to say on the legality of his marriage to Queen Catherine. By this time

Wolsey had resigned as Bishop of Durham and taken the even more valuable see of Winchester, though his supreme position in church and state was soon to be undone. The new Bishop, Cuthbert Tunstall, did not take office until March 1530. He continued to allow Anne Bolyen's father, now created Earl of Wiltshire, to live in Durham House, and in 1532 the future Queen was herself in residence In 1536 he was persuaded by Henry VIII to exchange the house for a rather smaller town residence in Thames Street. Thus Durham House began its first period of secular ownership which would last for twenty-seven years.[2]

King Henry, who moved his court from place to place with bewildering rapidity, often made use of Durham House for the entertainment of ambassadors and others. One of the most spectacular of these entertainments took place in May 1540 when the knights who had been taking part in a tournament at the Palace of Westminster rode to Durham House, where they 'feasted the King's Majesty, the Queen's Grace and her ladies with all the court' serving them 'delicious meats and drinks'. This Queen would have been Henry's fourth wife, Anne of Cleves, whose marriage was to be annulled some two months later. Prince Edward, son to King Henry by his third wife Jane Seymour, lived in Durham House in the latter part of the reign. Various royal retainers also occupied parts of the property, notably Nicholas Fortescue, 'groom porter of the King's household', who was granted 22 messuages and gardens between Durham House and Ivy Bridge Lane in 1544. King Henry, who died in 1547, had left Durham House to Princess Elizabeth, his daughter by his second wife Ann Boleyn, but the new young King Edward VI did not honour this bequest until 1550, by which time he had already established a royal mint in part of the palace.

In the same year, 1550, Durham House was made ready to receive the French Ambassador, being, as the contemporary account puts it, 'richly hanged' with tapestries and fine wall cloths, the cellars stocked with wine and 'in the court of the same, for a present from the King's Majesty, certain fat oxen, calves, sheep, lambs and all manner of wild fowl of every sort – and also all manner of fresh fish of the best that might be gotten'.[3] In 1551 the King's Privy Council met at Durham House. The dominant figure in the realm was now John Dudley, Earl of Warwick and Duke of Northumberland. Early in 1553 he took possession of Durham House, to the dislike of Princess Elizabeth. He used the house for a magnificent entertainment in May 1553 on the occasion of the marriages of his son, Lord Guildford Dudley to Lady Jane Grey, of Jane's sister to Lord Herbert, and of his daughter Catherine to the Earl of Huntingdon. On 6 July 1553 Lady Jane learnt that she had been bequeathed the Crown. She is said to have embarked by barge for the Tower of London from the steps of Durham House with an air of sadness and foreboding. Her reign ended some nine days later when Mary, daughter of Henry VIII and Catherine of Aragon, was acclaimed as Queen. Mary restored Durham House to Bishop Tunstall who had held steadfast in his faith in spite of imprisonment in 1551 and the imminent plunder of his diocese by the Earl of Northumberland. The Bishop allowed the Spanish Ambassador to use the house in January 1554 and later in that year King Philip himself was in residence.[4]

When Elizabeth came to the throne in 1558 Bishop Tunstall declined to take the Oath of Supremacy and was deprived of his see. Durham House was again at the disposal of the crown. The Spanish Ambassador lodged there from 1559 to 1563 and English catholics occasionally attended mass in his chapel. The House was still considered fit for royal entertainment. Queen Elizabeth supped there in July 1565 when Margaret Cave, daughter of Sir Ambrose Cave, Chancellor of the Duchy of Lancaster, married Henry Knollys, son of Sir Francis Knollys. From 1565 to 1579 Sir Henry Sidney, father of Philip, lived at Durham House. His brother-in-law was the Earl of Leicester, the Queen's favourite, and he entertained both Leicester and the Queen. Sir Walter Raleigh used the upper part of Durham House from 1584 to 1603 and his wife's cousin, Sir Edmund Darcy, occupied the downstairs rooms. The 17th century antiquary John Aubrey described Raleigh's study in Durham House: it 'was a little turret which looked into and over the Thames, and had [a] prospect which is pleasant perhaps as any in the world, and which not only refreshes the eyesight but cheers the spirits and (to speak my mind) I believe enlarges an ingenious Man's thoughts'.[5]

Christopher Marlowe seems to have been a welcome visitor to Durham House, in 1592/3 enjoying the company of Raleigh's free thinking circle. Dr John Dee, the mathematician and astrologer, noted in his diary for October 1595 that he 'dined with Sir Walter Raleigh at Durham House'. Raleigh had a household of twenty persons and kept twenty horses. In 1600 his wife described the damage caused by a fire which she blamed on 'my cousin Darcy's servant, a woman that dwelleth just under our lodgings, and annoyeth us infinitely'. These particular rooms faced the Strand and were not far from 'The Bishop's old stables' which Sir Robert Cecil, who was himself building a house in the Strand, wished to rebuild and possibly acquire together with a strip of the Bishop's garden. Cecil was by now concerned above all with the likely succession of the King of Scots and he looked on Raleigh as a dangerous rival and poisoned the ear of King James against him. Indeed it would be asserted after the Queen's death in 1603 that Sir Walter and his friend Sir Henry Cobham conspired at Durham House 'to advance Arabella Stuart to the Crown and Royal Throne of this Kingdom'.[6]

The Early Stuarts and the Interregnum

King James took no time in evicting Raleigh and Darcy from Durham House and in restoring the property to the see of Durham. This enabled Cecil to obtain from the Bishop, the by now ruinous stables and gatehouse and to develop the Strand frontage as a business and public enterprise. The 'New Exchange' or 'Britain's Bourse' as the King called it, was begun in 1608. Intended as a rival to the City's Royal Exchange, it was a handsome arcaded structure, which succeeded as a centre for retailers of luxury goods, but not for serious mercantile transactions. A new gate house for Durham House was built further to the east and would survive until the end of the succeeding century. A right of way from the new gate house to the River was secured and a portion of the Bishop's outer courtyard at the back of the old stables, and a strip of his gardens adjoining Ivy Bridge Lane were also obtained. Cecil added the latter to the grounds of his own Thameside mansions, and the former was used in part for a roadway to the river and as the site for a small private residence.[1]

To the west York House would undergo a major transformation. The medieval palace of the Bishops of Norwich had been granted by Henry VIII to Charles Brandon, Duke of Suffolk. Suffolk's heirs had surrended it to Mary I who granted it to Nicholas Heaton, Archbishop of York. In 1558 the Archbishop, who was Lord Keeper of the Great Seal, gave up his charge to Nicholas Bacon and with it the possession of 'York House'. In 1622 James I compensated the then Archbishop of York for the loss of the property and presented it to his favourite, George Villiers, 1st Duke of Buckingham, who removed the buttresses from the external walls, embellished the interior galleries, replanted the gardens and employed Nicholas

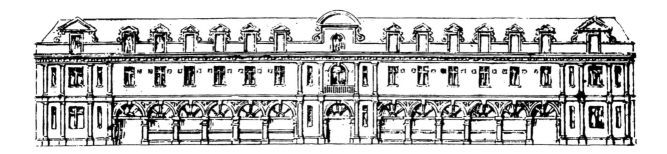

2. The New Exchange c.1609 to c.1737 from an engraved view of the Strand front.

19

Stone to build the magnificent Palladian watergate which has survived to this day, still ornamented with the Villiers arms and the anchors which indicate that the Duke was Lord High Admiral of England. Through this gate, alighting from barges rowed by His Grace's watermen, came a stream of visitors to be entertained by an enormous household of servants and retainers.[2] The once semi-rural environment of the Bishop of Durham's Palace was now becoming crowded by an occupationally mixed and populous neighbourhood and nowhere would this be more evident than on the opposite side of the Strand, where the Earl of Bedford's development of Covent Garden would soon take place.

Yet Durham House itself, with its great hall, chapel and riverside apartments, its inner and outer courtyards and still extensive gardens remained a residence fit for prelates, ambassadors, and as a setting for ceremonies of state.

The final arrangements for the restitution of Durham House to episcopal use were made by William James (Bishop 1606-1617). Since he is known to have restored the chapel of his palace at Durham he may well have done the same in London. Like his pre-Reformation predecessors he allowed Durham House to be used at the pleasure of the King. On the occasion of Prince Henry's investiture as Prince of Wales in 1610 twenty-five young men of noble descent were designated as Knights of the Bath. On the night of 1 June these patriotic Knights were lodged at Durham House and on the next day they went in procession to Whitehall Palace. After their ceremonial baths and a night spent in the Grand Chamber they returned to Durham House by river clad in robes of crimson taffeta and white sarsenet. Then, presumably in the outer courtyard, they armed themselves and mounted their steeds to ride in procession back to Whitehall, trumpeters sounding before them, until they come into the King's presence and were formally knighted.[3]

William James's successor, Richard Neale (Bishop 1617-28) was a Prince Bishop of the old type. He beautified his palace in Durham and entertained lavishly both there and in London. 'That which gave him most content', wrote a contemporary, 'was his palace of Durham House in the Strand, not only because it offered him convenient room for his retinue but because it was large enough to allow sufficient quarters for Buckeridge, Bishop of Rochester, and Laud, Dean of Gloucester…[and for]…such learned men…as came from time to time, insomuch that it passed by the name of Durham College'. The House must indeed have been like a crowded Oxbridge College in term time. For as well as the clergy there were also the numerous diplomats staying in various apartments as guests of the King and Bishop.[4]

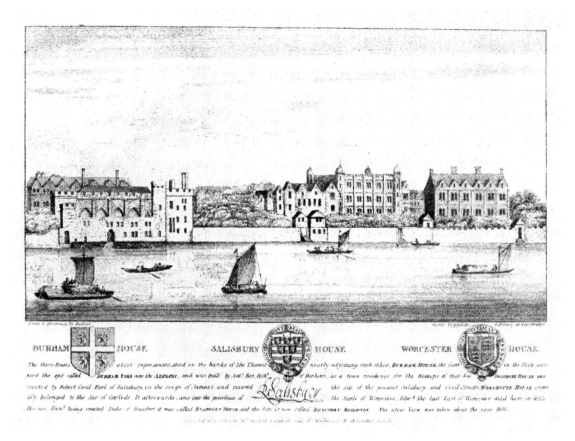

3. Durham, Salisbury and Worcester Houses from the River as they appeared in the mid-17th century, with the back of the New Exchange. From an engraving after the drawing by Wenceslaus Hollar (1607-1677).

In 1619 it was said that in Durham House there were three resident ambassadors: from France, from Savoy and from the United Provinces; three agents, one a friar sent by Spain, one a gentleman from the Elector Palatine and another from the Archduke of Austria. There was also a 'Secretary from Venice in the manner of Agent'. Four years later Durham House was designated as a residence for the Spanish grandees who would come in the train of Prince Charles and his bride, the Infanta of Spain. Magnificent new furnishings were installed in the House, but since nothing came of this 'Spanish Match', and since during the plague outbreak of 1625/6 Durham House stayed free from infection, Bishop Neale gave up 30 rooms to the new French Ambassador, Monsieur de Blainville in 1626. This Ambassador was to be concerned in a diplomatic crisis which caused the English Privy Council to examine the topography of Durham House in considerable detail.[5]

On Sunday 26 February 1626 a number of English catholics entered Durham House and attended Mass in the Ambassador's lodgings. As they passed from the outer courtyard to the Strand Gateway they were seized by armed constables. Some of the Ambassador's men went to their rescue and a fight ensued. Had not Bishop Neale emerged from his apartments a major riot might have taken place. The Ambassador claimed that his diplomatic privileges had been violated and the Privy Council, who were anxious to mollify him, investigated the affair. A plan was drawn up with captions in English and French which still survives amongst the State Papers in the Public Record Office. It shows the position of the 'Great Strand Gate' to the east of 'Britain's Bourse' with 'The Common passage from the water's side' running from a side opening in the Gate House, behind the Bourse and then along the western edge of the

4. A detail from illustration 3. Durham House from the river as it appeared in the mid-17th century, as on the previous page.

courtyard wall down to the Thames. Another route is marked as going through the 'Bishop of Durham's outer court – common to himself and others as well as to the Ambassador'.[6] It seems that the Ambassador was satisfied with an apology and it is not surprising that in the following year Bishop Neale was himself sworn to King Charles's Council and translated early in 1628 to the even richer see of Winchester. The Bishop of London was then moved to Durham and after three months made Archbishop of York.

John Howson, former Bishop of Oxford and a keen Laudian was Bishop of Durham from July 1628 until his death in 1632 and Thomas Morton, who would be the last Bishop to use Durham House, held the see from 1632 to 1659. Bishop Howson was buried at St Paul's Cathedral which suggests he was living at Durham House at the time of his death. Bishop Morton probably spent most of the early years of his reign in the north, but when the Scots convenators occupied Durham in 1640 he moved to London and lived in Durham House while attending the early session of the 'Long' Parliament. He appears to have agreed to a proposal made in 1641 that the house should be granted to Philip Herbert, 4th Earl of Pembroke in return for an annual rent charge of £200. This transaction was approved by an Act of Parliament and it may be that the Earl was for a time in residence together with the Bishop. A painting exists which shows the Earl as Lord Chamberlain receiving King Charles I at what is said to be Durham House. This cannot be later than 1641 since the Earl did not hold the office after that year – he sided with Parliament in the Great Rebellion. A design by Webb, the pupil of Inigo Jones, for a large mansion to be built on the site of Durham House for the use of the Earl was never carried out. Bishop Morton, who had been sent to the Tower by order of the House of Commons on 30 December 1641, was released in April 1642 and allowed to live peaceably at old Durham House until 1645 when he was again put in prison. In 1646 he returned to Durham House although all Bishops' properties had been declared confiscated by Parliament and Lord Pembroke and the second Earl of Salisbury had both bought out their rent charges on the Durham House estate. The Bishop claimed he was owed four years rent by Lord Pembroke and he determined to remain in residence. In 1648 he was forcibly removed by soldiers of the Parliamentary army. Though Parliament had abolished episcopacy he defiantly declared 'I am Bishop in spite of all your votes'. For the next eleven years, until his death in 1659, he remained in hiding in the country, secretly exercising his canonical functions and ordaining priests according to the (then) forbidden rites of the Church of England. He was the last of the long series of Bishops who for five centuries or more had occupied and embellished the Palace of Durham House on the Thames.[7]

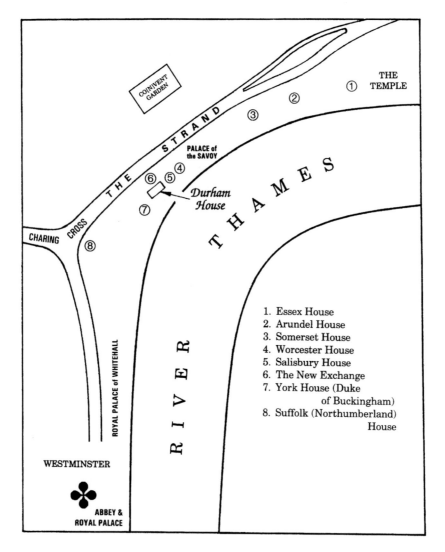

Map c) North bank of the Thames between Westminster and the City in early 17th century.

In the meantime London and the nation had to endure a decade of Puritan rule. The Earl of Pembroke died in 1650 and Durham House was used by the army in the same year. Houses were built in the garden on the eastern side of the property. The chapel was given over for the use of French Protestants. Though theatres were banned and the use of taverns restricted, human nature demanded some sort of public entertainment. From 1655 to 1658 there were displays of acrobatics and fairground wonders in the outer courtyard of Durham House. In September 1657 John Evelyn was amused at the agility of a rope-dancer called 'The Turk'. On Christmas Day of that year he had a less pleasant experience on the other side of the Strand. He and his wife attended communium in the chapel of Exeter House when soldiers entered and broke up the service declaring it to be idolatrous and 'Popish'.[8]

Trade in the New Exchange, which had been depressed during the Civil War, began to revive in the 1650s. An especially prosperous shop was kept by Anne Clarges who in 1651 married General George Monk and in later years would become Duchess of Albemarle. On the western side of Durham House the great palace and splendid watergate built by George Villiers, Duke of Buckingham, in the reign of James I, remained intact. It was occupied during the Interregnum by the Earl of Northumberland, who had supported Parliament in the Civil Wars. Similarly the second Earl of Salisbury remained in possession of Salisbury House. Worcester House, on the other hand, was used to store valuables confiscated from persons loyal to the King and Somerset House was garrisoned by the army.[9]

The Maypole outside St Mary in the Strand pulled down in 1644, would be replaced at the Restoration in 1660 and on the site of Queen Eleanor's monument at Charing Cross which Parliament had demolished, Le Sueur's statue of King Charles I, with a pedestal designed by Wren and ornamented by Grinling Gibbons, was eventually erected.

CHAPTER FOUR

Reconstruction and Decay:
From the Restoration to the
First Decade of George III

The later 17th century saw the pulling down of a range of great riverside mansions. Some like York House (demolished 1672) and Salisbury House (demolished 1673) had been built earlier in the century. Others like Arundel House (demolished 1678), Essex House (demolished 1680), and Worcester House (demolished 1694) dated from Tudor times. But perhaps the most striking survival from the ages of Bishops' palaces was Durham House and although the rent charge on this property was restored by King Charles II to the epsicopal see and was therefore due to be paid by the 5th Earl of Pembroke, the Earl's inheritance of the estate was confirmed and within a year of the Restoration, he demolished the ancient structure and leased the site in building plots. Houses of various sizes were built with gardens stretching towards the river, and for a decade or more the area was quite fashionable. Lord Denbigh occupied one of the larger residences in 1663. In 1669 Pepys recorded a visit by 'The King and Court' apparently to see the house of Lady Hungerford which was 'newly furnished' but which caught fire 'by the carelessness of the girl sent to take off a candle from a bunch of candles'. The King stopped the fire from spreading by ordering the neighbouring house to be blown up. In the 1680s Sir Godfrey Kneller and the Dowager Lady Herbert of Chertsey were among the more fashionable residents.[1]

Pepys himself settled in nearby Buckingham St in 1679 living at no.12 until 1688 and then at no.14 until 1700. Buckingham St had been laid out in 1675 when George Villiers, 2nd Duke of Buckingham, decided to develop the site of York House and its gardens. Four streets and an alley commemorated his name and title: Villiers St, Buckingham St, and George St (today called 'York Buildings') running towards the river and Duke St, with the adjacent 'Of Alley' (today respectively 'John Adam St' and 'York Place') running parallel. The Watergate remained intact and a tree lined garden walk was retained at the riverside. A waterworks was constructed at the west end of the walk for the benefit of the residents. In 1692 a 70 foot high

Map d) York buildings and Durham Yard in the mid-18th century. (From the map by Horwood.)

water tower in a classical style was built and for some years in the early 18th century it was worked by steam power.

Since no provision was made for repairing the stone paved landing steps and gate they were gradually undermined by the tidal waters of the Thames. In 1756 the local inhabitants applied to Parliament for permission to dismantle and dispose of the Watergate or alternatively to levy a rate for its repair. The Speaker intervened, objecting strongly 'to pulling down a Building of such admirable Structure and so great an Ornament to the River Thames'. An act was passed enabling the York Buildings residents to raise money by tax, and the terrace and Watergate were restored.[2]

As was customary in the later 17th century the houses on the York Building estate varied in size and value. Pepys' former house at 14 Buckingham St, adjacent to the Watergate, was considered suitable as a residence from 1701 to 1714 by Sir Thomas Harley, MP and later Earl of Oxford. Lord Torrington lived there from 1714-1716 and was succeeded by the Earl of Lichfield. Sir Thomas Harley's Librarian, Humphrey Wanley, famous as a bibliographer and antiquarian, lived in a more modest house: 4 Duke St. The area was much favoured by wine merchants who used the extensive cellars beneath the riverside houses. A Mr Brisden of Durham Yard sold wine to Voltaire in the 1720s. Four decades later J J Rousseau and David Hume lodged at 10 Buckingham St near the house of the celebrated wine merchant Archibald Stewart, MP (at no.11 from 1743-65) whose apprentice, Caleb Whitefoord went into business on his own account in nearby Craven St in 1754 where he would later become a neighbour of Benjamin Franklin. Craven St was developed in the 1730s and was on the other side of Hungerford market from Villiers St. The market had been built in 1682 on the riverside gardens of Hungerford House, destroyed by fire in 1679.[3]

On the Strand the New Exchange also fell into decline. By the end of the 17th century the shop girls were known to be available for prostitution, dressing 'themselves up for sale to the best advantage, as well as the Fripperies and Toyes they deal in'. In the early 18th century rents on the shops began to be reduced, yet more and more stood empty. The Exchange was finally demolished in 1737 and eleven houses built on the site.[4] Although prostitution continued to be a feature of life in the Strand and would prompt Jonas Hanway, who lived above the Durham Yard Gate House from 1750 to 1764, to campaign for a 'Magdalen' Hospital, the street contained the combined shops, offices and residences of many prosperous tradesmen[5]. There was also a lodging house called 'The Black Boy' whose address was 'over against Durham Yard', where Samuel Johnson lived in 1741 before moving to Bow Street. For those who could not afford a Strand frontage, Durham Yard was a convenient approximation. When the young David Garrick sought to set up as a wine merchant in 1738 he chose accommodation in Durham Yard because of the availability of cellars and because he hoped to find a market in the coffee houses and taverns of Covent Garden. Garrick moved away in 1743 and returned again to a transformed area in 1771.[6]

A proposal to redevelop the Durham House estate was made by John Gwynn in his imaginative *London and Westminster Improved* which he published in 1766. He suggested that regular streets should be built leading from the Strand to an embankment or public quay, or alternatively that a riverside square should be built to house the market, which would be moved from Covent Garden where it was proving a nuisance to residents.

5. Durham House Gateway in the 18th century. From the engraving done before the demolition in 1790.

6. York Building and Durham Yard from the Thames c.1750. From the engraving by Nathaniel Buck (1727-53).

By this date the estate was certainly ready for development. The 1767 Land Tax Assessment for Durham Yard names only the occupiers of the two riverside wharves and has a note 'all the rest ruins, no houses'. The ground landlord was now the 3rd Duke of St Albans, whose family had obtained the estate early in the century from the representatives of Sir Thomas Mompesson, who had himself purchased it from the Earl of Pembroke. In 1768 the Adam brothers negotiated a lease of the property from the Duke's trustees, the Duke being at this time bankrupt, and a new chapter in the area's history was begun.

7. N Buck's view modified to show the Adelphi development c.1774. From the engraving published by Samuel Buck (1696-1779).

CHAPTER FIVE

'The Adelphi'
A Speculation and a Monument

8. Robert Adam MP FRS FSA **(1728-92).**
From the medallion by James Tassie (1735-99).

In 1757 Robert Adam, the second of the four sons of a highly successful Scottish architect, was in the final year of his prolonged 'Grand Tour', which he hoped would qualify him for a brilliant social and professional career when he returned to Great Britain. Having studied in considerable detail the remains of ancient Roman public buildings and temples in the mainland of Italy, he had obtained permission from the Venetian authorities to survey ruins of the retirement palace of the Emperor Diocletian at Spalatro – the present day Split – in

9. Ruins of Diocletian's Palace at Spalatro in the mid-18th century. From the plate in Robert Adam, *Ruins of the Palace of the Emperor Diocletian at Spalatro in Dalmatia*, (1764).

Dalmatia. The great edifice rose from the waters of the Adriatic above wharves and warehouses. A plate from Robert Adam's magnificently produced book *Ruins of the Palace of the Emperor Diocletian at Spalatro in Dalmatia* shows how it influenced the mind of the young architect, when some ten years later he considered the redevelopment of the Durham House estate on the banks of the Thames in London.[1]

By that time Robert Adam had already established a successful architectural practice in partnership with his younger brother James. He could generally count on financial support from his elder brother John, who looked after the family estate and business in Scotland, and could draw on the resources of William, the youngest of the four, who carried on the building materials side of the family's multifarious activities. All four became involved in the 'Adelphi' estate project, as Robert now called the Durham House area, but it was Robert and James who did most of the work and it was those two whom David Garrick, using the Greek word for brothers, addressed as 'My dear Adelphi'.[2]

The area to be developed was over 140,000 square feet of irregular and sloping sites. The Strand level was about 40 feet higher than the old riverside wharves which were just above high water mark. Facing the river the brothers built a terrace to that height supported by giant arches which opened into warehouses above which were a range of small chambers known as the 'Adelphi cottages'; this was the working and commercial level. Above again were the private residences each with four stories rising from the terrace level and having two below. There was a range of eleven houses facing the river with the centre and ends ornamented with the rectangular pilasters of artificial stone bearing the Grecian decorative motifs so much loved by Robert Adam and already used by him on the garden front at Kenwood. The houses backed onto a central court behind which was another range of houses facing the newly created 'John Street' (now John Adam St) and to the sides of which were linking houses facing 'Robert St' on the west and 'Adam St' on the east. The latter streets were completed by ranges of residences running from John St to the river where they terminated in two projecting bays ornamented with pilasters which matched those on the central block but which were capped with pediments to emphasise their rôle as markers in the riverside composition. Within each pediment were placed the Adam family arms and this combination of pilasters and pediments and arms was also used on the house terminating the eastward view along John St to Adam St. This house and the river end of Robert St can still be seen. Adam St itself cut through the former 'Theobald's' court to the Strand and this provided a level entrance for 'carriage folk'. Alternatively they could go through the still surviving 17th century gateway of Durham House and turn left into 'William St' then right into 'James St' and crossing John St reach the terrace via Robert St. The houses in the upper level gleamed with the white of new stock brickwork and stucco ornament. The front doors were crowned with the characteristic 'Adam' fanlights and iron balconies of the architect's own design were attached to the principal windows. From the river the 'Adelphi Buildings' had the appearance of a brilliant new palace: a worthy successor to the episcopal, royal and noble residence which had once stood on its site.

Beneath this concentration of luxury and taste lay a vast underworld of servants' accommodation, cellars and vaults. The houses themselves, as has been mentioned, had two basement stories and there were also the so-called 'cottages' beneath the terrace. Supporting all these was a network of underground vaults getting ever deeper as the land sloped towards the river and to the west. The giant brickwork arches recalled the immense drainage system of Ancient Rome and there can be little doubt that Robert Adam was influenced in the design of these internal galleries by the archaeological remains he had seen in Italy and Dalmatia.

10. The Adelphi looking towards Westminster 1791. From the engraving by Benjamin Green (c. 1736–1807).

Entry to this lower level from the Strand was through Durham House gatehouse in the Strand, from which there had been a public right of way to the river's edge. The Adams replaced this by an underground road, starting with a sloping tunnel called 'Durham Hill', above which they would build a house for the [Royal] Society of Arts, and then running into 'lower John [Adam] St' which turned at its eastern edge into the ever descending 'lower Adam St' and eventually reached the riverside.

Through their family connections the brothers brought to London Scottish building labourers to lay the foundations and work as bricklayers on the great arches. Pipers were employed to spur them on to their work, but they became restless and demanded higher rates of pay. When these were refused many left, grumbling, it was said, at 'the curse of Adam'. So some 2,500 Irish labourers were employed instead. The Irish also complained of their wages saying that instead of pipes they were given 'the fiddle'.[3] To problems with labour were added those of flooding at high tide. The Brothers believed that the engineering problem of keeping damp from

34

the warehouses would not be serious but subsequent high tides revealed that their calculations for the height of the wharf were slightly too low for the water level. They therefore needed to embank the muddy foreshore of the Thames at a vulnerable bend in the river but this brought about further difficulties since the City of London claimed rights as conservators of the river bed. The costly procedure of obtaining a special Act of Parliament was therefore undertaken.

The Act 'for enabling certain Persons to enclose and embank Part of the River Thames, adjoining to *Durham Yard, Salisbury Street, Cecil Street* and *Beaufort Buildings* in the county of *Middlesex*' was passed in May 1771. Its preamble pointed out that the width of the bend of the river between Westminster Bridge and the 'New Bridge at Black Friars' causes 'an accumulation of mud and silt…and…a very extensive Sand Bank' and went on to recite the public and private advantages of building an embankment on the north side of the river 'by advancing the unequal and irregular Fronts of the…Wharfs and Grounds into a uniform line'. Named as petitioners were John, Robert, James and William Adam, together with James Paine who was developing part of the Cecil estate, and the owners of some of the wharfs.[4]

The City Fathers who had not before bothered about the neglected state of Durham Yard thought the Act 'violent', 'unjust' and a 'peculiar invasion' of their immemorial right 'in the soil or bed of the river'. The matter took on a political flavour. The City was an opposition stronghold whereas the Adams were identified with the King and Government of the day. The ensuring controversy had at least the advantage of giving publicity to the Adelphi scheme, but may have turned away certain potential tenants for the warehouses which even the Adam's ministerial friends now thought would be unsuitable for naval and military stores.

Some tenants were found from persons already established in the area. Alexander Eddie, the seed merchant, whose firm of Eddie and Dupont had occupied no.71 the Strand, now had new offices built at no.68, and a splendid private residence at no.3 John St (now no.6 John Adam St), as well as leasing wharves on the river front and warehouses under the arches.[5]

In addition to the warehouses the Brothers built underground stables, some of which were large enough to accommodate sixteen horses. By 1773 they had found several prominent tenants for these coach-houses and stables, among them were Sir Watkin Lewes, Sir Richard Hotham and Sir Edward Baynton. Other vaults were available as livery-stables and these would have been in demand by the residents of William Osborn's 'Adelphi Tavern and Coffee House' which would later became famous as Osborn's 'Adelphi Hotel'. As early as 1770 Robert Adam had designed ceilings for Osborn, and in 1772 the tavern opened on the north-east corner of John St and Adam St and Osborn himself seemed to have resided in a house adjoining Alexander

11. Elevation of the Society of Arts House c.1772. From the drawing in the RSA's bound collection of 'Original Plans ... by the Brothers Adam'.

Eddie's private residence. Osborn took great pride in the food available for his guests. He used to call his kitchen his 'Elaboratory'. One of his earliest functions was to entertain members of the Society of Arts – to which both he and Eddie belonged – on 28 March 1772, after the foundation stone of their new building further down John St had been laid.[6]

Negotiations between the Society of Arts and the brothers had begun in October 1771, soon after the Society had failed to negotiate an extension to the lease of its premises in Denmark Court on the north side of the Strand. Robert designed a splendid temple-like façade using a composite order he had employed on the north front of Kenwood, and with an entrance porch derived from the Tower of the Winds at Athens. Above the porch and between the two central columns is a Venetian window surmounted by the decorative fan device which became a trademark of the architect's designs. On the east side of this 'main house' (now 8 John Adam St) would be one for the Society's Secretary matching Eddie's private residence which it would adjoin. The ground floor of the 'main house' would contain a large 'Repository' for the display of prize winning machines and other objects, and a parlour for the officer in charge of the collections. On the first floor there would be a so-called 'Great Room' where meetings would be held. This rose to the roof of the building and was lit from above by a skylight. A second floor of offices ran between the façade and the upper level of the Great Room and there was another room behind the *oeil de boeuf* in the pediment. James calculated that it would cost £5,000 to build the two houses which would mean an annual rent of £300 plus a ground rent of £59 13s. He pointed out that 'my brothers and I have long been members of the Society [and] that an Elegant and established Residence, would give to the Society a greater appearance of permanency and Éclat'. After some haggling the rent was reduced to £270 if the Society would pay £1,000 to the Brothers. A building agreement was signed on 21 March 1772 and at the foundation laying ceremony on 28 March 'the sum of one Thousand pounds was paid to Messrs Adam', and Lord Romney, the Society's President, gave ten guineas to be distributed among the workmen. Under the first stone laid at the west end of the south front of the new building a glass vessel containing a drawing of the elevation, some official documents of the Society, specimens of its medals and coins of the realm, was placed in a stone container filled with charcoal dust and covered in tin foil. The company 'then proceeded to dine at the Adelphi Tavern where the remainder of the day was spent with…Harmony and Good Humour'.[7]

While this jollification was in progress the most famous of the Adam Brothers' private tenants was settling into his house at no.5 on the riverside terrace. David Garrick had come a long way since he struggled as a wine merchant in Durham Yard. Now a famous actor, he

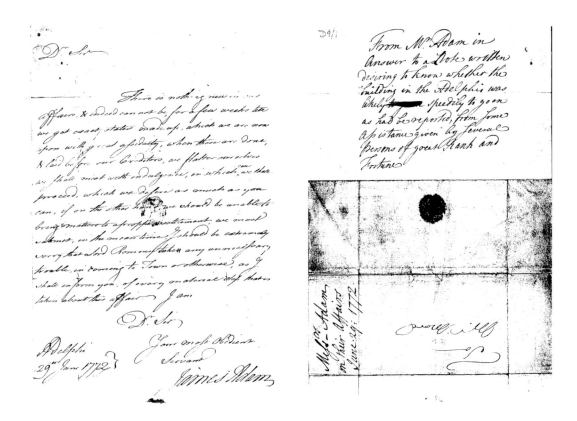

12. Letter from James Adam to Samuel More, 29 June 1772, referring to financial difficulties caused by the Adelphi project. From RSA Loose Archives D9/1 AD.MA/305/10/17.

returned to the site and we cannot say whether his professional engagements or the bustle of the move, which so fatigued his wife, allowed him to join his fellow members of the Society of Arts in the Adelphi Tavern. A long standing friend of – as he jokingly called them – 'those unprincipled Gentlemen and vile Architects the Adams' he had allowed his name to be used in a 'puff' for the Adelphi which had appeared in the *Town and Country Magazine* for June 1771. In the magazine article which was headed 'An Account of the New Buildings in the Adelphi' reference was made to 'the grand front towards the river Thames' in which 'one of the centre houses is purchased by Mr Garrick, and is almost completely fitted up in a truly classic style. The ceiling of the front room on the principal floor is painted by Zucchi, in the middle of which [are] represented the Graces attiring Venus, Cupid standing by her. The chimney piece in this apartment is of white marble, finely sculptured, and is said to have cost three hundred pounds'.[8] No other tenants are named in the 'puff', unless we count Zucchi who moved into no.4 John St exactly opposite Alexander Eddie's house. Antonio Pietro Zucchi had travelled with Robert Adam through Italy and Dalmatia. In 1766 Robert invited him to England and employed him on the interior decoration of many of the great houses he built, such as Luton Hoo, Syon House and Kenwood. A footnote in the magazine says that he has 'painted the principal apartment of each house in the Adelphi with subjects taken from Heathen Mythology'. As well as Garrick's ceiling, which survives in the Victoria & Albert Museum, two interesting examples remain *in situ* at what is now no.18 Adam St in the former coffee room of the 'Adelphi Tavern and Coffee House' and which is now part of the RSA building.

Moving into another of the riverfront houses at the same time as the Garricks was the Honourable Topham Beauclerk, and his wife the former Lady Diana Spencer. A friend to both the actor and the architects, Beauclerk belonged to Dr Johnson's literary club and had the sort of aristocratic connections which the Adams hoped might bring other persons of rank to live in the Terrace. The Beauclerks leased no.3 to the east of the Garricks who were at no.6. Beauclerk paid an extra £35 10s a year on top of his house rent of £264 13s, for an underground stable and coach house. A less socially distinguished tenant but one considered indispensable to men of taste was Thomas Becket, bookseller and publisher, who thanks to Garrick's intervention obtained in 1773 the lease of the house built by the brothers at the north-east corner of Adam St and the Strand. 'My dear Adelphi' Garrick wrote to Robert and James in 1772 'We shall all break our hearts if he is not bookseller to the Adelphi and has not the corner house that is to be built – Pray, my dear and very good friends, think a little of this matter, and if you can make us happy by suiting all our conveniences we shall make his shop…the rendezvous of the first people in England. I have a little selfishness in this request – I never go to coffee houses, seldom to taverns, and should constantly (if this scheme takes place) be at Becket's at 1 at noon and six at night'.[9]

Another early tenant who used his house for business and residential purposes was John Arnold the clockmaker who lived at 2 Adam St from 1771 to 1782. Arnold played a major part in developing the marine chronometer of John Harrison into a standard form which could be produced in large numbers at an acceptable cost.

For the spiritual health of the Adelphi the Adams contemplated the building of a church or chapel. Robert Adam put on paper two fanciful designs but the structure actually erected seems to have been rather plain and to have been used by a dissenting congregation. It was situated on the corner of James St and William St not far from the back of Thomas Coutts's house in the Strand and the opening into John St which preserved Coutt's river view. The chapel eventually became part of the banker's premises.

Coutts had moved to the family's banking shop at no.59 Strand, the centre house of New Exchange buildings in 1761 and he employed the Adam brothers to enlarge and decorate his living apartments. In 1775 he leased 17 John St, which the brothers had built as part of the Adelphi estate and to this was added no.16 in 1788. The bank's growing business eventually required still more accommodation and in 1799 nos. 1 and 2 William St were acquired. By a private Act of Parliament Thomas Coutts was permitted to build an enclosed upper walkway across William St which was, as we have seen, a public right of way. It was designed in a neo-classical form by William Adam and it connected 59 Strand with the outlying premises.[10]

Another variant in the planning of the Adelphi was the building of what today would be called a block of flats. On the outside they looked like houses and stood on the north-west corner of Robert St and consisted of five chambers: ideal for bachelors or persons looking for a London pied-à-terre.

Water was laid on from top to bottom of most of the private residences on the estate and all had the benefit of fire protection 'much beyond' as the architects announced 'any other houses in London'. A water tower connected to the river was built. Its pipes were, it was said, able to keep three fire engines constantly supplied 'upon a minute's notice'. On the roofs of the houses there were 'easy and safe walkways to enable persons to escape from fire'.

It was a time when there was much public discussion about the dangers of lightning. Experiments with lightning conductors reported to the Royal Society would have been familiar to many potential residents of the Adelphi. Robert Adam, himself FRS, made sure that lightning conductors were placed 'on the top of the water tower and other parts, so that every possible precaution against those dreadful accidents have been attended to'.[11]

Iron balconies or 'balconettes', as Robert Adam called them, were both an amenity and a decorative feature and the same could be said of the area railings. For the balconies Adam would use vertical rods with a leaf or two at the bottom to break the line, or geometric patterns, or lines crossing in an X shape, some arched, some in a scroll shape of free and flowing design. The area railings were topped with flat spear heads or pointed arrow shapes and punctuated with more prominent headings in the form of Greek vases. Graceful iron lamp standards were also provided. The Adelphi ironwork was made by the Carron Company in Scotland of which John Adam was himself a director. In this as in many aspects of the Adelphi project the whole family were financially involved.[12]

In August 1772 an Irish clergyman who had heard a distorted story about ministerial patronage of the Adams but who could not withhold his admiration for their work, described in his diary a visit to the Adelphi site:

> August 26 1772. Took a trip this morng through Leicester Fields to Covent Garden…I marched to the street on the quay called the Adelphi where formerly Durham Yard was placed. This though vested in the Crown has lately been granted by the influence of Lords Bute and Mansfield to one Adams, a Scotchman and a meer Creature of their own. Under the specious cloak of whose name is Architect a Noble Group of Buildings, these 4 or 5 years past [erected] has been carrying both above and Below Ground fit to Entertain princes. The whole of this extensive yard is vaulted with strait and cross vaults running into each other, so capacious and deep at the very Edge and Brink of the Thames; it would afford sufficient stowage for all the Rich Commodities of Both the East and West Indies. Upon the top of each Arch is a Counting House for Clerks and Brokers to transact Business in and Above All a Regular Range of Noble Buildings of Brick 4 stories High faced with cut stone neatly carved and figured and the Roof seemingly supported upon Corinthian pillars at proper intervals in the Front; and the Drawing Rooms of the Whole Range have their windows defended with Venetian Grates of cast metal of the most Beautiful form as also the Palisades that front the Houses are in the same taste. Whether the two Noble Lords who procured from His Majesty the Grant of the Ground are to be Sharers in the Profits arising from this Grand Scheme, politicians do not pretend to determine. But though the public is much distressed on account of the Late Failures, this great work has never yet stood still for want of cash as some of the workmen informed me.[13]

The pressures to succeed on Robert and James was particularly great and before long they would be required to put all their resources at risk. Although the uncompleted estate was valued at £210,310 at the beginning of 1772, the brothers – or more properly William Adam and Company – owed almost £124,000 and this excluded a loan from John Adam who came down from Scotland to help out Robert and James. The brothers hoped to obtain a mortgage of £70,000 on the Adelphi estate but a wave of bank failures in the summer of 1773 prevented this. 'Of all the sufferers' wrote David Hume to Adam Smith, 'I am most concerned for the Adams…to me the scheme of the Adelphi always appears so imprudent that my wonder is how they could have gone on so long'. The brothers spent at least £100,000 a year on the construction works and found it difficult to keep exact accounts owing to the complexity of the enterprise. 'In a work so very extensive' they admitted, 'where such a number of hands were daily employed in various places, and such a quantity of materials used…the actual expence upon each particular building could not be ascertained with any degree of precision'.[14]

In February 1773 Robert and James held a three day's sale of their works of art. Fanny Burney who eleven month's earlier had visited Garrick's 'new house in the Adelphi buildings, a sweet situation' now recorded in her diary that 'Mr Adam and his brother…exposed to public sale a large and valuable collection of busts, statues, bas-reliefs, pictures, etc, which they purchased many years since in Italy. These gentlemen, with another of their brothers…built the Adelphi – so called from the three brothers being engaged in it. The undertaking was, I believe, too great for them, and they have suffered much in their fortunes. I cannot but wonder that so noble and elegant a plan should fail of encouragement'.[15] The brothers then hit on the desperate expedient of a public lottery in which they would offer the unsold houses in the Adelphi as prizes. After much debate, a petition for an Act of Parliament, sponsored by their friends in the House of Commons, was passed in July 1773. It allowed them to dispose of their unsold property 'by way of chance in such manner as may be of most benefit to themselves and their creditors'. This use of a lottery earned the scorn of Horace Walpole, who like others had felt that Robert and James were rather too boastful in their claim to be the arbiters of taste. The Adams greatest rival Sir William Chambers, who would shortly begin to build his own great Thames-side structure, the new Somerset House, took exception to the claims made in the preface to the first volume of *The Works in Architecture* in which Robert and James 'boast[ed] of having first brought the True Style of Decoration into England and that all the architects of the present day are only servile copiers of their excellence'. The poet, William Mason, on reading the preface commented to Horace Walpole 'Was there ever such a brace of self-puffing Scotch coxcombs?', and Walpole replied in the same sarcastic vein calling the preface 'a specimen…of modesty and diffidence' and expecting more of the same from the Adams' announcement of their Adelphi lottery: 'What patronage of arts in Parliament, to vote the City's land to those brothers, and sanctify the sale of the houses by a bubble!'[16]

Of course if the brothers were to rescue their scheme they needed to publicise the Adelphi lottery and this they did by means of a prospectus which began by justifying their enterprise:

> The Messrs Adam engaged in this undertaking, more from an enthusiasm of their own art than from a view of profit; at the same time being eager to point out a way to public utility, though even at an extraordinary expense; they will be perfectly satisfied if they should only draw, from this lottery, the money laid out by them on a work which, they readily confess, they have found to be too great for their private fortunes. [17]

The fairness of the valuation they put on their properties was guaranteed in bonds lodged with the eminent Roman Catholic conveyancer, Matthew Duane, who had handled their dealings with the [Royal] Society of Arts. There were eight principal prizes ranging in value from 12 fine houses worth in total £50,080 to 6 small properties valued in all at £4,960. Some of the houses were still being built but the brothers undertook to complete them by 24 June 1775. Tickets were to be sold at £50 each, which added up to £218,500 and equalled the total of the prizes. They could be bought at the Adam office and in coffee houses all over town. The brothers hoped that the Lord Mayor would allow the lottery to take place at the Guildhall and David Garrick employed John Wilkes to use his good offices on their behalf. Failing in this they asked the Mercers' Company for use of their hall but were again unsuccessful. Eventually they hired the Great Room in Exchange Alley, Cornhill (formerly Jonathan's Coffee House) and the lottery began on 1 March and continued for four weeks. Some tickets were bought as a speculation and some unfortunates paid a premium for tickets on sale after 9 March or for portions of tickets. An auction of prize-winning tickets held at the Adelphi Tavern on 11 July showed that the properties had been overvalued by the brothers. Yet from their point of view the lottery had been a success since it enabled them to pay off their debts and complete their building work.[18]

Life in the Adelphi in the years immediately following the lottery was vividly evoked by Frederick Reynolds who was a schoolboy at Westminster when his family moved into a house in John St in 1775:

> With the Adelphi, I was delighted. The Thames, the wherries, and boating, were all novelties to me. Day after day, I ran over the still unfinished buildings in John Street, incapable of fatigue, deeming myself a man of bustle and business: now stopping with the workmen, to chop wood, and my fingers, and then running to chatter in the technical terms of carpentry to Terence, the foreman, who, answering all my boyish inquiries with incessant good humour, I was scarcely ever so happy as in his company.

Recording that Terence was 'foreman to the three Adams, who built the Adelphi,' he tells us that his father's house was 'opposite to the back of Garrick's'.[19] The Adams themselves were still busy with their professional and business ventures. Robert and James stayed at their house in the Terrace until 1778 when they moved to no.3 Robert St, a house which still survives. William Adam who had started out in 6 Adam St moved to 12 John St in 1774. This was also the Adam Office, where Robert Adam's pupils and draughtsmen worked. It was from these

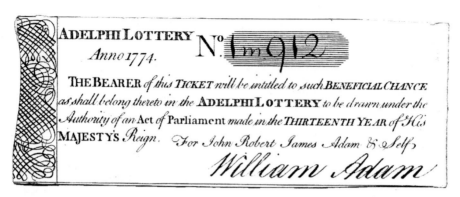

13. A Ticket for the Adelphi Lottery. From an original specimen preserved by the RSA. AD, MA/305/10/73.

venues that designs poured out for English country houses, London exteriors and interiors, public buildings in Scotland and numerous ornamental adjuncts. Many of the sketches and finished drawings and plans carry an inscription noting that they were executed in the Adelphi. Such was the drawing for a pianoforte for the Empress Catherine of Russia marked 'Adelphi 1774' and the 'Plan of the New Town of Bath for William Pulteney, Esq. An exact copy of this delivered to Mr Pulteney, Adelphi June 20 1777'. The superbly engraved plates of the second volume of *The Works in Architecture* (1776-77) were published during these years.[20]

David Garrick's brilliant career as the greatest and most successful actor of his time was now drawing to a close. His last appearance on the stage was in 1776 and he died in 1779. The procession of carriages at his funeral (Robert Adam was in carriage number 24) reached from the Adelphi almost to the door of Westminster Abbey. His widow continued to live in the Adelphi until her death some years later and had as her frequent visitor the authoress Hannah More. Boswell recorded a memorable occasion on 20 April 1781 when he spent with Johnson 'one of the happiest days that I remember to have engaged in the whole course of my life. Mrs Garrick, whose grief at the loss of her husband was sincere, had this day, for the first time since his death, a select party of his friends to dine with her. The company was Miss Hannah More, who lived with her and whom she called her chaplain; Mrs Boscawen, Mrs Elizabeth Carter, Sir Joshua Reynolds, Dr Burney, Dr Johnson and myself'. After the dinner and the evening party which followed it Boswell and Johnson 'walked away together: we stopped a little while by the rails of the Adelphi, looking in the Thames, and I said to him with some emotion, that I was thinking of two friends we had lost, who once lived in the buildings behind us, Beauclerk and Garrick: "Ay Sir (said he, tenderly) and two such friends as cannot be supplied"'.[21]

CHAPTER SIX
'Arts and Sciences'

The Society of Arts' move from Denmark Court, Strand to its newly built house in the Adelphi is usually and rightly associated with that harmonious mixture of artistic elegance and functionalism which characterized so much of London life in the eighteenth century. The two talented architects had provided a building in the centre of the members' favourite London area that was exactly suited to the needs of the institution. Yet the actual circumstances of its move to the Adelphi vividly illustrated Smollett's famous warning regarding its 'democratical' form. For the unfortunate official who was in charge of moving the extensive collection of works of art and machines found himself accused of defrauding the Society and in spite of attempts made by his friends amongst the members to block the proceedings, was subject during the spring of 1775 to an investigation by the Committee of Accounts which revealed a spirit of vindictive thoroughness worthy of a parliamentary impeachment.

Alexander Mabyn Bailey, Register of the Society for the encouragement of Arts, Manufactures and Commerce since February 1773, was no national figure, though he occupies a small niche in the history of technology, having assisted in producing and subsequently enlarging his father's important book of *Machines*. The story of his alleged misconduct as recorded in the minutes of the Committee of Accounts' investigation with its references to the Society's 'Black Servant', to the working conditions of John Turner, an unemployed bookbinder who served as a porter in the move alongside 'Pettigrew, a Watchman, a soldier whose name he does not know, a man they called the Barber, [and] a Deaf Man called George', also to meetings of 'Witnesses' in the 'Cock and Bottle', a conveniently situated public house, and to depositions before Sir John Fielding, are vivid illustrations of life in what has been called the 'Other London' of Georgian times.

At the Society meeting on 5 April 1775, a motion was carried, 'that it being represented…that cause has arisen to suspect there have been some abuses in the Office of Register…it is referred to the Committee of Accounts, to examine into the Grounds of the suspicion'. The Committee met on 13, 21, 28 April and finally on 17 May when the matter was again taken up by the full Society. Witness after witness seemed to testify that they had

14. Society of Arts' Great Room at the end of the 18th century showing James Barry's wall paintings. From the engraving by A C Pugin and T Rowlandson published by Ackermann, 1808.

been short-changed by the Register. At the last meeting of the month (held on 31 May) the Society heard and accepted, after some debate, a memorial Bailey had written making his 'humble submission' and explaining 'that whatever has hitherto appeared faulty or negligent...may be Imputed to the embarrassing Circumstances which I lay under with respect to Health, hurry of business and other difficulties'.

Bailey held on to his insecure office until 1779, when he was succeeded by George Cockings, Poet *manqué* and former holder of the humble post of Porter, who had once before tried to oust Bailey from his office and now established a dynasty in the service of the Society which lasted into Victorian times. The whole episode is a curious reminder that at the heart of a national and international membership of outstanding social and intellectual distinction had lain a parochial network of ingenious and often gifted tradesmen, tied to the Strand area by long-standing business and family connections. The building of the Adelphi introduced a superior note into the district which undoubtedly benefitted the Society. Many of the occupants of the Adam Brothers' splendid residences became members of the Society of Arts, and by the nineteenth century the institution was universally known and respected as 'the Society in the Adelphi'.

If some magic formula could distil the words spoken and ideas propounded in the Great Room of the Society since its completion by the Adam brothers, the intellectual development of the nation and perhaps of mankind could be unfolded. To provide a background for these exchanges was the self-appointed task of the Irish born artist, James Barry. Together with nine other prominent artists Barry had been invited by the Society to contribute a work for exhibition and subsequent retention in the Great Room. As a body the artists refused to cooperate in the project but Barry, in 1777, offered without payment to decorate the Great Room 'with a series of pictures analogous to views of the institution'. His six paintings which were first exhibited in 1783 and not finally completed until 1801, tell the story of mankind from 'Orpheus instructing his savage listeners', through a 'Grecian Harvest Home', a superb 'Olympic Victors', an idiosyncratic 'Triumph of the Thames', a Society of Arts' prize giving to 'Elysium, or the state of final retribution', in which the gigantic angels pleased even the critical Walpole, and from which the young William Blake drew inspiration. Barry's 'Adelphi pictures' as they were often called, became one of the sights of London, and though English 'history' painting went out of fashion for a while, they are today regarded as major works of art.[2]

The first resident secretary of the Society of Arts who lived in the Adelphi premises was Samuel More (d.1799). He was well known to a distinguished circle of scientists and industrialists amongst whom were Joseph Priestley, Matthew Boulton, Josiah Wedgwood and Richard Arkwright. Wedgwood, who included More in his series of cameo heads of 'eminent moderns', considered opening a show room in the Adelphi, and he asked More to undertake secret chemical experiments in the Adelphi vaults. Arkwright actually took a house in the Adelphi in 1788. It was no. 8 Adam St and he used it when in London for his various law suits in which More appeared as a technical expert. Today it forms a part of 'Adam House'.

After More's time a great deal of the administrative work of the Society was carried on by the Housekeeper and Register, the formidable Miss Ann Birch Cockings who succeeded her father in 1802 and worked until her death in 1844. The story is told of an occasion during Arthur Aikin's secretaryship (1817-1839) when she retorted to an importunate visitor to the Adelphi

1. Arthur Young.* 2. Samuel More. 3. Charles Marsham.†
4. William Shipley.* 5. An unnamed 'farmer'. 6. Lord
Romney.† 7. Owen Salusbury Brereton.† 8. Prince of Wales
and hidden behind him, Joshua Steele.† 9. Duchess of
Northumberland.§ 10. Earl Percy.* 11. Sir George Savile.†
12. Dr. Hurd, Bishop of Worcester. 13. Mrs Montagu.§
14. Unnamed head. 15. Soame Jenyns* 16. Unnamed 'young
female'. 17. James Harris. 18. Unnamed female head.
19. Unnamed girl holding a medal of the Society of Arts.
20. Duchess of Rutland. 21. Dr. Johnson.* 22. Duchess of
Devonshire. 23. Unnamed female figure (possibly Lady
Betty Germaine §). 24. Dejected boy. 25. William Lock.*
26. Premium-winning boy. 27. Duke of Northumberland.†
28. Dr. William Hunter.* 29. Edmund Burke.* 30. Duke of
Richmond.† 31. 2nd Earl of Radnor.† 32. Edward
Hooper.† 33. Keane Fitzgerald.† 34. Dr. Stephen Hales.†
35. Lord Folkestone.† 36. 1st Earl of Radnor.†
*Ordinary members (male) †Vice-Presidents and Presidents
§ Lady members

15. 'The Distribution of Premiums in the Society of Arts'. From the oil painting in the Society's
Great Room, 1783-1801 by James Barry (1741-1806).

who demanded to see the senior officer 'one old woman ought to do as well as another'. Aikin, a distinguished man of science, never married but was an active and benevolent uncle. His niece, Anna Le Breton, recorded the happy visits which she and her sister paid to the Adelphi:

> The house of the Society of Arts, which communicated with my uncle's by a door in the staircase, was very interesting to us children. We were allowed to roam about in it whenever there were no meetings of members. The housekeeper, a kind, clever woman, who had been born in the place, was as indulgent to us as my uncle, and was liked and respected by all, from the President, the Duke of Sussex, to the humblest official.
>
> The walls of the large room where the meetings were held were painted by the great artist James Barry, in life size figures, representing the victors of Olympia, Elysium, and other subjects, all vividly impressed upon my mind.[3]

Moving across the street to the Adelphi Terrace reference must be made to the 'Temple of Health' which the extraordinary quack doctor James Graham opened in 1779 at no.4, the former home of Robert and James Adam. Spending vast sums on what was already a splendidly decorated residence, Dr Graham guaranteed cures for a multitude of illnesses and the restoration of sexual vigour to those who spent the night in the 'celestial bed'. The entrance hall was filled with the testimonials of cured patients. Light from stained glass and perfume from incense burners gave character to the interiors. One chamber was called 'The Apollo Room', another the 'Temple'. Tall footmen with immense gold leafed cocked hats stood at the front door giving away handbills announcing:

> Temple of Health Adelphi
> To their Excellencies the Foreign Ambassadors
> To the Nobility, Gentry, and Persons of Learning and Taste
> This evening exactly at eight o'clock
> The Celestial Brilliancy of the
> Medico-Electrical Apparatus in all the Apartments of the Temple
> Will be exhibited by Dr Graham himself
> Admission by night 5s., in the day 2s 6d

Once inside customers could be charged £100 a night for the use of the celestial bed and £50 for 'magno electric' treatment. The earth bath was quite cheap at one guinea but the 'Elixir of Light' also cost £100.[4]

16. John St (now John Adam St), Adelphi in 1795. From the aquatint by Thomas Malton the Younger (1748-1804).

A less expensive annual attraction (from 1787) were the prize giving ceremonies held in the Society of Arts 'Great Room' in John St. Members were allowed to bring guests and the relatives of the recipients also attended. Around the President's chair were grouped the senior officers of the Society and seats were reserved for the foreign diplomats. The first occasion was presided over by an Adelphi tenant, already mentioned, Sir Watkin Lewes, Vice-President of the Society and distinguished MP for the City of London, but as a rule it would be the Presidents who would hand out the awards. In her pocket diary for May 1794 the young artist, Georgiana Keate, describes how she went in a carriage with her father, a sometime enthusiast for the work of the Adams, from their house in Bloomsbury down to the Adelphi and saw their friend Captain Bligh receive the Society's gold medal from the Duke of Norfolk. The Keate's were introduced to the meeting by John Henderson, a member of the Society who lived at 4 Adelphi Terrace, after Dr Graham had moved to Schomberg House in Pall Mall. Henderson's name occurs frequently in the diary and it comes as no surprise to learn that, in spite of her father's opposition, he later became Georgiana's husband. Though a lawyer by profession, he was a keen connoisseur of the arts and he introduced Girtin and Turner to Dr Thomas Monro, a wealthy physician who kept a famous private drawing academy at no.8. Henderson and Georgiana's father also knew Caleb Whitefoord, who like Garrick had started out as wine merchant, when he had been Benjamin Franklin's neighbour in Craven St, but was now an art collector of independent means living in James St. Whitefoord was a Vice-President of the Society of Arts and had served as chairman of its Committee of Polite (i.e. Fine) Arts.[5]

Amongst the youthful artists who came to receive their awards from the Society were W M Turner (1793), J S Cotman (1810), Edwin Landseer (1816, 1817), William Ross (1816, 1817), W P Frith (1836, 1837) and J E Millais (1839, 1840, 1841, 1846, 1847). Landseer was only eleven when he received the first of his prizes and Millais was ten when he received his. The latter's brother, William Millais, described how the young John came to the Adelphi in 'a white plaid tunic, with black belt and buckle; short white frilled trousers, showing bare legs, with white socks and patent leather shoes; a large white frilled collar, a bright necktie and his hair in golden curls'. When the little boy stepped up to receive his prize from the Duke of Sussex it was some time before the short-sighted and corpulent President could make out who was standing before him.[6]

The Duke of Sussex died in 1843 and was succeeded by his niece's husband, Prince Albert, as President of the Society. It was at the prize distribution held on 14 June 1849 that the then

17. Samuel More, Secretary of the Society of Arts and Adelphi Resident, 1796. From the painting by Benjamin West PRA (1738-1820).

Secretary, John Scott Russell, in the presence of the Prince and with the Prince's approval, referred to 'the probability of a large National Exhibition of specimens of Manufactures and Art taking place in 1851'. The Society, having long maintained a permanent exhibition of inventions in the 'Repository' on the Ground Floor of its house and having held since 1847 annual exhibitions of 'British Manufactures and Decorative Art', now came forward as the sponsors of a gigantic exhibition which Prince Albert himself said should include the products of all nations. Thus it can truly be said the Great Exhibition of 1851 was conceived and born in the Adelphi.[7]

Of course the Great Exhibition was far too extensive to be held in the Society of Arts' premises. At first Leicester Square was suggested and eventually the site in Hyde Park was chosen. When the Crystal Palace was moved to Sydenham in 1852 the Secretary of the Society, George Grove – the last resident in the Adelphi house – became its manager.

Small annual exhibitions of inventions continued to be held in the Society's 'Repository' until 1861 and the first ever British exhibitions of photography was held in the Great Room in 1852. Fine art exhibitions were also held in the Society's house including a display of the works of William Etty (1849) who lived in nearby Buckingham St and of the miniatures of Sir William Ross (1860), which prompted a visit by Queen Victoria, the first occasion on which a reigning British sovereign had been seen in the Adelphi and Durham House area since the 17th century. In the following year her husband died and though her son, the Prince of Wales also became President of the Society, he did not visit the Society once he had ascended the throne as King Edward VII. George V did not come when King, though Queen Mary did. Queen Elizabeth, the Queen Mother and her present Majesty have each visited what had been called, since 1908 thanks to King Edward, the *Royal* Society for the encouragement of Arts, Manufactures and Commerce.[8]

CHAPTER SEVEN

Coffee Houses, Taverns, Clubs, Companies and Tradesmen

When the Adam brothers purchased the Durham House estate they became the ground landlords of the New Exchange Buildings and thus of the 'New Exchange Coffee House' at no.69 the Strand. This seems to have been a flourishing concern which the Adams described as 'greatly underlet' in the prospectus for the Adelphi Lottery. A pocket guide to London dated 1793 suggests a rather raffish clientele:

> A set of jovial bucks do here resort. With Bacchus flush'd and reeling ripe for sport...For many years kept by Old Townsend and his ancient wife and even in its early days, remarkable for good things especially if the female attendants be included. Nelly, the present proprietress, though not highly ornamented by nature or education yet, when in the humble capacity of bar-maid had the art of pleasing all...[1]

By 1803 it was said to be 'frequented by professional gentlemen' but it is doubtful if it could compete in gentility with Osborn's 'Adelphi Tavern and Coffee House' already mentioned. After 1781 Osborn's main premises were on the south east corner of John St and became well known as 'Osborn's Adelphi Hotel'. In *The Pickwick Papers* Wardle and his daughters came to stay at Osborn's after Pickwick's release from the Fleet Prison. The whole episode of Mr Snodgrass's being accidentally confined to Wardle's bedroom, of the Fat Boy's valiant attempts to bring Pickwick to his aid and Wardle's ultimate acceptance of him as his son-in-law, would have taken place in interiors still embellished with Adam chimney pieces, splendidly decorated plaster ceilings and finely carved door casings. 'Below stairs' where Mary entertained the Fat Boy was less ornate: a sort of half way house between upstairs splendour and the dreadful caverns below.

In real life Osborn's Adelphi Hotel continued until the demolition of the Terrace block. Isaac Disraeli had stayed there after his marriage in 1802 and the King and Queen of the

18. Adam St, Adelphi in 1795. From the aquatint by Thomas Malton the Younger.

Sandwich Islands were at the hotel in 1824, where the unfortunate Queen contracted smallpox and died. The King then moved to the Caledonian Hotel where he also died of the disease. When Alexander Graham Bell demonstrated his newly invented telephone in the Society of Arts' Great Room in 1877 a connection was made with an instrument in the Adelphi Hotel opposite and there can be little doubt that members of the Society made frequent use of both the Adelphi and the Caledonian hotels. The Caledonian had been established at no.3 Robert Street – Robert Adam's former home – at the end of the 18th century. It flourished during the Victorian era and was for a time under joint management with the 'Adelphi', the proprietor of both establishments being William Chaplin, who like Osborn before him was a member of the Society of the Arts. In an 1840 directory it is called 'Osborn's Caledonian Hotel'. By this period there were also a selection of lodging or boarding houses in Adam St: Miss Ann Ramsay at no.3, Mrs C M Wallace at no.8 and William Bliss at no.19. The boarding house at no.19 eventually became Sherwood's private hotel which is listed in the directories until as late as 1905. Adam St also had the 'Adelphi Wine Shades' at No.11 and the 'Regina Tavern' at no.12. Other taverns in the area were the 'Salisbury Arms' at 1-3 Durham St, 'The George' in George St, and 'The Fox under the Hill' which was built precariously on the riverfront at the south end of Ivy Bridge Lane. Dickens knew the 'Fox' well; he described it in his *Sketches by Boz*, and introduced it into *David Copperfield* as the 'tumble down public house' with wooden stairs from which the Micawber family commenced their voyage of emigration to Australia. A correspondent of the *Times* in 1895 contributed a vivid recollection:

> On the southern side of the Strand I saw last week still remaining the entrance to a long and dismal lane, which forty years ago ran from the Strand to the river shore. The lane skirted the eastern side of the Adelphi Dark Arches, and led to an old-fashioned riverside Public-house, The Fox under the Hill, described by Dickens in one of his *Sketches by Boz*. The house, I think, was on the shore but in front was moored a barge with alcoves something like the old fashioned tea-gardens. By the side of the public-house a rickety gangway led across moored barges to the pier of the 'apenny boat' which plied between the Adelphi and London Bridge (the old fashioned steamers which performed the service being called, I think, Venus, Jupiter, and Endeavour respectively). The building of the great hotels on the Thames Embankment is causing the disappearance of this and other old London landmarks. The curious may find the entrance to the passage on the south side of the Strand by the side of of a restaurant nearly opposite the *Adelphi Theatre*.[2]

19. Adelphi Terrace in 1795. From the aquatint by Thomas Malton the Younger.

Dickens, who was well acquainted with taverns and lodging houses, was equally familiar with societies and clubs. The Pickwick Club had many of the adjuncts of a scientific society. Like the Society of Arts of which Dickens was a member, it had 'corresponding members', 'perpetual members' 'Chairmen' and 'Vice Presidents' and it published its proceedings in volumes which were called *Transactions*. Of course the club had no permanent lecture theatre as was the case with many institutions which used the Society of Arts' Great Room for their meetings. In this way a stream of photographic amateurs, social scientists, industrial chemists, school teachers, electrical engineers and philanthropists of all sorts were brought to the Adelphi.[3]

Other institutions rented office space and boasted Adelphi addresses. The Institution of Civil Engineers, which had begun in Kendal's Coffee House, Fleet St in 1818, was at 15 Buckingham St from 1820 to 1832, letting its rooms for meetings by the Phrenological Society which proved an uncongenial tenant. At no.18 Adam St, where Osborn had originated his hotel, the Naval Charitable Society was established in 1832 and stayed there for 114 years by which time it had become the Royal Naval Benevolent Institution. It shared the premises with numerous other bodies. For example in 1878, the Wine Importers Association, the Freedman's Museum Aid Society, the Church of England Temperance Sick and Burial Society, the *Naval Chronicle* and the *Wellington Gazette* were all listed as being at no.18. Close by in John Street, the Lord's Day Observance Society had its headquarters at no.20 from 1860 to 1881 and the Index Society was further down the same street at no.8 in 1885.[4] Back across the road at 7 Adam St the Evangelical Alliance, a bastion of Anglican and Non-Conformist Protestantism waged its campaign against 'Popery' from 1846 to 1926. The elegant Adam façade of no.7 was modified by the addition of a horizontal plaster band between the pilasters below the second floor which can still be seen. It carried the name 'Alliance: 1846: House'. At 1 Adam St the Imperial Institute, in many ways a child of the Society of Arts, was established in 1890 before moving to its headquarters in South Kensington. In Adelphi Terrace itself the London Bible Mission was at no.2 from 1880 to 1907 and the Police Institute at 1a from 1897 to 1936. The Statistical and Economic Societies both to be granted the prefix 'Royal' were at no.9 from 1888 and 1895 respectively and this building was also shared by the Institute of Actuaries and the Institute of Chemistry.[4]

The area had its fair share of clubs. As a result of a rift in the Junior Garrick Club which had been at 1a from 1877 to 1888, the Green Room Club was established at 10 Adelphi Terrace where it stayed until 1883, returning to the area after several moves in 1955. The actors who joined the institution included the leading personalities of the Victorian stage: Sir

20. View from west corner of Adelphi Terrace in the late 18th century. From the watercolour by Thomas Girtin (1775-1802) in the A H Baldwin collection.

Henry Irving, Sir Herbert Beerbohm Tree (at that time he used the name of Herbert T Beerbohm), Edward Ledger (The Editor and proprietor of the *Era*), H J Loveday (for many years Irving's stage manager), Sir Johnstone Forbes Wyndham Robertson, and Sir Christopher Wyndham. The Club's founder, Murray Marks, was a dealer in *objets d'art* with a passion for the theatre. He spent his own money in decorating the premises and persuaded Norman Shaw to design a hat stand for the club.[5] Many of the club's members performed at the neighbouring 'Adelphi Theatre' which was on the opposite side of the Strand from the end of Adam St. Opened in 1806 as the 'Sans Pareil' it took the name Adelphi in 1819. It was rebuilt in 1858 to look like the Opera Comique in Paris and in the 1880s and 1890s was famous for the production of melodramas.

The 'Arundel Club' and the 'French Club' are listed as being at no.1a in the 1880s but the most famous of the area's clubs was undoubtedly the 'Savage'. Founded in 1857 at the suggestion of the journalist G A Sala it was named after the poet Richard Savage, though it later decorated its premises with spears and shields to suggest the other meaning of its name. Initially peripatetic it found a permanent home at 6 and 7 Adelphi Terrace in 1888 where it remained until the demolition of 1936. It was famous for its gregarious character and its dinners were important social occasions. Many notable figures have belonged to the club, amongst them G A Henty, Sir Edward Elgar, Sir Arthur Sullivan and Sir Henry Tate.[6]

Leaving the world of entertainment and leisure, and of societies and clubs, we are reminded of the source of wealth which sustained them by the names of the numerous businesses which had their offices in the neighbourhood in Victorian times. Railway companies abounded at 5 and 12 John St, 1 Robert St and 11 Adam St from the late 1830s onwards. The 'Equitable Gas Company' was at no.21 John St from 1832 to 1869. The 'United Kingdom Electric Telegraph Company' at 1 Adelphi Terrace from 1857 to 1869. The growth of Empire was reflected in 'the African Expedition Office', and the 'Australian Rooms Agency Office' at 4 Adam St by the 'New Brunswick and Nova Scotia Land Company at 18 Adam St, and by the 'Colonisation Company for South Australia' at 6 Adelphi Terrace, all listed in the directories for the period.

As well as railway companies some very eminent railway engineers were residents from the 1840s onwards. William Bridges Adams, engineer, inventor and entrepreneur, lived at no.1 Adam St. Joseph Locke, sometime pupil of George Stephenson and engineer for the Grand Junction Railway connecting the Liverpool and Manchester Railway with Birmingham was at no.11. John U Rastrick of no.1 Robert Street had been an adjucator at the Rainhill trials and had constructed the London to Brighton railway lines, being famous for the Balcombe viaduct (1841) and the London Road Viaduct (1846) at Brighton. C F T Young, author of *The Economy of Steam Power* (1860) was at 5 Adam St and W C Siemens was at 7 John St; other engineers could be found at 8, 11, 18 and 19 Adam Street, at 9 and 12 John St, at 2 and 5 Robert St and at 1, 5 and 8 Adelphi Terrace. T R Crampton was at 10 Buckingham St when his railway engines earned him a medal from the Society of Arts and he designed the first practical submarine cable to be laid between Dover and Calais.

Wine merchants, continuing a tradition dating from Garrick's early years, were in John St and Adam St and at the Adelphi Wharfs where coal merchants also congregated. Solicitors and attorneys seem to have been omnipresent. There were physicians at 8 and 13 John St and surgeons at no.14 and at 6 Robert St and at no.5 in the Terrace. Agents of all sorts – medical, clerical, navy and others – could be found at various addresses. A Miss Harriet Bernard, 'Professor of Phalachromiasy' was at 14 John Street and an undertaker at 1 George St.

There were tailors at 12 John St, at 12 and 15 Adam St and at 10, 19 and 21 George St, but not in the more exclusive professional parts of the estate. George St indeed had a remarkable variety of tradesmen: a flint and glass cutter and dealer at no.2, a jewellery case maker at 3, a bookbinder at 4, a jeweller and pearl worker at no.5, and the manufacturer of a patent knife cleaner at 13. The most beautiful retail shop was undoubtedly Rudolph Ackermann's 'Repository' at no.96 Strand on the corner of Adam St. This had been Beckett's bookshop, already mentioned as Garrick's favourite adjunct to the area. Ackermann began there in the late 1790s and then moved to 101 Strand. In 1827 he returned to no.96, which he had rebuilt in the Adam manner by J B Papworth. One of Ackerman's collaborating artists had been Thomas Rowlandson who had lodged at various times in Robert St and John St. Less spendthrift and more permanently established artist-residents will be considered in the next chapter.

CHAPTER EIGHT
Some Victorian Residents and Habitués

As a socially select area for private residences the Adelphi underwent a long and slow decline during the 19th century. The tide of fashion moved ineluctably westwards. Mrs Arbuthnot was anxious that her husband should not accept a particular government appointment from her friend the Duke of Wellington because it carried with it a residence near the Strand. The change was for long imperceptible. Dickens, for example, imagined 'Cornelius Brook Dingwall, Esq MP' living in the Adelphi and maintaining 'a red hot looking footman in bright livery'. Dingwall 'was wonderfully proud of the MP attached to his name'.[1]

Judge William Bolland (d.1840), amateur bibliographer and founder of the Roxburghe Club, who had lived for many years at 4 Adelphi Terrace, earned a knighthood as a result of his professional services. Yet by 1846 the Court Directory listed 105 Adelphi residents designated as 'Esquires' none of whom could boast the further addition of 'Member of Parliament' and it listed no knights, baronets or noblemen as living in the area. There were of course still persons of means and standing who clung to their graceful Adam residences: George Blamire, the wealthy barrister, who owned large estates in Cumberland and South Wales, lived the life of a recluse at 1 Adam St. For at least twelve months before his death in 1863 he never left his private apartments. His housekeeper used to leave his meals on a tray outside his door. When he was unwell he would refuse medical aid, and have medicine brought in from a neighbouring chemist. At length, when for two days his housekeeper failed to get any reply to her knocking, she sent for the police, who found Mr Blamire dead in his arm chair, surrounded by newspapers and with scientific and legal books strewed on the floor. The handsome furniture was covered with dust, packages of candles and clothing were heaped up in confusion, and there were three large bags filled with new books. Unlike Ebenezer Scrooge in his first incarnation George Blamire had the reputation of being a very honourable and charitable man.[2]

When Richard D'Oyly Carte, the successful impresario and builder of the Savoy Theatre (1881) moved to 4 Adelphi Terrace in 1888 he found the surviving Adam decoration far too restrained. He added gilding and colouring to the principal rooms so as to be in keeping, it was said, with his theatrical tastes. He was assisted by his friend James McNeil Whistler who not only drew up schemes of decoration but actually mixed paint for the famous 'Yellow Room' which would become a gathering place for personalities associated with music, drama and the arts. From it French windows opened onto a balcony where the view of the river could be enjoyed on summer evenings. A sofa presented by Arthur Sullivan had pride of place in the room. D'Oyly Carte also fitted up a billiard room which Whistler painted a rich green to match the colour of the baize. In the dining room Carte would entertain his friends to meals cooked by chefs from the Savoy Hotel kitchens. He also installed an electric lift, the first to be used in a private house in England. He lived at no.4 until his death, which took place on the Yellow room sofa in November 1903.[3]

William Henry West Betty, the famous youthful actor, lived on the fortune he had earned in his teens in Regency times, first at 14 John St and from 1835 to 1845 in chambers at 1 Robert St, where Henry Ryall, honorary engraver to the Queen, also had accommodation from 1841 to 1850.

Artists and architects abounded, and were to be found chiefly in John St, Adam Street or on the Terrace, though the great William Etty had lived for many years in Buckingham St, where John Francis Bentley would also have an office. William Dyce, the fresco painter, with Thomas Taylor and Charles W Claus was at 1a Adelphi Terrace, and Owen Jones, his fellow enthusiast for ancient colouring and ornament was at 9 John St. William Butterfield, the celebrated church architect was at no.4 Adam Street and Henry Roberts, designer of school buildings at no.18. An architectural intrusion into the late 17th century and early 18th century regularity of the Duke St, as the western continuation of John St was then called, was 'Canova House'. This strange Italian Medieval style building survives to this day, preserving the roof line of the neighbouring houses but with a distinctive pitch roof and 'loggia' like porch. The architect was R P Pullan, brother-in-law of William Burgess, and it was used by Burgess as his office.

Another successful exponent of revival styles, Arthur Blomfield, moved his expanding practice to 8 Adelphi Terrace in 1863. One of his pupil-assistants was the young Thomas Hardy, who drew and studied just inside the easternmost window on the first floor. Occasionally Hardy would go out onto the balcony and look down on the riverside scene, which reminded him of a coastal town in his home county of Dorset. He and his fellow assistants and pupils were full of high spirits in their new environment and showed little respect for the graceful interiors which surrounded them, scrawling caricatures on the white marble Adam fireplaces and using the iron balconies as vantage points to annoy members of the Reform League, who had their offices on the ground floor.

The darker side of London life which impressed both Hardy and Dickens and an earlier Adelphi writer, Thomas Hood who had lived at no.2 Robert St from 1828 to 1830, could be found just beneath the Adam streets and terraces, but was only noticed by persons of imagination and human sympathy.

'Thousands who pass along the Strand' wrote Thomas Miller in 1849 'never dream of the shadowy region which lies between them and the river'. They see 'huge, broad-chested steeds...dragging the heavily laden coal waggons up those steep passages which lead into the Strand'. 'Cows' continued Miller, 'are also kept there deprived throughout their lives of daylight, but calving and giving milk to a good old age'. The Adelphi arches seemed, he thought 'to form a little subterranean city; there is nothing like it in London: in some places you catch a glimpse of the river; a small loophole then lets in the light like the end of a railway tunnel, yet seeming to diminish more than those tunnels, on account of the steep descent, until one of the steamers in passing, appears to fill up the opening like a half-closed door. Besides these arches, there are narrow passages which go dipping down to the water side, where on either hand houses stand looking at one another in the openings between the darkness. There is a dismal and solitary look about these tall imprisoned houses; you cannot conceive how they are entered, for there appears to be no way to them and you conclude that they are empty. Or, if they are inhabited, you wonder if the people ever look out of these dim, dirt-ditched windows at the dead-looking walls opposite'.

John Timbs, a year later, wrote of 'the grim vastness' of the arches and their reputation as a haunt for outcasts and criminals, where 'the most abandoned characters have often passed the night nestling upon foul straw; and many a street-thief escaped from his pursuers in those subterranean haunts, before the introduction of gas-light and a vigilant police'.[4] The arches were used to house a battery of guns ready for deployment against the Chartists in 1848 and later as a place for military band practices. A shooting gallery was also established and flourished for a while, but so vast was the underground area, that vagabonds and criminals could easily hide in it without detection.

Names such as 'Jenny's Hole' and the 'Devil's Bridge' below the Robert St area, and 'The Thieves Kitchen' below Adam St recall the setting that Dickens created in *Oliver Twist*. When as a boy the great novelist had been forced to work in the hated blacking factory at

Hungerford stairs he would sometimes escape into the subterranean world. In *David Copperfield*, he makes his hero undergo similar experiences:

> I was fond of wandering about the Adelphi, because it was a mysterious place, with those dark arches. I see myself emerging one evening from some of these arches on to a little public-house, close to the river, with an open space before it, where some coal-heavers were dancing; to look at whom, I sat down upon a bench. I wonder what they thought of me![5]

This public-house was the 'Fox-under-the-Hill' at the bottom of Ivy Lane which has already been mentioned.

Just after Christmas 1863 the young Quintin Hogg met two boy crossing sweepers in the Adelphi arches and with a beer-bottle and a tallow candle for light and two bibles as school books tried to teach them to read. He was interrupted by the police and later disguised himself as a shoe-black so that he could make friends with the boys. In 1864 he opened a 'ragged-school' for them in 'Of Alley' and in later years he would say that his famous 'Polytechnic Institution' grew out of this Adelphi enterprise.[6]

Victorian political economists, as Scrooge knew so well, often doubted the value of charitable endeavours, but William Bridges Adams, the railway company director and Adelphi resident (see Chapter 7), speaking at the Society of Arts in 1854 had denied the proposition which he saw as widely held that 'degrading human labour is essential to national prosperity'. During the succeeding decades the Society campaigned for improvements in public health, the housing and diet of the poor, and in artisan education. It was the only non-political body which Karl Marx joined and we can imagine the 'Red' Doctor coming down to the Adelphi to attend the Society's meetings soon after his election in May 1869.[7] The [Royal] Statistical Society which frequently met in the Society of Arts' rooms and Charles Booth, both to have offices in 9 Adelphi Terrace, collected facts and figures on the London poor which spurred on the philanthropic spirit of the age. In the first decade of the succeeding century the Moral Education League, 7 York Buildings, and the Women's Industrial Council, 7 John St, used the facilities of the Society of Arts.

The lease of the Society of Arts' house had come to an end and been renewed for a further thirty years by the ground landlords – the Drummond family – from Lady Day 1867. Victorian schemes of decoration, including the mosaic pavement in the main entrance hall and on the main staircase, 'ugly and useless' glass cases – as a contemporary called them – replacing Adam's pillars in the Repository, and a drastic rearrangement of the Great Room, were to be a permanent backdrop to the Society's multifarious activities until the 1920s.[8]

Fortunately the Victorian urge to ornament was not allowed to alter the external appearance of the building, though architectural critics rejected Thomas Malton's verdict that it was 'beautifully simple without meanness and grand without exaggeration'. W H Leeds writing at the beginning of the Queen's reign showed his dislike of the facade with devastating frankness:

> The real truth is, it has no pretensions whatever to grandeur; and even its simplicity is of a very spurious kind, for it partakes far more of nakedness and poverty, than of that subdued elegance and unity of expression, which are essential to aesthetic simplicity. Here, on the contrary, we behold two utterly distinct and even adverse styles brought into contact, without any attempt being made to reconcile, much less to amalgamate them.[9]

Yet if what John Gloag once aptly called 'Georgian Grace' was rejected, 'Victorian Comfort' made some amends. Gas was first used in the interior of the building in 1847, when a fitting was installed to light the staircase. In 1848 gas lighting was introduced into the Repository and a 'handsome' Boccuis fitting 'with Burner and Chimney Glass complete' was hung from the ceiling of the Great Room – the Boccuis 'Light Office' being conveniently situated at 6 John Street. A year later the entrance hall and committee room were also given gas lighting. In 1853 it was decided that the four hanging ornamental lamps in the Great Room should be converted to gas burners, and, in 1854, that the Boccuis fitting should be replaced by a central 'sunlight' gas lamp.

Electric light operated by chemical batteries had been hired for two evening 'promenades' during the Society's exhibition of select specimens of British manufactures and decorative art in 1849. But three decades were to elapse before the 'electric light' was to replace gas as the regular source of illumination in the Society's Houses. On 4 December 1878 a paper read to the Society on methods of lighting was accompanied by working demonstrations of a Hallé lamp in the Entrance Hall and a Suisse lamp in the ante room, which were supplied from the Repository by a Gramme dynamo driven by a Crossley gas engine, while the Great Room was lit by a Siemens lamp supplied by a Siemens dynamo, driven by a Brotherhood steam engine in the Durham Street yard. Similar meetings were held in 1881, and the need for heavy equipment to supply the demonstrations led a group of Council members to present to the Society a Crossley gas-engine, which was installed in a cellar. Soon afterwards a Siemens generator was purchased, and a general electric lighting system was permanently installed in time for Sir William Siemens' inaugural address as Chairman of the Council in November 1882. The Society's house and the newly built Savoy Theatre nearby were the first public buildings in London to be permanently lit by electricity. The system was improved in 1886 by the purchase of a storage battery and it remained in use until 1899 when the current was taken from the then newly-established street mains.

Up to 1877 the only form of central heating in the Society of Arts' house came from a furnace in the lower basement which was supposed to send up hot air through gratings into the Great Room. Otherwise the members and officers relied for warmth on open fires and stoves. A central heating system based on pipes was introduced in 1877 and remained in service until 1966 when it was dismantled and given to the Science Museum. The Clean Air Act of 1956 brought to an end the coal fires which had burned merrily in the Adam grates during a hundred and eighty two years.

Standards of hygiene and propriety in regard to drainage change with the generations as much as do standards of comfort in regard to light and heat. In the 1770s the Adelphi estate was considered to possess especial advantages in its water supply, and the building agreement between the Adam brothers and the Society provided for a 'Water closet…completely fitted up and water laid into it'. A 1779 inventory records that in the Great Room there was a 'baize screen and a copper urine pot and stand', a convenience which in the next century was sacrificed to the interests of decency. The Society's Housekeeper reported in 1846 on 'the very unwholesome atmosphere which came up through various openings in arches below the Society's House'. Sanitation in general became a concern of the Society. In 1852 it experimented with the establishment of a public lavatory at Bedford St, Strand and in the 1870s it offered medals for 'the best sanitary arrangements in houses in the metropolitan area'. This prompted it to set its own house in order. In 1881 a professional examination of the drains revealed them as defective and unhygienic and much needed improvements were put in place.[10]

On 10 February 1864 the diarist A J Munby recorded the impending end of the river scene which Dickens had known so well and which had delighted the young Thomas Hardy. Noting that it was 'a fine cold day with a slight fall of snow towards evening' he described how, as he walked:

> round by the Adelphi Terrace about sunset, I lingered a little to look down upon the wharves and shipping below. Some of the 'bits' here are very picturesque. There was one little dock just

under where I stood: and old quay by the side of it, and upon the quay a block of low eighteenth century buildings, containing a little counting house with quaint bow windows and a range of sheds built of rough blackened timber and tiled with old dun tiles: and in the river – it was high tide – three brown sailed green painted barges lying around with their sterns to the quay; and sailor like men going aboard them; and casks and kegs heaped all about; and one tree the top of which showed above the tiles against the dim mainstream of the Thames, whereon other craft were floating down the tide. One such simple scene a day would do a man good to look upon but this also is doomed. The embankment is coming and the hideous bridge and station of Charing Cross are already there; in full view.[11]

CHAPTER NINE
The Adelphi Embellished
1862–1918

The Victoria Embankment built between 1864 and 1870 pushed the Thames far back from the Adelphi Terrace and the picturesque shanties admired by Munby. Old London Bridge had held back the river in this area so that in the Adams' time it had lapped the edge of their terrace at high tide. After the new bridge was opened in 1831 the water level fell so that when Victorian engineers built up the embankment and its gardens they had extensive mud banks as a starting point. The trees and flower beds they planted helped to modify the foggy and sooty atmosphere of the area, which Dickens had noted as prevalent in Buckingham St and which had encrusted the Adam ornamentation on the riverfront. The Adelphi was now a hundred years old and was found to be sinking. Extensive underpinning of the arches was carried out between 1872 and 1874 and at the same time the architectural firm of Scurry and Wright was employed by the new ground landlords to embellish the façade. Their object appears to have been to give extra architectural emphasis to the river front which seemed at the time to be an ordinary example of the numerous graceful but repetitive late Georgian streetscapes which could be found throughout the capital. A central pediment, various Italianate window entablatures, and balconies were added, and the multi-paned windows were replaced with the Victorian single pane type, and with French windows on the principal floor. At the time it must have seemed refreshingly modern but it was not long before it would be regarded as desecration.

In the gardens below statues and monuments began to be erected amongst the trees and flowerbeds and on the riverside. The iron lamp standards of 1870 with dolphins twined around seats, and other seats with ornamented sphinxes and camels, were soon joined by 'Cleopatra's Needle', an ancient obelisk brought to London from the sands of Egypt and put up by the river with appropriate adjuncts in 1878. Statues of Robert Raikes standing (1880) and of Robert Burns sitting (1884) were strictly realistic. The Fawcett Memorial (1886) and the Arthur Sullivan memorial (1903) were both emblematic and ornamental.[1]

21. The Adelphi area at low tide in early Victorian times. A reconstruction by Corrie Lamberth based on the painting by Louis Thienon (1836) and prints from the 1840s and 1850s.

The bridge and station had only just been built and were themselves replacements of features unknown in the boyhood of Dickens. Hungerford Market had been rebuilt in 1833 and been connected with the south bank in 1845 by a suspension bridge designed by Brunel. In 1851 a bazaar and art gallery was added to the market but pressure from the South Eastern Railway Company, which wanted a terminus on the north bank, caused all this to be swept away in 1863. Sir John Hawkshaw, the Company's consulting engineer, designed a new bridge to carry the tracks, retaining Brunel's central piers, with a footbridge on the east side. The station was built over brick piers with six platforms surmounted by a single great arch of 164 foot span, rising to nearly 100 feet above the platform level. To the north were booking offices surmounted by an enormous hotel.

The new station seemed to isolate the Georgian houses in Craven St from the Adelphi. To pass from one to another, dark and mysterious passages would need to be used. The district has always been full of contrasts. In *Oliver Twist* Mr Brownlow had a comfortable home in Craven St whereas Mr Peggoty and Mr Dick in *David Copperfield* used humble lodgings above a chandler's shop in Hungerford Market. R L Stevenson described the sinister quality of the area in his blood chilling stories of 'The Suicide Club' (1882). The club had its headquarters in a house in 'Box Court', an invented locality which is given reality when he writes that 'A single tall window looked out upon the river and the embankment; and by the disposition of the lights they judged themselves not far from Charing Cross station'. One of his characters stays in the Craven Hotel, Craven St, an actual location where 'the yellow coffee room' and the 'smoking-room…[a] black, gas-lit cellar' seems particularly Dickensian. The

22. Building the Embankment. From a photograph in the A J Stirling collection.

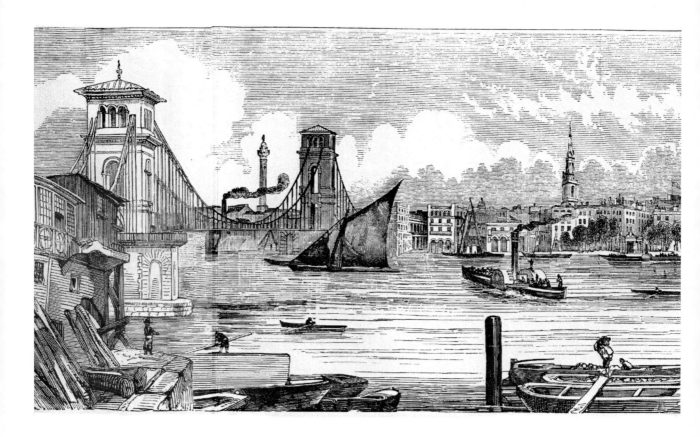

character in question is in possession of a sinister heavy trunk which 'was carried before him by several stout servants' from Craven St to Box Court. The Court is further described as 'opening off the Strand...it was too narrow for the passage of a coach; it was a mere footway between railings'.[2]

The Charing Cross Hotel, built above the railway station by E M Barry in 1863-4 must have taken custom away from the long established 'Adelphi' and the 'Caledonian'. The latter ceased business in 1908 while the former survived in its historic Georgian home until the 1930s. Even closer were the gigantic Cecil (1886) and the Savoy (1889) hotels. Their construction led to the demolition of the houses which had been built on the Salisbury estate in the 17th and 18th centuries and of historic fragments of the medieval palace of the Savoy. Oscar Wilde, who frequented the Savoy Hotel when he was rich and famous in 1895, had begun his career as a writer in London fourteen years

23. View from the river east of the Hungerford Suspension Bridge built c.1841-45.
From a Victorian line engraved panorama.

before at 13 Salisbury St, an untidy and romantic house which, with the rest of the street, would be pulled down to make way for the Cecil. The new hotels towered above the Adams' Adelphi and caused gusts of wind to blow into flues and chimneys in uncomfortably new directions. W Bottomley wrote from his builder's office in York Buildings to the Secretary of the Society of Arts in February 1902 suggesting that the down draughts in the Society's house had become a problem 'since the high Cecil Hotel disturbs the current between there and Charing Cross Hotel'.[3] These new buildings were not only gigantic in size but were eclectic in their use of architectural styles. Charing Cross Hotel was Parisian, the Savoy vaguely Italian and the Cecil Viennese. Perhaps the most extraordinary structure in the neighbourhood was the Tivoli 'Theatre of Varieties'.

Adelphi Terrace
& Hotel Cecil
from Embankment
Gardens.

24. The Adelphi and the Hotel Cecil viewed from the Embankment c.1911. From a sketch by
Howard Penton.

In 1876 a restaurant and beer garden had been opened in the Strand in the middle of the
block bounded by Adam Street to the east and Durham Street to the west. It was called the
'Tivoli' and singers and comedians were engaged to entertain the customers. The enterprise
was a success and the whole block was purchased leading to the demolition of Robert Adam's
fine corner building in Adam Street and of some more modest 18th century survivals on the
Durham Street side. The new Tivoli Theatre was an ebullient melange. Costing £300,000,
roughly twice as much as other new West End theatres, it had Tudor windows, French empire
pilasters, and Romanesque arches. The ground floor buffet was in Indian style, there was also
a palm room ornamented with alabaster swans and cupids. The auditorium was largely
'oriental' in ornamentation but the entrance vestibule was panelled in oak and had a staircase
of the 'Francois Premier order of art'. Two years later further embellishment was carried out:

25. John St (now John Adam St), looking into Adam Street, 1927. From the drawing by Hanslip Fletcher (1874-1955).

26. The Prince of Wales on the Embankment in the Winter of 1881. From a photograph of the painting by William Small (1843-1900) in the A J Stirling collection.

the entrances and saloons were said to have been, thoroughly redecorated, but in difference styles from the rest of the building – the balcony saloon being in Louis Quinze style, and the stalls saloon 'in [the] Japanese'.[4]

A more refined venue for dramatic presentations was the 'Little Theatre' which opened in 1910, a short walk away from the Tivoli. The auditorium was constructed behind the walls of the one storey building in John Street which had been linked by an archway to Coutts's premises in the Strand in 1799 and had served as extra offices and strongrooms for the bank until it moved to the former Lowther Arcade in 1904. Part of 17 John St was incorporated in the new theatre's building. The architects responsible for the work, Hayward and Maynard, copied examples of Adam work elsewhere in the Adelphi and incorporated original ceiling paintings by Angelica Kauffman. The 'Little Theatre' was leased by Gertrude Kingston who played Lysistrata in the opening production. Her friend and adviser was George Bernard Shaw who became an Adelphi resident in 1910. His 'Fanny's First Play' opened at the Little

27. The Tivoli Site in 1915. From a sketch by S T C Weeks printed in the sale prospectus.

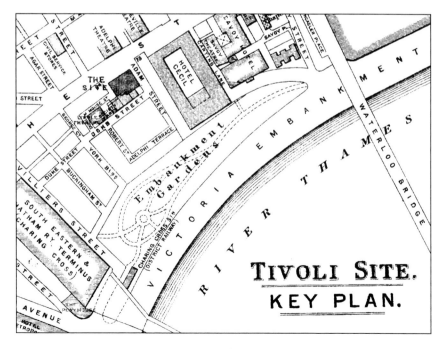

map e) The Tivoli site in 1915. (from the sale prospectus).

Theatre on 19 April 1911 and was his first commercial success. Early in that year Noel Coward had made his first stage appearance as Prince Mussell in 'The Goldfish', a children's play. In 1917 the theatre was damaged in an air raid and remained ruined and empty until 1919 when it was rebuilt to the original designs. It reopened in 1920 and between the wars became a centre for many innovative productions. In April 1940 'The Country Wife' was produced with Alec Clunes and Hermione Badderly, and The Ballet Group gave lunchtime performances between October 1940 and February 1941. The air raid shelter in the old vaults of the bank was advertised as one of the safest in London. The theatre was almost totally destroyed on the night of 16 April 1941, a rare example of German bombs hitting the same place in London twice during the course of two world wars. In 1949 the surviving walls were demolished and 'The Little Adelphi' built on its site.[5]

The air raids on London during the first world war received far less publicity than those of the second. They were also far less dangerous. From the roof of her flat in 14 Buckingham St, Christopher Isherwood's grandmother, Mrs Mackell Smith, who was in her 80s, regarded them as entertainment. Reclining in a deckchair, she watched the raids though a pair of opera glasses with a long handle like a lorgnette. J M Barrie was once forced to take shelter during an air-raid with a group of his literary guests amongst whom were Arnold Bennett, John Galsworthy and H G Wells, but does not seem to have broken up the party.[6]

Wells like Barrie's neighbour G B Shaw saw the education of the masses as the key to a brighter future for mankind. In this they had long been anticipated by the Society of Arts which had held examinations for the poorer classes in a wide range of subjects since the 1850s. In 1881 the young Sydney Webb distinguished himself by winning the first prize in the Society's Political Economy examination. Some years later he addressed the Society on the need for a special institution to study the subject and in 1895 he assisted in the foundation of the London School of Economics and Political Science. The LSE opened in three rooms on the ground floor of 9 John St and used the Society of Arts' meeting room for its lectures. After two years it moved to 10 Adelphi Terrace which had been leased by Miss Charlotte Payne Townshend, a wealthy friend of Sydney and Beatrice Webb. The ground floor and basements were used for teaching, the first floor as a library, and Charlotte (by then Mrs Bernard Shaw) lived in the upper floors with her famous dramatist husband. The LSE moved to Clare Market in 1900 but the Shaws continued in the Adelphi until 1926.[7] The London Vegetarian Society, another of Shaw's interests, was at 8 John St from 1920-25.

These literary and educational associations of the area were continued by the Workers'

Educational Association which was at 18 Adam Street in 1910, and by J M Barrie and John Galsworthy. Barrie and Galsworthy lived in 'Adelphi Terrace House' which was the name given to 1-3 Robert St, the range of chambers formerly occupied by the Caledonian Hotel, and still preserving its Adam exterior and many matching internal features, though the Booth shipping company inserted a large plate glass window at ground floor level and there was a lift at the side of the grand staircase. J M Barrie had a flat at no.3 from 1909 to 1919. It was on the third floor and had a dining room decorated in blue and a booklined study. Maurice Maeterlinck once visited Barrie and wrote on one of his study walls:

'Hommage d'Admiration au Pére de Peter Pan, Grandpére de l'Oisea Bleu.[8]

Maeterlinck's own works were performed at the Little Theatre where Barrie's close friend H Granville Barker had a private flat. Above Barrie in Robert St lived Joseph Pennell, the artist and Elizabeth, his literary wife. They had moved there from 14 Buckingham St in 1908.

The Pennells have both left records of the area as it was at this time. Joseph in his forceful lithographs showing the view over the river from his studios in Buckingham St and Robert St and the tunnel like gloom of Ivy Bridge Lane, and Elizabeth in her book *Our House* (1911) and her biography of her husband (1930).

Elizabeth describes the delight she and her husband felt when after house-hunting for weeks and months from Chelsea to Blackfriars they came across 14 Buckingham St:

> It was all that we could have asked for: as simple in architecture, with bricks as time-stained as the courts of the Temple or Gray's Inn. The front door opened into a hall twisted with age, the sloping roof supported by carved corbels…three flights of time-worn white stone steps led to the windows, with behind them a flat, called chambers, decorated by Adam!

The book contains pen portraits of her various domestics on whom she often waited as much as they did on her, of the beggars and confidence tricksters who knocked at her door, and of the more welcome visits she received from Whistler, Henley, Phil May, Edmund Gosse and other famous artists, writers and actors. She and her husband fought back without rancour at the noisy suffragettes and were amused at the growing wealth of the 'Socialist' as they called their Adelphi neighbour Shaw. They were grateful when the police stopped the German band from playing in the neighbourhood and showed compassion for the genuinely poverty stricken in 'the hunger line' on the Embankment.

28. The Adelphi Terrace in 1936. From the watercolour drawing by Francis A Taylor (b.1899), done before the demolition.

The studio above Barrie in Robert St had been constructed on the roof at Joseph Pennell's suggestion. The landlord's agent for Adelphi Terrace House built an entire fourth floor divided into three flats, and for two of them Pennell signed a lease of twenty-one years. He chose for his studio the flat on the river front, partly hidden behind Adam's pediment but with wonderful views of St Paul's to the east and Westminster to the west. The walls sloped inwards and the windows rose vertically to the ceiling giving the feelling of an Admiral's cabin in an ancient ship of war, an effect which delighted Barrie. Elizabeth described the decoration; the walls of the studio were papered in grey with a single print above the chimney piece, Toulouse-Lautrec's *affiche* for *L'Estampe Originale*. The 'white and rose on the other walls' she wrote 'made a good background for the few Whistlers and Pennells hung. The rooms were as empty as needs allowed, a few rugs on the well polished floors, a few pieces of indispensable furniture'.[9]

Other writers and graphic artists gathered at the Savage Club which had occupied 6 and 7 Adelphi Terrace since 1889. The structural repairs and alterations necessary to convert the houses into a club cost nearly £4,000 and to raise further funds and increase the membership a lavish series of 'Ladies' Nights' were held in the summer of 1891. It was said, forgetting Dr Graham's 'Temple of Health', that 'nothing like it had been seen before at Adelphi Terrace'. There was red carpet at the door, an awning over the entrance, and the vestibule and staircase were loaded with flowers and greenery. An entertainment of music and recitations was given in accordance with the practice of the Club but as the Savages' historian put it: 'nobody suspected that, under the fascination of a Savage Club night, some wives would wish to stay at the Club later than their husbands…the Ladies' Nights were soon abandoned. Instead a Ladies' Banquet was inaugurated annually'. The menus and souvenir programmes of the Savage Club were drawn by the artist members. That for 15 November 1913 was by John Hassell and shows a Canadian Indian drying a buffalo skin upon which are listed the dishes for the evening:

> *Soup*; hare, *Fish*; Fillet of Whiting, Sauce Supreme, *Joint* ; Saddle of Mutton, Red currant jelly, *Poultry*; Roast Capon, Bread Sauce, Cumberland Ham, *Vegetables*; Brussel Sprouts, Spinach, Potatoes, *Sweets*; Compote Pears, Wine Jellies, *Savoury*; Devilled haddock on toast.

The Great War which followed in the summer of the following year did not seriously limit the social activities of the club. The hours during which alcoholic liquor could be served in the bar were curtailed and by 1917 food shortages became noticeable. Yet the Saturday night dinners and the annual banquets continued as before. In 1916 a 'Shakespeare Tercentenary Dinner' was held with Courtice Pounds in the Chair and F R Benson and Edward German as guests, and in 1917 the Lord Mayor and the American Ambassador were entertained. There was, of course, the inevitable display of xenophobia. Enemy aliens were removed from the membership: a step which was also, and rather more surprisingly, taken by the Royal (as it had been since 1908) Society of Arts in John Street.[10]

CHAPTER TEN
The Last of the Old Adelphi
1918–1938

One proposal to commemorate the first world war was to revive a scheme put forward as long ago as 1906, to remove Charing Cross Station to the south bank and to rebuild Hungerford bridge. A 235 foot 'Tower of Victory' was proposed in 1919, a 'Victory bridge' in 1926 and a 'War Memorial Bridge of Empire' in 1927. Lutyens proposed in 1929 a new 'double-decker' bridge comprising a roadway over the railway capped by a concourse of workers' apartments, restaurant and roof garden. None of the schemes came to fruition and J M Barrie used to say that although Hungerford bridge was the ugliest of the bridges he could see from his windows it was none the less precious to him because it had once carried the troop trains on their way to France.[1] Yet on the Embankment the moving Belgian War memorial, Lutyen's severely classical screen with seats and flower garden, and the finely modelled Camel Corps statuette provide tangible reminders of the dreadful conflict.

A period of change, comparable to those which had occurred in Restoration and mid-Georgian times, was about to begin for the Adelphi area. The Drummond estate who were the ground landlords sought to increase rents wherever possible to keep pace with post-war price rises. The Royal Society of Arts, still occupying the premises built for it by Robert and James Adam in the 1770s was especially vulnerable. The Society's house was held on a tenancy agreement terminable on either side at two years notice. In March 1920, George H Drummond gave formal notice that he was unable to continue the lease after March 1922 and offered to sell the freehold to the Society for £50,000, this figure being subsequently reduced to £42,000.

The RSA had no capital funds to draw upon, but although at various times in the 19th century and into the early 1900s it had considered moving from the Adelphi, such a move was now said to be 'unthinkable'. Sir Charles Parsons, the great marine engineer, with other members of the Society's Council subscribed about £10,000 and then the recently appointed Secretary, George Menzies, learnt of a mysterious benefactor, whose anonymity has been preserved to this day and who was willing to subscribe a further £30,000. After an appeal had

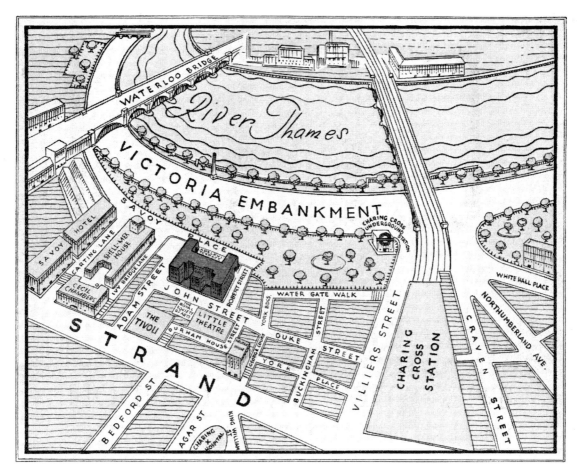

map f) The Adelphi area in 1936. From the prospectus for the New Adelphi.

been made to Fellows enough money was collected to buy the freehold and to employ Arthur Bolton, Curator of the Soane Museum and expert on the work of the Adam Brothers, to restore the interior of the building and supervise structural repairs.[2]

Edward McKnight Kauffer, the brilliant commercial artist, thought of the RSA's home as 'a kind of sanctuary – a resting place of the mind, once inside the door the noisy traffic of the Strand was silent'. Kauffer and his companion, the Swedish designer Marion Dorn, lived in flats at 6 John St (opposite the Society) in 1924 and at 12 Buckingham St from 1925 to 1930.[3] The young Harold Acton noted the décor as 'all beige and aluminium, ultra-modern, austere yet comfortable with discreet lighting and the latest gadgets'. Acton, whose own tastes ran to the Baroque and the oriental, had a flat at 5 John St which like Kauffers' first flat was on the north side of the central Adelphi block, and was next door to the Adelphi Hotel.[4] Other occupants of no.5 were various daytime businesses: Sindix Ltd, toilet brush manufacturers; Case and Hammond, theatrical agents and, especially congenial to Acton, Martin Secker, the publisher.

Secker had started his firm at no.5 in 1910 and was by this time well known as the publisher of Compton Mackenzie, Hugh Walpole and D H Lawrence. He might have been drawn to the Adelphi through the example of Sidgwick & Jackson who were at 3 Adam St from 1910 to 1925 and who were succeeded at the same address by A D Peters' long lasting literary agency. All were familiar with the work of 'The Publishing Unwins' to use Philip Unwin's evocative title and looked upon Thomas Fisher Unwin as the doyen of their profession. It is worth pausing in our historical wanderings to quote Philip's charming account of his first day of work at the office of his 75 years old 'Uncle Fisher' at 1 Adelphi Terrace:

one sunny September morning in 1923 I walked to my first day's work across Hungerford Bridge, alongside the old South Eastern & Chatham Railway. The line had just become part of the newly created 'Southern', but the initials SE & CR still decorated the sides of the smoky little tank engines and four wheeled carriages as they bumped along beside me into Charing Cross Station. Rennie's lovely stone-built Waterloo Bridge, exactly matching Somerset House, stretched across to the east, its middle piers beginning to subside into the river bed. My destination, the old Adam-built Adelphi Terrace, lay low and elegant, just to the west of the Hotel Cecil, showy and bulbous and soon to make way for the austere lines of the Shell building…and so by way of John Street into Adelphi Terrace…I was received in the stone-flagged hall by the Commissionaire, an ex-sergeant of Marines. That gave authors a good impression; few publishers had commissionaires. He led me up the graceful, easy, eighteenth-century flying staircase, at one end of which the stone steps seemed to rest on air, and up to the door of my uncle's office. On the landing wall outside hung two boldly coloured posters depicting what seemed to me strangely misshapen females. They were Aubrey Beardsley originals, commissioned with some enterprise, to advertise Fisher Unwin's Pseudonym Library in the 1890s. So just before nine o'clock I entered my first publisher's office. Architecturally it was probably one of the most beautiful in London. It lay on the first floor and had been the drawing-room of the original private house. From the full-length french windows one looked over the Embankment gardens and onto the river, the thunder and thud of the LCC's chocolate-coloured trams partially muted by the trees. The original Adam ceiling and marble fireplace were still there and TFU worked at an imposing, mahogany partners' desk, which had belonged to his father-in-law, Richard Cobden, whose bust looked on gravely from a side table. To complete the picture of an ideal publisher's office, one wall was lined with books, mainly his own publications, many of them specially bound in white buckram; even the ordinary pre-1914 bindings, with their lavish gold blocking, looked more sumptuous than is the case today. Promptly at nine o'clock Uncle Fisher entered from his flat at no.3 Adelphi Terrace, where he always breakfasted in bed. He was an imposing figure of fair height, substantial build and remarkably erect carriage, rather like a horse with a bearing rein; he held his back very stiff. His piercing blue eyes, long, well-trimmed wavy beard and the invariable morning coat, with which he always wore a floppy, yellow bow-tie, gave him an undoubted if curious air of distinction. He handled and sorted all the incoming mail and it became my morning job to sit on the opposite side of the great desk slitting the envelopes on three sides and passing them over to him, while he sang to himself over and over again, 'yes-yes', mostly in octaves and sometimes quavering. Occasionally he would interpolate a run of 'I don't think so', repeated several times....[5]

Leaving young Philip to complete his first day's work and returning to John St we find that below McKnight Kauffer's flat at no.6 there were the offices of Howard Rumney, solicitor, of Mansons, translators, of *The Economic Review*, and of the British Science Guild. At no.7 where the artists George Mansell and Percy Smith had their studios the mysterious 'CBC' Society was established, and at no.8 the more obviously named London Vegetarian Society could be found. *The National Review* offices, also at 8 John St, would have been well known to Violet, Viscountess Milner, who took over the editorship in 1932. Her love for the historic architecture and special character of the area was expressed in the preface she wrote for Charles Pendrill's book, *The Adelphi or Old Durham House in the Strand*.[6]

When the numerous office workers had departed for the suburbs catching trains from Charing Cross Railway Station or from the confusingly named Charing Cross Underground Railway Station, or had begun long slow tram or bus journeys starting in the Strand or Embankment, the guests of the private residents would arrive from Chelsea, Bloomsbury or Hampstead. Then the Adelphi would once again be redolent of the atmosphere which caught the imagination of so many artists and writers. At Harold Acton's flat they would enjoy or disdain, according to their tastes, the succulent meals served by his Chinese cook valet, Chong Sung, or attend the soirees held by Anita Berry and her Chilean aunt, Tia Martinez, who lived 'at the corner of Robert St' in Adelphi Terrace House. In this way we learn from Acton's memoirs, the painters John Banting, Lett Haynes, Cedric Morris, and the authors Cyril Connolly and Peter Quennell frequented the area.[7]

The widening of the Strand in 1924-6 saw the final demolition of the old New Exchange range with the former Coutts building of 1903 and its replacement further back from the road by Val Myer and Watson Hart's stark mini-sky scraper for the Halifax Building Society (1932-4), and a neo-Adam building designed by Yates, Cooke and Darbyshire for Saxone shoes (1924-6).

With these changes, the back of the RSA, reached by steps down Durham House Street, now came prominently into view and was ornamented by the firm of Aston Webb in 1926 with an applied portico reflecting Robert Adam's design for the John St façade. The ornamental plaques were designed by E J and A T Bradford and the pediment sculpture by Walter Gilbert. Further east the vacant Tivoli site which had been auctioned in 1915 had been used for building a gigantic 'Picture House' with a neo-Palladian façade (1924) and beyond Adam St was the elaborate Strand frontage of the now defunct Hotel Cecil and of its neighbour and more successful rival the Savoy, whose art-deco entrance dates from 1929-32. The river front of the Hotel Cecil was replaced by an enormous office building: Messrs Joseph's Shell Mex House (1931-3), whose clock tower earned it the name 'Big Benzene' and made it a totally inappropriate neighbour for the increasingly forlorn Adelphi Terrace.

A lecturer at the Royal Society of Arts in November 1922 spoke of 'disquieting rumours that the Adelphi Terrace may be sold for the erection of a new Masonic Hall' and he trusted that 'every effort will be made to prevent it'.[8] Letters and articles in the press, and agitation by the Society for the Protection of Ancient Buildings could not persuade the freeholders to save the terrace. The sale took place in October 1931 with the site described as 'ripe for redevelopment' and as 'in the heart of the Strand district which is increasing in value rapidly and which on completion of the new Shell Mex building must assume fresh significance'. The iconoclasts (as J A Milne called them) who purchased the estate kept their names out of the public domain, but pressure to save what the *Times* called 'a monument to Georgian England' continued. 'Must the Adelphi go?' asked the *Architectural Review* and even *The Builder* deplored the sight of the Adelphi 'ravaged and forlorn'. That hope was gone appeared from the announcement of a sale of fixtures to be held 'at 6 and 7 Adelphi Terrace, Strand, at present in occupation of the Savage Club on Thursday 2nd April 1936'. The result was the dispersal of numerous 'Marble and Wood chimneypieces, fire grates, wainscoting and doors believed to be the original designs and works of the renowned architects and builders, Robert and James Adam'. Top price was £200 given for a white marble mantelpiece from 3 Adelphi Terrace with fluted frieze and sculptured centre panel. Another white marble mantel from no.4 made 190 guineas and a third from no.8 made 120 guineas. A painted pine chimney-piece from the

29. The Durham St entrance to the RSA. From a recent photograph.

ground floor room of no.5 was knocked down at £86 to the National Art Collections Fund for presentation to the Victoria & Albert Museum. The Fund also acquired for the Museum two original iron balconies, one from 12 John St and the other from 5 Robert St, together with the front door of 10 Adelphi Terrace, with its graceful fanlight and portion of iron railings – prompting a newspaper headline 'Mr G B Shaw's front door for Museum'. The directors of the new 'Adelphi Estate Company' tried to salve their consciences by presenting the V&A with the plaster ceiling containing painted panels by Zucchi from the former drawing room of David Garrick at 5 Adelphi Terrace. The room has been carefully recreated in the Museum.[9]

The members of the Savage Club preserved their good humour to the last. Though knowing their lease would eventually terminate they had held their usual round of festivities in the 1930s. 'The Savage Parade', a theatrical entertainment held for the benefit of charities, took place at the Little Theatre on 26 November 1933 with its programme decorated with a view of the Adelphi Arches.[10] Sir James Barrie, called their 'near neighbour', described how from his 'eyrie so near the club that through my windows I can note the Savages going in and out as if I were in a lofty private box. They look so happy and waft such gaiety on still Saturday nights'.

In 1919 Barrie had moved up a floor in 3 Adelphi Terrace House to the Pennell's former apartments, which were remodelled for him by Lutyens. A corner of the big studio room was partitioned off to form a kind of private or personal kitchen ornamented with old blue and white Delft tiles. This area served as a secretary's office and was subsequently reabsorbed into the main room. An enormous inglenook fireplace on raised dais was built on the east wall. In it was what visitors described as the 'excruciatingly uncomfortable high backed wooden settle' and a 'little less uncomfortable' leather covered sofa. The floor was covered with matting and oriental rugs and the curtains were grey and red. Bookshelves lined the walls and Samoan carvings, presents from R L Stevenson and caps won at Eton by Barrie's favourite boys, helped to create a magical background to the hours of story telling and entertainment which the owner lavished on his friends. Urged to follow Shaw's example, who had moved to Whitehall Court in 1927, Barrie would deny rumours of the threatened demolition of the central terrace. When the Hotel Cecil was pulled down in 1931 to make way for Shell Mex House he fell into a mood of depression, but his spirits revived in the following year when on 4 May 1932, he gave 'the lunch party to beat all others', to celebrate Lord Grey of Falloden's 70th birthday. Thirty four guests including the Prime Minister, the Archbishop of Canterbury, Lord Grey, Stanley Baldwin, John Buchan and Winston Churchill crowded into his Adelphi flat. Barrie retained his foothold in what he called 'our Latin Quarter' until his death in 1937, joining we may imagine those ghosts he had once visualised as swirling round the area below:

> I see Dr Johnson and Mr Boswell coming out of Garrick's house…The Brothers Adam patrol the Adelphi still in the small hours, ready to hand over to the watch anyone who may be presuming to alter their designs and they would ascend to my eyrie to ask who had dared to put it here were it not that they are frightened at the lift. They look with suspicious eye on three revellers, Mr Micawber, the Fat Boy and Charles Lamb, who have just left Rowlandson's corner and are disturbing by their shouts another ghost at a window, who is Gibbon, very busy correcting the proof sheets of the *Decline and Fall*.[11]

Less whimsical in his attitude would have been Barrie's fellow Scot, William Douglas Weir, industrialist, public servant and creator of the Royal Air Force. Ennobled in 1918, Lord Weir was the last peer of the realm to live in the terrace and the first since the early 19th century. He leased 3 Adelphi Terrace as his town residence from 1919-36. He appreciated both the grace and dignity of the architecture and the convenience of the situation and was presumably in the country when the Savages had their gala nights and was no doubt undisturbed by such neighbours as the *Christian Science Monitor* (no.2), the National Radium Commission (no.5), Godfree's Wine office (no.8) and the Royal Statistical and the Royal Economic Societies (no.9). Soon all would depart from the Adelphi.

'The Passing of the Adelphi' and 'The Last of the Adelphi Terrace' were recorded by *The Sunday Times* in pen and ink views by Hanslip Fletcher. They showed the buildings still intact, but soon demolition would begin. By June 1936 Arthur Pile had recorded in a series of pencil sketches the awe-inspiring sight of the arches and vaults exposed to view and looking like some great ruin from classical times. A valiant struggle to keep the 'perpetual licence' of the bar of the Adelphi Hotel was noted in the *Evening Standard* for 1 July 1936:

> Amidst the desolation of falling timbers and tumbling bricks, where every five minutes the blow of a pick shudders the walls and the floor, five people are bravely preserving the last bit of unspoilt Adam architecture left in the Adelphi.
>
> Nowhere else in the whole of the famous block remain delicately-carved mantelpieces and pillared shelves and mellow wainscoting. All around the collectors have carried off the treasures, and the housebreakers have hacked away the walls.
>
> It is not, however, devotion to art that preserves this one memento of a lovely building, but devotion to a perpetual licence. For this one room is the bar of the old Adelphi Hotel in John Street. Whatever happens to the rest of the block, from the moment the first pickaxe was laid to the arches to the moment when the new block is completed on the site, there will

always be a bar open there, and always the five people to keep it running. In no other way can the perpetual licence be held. At present the bar is still in its picturesque old quarters. Soon they, too, will have to be destroyed, and then the bar will migrate to a builders' hut moved here and there on the site, probably, by a giant crane, so that demolition and building may go on. The five people who are holding the fort in a continual din of falling buildings, are the manageress, the barmaid, two porters and the charwoman'.[12]

Two architects proposed designs for a replacement building which were exhibited at the Royal Academy in 1934. J J Joas wanted to compete with Shell Mex House and drew a 'super cinema/town hall' style structure with a stress on horizontal forms and a modernistic central tower. Arthur Davis and Robert Lowry combined to produce a more traditional design. Five floors higher than the original building, its vertical divisions echoed Adam's pilasters and its rusticated arches resembled those of Somerset House.[13] The developers rejected both these schemes and chose instead the present building by Stanley Hamp of the firm of Collcutt and Hamp.

30. Demolition of the Adelphi Terrace: rear of the Adelphi Hotel, 1936. From a drawing by Albert Pile (1882-1981).

Hamp's building described as being 'in the modern perpendicular style', was like the Royal Academy exhibition designs, on the same scale as Shell Mex House. This meant that it dwarfed the surviving 18th century street frontages notably the RSA house in John Street, where its main entrance, conceived on the lines of Fitz Lang's 'Metropolis', seems a constant insult to Adam's 'Temple of Arts'. On the river side it was more successful with projecting side towers supported by statues built over a new terrace. Its recessed metal windows were an innovation for 1930s offices and some ornamental features – small animals, the coats of arms of cities and their names added interest at street level. The Dutch brickwork with its wide joints of which only a limited number of curves could be laid in a day, slowed progress on the site and annoyed the contractors who had already tried and failed to modify Hamp's siting of the statues.

31. Demolition of the Adelphi Terrace: view of the arches, 1936. From a drawing by Albert Pile.

32. Demolition of the Adelphi Terrace: general view, 1938. From an original photograph taken from the RSA House.

Inside the new building there were impressive 'Art-deco' staircases of travertine marble. Built as a luxury office block on twelve floors, it offered running water, porterage, lift service, central heating, window and office cleaning, and 'letter chutes and towel services' to its tenants. Floor space was to be divided and partitioning erected 'to suit the reasonable requirements of tenants'. Kiosks and larger shop sites were available in the ground entrance hall and garage and storage space in the former vault area could be hired by the tenants 'at moderate charges'.[14]

Completed in 1938 and designed for the age of the motor car, the new Adelphi soon found an unlooked for function as a headquarters for wartime organisations – notably the British Red Cross Society – and, in its lower levels as a gigantic air-raid shelter.

33. Stanley Hamp's Adelphi: the River front entrance. From a drawing for the 1936 prospectus.

34. Stanley Hamp's Adelphi: the John St elevation [now John Adam St]. From a drawing for the 1936 prospectus.

35. Stanley Hamp's Adelphi, the Adam St elevation. From a drawing for the 1936 prospectus.

CHAPTER ELEVEN
Warr, Post War and Four Decades of Threatened Demolition and Successful Conservation 1949–1989

In 1939 a new street name appeared in the area. 'John St' which dated back to the Adam brothers' layout in the 18th century and 'Duke St' which derived from George Villiers' redevelopment of his paternal inheritance in the 17th century, were now declared by the LCC to be one street and were given the name 'John Adam St'. This change gave some annoyance to the RSA whose historic postal address was altered as a consequence. The other Adelphi streets; Adam St and Robert St, retained and retain their original names as did and does Buckingham St and Villiers St. York Buildings which had been 'George St' until 1852, and Durham House St which had long since absorbed James St, and George Court survived and survive. The sign in York Place still records the fact that it was once called 'Of Alley'.

Before the area could settle down to these name changes and to the consequences of having a vast new business centre in its midst war brought further and unintended demolition and disruption. On government advice many institutions and firms planned to leave London as soon as war was declared. The RSA found temporary offices in the outbuildings of Buxted Park, Sussex and sent its historic archives for safe keeping in Wales. RSA meetings began in John Adam Street as usual on 1st November 1939 and in May 1940 the staff were bought back to London though the Society's pictures and more valuable books were sent to join the records in Wales. When serious bombing began in the autumn of 1940 a second evacuation was decided upon, this time only of the RSA examinations department and printing press which were sent to the village of Upper Quinton in Warwickshire. The Society's lectures which in pre-war days had been held in the evening, were given in the afternoon and, at the height of the Blitz, at lunch time. Often disturbed by the sound of an alert, both speakers and audiences soon learned to ignore the sirens.

36. The Adelphi area in wartime: bomb damage in John Adam St looking north-west. From a drawing by Ronald Fuller, 1942.

In April 1941 a parachute mine fell on the Little Theatre. The theatre itself and the building opposite, on the corner of York Buildings, were damaged beyond repair. The blast also broke most of the glass in the RSA house and damaged much of the roof and general woodwork. For a few weeks lectures had to be held at the Institution of Electrical Engineers on the nearby Embankment, then the RSA Library (today 'The Benjamin Franklin Room') was patched up and used for meetings. A photograph of the presentation of the Albert Medal to Winston Churchill in 1945 shows the room with a temporary war-time ceiling.

After the war the damage to the RSA house was repaired and the interior re-furbished under the direction of Oswald P Milne. The Lecture hall or 'Great Room', which had been unserviceable for six years, now again displayed James Barry's great canvasses. It was formally reopened by the then President of the Society, Princess Elizabeth (now HM The Queen) in November 1947. The Library and other rooms were redecorated and the Society began to prepare for two historic commemorations, the centenary of the Great Exhibition (1951) and the bicentenary of its own foundation (1954). The planning of the Festival of Britain which would include a transformation of the opposite bank of the River Thames which continues to this day took place in the RSA house and in 1951 the building was the scene of a special 'Exhibition of Exhibitions'. The bicentenary celebration saw a gathering of representatives of learned and artistic societies from throughout the world coming to the Adelphi to felicitate what to many of them was the parent body. The RSA's work and membership increased as each year went by so that when, in 1957, the opportunity came to buy a 99 years lease of the range of surviving Adam houses adjoining its building on the east side, 2-4 John Adam St and 18 Adam St, funds were raised to obtain it and to create a new council chamber, Secretary's office and exhibition gallery on the first floor, and to use the upper floors for the ever expanding Examinations Department which had been in separate offices in Victoria St since the end of the war. Some of the rooms in 18 Adam St were sublet to institutional tenants and in this way the Wiener Library and the Institute for Strategic Studies spent their formative years in the Adelphi.[1]

On the west side of the RSA building Collcutt and Hamp made some amends for their pre-war vandalism. Where the bomb-damaged Little Theatre had stood, they built, in 1951-2, an office block which was as much in keeping with the RSA house as the dictates of post-war austerity would allow. It was called 'The Little Adelphi' and though the fenestration was plain its main entrance porch entirely matched that provided by the Adam brothers for the Society. An original fanlight, rescued perhaps by the architects from the central terrace was fitted above the front door. The so-called 'Durham House', a brick structure of the early 1900s just

37. The Adelphi area in wartime: view of York Buildings with barrage balloon in the distance. From a drawing by Ronald Fuller.

to the west of the Little Adelphi was given an extra storey and fitted out as flats and offices. The Little Adelphi itself became the headquarters of the Ministry of Pensions and other government departments moved into Hamp's monolith. The area became full of civil servants who mingled with the staff of *The Lancet*, which had been at 7 Adam St since 1926 and the members of the 'Adelphi Guild', tenants of no.8 and no.9 since 1939, to make use of the 'Adam' tea house in the basement of no.10. Actors who had once been so prominent in the area as members of the Savage, returned when the Green Room Club took over the basements and under street areas of 8 and 9 Adam Street in 1955 and the literary traditions were carried on by Kingsley Martin who had a private flat in Robert St.[2] On the vacant bombed site at 13-15 John Adam St a block was put up called 'Ingram House' in 1959 and the famous *Illustrated London News* had its editorial offices there until 1965.

Collectors of coins and medals had long been led to the area in search of A H Baldwin and Sons Ltd. Established in Duncannon St on the north side of the Strand in 1900 the firm soon afterwards took additional accommodation in 14 Craven St. In 1920 it moved to the first floor of 3 Robert St, below J M Barrie's earliest flat, using as its main coin room the former ballroom of the Caledonian Hotel, then called the 'Adelphi Terrace House', a magnificent Adam interior, now preserved by the Chartered Institute of Public Finance and Accounting. Here Baldwins remained until 1963 when they took offices in the 1930s Adelphi block on the ground floor, east of the main entrance, facing the RSA. The continued prosperity of the firm enabled it to make a final move in 1971 to the 'Adam pastiche' Edwardian dining room (1906) of the former hotel. This has a balustraded roof terrace and projecting bay overlooking the river, standing above the riverside façade of a late 18th century residence which incorporate portions of the original Adelphi 'cottages' with arched storage cellars below.[3]

Aficionados of French, German and other continental language books made their way to Grant and Cutler at 11 Buckingham St. Begun before the war as the 'International Book Club' it was transformed in the late 1940s into a bookshop whose growth seemed unstoppable. The firm eventually came to occupy the entire ground floors of both 11 and 12 Buckingham St, the latter the one-time home of Samuel Pepys. It was a sad loss for the area when the leases terminated in 1986 and the 75 year old Frank Cutler moved his rabbit-warren of treasures to Great Marlborough St in the West End.[4] However the historic Buckingham Street houses were meticulously renovated which would not have been the case had the move taken place twenty years before.

In 1962 the splendid art-nouveau block of chambers (1908) at 15-16 Buckingham St which also faced onto the Watergate gardens was demolished and replaced by the existing

38. The RSA block in 1978, showing the basement floors and the former wine vaults below street level. From an isometric drawing by Alan Robson.

Burdett House. Treherne and Newman, the architects used stone and triangular headed windows to suggest, in a 20th century idiom, the medieval character of the riverfront. At the same time it was proposed to demolish the remaining Adam wing of the Adelphi on the west side of Robert St. This was of great architectural and historical importance since not only had it been the residence of many of the literary and historic figures already mentioned and contained several fine original interior features, but it had at its south-west corner the last surviving fragment of the Adam's riverside façade complete with pilasters and pediments, its companion wing on the south-east corner of Adam St having been demolished in 1937. Another argument in favour of preservation put forward at the time was that 1-3 Robert St contained the first purpose built set of 'chambers' or flats to have been built in London outside the Inns of Court. The LCC therefore placed a preservation order on the building which was supported in a letter to the *Times* (21 June 1962) signed by amongst others John Betjeman, Hugh Casson, Kenneth Clark, Jane Drew, Maxwell Fry, Frederick Gibberd, Osbert Lancaster, Raymond Mortimer, John Piper and Basil Spence. The owners appealed against the preservation order to the Ministry of Town and Country Planning, whose inspector upheld their appeal arguing that:

> as so much of the original Adelphi has been dissolved that it is not possible to consider these buildings in relation to what was once a finely conceived whole and their claims to preservation must therefore depend solely on their intrinsic architectural or historical interest. In this respect, apart from being the work of the Adam brothers, they are little different from surviving fragments of 18th century terraces. Externally…the buildings are entirely lacking in interest.

The same sort of arguments were also used to sanction the demolition of a large part of Harley St. Kingsley Martin wrote:

> The case seems to me to raise an issue that must trouble every Londoner who watches what is going on around him. The LCC plans to keep a proportion of beautiful and historic buildings in which people can live in the middle of London. Should not its decision be enough? Must it prove in each case that the building which it wishes to preserve are museum pieces? At the present rate London will soon become indistinguishable from any large modern city in any continent, a collection of vast functional boxes, differing little from each other relieved only by the almost hidden existence of a few dwarfed churches (including St Paul's and Westminster Abbey) and some other ancient monuments which tourists may find with the aid of a guide book.[5]

39. The surviving Adam range in Robert St. From a recent photograph.

40. The surviving Adam range in John Adam St. From a recent photograph.

Fortunately general restrictions on new office building made the developers think again and in 1966 a partial restoration of the building was undertaken. Seventeen years later the Chartered Institute of Public Finance and Accounting purchased 1-3 Robert St and at once appreciated the historic legacy they had acquired. Two major problems had to be faced, the need for floor strengthening and dry rot. Some beautiful decorative ceilings dating from the Adams' time were found to have survived when the Institute purchased the property but were in a very poor condition, the previous occupants having damaged the plasterwork by suspending fluorescent tubes as light fittings. The GLC's historic building experts insisted that in view of the structural work required immediately above the ceilings, shoring must be used to support them. The entrance hall also needed a great deal of work as the original staircase had been removed. A new central staircase was built flanked by marbled columns.

103

Original patterned cornices were replaced and plaster mouldings restored. The marble chimney pieces in the council chamber and dining room were opened up and cleaned.[6]

Under the terms of the lease granted to the RSA for 2-4 John Adam St and 18 Adam Street in 1956 the Society had the right to purchase the freehold of the premises at an agreed price at any time up to 1978. In 1977 it exercised the right and appointed the architects Messrs Green, Lloyd and Adams to undertake a major scheme of restoration and reconstruction. Suites of intercommunicating rooms were created on the ground and first floors which were linked to those in the original premises. A gallery was built for the design department in the basement and an attic floor added to the top of 6 and 8 John Adam Street and joined to that on the adjoining range. In 1982 the Society obtained possession of the wine vaults from H Sichel & Sons, who had found that the container lorries bringing the produce of their Rhenish vineyards could no longer negotiate the Embankment approach. Sam Lloyd was invited to draw up plans for their development. In 1988/90 the vaults were converted into a restaurant and exhibition area and at the same time a secondary lecture theatre called 'The Durham Street Auditorium' was created out of the surviving fragment of the underground roadway running below the cellars of 8 John Adam St. The outside area at the rear of no.6 – the former Suthers Court – flanked by the wall of no.8 (the Society's main house) was converted into a glass roofed atrium. A light steel staircase with treads of unpolished oak runs from the landing of no.4 and the Great Room down to the Benjamin Franklin Room. The staircase then descends to the paved floor of Suthers Court, from where there is an opening into the entrance lobby of the Durham Street Auditorium which gives access to Durham House St, and the steps up to the Strand.[7]

CHAPTER TWELVE

Post-Modernism and Embellishment at the Turn of the Century with a Walk around the Area

Any hope that the 1930s Adelphi Terrace might itself follow the fate of its famous Georgian predecessor faded when the interior was refurbished in the 1980s and prosperous undertakings connected with oil and petroleum replaced penny pinching government departments as its principal occupants. In 1993 Sepica Industries employed the architectural firm of Scott Brownrigg and Turner and the old established Sussex builders, James Longley and Co, to design and build a two storey extension at twelfth and thirteen floor level plus plant rooms at fourteenth floor level. Construction at this height was full of problems. Seven passenger and two service lifts had to be taken out of commission in sequence and returned to use while extended shafts were being built. The plant for the existing building services was on the floor area of the new structure and had to be kept running until the new superstructure had been completed and replacement plant installed at fourteenth floor level. The lower floors remained fully tenanted during the work, so stringent noise restrictions were enforced. Internally marble clad cloakrooms, staircase and lobby areas were constructed, and doors with a curled mahogany veneer, lacquered to give a full gloss finish, were installed. The floors of each incorporated a special star design worked in marble. Outside, the new extension replaced Hamp's square roof line with a graceful arched effect, which works well when seen from the River, though from street level the increase in height inevitably overshadows the surroundings even more than the 1930s giant.[1]

Facing the Adelphi Terrace's main entrance, whose Fascistic stone-incised name had now had its gigantic letters brushed with gold, and whose lobby now seemed to owe more to the style of Louis Quinze than to that of Benito Mussolini, was the Adam's surviving masterpiece: the Royal Society of Arts. Tourists and other visitors who had come to admire the façade over the years may not have noticed that the pediment had a masonry base at its top and two slightly raised platforms at each end. These features were barely visible at ground level though they can be clearly seen in Thomas Malton's aquatint of 1795 and in various later views of the building. Few realised that they were not as might have seemed chimneys, but were inserted to support statues emblematic of the Society's aims, proclaimed in the inscription below the pediment: 'Arts and Commerce Promoted' (see above, illustration no 16).

For Robert and James Adam it would have been a matter of course to ornament the pediment in this manner. Precedents abounded from Classical and Renaissance times and in Great Britain, in their own day, architects such as Colin Campbell and John Vardy made use of the form. Robert Adam's designs for General Bland and for the Edinburgh Royal College of Physicians, both dated 1758, are striking anticipations of what he intended for the Society of Arts.

41. Stanley Hamp's Adelphi enlarged. From a photograph taken in 1993: collection of James Longley & Co.

That he envisaged the use of statues in the design of the Society's façade is shown firstly in his preliminary pencil sketch and secondly, in a wood engraved vignette used to illustrate William Bailey's 1772 book of machines. Both show the central statue as Minerva holding shield and spear, but in the sketch only one statue is indicated and, as in the vignette where a third is shown, few other details can be made out.

Then in the finished water colour drawing of the façade bound in the *Original Plans...by the Brothers Adam* (see above, illustration no 11) 'Arts, Manufactures and Commerce' are seen to be clearly personified. A Minerva with her shield bearing the Gorgon's head is flanked on the west by a figure holding a spindle and to the east by another carrying what is probably a length of cloth. The flanking figures appear in a modified form in the drawing used by Robert and his brother James in their *Works in Architecture* and engraved for them by Thomas Vivares. Here we see 'Commerce' to the west standing on a rocky shore and holding in one hand a length of cloth and in the other a bag of bullion. To the east the arts of forestry, husbandry and fishery are personified by Ceres holding a young oak tree. At her feet is a harpoon for catching whales; an invention and an industry encouraged by the Society.

In 1790 the Society published an elevation of its house engraved by Isaac Taylor which was based on a drawing by Robert Adam. Though no statues had been erected on the building itself the engraving once again showed a Minerva in the centre of the pediment with a clearly recognisable figure of Mercury to the west and Ceres to the east. The architect's wish that the façade should be crowned with statues and be ornamented with festoons and roundels is once again made evident. Yet no steps seem to have been taken to realise this design.

Lack of funds was the undoubted cause for this state of affairs. It had not been easy for the Society to finance the building of the House and the detailed agreement negotiated with Robert and James Adam made no provision for luxurious ornamentation of the sort they supplied to their wealthy private patrons. Statues are not mentioned in the text of the agreement and do not appear in the small scale elevation which accompanied it. Presumably they were to be added by some generous benefactor at a later date.

That this was a possibility had been demonstrated by John Francis Moore's present in 1766 of his marble relief 'Britannia, Reviver of antique and prompter to modern arts' and would be further exemplified in 1793 when Agostino Carlini's statue of Dr Ward was given to the Society by the sitter's heir. Yet masonry statues which would have suited the site would have been expensive items. Carlini had been paid £240 in 1778 for his Portland stone statues of 'Prudence' and 'Justice' which can still be seen adorning the Strand façade of Somerset House.

42. Statues on the RSA House with a view over the roof to the Strand. From the drawing by Ron Sandford RDI.

More within the Society's means or those of some generous members would have been a set of statues from Mrs Coade's Manufactory. Coade stones statues would have been especially suitable since they were generally cast from designs by John Bacon RA, the neo-classical sculptor whose early career had been fostered by the Society, and who had presented his 'Mars' and 'Venus' to the institution in 1778. Yet a century and more went by and still there were no statues on the Society's House. Then in 1926 Sir George Sutton, an active member and Vice-President of the Society paid for the decoration of the rear elevation of the building in the manner already recorded.

43. The Little Adelphi embellished. From a recent photograph.

In 1980 duplicate casts of a late eighteenth century roundel depicting 'Priam's Appeal to Achilles for the Body of Hector' which belonged to the Society and matched in size those suggested by the Adams were affixed to the principal façade. Fourteen years later in 1994 the Adam's proposal for statues on the pediment were finally carried into effect as a result of Sebastian de Ferranti's generosity and the skills of the firm of Plowden and Smith. Fibre glass with the appearance of masonry was used to make enlarged three dimensional copies of the 'Mercury', or 'Commerce', of the Minerva and of the Ceres, as shown in the *Works in Architecture*, and they were hauled up by crane and fixed to the pediment. All that now remains is the festoon on the *oeil de bouef*. Then the RSA's house, like Kenwood, will appear fully ornamented in the manner its brilliant architects had suggested.

Internally of course modern needs had to be catered for. In 1996 air conditioning was

44. Heron House. From a prospectus for the office block built in 1998 on the sometime Tivoli site.

45. Benjamin Franklin House in Craven St. The restored exterior. From a recent photograph.

introduced into the Great Room and a circular skylight designed by Troughton McAslan inserted in its roof.[2] The Little Adelphi, the Society's westerly neighbour, was transformed both internally and externally at the same time (1996/7). The John Adam St façade was tempered by balconies and rustication designed by BUJ architects so that it harmonized with the surviving Adam range to the east of the RSA's pedimented main house. Luxuriously appointed private flats were created in the interior, thus bringing private residents back into the heart of the Adelphi, and a small lawn area was planted at the back in Durham House Street. 'Durham House' itself had some time before been given a new front door to emphasis its Edwardian 'Queen Anne' design and had also been turned into luxury apartments and offices. Another welcome introduction of greenery was to be seen at the back of the new 'Heron House' which replaced the former New South Wales/Peter Robinson building on the Strand. Demolition and construction lasted from 1992 to 1997 and the end product, designed by the Fitzroy Robinson Partnership, was an impressive stone clad office block with a simple eaves cornice and polygonal corner to Adam St. The architects took especial care to harmonise the approach to the RSA's north façade. Heron House has become the headquarters of the long established pharmaceutical company, Smith and Nephew, known for its pioneering medical research which brings back to the area the tradition of the *The Lancet* days.

Another dignified post-modern structure was built on the corner of York Buildings in 1998/99. The vertical lines suggest, without copying, the styles of the Adams' Adelphi and it harmonises with its neighbours. Like the Little Adelphi it was designed for private residents whereas the beautifully restored former 'Lancet' Building and neighbouring houses in Adam street now called 'Adam House' provides a furnished office service.[3]

* * *

Having reached the end of one century and the beginning of another the time has come for a final walk around our area. Let us begin our tour at the top of Villiers Street and, traffic permitting, glance east towards St Mary Le Strand which still provides a focus point for the ever busy thoroughfare. We shall return later to this northern boundary of our area but first we turn west and pass the fore-court of Charing Cross Railway station noting the Victorian façade beloved by Betjeman and Sir Giles Scott's version of the medieval Eleanor Cross. King Charles and Whitehall might tempt us to go on towards Westminster but we take a sharp turn into Craven St where we are suddenly back in the 18th century. Passing Benjamin Franklin's house so beautifully restored in recent years we continue down Craven St until we are able to

46. The York Buildings Watergate from the Embankment Gardens. From a recent photograph.

47. A view of Buckingham St. From a recent photograph.

turn east once more and, passing between the two halves of 'The Ship and Shovell', go through to the shopping arcade which has been made out of one of the great brick arches which date from the mid-19th century when the Charing Cross Terminus was built. We soon find ourselves once more in Villiers St – a rather dark and busy street in spite of its being for pedestrians only. On one side it has the enormous height of the arches and Terry Farrell's Station building (1990) with its futuristic glass roofline rising above the earlier brickwork, and on the other side a range of mainly late Victorian façades imposed on earlier domestic structures with the ground floors used as cafes and tourists shops. At the south end we see 'Kipling House' where the poet and travel writer endured two years of London gloom after his return from India in 1889, and towards the north turning which will take us into John Adam St there is the Royal Adelphi Hotel, a small and comfortable establishment which carries on the traditions of its famous predecessor. In John Adam St we notice that the buildings on the south side begin by following the earlier rooflines whereas those on the north

48. A view of John Adam St. From a recent photograph.

are much higher. First on the north side is the stock-brick 'Charing Cross Chambers' contemporary with the Victorian station and Hotel buildings we have already seen. Behind them is York Place interesting only because of its name plate saying that its was 'formerly Of Alley', and then there is the even taller 1950s 'Villiers House' now called '40 Strand' and a stepped up arcade made out of what was once a continuation of Buckingham St. Part of the John Adam St frontage is a lower level wing of the Strand block which has been used as a pub and restaurant under differing names in recent years (it is currently called *Theobald Bullfrog*). At this point the roadway begins to rise, reflecting the gigantic subterranean structures beneath the Adelphi and we can glimpse the pediment with the statues of the RSA house and the pilastered façade of Adam House. But before climbing the hill let us cross the street and examine the buildings on the south side.

Starting again from the Villiers St end we come to a range of much smaller houses and offices. The building on the west corner of Buckingham St is an interesting Adam revival block of 1924, which harmonises quite well with the earlier buildings which stretch down to the river. A room at the back of no.6 contains fragments of the medieval Bishop's palace which once stood on the site.

Notice the range of differing earlier doorways as we move down to no.12 where Pepys resided, as a plaque informs us, and finally to no.14 which was the site of another of his residences and is an elegant set of chambers built c.1792 by Peter Bogue and has an impressive front door with Doric columns in Buckingham St and a river front which is ten bays long. We could, if we wanted, walk down into Watergate walk and imagine ourselves taking a barge from where the now stranded Palladian masterpiece stands on the edge of the Embankment Gardens, and perhaps be tempted into the adjacent wine vaults, once the scene of Jacobite intrigues.

Refreshed or otherwise we can now go back up the east side of Buckingham St admiring the Georgian doorways and peering into late Stuart interiors. The ornamental iron railings with torch extinguishers are worth noting and, when we once more arrive at John Adam St and reaching the Victorian 'Italian medieval' corner house, we look at the recently cleaned tiled frieze below the roof, and coloured foliage capitals in the porch, before climbing the hill towards the Adelphi and reaching 21 John Adam St, the home of the Business Exchange. This house dates from the 1670s and is one of the properties put up after the demolition of York House early in the reign of Charles II. Though the window glass is later and the brick walls have been rendered in painted cement, the interior has retained more original features than most of the premises in the area. The staircase with its stout turned balusters and moulded dado and the finely panelled rooms evoke the atmosphere of the 17th century so redolent still in nearby Buckingham St.

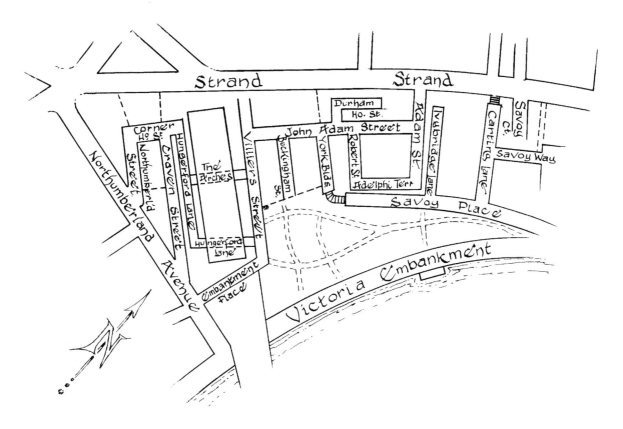

map g) The area the the beginning of the 21st century. (Drawn by John Blundell.)

Passing the post-modern flats (nos.17-19) and crossing to the end of York Buildings, with the juxtaposition of Ingram House and the intact Adam range of Robert St, we look over the road at the so-called 'Durham House' whose name and plaque to Rowlandson reminds us both of medieval and Georgian history, and to the Little Adelphi and to the RSA range. York Buildings itself has some old doorways on the west side but has been extensively rebuilt on the east. There is however an evocative fragment of the old Adelphi underworld to be found if you venture into Lower Robert St.

Walking down Robert St on the upper level we see the 1930s block on the east side and can read the tablet to the Adam brothers, to J M Barrie and to John Galsworthy on the west. At the river end, below the Adam front is the interesting projecting building created in 1906 and now the home of Baldwin's the medallists. Turning round to the river front there is the splendid view over the gardens to the South Bank and one can read another memorial tablet,

117

49. A view towards the area in the 21st century. From a recent photograph.

this time to the Adelphi as a whole. Continuing back down Adam St towards the Strand we pass 'Adam House', at the back of which is Ivy Bridge Lane now blocked at the north end but still reached from the Embankment. A last glimpse at the RSA façade in John Adam St and the entrance front of 18 Adam St provoking thoughts of Osborne's Tavern and Coffee House leads us to Heron House and we are once more in the Strand. Turning west we continue along the pavement remembering that the road was narrower in earlier times, the buildings reaching to the present pavement's edge. Heron House ends at the steps which lead down to the back of the RSA House. The arched entrance once led into the Adams' underground roadway, a fragment of which has been converted by the Society into the Durham St auditorium. Looking upwards to the large window it is difficult to realise that this is the ground floor of the Society's House and is on a level with the Adelphi Terrace overlooking the Embankment and the river. And, as time unravels in our mind we realise that we stand in what would have once been the outer courtyard of the Bishop of Durham's palace. At our back on the edge of the Strand would have been the Hospicium and great gatehouse and in front of us, beyond the courtyard's inner wall, would have been the great hall and the chapel. The noise of modern traffic awakes us from our reveries and we look for sanctuary in the Society's research library.

References

1 A Note on the Topographical Setting

1   Quoted I Darlington and J Howego, *Printed Maps of London* c.1553-1850 (1964) p.1

2   J Evelyn, *Fumifugium* (1661), pp.4-5

2. Medieval Splendour

1   C Pendrill, *The Adelphi or old Durham House* (1934), pp.5-6, hereafter cited as *Pendrill*

2   London County Council, *Survey of London XVIII. The Strand Part II* (1937), (cited hereafter as *Survey*), p.85

3   *Pendrill*, pp.16-17 quoting Norden, 1593

4   *London Topographical Record* X (1916), pp.107-11; W Jenkinson, *The Royal and Bishops Palaces in Old London* (1921) under 'Durham House' and 'Durham Place'; J Schofield, *Medieval London Houses* (1995), pp.212-3

5   *Pendrill*, p.18. See also E F Jacob, *The Fifteenth Century* (1961) pp.33, 478, 496

6   J D Mackie, *The Earlier Tudors* (1952) p.232

3 Politics and Religion in the 16TH & 17TH Centuries

THE TUDORS

1   *Pendrill*, p.20

2   *Ibid*, p.22

3   Quoted *Survey*, p.88

4   *Pendrill*, p.29

5   Quoted in *Survey*, pp.89-90. See also *Pendrill*, p.37

6   *Survey*, p.90

THE EARLY STUARTS AND THE INTERREGNUM

1   See L Stone, 'Inigo Jones and the New Exchange', *Archaeological Journal*, CXIV (1959), pp.108-11, and *Family and Fortune* (1973), pp.95-109

2   C R Cammell, *The Great Duke of Buckingham* (1939), pp348-9

3   *Pendrill* p.44; G P V Akrigg, *Jacobean Pageant* (1962), p.126

4   See article on Richard Neale in the *DNB*

5   *Pendrill* p.69

6   *State Papers Domestic* 31 December 1625 reproduced in *Survey*, p.92; *Pendrill*, pp.71-3

7   *Survey*, p.93; article on Thomas Morton in *DNB*

8   J Evelyn, *Diary*, 15 Sept, 25 Dec 1657; *Survey*, p.93. Many years later in the winter of 1683/4. Evelyn would lodge in the newly created Villiers St. See *Diary* 17 Nov 1683 and *Survey* p.62.

9   *Pendrill*, pp.59-63

4 Reconstruction and Decay: From the Restoration to the First Decade of George III

1   *Survey*, p.94

2   H Phillips, *Mid Georgian London* (1964), p.111; J H Appleby, 'James Theobald and the Chronological Register', *Antiquaries Journal* LXXVI (1996), pp.209-10

3   Phillips, pp.122-4; *Survey*, pp.32-4, 134

4   *Survey*, p.98; E Ward, *The London Spy* July 1699, p.10 quoted L Stone, 'Inigo Jones and the New Exchange', pp.120-1

5   J S Taylor, *Jonas Hanway: founder of the Marine Society* (1989), p.40

6   *Pendrill*, p.91; R W Chapman ed, *Letters of Samuel Johnson* 1719-74, I (1952), p.26

5 'The Adelphi': A Speculation and a Monument

1   *Survey*, p.99; R Adam, *Ruins of the Palace of the Emperor Diocletian, at Spalatra, Dalmatia* (London, 1764), passim; J Bryant, *Robert Adam 1728-92. Architect of Genius* (1992), pp.13-15

2   A J Bolton, *The Architecture of Robert and James Adam* (1922), II, (cited hereafter as Bolton) Chapter XVIII

3   Cited in A E Richardson, 'Must the Adelphi go?', *Architectural Review* 73 (1935)

4   XI Geo III cap.34

5   Survey p.100; *Pendrill*, p.83

6   Bolton, *loc cit; Survey* p.71; D G C Allan, *The Houses of the Royal Society of Arts, a history and a guide*, 1974 (cited hereafter as *Houses*), p.25

7   RSA Ms Minutes 28 March 1772; *Houses* pp.6, 14, 28-9

8   *Town and Country Magazine*, June 1771

9   Quoted *Pendrill* p.92

10   R M Robinson, *Coutts': the history of a banking house* (1929), pp.36-38

11   Quoted *Pendrill*, p.87

12   D Stephenson, 'Surviving Adelphi Ironwork', *Jnl RSA* CXXV (1977), pp.208-11. See also P Fitzgerald, *Robert Adam, Artist and Architect* (1904), *passim*

13   Anonymous diary in British Library, Additional Mss.27951. See H Creaton, 'London Diaries', *London Topographical Record*, vol. 28 (2001), pp.137-52

14   A Rowan, 'William Adam & Co', *Jnl RSA* CXII, (1974), pp.659-678; David Hume to Adam Smith 27 June 1772, printed in E C Mossner and I S Ross, *The Correspondence of Adam Smith* (1977), pp.161-3; *Pendrill* p.88; J Swarbrick, *The Works of Architecture of Robert and James Adam* (1959), p.vi

15   Quoted *Bolton*, p.22

16   The act was XIII George III cap 75. See also J Bryant, *Robert Adam*, p.51 and W S Lewis ed, *The Yale Edition of Horace Walpole's Correspondence* (1937-) 29, pp.107-8

17   Quoted *Pendrill*, p.86

18   *Pendrill*, pp.88-91; D Yarwood, *Robert Adam* (1970), p.146; *Houses* p.12

19   F Reynolds, *Life and Times of Frederick Reynolds* (1826); see Bolton, *loc.cit.*

20   J Swabrick, *op.cit* pp. 17-19

21   G B Hill, ed, rev. L F Powell, *Boswell's Life of Johnson* (1934-50), IV, p.99

6 Arts and Sciences

1   In 1774 109 members of the Society of Arts had addresses in the area; 38 in streets leading off the Strand, 27 in the Strand itself, 21 in Covent Garden, 10 in St Martin's Lane, 7 in the Adelphi and 6 in Charing Cross. The 'Cock and Bottle' was on the east of Durham Yard at 83 Strand. For a more detailed account of the episode see D G C Allan, 'The Move to the Adelphi', *Jnl.RSA* CXXII (1974), pp.383-454.

2.   W Presley, *The Life and Art of James Barry, passim, Houses* pp. 17-19

3.   B Rodgers, *Georgian Chronicle*, (1958), p.176. See also G E Mercer, 'Mr More of the Adelphi', *Jnl RSA* CXXVII (1979), pp.96-103, 173-79, 237-44; J K Des Fontaines, 'The Society of Arts and the early Wedgwoods', *Jnl RSA* CXIX (1971), pp.327-31, 407-10

4   Bolton, *loc.cit*

5   *Houses, loc.cit*; Georgiana Keate's Mss diary; *Bolton loc.cit*; D G C Allan 'Caleb Whitefoord, FRS, FSA, 1734-1810', Jnl RSA CXXVII (1979), pp.306-309; 371-375

6   D Hudson & K W Luckhurst, *The Royal Society of Arts* 1754-1954 (1954), pp.50-51

7   *Ibid*, pp.196-7

8   *Ibid*, pp.52-3, 264, 290, 353; A J Stirling, 'Early happiness recalled: Sir William Ross, miniature painter to the Queen', *Jnl RSA* CXXXV (1987), pp.578-82

7 Coffe Houses, Taverns, Clubs, Companies and Tradesmen

1   Quoted B Lillywhite, *London Coffee Houses* (1963), p.393
2   W J Fitzsimmons in *The Times* 23 Oct.1895. For the Adelphi and Caledonian Hotels see *Survey* and for Alexander Graham Bell's experiments see *Jnl RSA* vol.XXVI (1878), pp.17-24
3   D G C Allan, "Barkiss is willin": some Dickensian associations of the Society of Arts', *Jnl RSA* CXLII (1994), pp.45-9; *RSA: a chronological history* (1999). The latter work lists the many kindred societies who used the Society's Great Room.
4   *Houses* pp.23-6. For the occupants of various premises see J P Bond's digest of Street Directories printed below and the rate book entries and notes in *Survey*, *passim*.
5   Ballard Berkeley, *The Green Room Club 1877-1977* (unpublished typescript, 1973)
6   See P Bradshaw, *'Brother Savages and Guests': A History of the Savage Club, 1857-1957* (1957)

8 Some Victorian Residents and Habitués

1   P Thorold, *The London Rich*, (1999), p.256; C Dickens, *Sketches by Boz* (Oxford Collected Dickens, 1957), pp.324-5
2   *Pendrill*, p.104
3   A Goodman, *Gilbert and Sullivan's London*, (1998), p.22
4   Miller and Timbs are both quoted in *Pendrill*, p.105–8
5   C Dickens, *David Copperfield*, Chapter IX
6   *Jnl [R]SA* XLI (1897), pp.857-8 and article on Quintin Hogg, *DNB*
7   RSA *Chronological History*, pp.86-91
8   H T Wood, *History of the Royal Society of Arts* (1913), p.66; *Houses, passim*
9   W H Leeds, *Illustrations of Public Buildings of London* II (1838), pp.229-31 quoted *Houses* p.37
10   *Houses*, pp.21-24
11   A J Munby, *Ms Diary*, Trinity College Library, Cambridge

9 The Adelphi Embellished 1862-1918

1   *Survey* p101; A Byron, *London Statues* (1981), under Victoria Embankment
2   R.L. Stevenson, *The New Arabian Nights: the Suicide Club* (1882), pp.7, 28, 29
3   RSA, Loose Archives, 21 Feb 1902
4   *The Era* 1890/91 quoted R Mander and J Mitcheson, *The Lost Theatres of London* (1915), pp.520, 526. For Wilde's 'Thames House' see R Ellman, *Oscar Wilde* (1987), p.105. For the hotels see A H Beavan, *Imperial London* ((1961), pp.275-77
5   R Mander and J Mitcheson, *op.cit.*, pp.247-53
6   C Isherwood, *Kathleen and Frank*, (1971), p.343; D Mackail, *The Story of J M Barrie: a biography* (1941), p.517
7   *RSA Chronological History*, pp.91, 105; *Survey*, p.108
8   D Mackail, *op.cit*, pp.417-8
9   *The Graphic*, 25 Feb 1911, p.276; E Pennell, *Our House* (1911), pp.253, 273; *The Life and Letters of Joseph Pennell*, II (1930), p.48
10   P Bradshaw, *op. cit*, p.41; D Hudson & K W Luckhurst, *op.cit*, p.366

10 The Last of The Old Adelphi 1918-38

1   P Hyett, 'All change at Charing Cross', *The Strand 1692-1992* (1992), p.29; C Asquith, *Portrait of Barrie* (1954), p.6

REFERENCES

2   *Jnl RSA* LXX (1922), p.586; *Houses*, p.24

3   *Jnl RSA* LXXX (1930), p.52. Information regarding E McKnight Kauffer supplied by Graham Twemlow

4   H Acton, *Memoirs of an Aesthete* (1948), pp.196-8

5   P Unwin, *The Publishing Unwins* (1970), pp.1-3

6   *Pendrill*, preface

7   Acton, *loc.cit*

8   J Slater, 'The Strand and the Adelphi: Their early history and development', *Jnl RSA* (1922), pp.19-30

9   *The Times*, 21 Feb 1933; *Architectural Review* vol.73 (1933); *The Builder* 17 April 1936; Adelphi Sale notice 2 April 1936; *Daily Telegraph* 3 April 1936

10   Drawn by Arthur Moreland and reproduced in P Bradshaw, *op.cit*

11   C Asquith, pp.6-8; D Mackail, *passim; Daily Telegraph* 21 November 1935

12   *Sunday Times* 16 February and 12 April 1936; Arthur Pile's drawings in RSA collection; *Evening Standard* under date

13   *The Builder* 1934, p.793

14   *Particulars of the Adelphi London*, managing agents Farebrother Ellis & Co, 1936

11 War, Post War 1939-49 and Four Decades of Threatened Demolition and Successful Conservation (1949-89)

1   *Houses, passim*

2   B Berkeley, *op cit*, p.79 and below no.5

3   Baldwin's Auctions Ltd, *125 Years of Baldwins* 1872-1997 (1997) *passim* and archives of A H Baldwin & Sons Ltd

4   See obituary of Frank Cutler in *The Times* July 1999

5   *The Times* 11, 21 June 1962; press cuttings collected in A Fox, 'The Adelphi: adaptation and change in the urban landscape', typescript dissertation (IV, 17)

6   Information supplied by CIPFA

7   D G C Allan, *The Houses of the Royal Society of Arts: a new guide* (1982), *passim*; S Lloyd, 'Converting the vaults and developing the Society's House, 1977-1990', *Jnl.RSA* CXXXVIII (1990), pp.734-737

12 Post Modernism and Embellishment at The Turn of the Century, with a Walk Around the Area

1   Information supplied by Mr Peter Longley OBE

2   D G C Allan, 'Statues on the Society's House; the historical background', RSA typescript (1994); H Pearson, 'The Great Room and the tradition of change', *Jnl RSA*, CLIV (1996), pp 22

3   Information supplied by Dr Simon Bradley, editor, revised *Westminster* volume of *The Buildings of England, Ireland, Scotland and Wales*

APPENDIX I
Further Reading

The pioneer works by H B Wheatley ('Durham House', *Transactions of the London and Middlesex Archaeological Society*, N.S. vol 2, 91, 1982 and *The Adelphi and its Site*, 1895) are still of value but the fullest treatment of the area is to be found in the London County Council, *Survey of London XVIII: The Strand Part II* (1937).

C Pendrill, *The Adelphi or Old Durham House* (1934) distils much of the information in the *Survey* and is of especial value regarding the Adelphi Lottery. The building of the New Exchange is reconsidered by L Stone in 'Inigo Jones and the New Exchange', *Archaeological Journal*, CXIV (1959), pps.108-111 and *Family and Fortune* (1973).

The period just before the Adelphi development is considered in H Phillips, *Mid-Georgian London*, (1964), and the development itself has frequently described in books on the Adam Brothers (see the works by A T Bolton, G Beard, A Rowan and D Yarwood, cited in the notes and those listed by J Bryant in *Robert Adam 1728-92: Architect of Genius*, 1992, p56).

The Victorian Adelphi is evoked in J Miller, *Picturesque Sketches of London*, 1849 and A Brereton, *A Literary History of the Adelphi and its neighbourhood*, (1907).

Several general books on London are useful for the later history in the area notably J and M Bone, *London Echoing* (1948), H Hobhouse, *Lost London* (1972), S E Rasmussen, *London: the Unique City* (1934) and F Sandwich, *London by Night* (1938).

For the RSA building see the author's work cited in the notes as well as the contributions to the *RSA Journal* by J Summerson (1954), S Lloyd (1990) and H Pearson (1996).

The dissertation in typescript by A Fox, *The Adelphi, adaptation and change in the urban landscape* (c.1985, RSA Library) collates references from *The Builder* to the 1930s development. The latest edition of the *Westminster* volume (edited by S Bradley) of *The Building of England, Ireland, Scotland and Wales*, covers the more recent architectural changes to the area. The documents c1667-1897 in the metal trunk marked 'George Drummond', sold at Sotheby's on 19 July 1993, (items 442) would repay detailed examination.

APPENDIX II
Lord Bishops and Counts Palatine of Durham
1099–1672

Ranulf Flambard 1099–1128
Geoffrey Rufus 1133–1141
William of St Barbe 1143–1152
Hugh de Puiset 1153–1195
Philip of Poitiers 1197–1208
Richard Marsh 1217–1226
Richard le Poore 1228–1237
Thomas Melsonby 1237–1240
Nicholas Farnham 1241–1249
Walter Kirkham 1249–1260
Robert Stichell 1261–1274
Robert of Holy Island 1274–1283
Anthony Beck 1284–1311
Richard Kellaw 1311–1316
Louis de Beaumont 1318–1333
Robert Graystanes 1333
Richard of Bury 1333–1345
Thomas Hatfield 1345–1381
John Fordham 1382–1388
Walter Skirlaw 1388–1406
Thomas Langley 1406–1437

Robert Nevill 1438–1457
Lawrence Booth 1457–1476
William Dudley 1476–1483
John Shirwood 1484–1494
Richard Fox 1494–1501
William Senhouse 1502–1505
Christopher Bainbridge 1507–1508
Thomas Ruthall 1509–1523
Thomas Wolsey [held in commendam] 1523–1529
Cuthbert Tunstall 1529–1559
James Pilkington 1561–1576
Richard Barnes 1577–1587
Matthew Hutton 1589–1595
Tobias Matthew 1595–1606
William James 1606–1617
Richard Neale 1617–1628
John Howson 1628–1632
Thomas Morton 1632–1659
John Cosin 1660–1672

Members of the Society of Arts with Adelphi Adresses
1774–1804

ADAM, James, Esq., Adelphi Buildings [No. 4 Adelphi Terrace, 1778], 1774, 1783*

ADAM, Robert, Esq., FRS, Adelphi Buildings [No.4 Adelphi Terrace, 1772-7; No.3 Robert Street, 1778-85], 1774, 1783

ADAM, William, Esq., Adelphi Buildings [No.6 Robert Street, 1775-82], 1783

ADAMSON, Mr David, *Painter*, Adelphi [No.7 Adam Street, 1774-6], 1777

AKERS, James, Esq., Royal Terrace, Adelphi, 1804

ANDERSON, Sir John William, Bt, MP, Adelphi Terrace [No.9 1798-1812], 1804

ANTROBUS, Edmund, Esq., Adam Street, Adelphi [No.7, 1784-7], 1787

BARNARD, Mr. Thomas, Adelphi, 1788, 1794

†BLAND, Mr. Robert, Adelphi Buildings [Surgeon, No.8 Adam Street, 1774-8], 1804

BROWN, John, Esq., John Street, Adelphi [?No.7, 1791-3], 1794, 1804

BROWN, Mr Thomas, Adelphi [No.17 John Street, 1790-1813], 1794, 1804

CAMPBELL, Duncan, Esq., Adelphi [No.3 Robert Street, 1786-1800], 1788, 1794

CLARKE, Ralph, Esq., Robert Street, Adelphi, 1794

CLELAND, Walter, Esq., Adelphi Terrace [No.2 1796-1803], 1804

CRAWFORD, Mr John, Surgeon, Robert Street, Adelphi, 1794

CRISP, John, Esq., John Street, Adelphi, 1788

D'AIGREMONT, Mr Paul, Jeweller, John Street, Adelphi [John D'Aigremont at No.9, 1775–97], 1777

DAVENPORT, John, Esq., John Street, Adelphi, 1788

D'ISRAELI, Isaac, Esq., James Street, Adelphi [No.2], 1801

DURNO, Sir James, Adelphi, 1804 [knighted 13th March 1799 after being HM Consul-General at Memel]

†DUNN, Samuel, Esq., Adelphi [No.13 John Street, 1782], 1788, 1794

DUNLOP, James, Esq., Adelphi Buildings [No.5 Adam Street, 1771-3], 1774, 1777

ERRINGTON, George, Esq., No.8 Adam Street, Adelphi [No.8 1783-4], 1783

FRANCO, Jacob, Esq., John Street, Adelphi [No.1 Robert Street, Court Guide, 1796], 1794

GARRICK, David, Esq., Adelphi Buildings [No.5 Adelphi Terrace, 1773-8], 1774, 1777

HENDERSON, Christopher, Esq., Robert Street, Adelphi [No.5 1786-8], 1788

†HENDERSON, John, Esq., Terrace, Adelphi [No.4 1790-7], 1794

IDLE, Christopher, Esq., Adelphi Terrace [No.6, Court Guide, 1805], 1804

LOUZADO-BARUCH, Emanuel, Esq., Adam Street, Adelphi [No.4, 1772-80], 1774, 1777

MORTON, Thomas, Esq., John Street, Adelphi, 1804

OSBORN, Mr William, Adelphi Hotel [19 Adam Street, 1785-1804], 1804

PARKYNS, Mr William, Adelphi Wharf [of Parkins and Thompson, Coal Merchants, Middle Adelphi Wharf, Kent's Dictionary, 1804], 1794, 1804

PAXTON, Mr John, 78 Adelphi, 1774

REES, George, MD, Adam Street, Adelphi [No.6, Court Guide, 1805], 1804

ROWLES, Mr James, Wine Merchant, Adelphi [No.14 John Street, 1779-90], 1777

†STEPHENS, Francis, Esq., FRS, FSA, Adelphi [No.10 John Street, 1786-97], 1788, 1794

SUTTON, Capt. John, Robert Street, Adelphi, 1783

†WHITEFOORD, Caleb, Esq., FRS, FSA, Adelphi [No.2 James Street, 1803-4], 1794

*Dates refer to the printed membership lists. In each case the fullest address is given and those in square brackets are taken from the list of rate-payers printed in the Survey of London, Vol.XVIII, or other stated sources. Excluded are ratepayers such as Sir Richard Arkwright, Sir Herbert Mackworth and Edmund Bearcroft who did not use their Adelphi addresses in the Society's lists.
†Indicates a Society of Arts Chairman

APPENDIX IV

Survey of Adelphi Occupants, 1836–1936

J P BOND

Introduction

This exercise was inspired by an interest in the conception of the Adam Brothers' Adelphi development and in its planning and architecture: it is designed to provide a substantial indication of the names and addresses of Adelphi occupants in the century before the demolition of the central block in 1936. It began with the extraction of entries from a copy of *Pigot and Co's London Alphabetical Commercial Directory, for 1836* in the possession of the writer. This meant searching through some 597 directory pages, a process only reasonably practicable in domestic surroundings. Initially the survey covered the actual streets formed in the Adams's development and some closely connected with it, namely George Street (now York Buildings), James Street and Durham Street (now merged as Durham House Street). George Street includes the entrance to Lower Robert Street which, with Durham Street, gave access to the Adelphi vaults and thence to the Adelphi wharves. The survey was later extended to include the wider Adelphi quarter drawing in the further streets to the south of the Strand and to the east of Hungerford Market – on the site of which Charing Cross Station was subsequently built. It is thus generally consistent with the area considered in the main text of the book. Directory entries are also given for Craven Street – to the west of Hungerford Market – for 1836.

The entries obtained from Pigot 1836 were reinforced by extraction of data from *Robson's London Directory, Street Key, and Conveyance List…for 1836*. This appears to be generally less substantial than the Pigot directory, and thus lacks a number of entries found in Pigot, but it did reveal others. Thus the 1836 information shown below is basically as derived from Pigot with additions from Robson. Occasionally data from both sources are shown where there is a substantial difference. The format of this section of the survey follows to some extent, but not entirely, that of the original directory, either Pigot or Robson. A few entries from the Robson directory in the following year (1837) have been added to illustrate the accelerating development of larger-scale commercial activity and the growing influx of offices of national organisations

From 1841 onwards the scope and the quality of the reference material is transformed with the introduction of the street directory section in the Post Office London Directory (Kelly). This continued over the whole of the remainder of the period covered − to 1936 − substantially unaltered in format. It should perhaps be noted that the directory coverage of the smaller streets and alleys is patchy. For example George Court is included, but not Off Alley as it existed before 1852, when it was merged with York Place. Even then only the more substantial occupiers in York Place seem to be listed. This incomplete coverage is revealed by inspection of the Rate Book records held in the Archives Centre of the Westminster City Library. In checking the period 1836 to 1850 some 20 to 23 houses were found recorded with their occupants. Interestingly it was found that several of the occupants also had businesses in the neighbourhood. For example in 1841 George Deakin Midgley at 1 and 2 Off Alley was listed as 'chemist & druggist, 49 Strand', while Thomas Bewlay at 3 Off Alley was listed as 'tobacconist & snuff manufacturer to the royal family, wholesale and retail, 49 Strand'. In 1845 Mrs Priscilla Davis at 1 Off Alley was listed as 'brush & sponge warehouse, & lodging house keeper, 49 Strand', while Thomas Bewlay continued at 3 Off Alley and 49 Strand. Additionally, in 1845, Henry Bath Michell at 5 Off Alley was listed as a builder at 4 Northumberland St. Strand. George Midgely, perhaps now retired, still occupied 2 Off Alley. In those years 49 Strand − indicated on map (h) one door away to the west from the entry to George Court − also accommodated a Post Office Receiving House, making it appear to be somewhat crowded. Thus while Off Alley housed numbers of people who were not recorded in the directories, it also appears to have provided something of a dormitory quarter for proprietors of local businesses.

In this survey the data extracted from the Kelly directories are presented in a format closely similar to the original material. Where there was scope to expand sometimes acutely condensed names and words this was done.

The various directories show interesting differences in routes to the Adelphi wharves. This is also the case within the run of the Kelly directories. Setting down a comparison of the routes over the hundred years covered provides an intriguing pastime, though the emphasis changed to the Adelphi arches following the embankment of the River in 1864-70.

Sources

Pigot and Co's London Alphabetical Commercial Directory for 1836
Robson's London Directory, Street Key, and Conveyance List…for 1836
Robson's London Directory, Street Key, and Conveyance List…for 1837
Post Office London Street Directory for (year) (F. Kelly, later Kelly & Co, then Kelly's Directories Ltd.)

Adelphi Area Map

The street map provided for the Adelphi area (map h) gives some guidance on street numbers. That portion of the map showing the Adam development and the closely connected streets was sketched mainly from a copy of Horwood's *Survey of London* (1807) kept at the Guildhall Library. The street numbering shown on the Horwood map is incomplete. Valuable further insight was obtained from the relevant Survey of London volume [London County Council. *Survey of London. Volume XVIII. The Strand.(The Parish of St. Martin's-in-the-Fields, Part II)*(1937)]. To some extent the location of some street numbers remains uncertain. For example the present writer guessed the location of 2 James Street and inferred the locations of 12, 13, 14 and 15 Adam Street, though being reasonably confident about the latter. As is stated in the Survey of London volume the original numbering of John Street was very irregular.

The Godfrey Edition reproduction of the relevant Ordnance Survey map of 1871 shows, in accurate detail, the main outlines of the street layout of the area up to the demolition of 1936, including the underground roadways [Godfrey, Alan. *The Godfrey Edition. Old Ordnance Survey Maps. London Sheet 7.73. Charing Cross & Trafalgar Square 1871* (1983). Original scale 1:1056 (60 inches = 1 mile)]. A small detail revealed by it is the public house in Durham Street, opposite William Street, which is very likely to be the *Salisbury Arms*.

Another detail perhaps worth recording is that numbers 1 and 2 Adam Street shared a single street entrance. At times these premises were occupied as a single unit, as number 1 Adam Street.

Map h) The Adams' Adelphi 1836-1936.

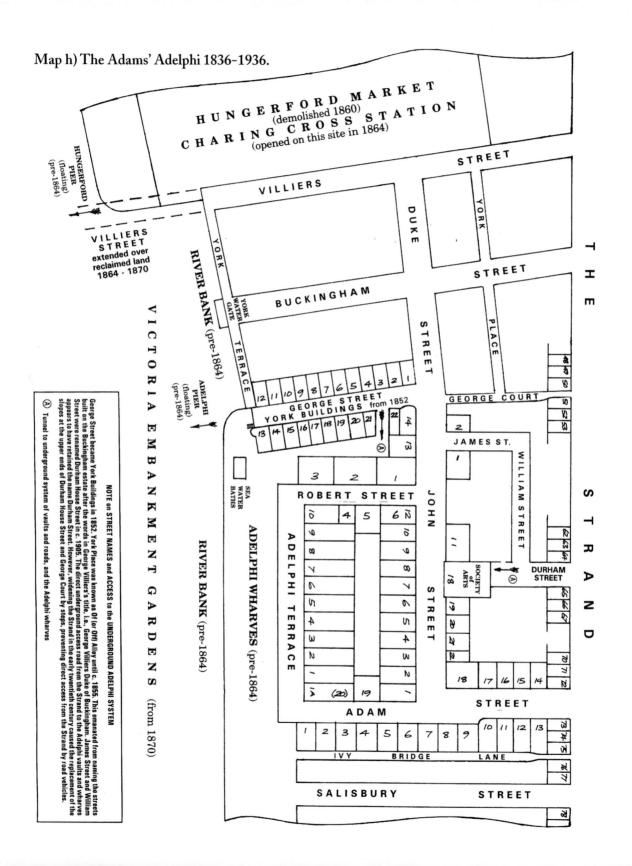

HUNGERFORD MARKET
(demolished 1860)
CHARING CROSS STATION
(opened on this site in 1864)

HUNGERFORD PIER (floating) (pre-1864)

VILLIERS STREET
extended over reclaimed land
1864 - 1870

RIVER BANK (pre-1864)

YORK WATER GATE

ADELPHI PIER (floating) (pre-1864)

VICTORIA EMBANKMENT GARDENS (from 1870)

RIVER BANK (pre-1864)

ADELPHI WHARVES (pre-1864)

VILLIERS STREET

BUCKINGHAM

YORK TERRACE

DUKE STREET

STREET

STREET

YORK

PLACE

GEORGE COURT

JAMES ST.

WILLIAM STREET

DURHAM STREET

SOCIETY of ARTS

THE STRAND

GEORGE STREET
YORK BUILDINGS from 1852

SEA WATER BATHS

ROBERT STREET

ADELPHI TERRACE

JOHN STREET

ADAM STREET

IVY BRIDGE LANE

SALISBURY STREET

NOTE on STREET NAMES and ACCESS to the UNDERGROUND ADELPHI SYSTEM

George Street became York Buildings in 1852. York Place was known as Of (or Off) Alley until c. 1855. This emanated from naming the streets built on the Buckingham estate after the words in George Villiers's title, i.e., George Villiers Duke of Buckingham. James Street and William Street were renamed Durham House Street in c. 1905. The direct underground access road from the Strand to the Adelphi vaults and wharves appears to have retained the name Durham Street. However, widening the Strand in the early twentieth century caused the replacement of the slopes at the upper ends of Durham House Street and George Court by steps, preventing direct access from the Strand by road vehicles.

Ⓐ Tunnel to underground system of vaults and roads, and the Adelphi wharves

The Survey

Directory Extracts 1836

The information in this section was extracted from *Pigot and Co's London Alphabetical Commercial Directory for 1836*, supported by information from *Robson's London Directory, Street Key, and Conveyance List…for 1836*. Unless denoted otherwise the data is from Pigot. Data from Robson is denoted by the key **[R36]**. A few entries from the Robson directory in the following year (1837) have been added to illustrate the accelerating development of larger-scale commercial activity and the growing influx of offices of national organisations. These are denoted by the key **[R37]**

ADAM STREET
Knox Vicissimus, barrister, 1 Adam st. Adelphi & 3 King's Bench walk, Temple
Donaldson S. John, scholastic agent, 4 Adam st. Adelphi
Lane, wine merchant, 4 Adam st. Adelphi **[R36]**
AFRICAN EXPEDITION OFFICE, 4 Adam st. Adelphi **[R36]**
Bidder G P C, engineer, 4 Adam st. Adelphi **[R36]**
Nicholson Joseph, attorney, 6 Adam st. Adelphi
Brookes William M'Intosh, architect & surveyor, 6 Adam st. Adelphi
Downing G, jeweller, 6 Adam st. Adelphi **[R36]**
Gafney John, *Adelphi Wine Shades*, 11 Adam st. Adelphi
Kelly Joseph, tailor, 12 Adam st. Adelphi
Andrews Jonathan, tailor, &c. 15 Adam st. Adelphi
Tucker William, surgeon, 17 Adam st. Adelphi
Morgan John Godfrey, wine and brandy merchant, 18 Adam st. Adelphi
Riddell John R. attorney, 18 Adam st. Adelphi
Roberts Henry, architect, 18 Adam st. Adelphi
Hancock Samuel, secretary to the Royal naval charitable society, 18 Adam st. Adelphi

ADELPHI TERRACE
Booth and Pettet, navy agents, 2 Adelphi terrace, Strand **[R36]**
Richardson Edward, attorney, 2 Adelphi terrace, Strand
Hill Rowland, secretary to the South Australian colonization commissioners, 6 Adelphi terrace, Strand
COLONISATION COMMISSION FOR SOUTH AUSTRALIA, 6 Adelphi terrace, Strand **[R36]**
Clementson Charles, 8 Adelphi terrace, Strand **[R36]**

BUCKINGHAM STREET
Walding James, green grocer, 8 Off alley, Buckingham st. Strand
Willers Samuel, fishmonger, 1 Buckingham st. Strand
Richardson Frederick. *Prince's Head, P.H.* 2 Buckingham st. Strand

Clewley Daniel, cowkeeper, 3 Buckingham st. Strand
Lilly James, green grocer and coal dealer, 4 Buckingham st. Strand
Darcy William, tailor, 5 Buckingham st. Strand
Shand William, artificial leg and arm maker, 6 and 7 Buckingham st. Strand
Cutler & Wilson, merchants, 10 Buckingham st. Strand
Cutler G.H. & Co. merchants, 10 Buckingham st. Strand
Wilson & Cutler, merchants, 10 Buckingham st. Strand
Paxton William Gill, wine merchant, 11 Buckingham st. Strand
Stafford William, attorney, 13 Buckingham st. Strand
Etty William, historical painter, 14 Buckingham st. Strand
Hayward Philip, solicitor, 14 Buckingham st. Strand **[R36]**
Forbes and Co. manufacturers of the Circassian hair dye, 16 Buckingham st. Strand
Withy Robert, attorney, 18 Buckingham st. Strand
Gargrave Ralph Burnock, attorney, 19 Buckingham st. Strand
Bevan Richard and John, civil engineers, 19 Buckingham st. Strand
LAND & ASSESSED TAX OFFICE, 19 Buckingham st. Strand **[R36]**
PRIVATE PERMIT OFFICE, 20 Buckingham st. Strand **[R36]**
Gibbon John Thomas, sculptor, 20 Buckingham st. Strand **[R36]**
Borgnis Joseph, drawing master, 21 Buckingham st. Strand
Hodgson Edward, attorney, 21 Buckingham st. Strand
Strachan John, wine and spirit merchant, 22$^{1}/_{2}$ Buckingham st. Strand
Vale Ann, dyer, 24 Buckingham st. Strand
Clarke James, straw hat maker, 25 Buckingham st. Strand
Lovell Ann, milliner, &c. 26 Buckingham st. Strand
Vickery Lawrence, tailor, 27 Buckingham st. Strand
Stone Richard, tallow chandler and melter and oil & colourman, 27 & 28 Buckingham st. Strand

CRAVEN COURT
Clarke Charles, grocer, &c. 2 Craven court, Craven st.
Cork Thomas, *Ship & Shovel, P.H.* 3 Craven Court, Craven St. Strand

CRAVEN STREET
Staunton Michael, stationer and bookseller, 1 Craven st. Strand
Monkhouse Cyril John, attorney, 3 Craven st. Strand
Davidson Robert, surgeon, 6 Craven st. Strand
DEBTORS' RELIEF SOCIETY, Lunn Joseph, secretary, 7 Craven st. Strand **[R36]**
Rees David, physician, 8 Craven st. Strand, and New Cross, Deptford
Price John, tailor, 10 Craven st. Strand
Collins I, milliner, 12 Craven st. Strand **[R36]**
Le Breton Philip Henry, attorney, 14 Craven st. Strand
Morrison John, tailor & draper, 15 Craven st. Strand
Wilkes Robert, bookseller, 16 Craven st. Strand
Potter J., silversmith, 17 Craven st. Strand
Leonard James, surgeon, 18 Craven st. Strand

Pittar Arthur & Co., jewel and precious stone merchants, 19 Craven st. Strand
Dodd Charles, attorney, 21 Craven st. Strand
Taylor Mrs, lodging-house keeper, 22 Craven st. Strand **[R36]**
Heath James Patten, physician, 24 Craven st. Strand
Morton Edward, short hand writer, 25 Craven st. Strand
Smith James, solicitor to the board of ordnance, 27 Craven st. Strand
Bell John, solicitor, 28 Craven st. Strand **[R36]**
Bell John B, publisher, 28 Craven st. Strand **[R36]**
Morris & Verbeke, attorneys, 30 Craven st. Strand
Shear Andrew & Nephew, tailors, 31 Craven st. Strand
Waterfield Thomas, physician, 31 Craven st. Strand
Kent John King, 33 Craven st. Strand
Price William Frazer, army agent, 34 Craven st. Strand
Dobson James, painter and paper stainer, 35 Craven st. Strand
Clemence Mark, tailor, 36 Craven st. Strand
Bentall J, wine merchant, 37 Craven st. Strand **[R36]**
Kay & Watson, wine merchants, 40 Craven st. Strand
Watson William, wine merchant, 40 Craven st. Strand
Clarke and Co, solicitors, 43 Craven st. Strand
Cork Thomas, *Ship & Shovel, P.H.* 3 Craven Court, Craven Street, Strand
Holland George, wine and spirit merchant, 44 Craven st. Strand
Tapster Stephen & Son, Craven Hotel, 46 Craven st. Strand
Cullington Daniel, attorney, 47 Craven st. Strand

DUKE STREET

Appleyard Flather, bookseller and newsagent, 1 Duke st. Adelphi
Gibbon John Thomas, seal engraver, 2 Duke st. Adelphi
M'Kenzie Stephen, wine and spirit merchant, 3 Duke st. Adelphi
Holland Henry, architect, 4 Duke st. Adelphi
Antrobus William, day school, 5 Duke st. Adelphi
Brown Benjamin, cabinet maker, upholsterer, &c, 5 Duke st. Adelphi
Watts James, fruiterer, 6 Duke st. Adelphi
Roberts Smith and Co. silversmiths and platers, 8 Duke St. Adelphi
Lowe James, Sheffield agent, 8 Duke st. Adelphi **[R36]**
Eaton John, tailor, 9 Duke st. Adelphi
Fairbairn Robert, bookbinder, 10 Duke st. Adelphi
Jones Evan, St. *Martins, P.H.* 13 Duke st. Adelphi
White Charles J, lighterman, 14 Duke st. Adelphi **[R36]**
Bryant Samuel, bath proprietor, 15 Duke st. Adelphi
Parr James Ebenezer, butcher, 16 Duke St. Adelphi
Hughes William, tailor, 17 Duke st, Adelphi

DURHAM STREET
Glasier Francis, *Salisbury Arms, P.H.* 1 Durham st. Strand
Pearce William, goldsmith, Durham st. Strand **[R36]**

GEORGE STREET
Lawrence, J. sea water baths, George st. Adelphi
Taylor George & Samuel, carpenters and undertakers, 1 George st. Adelphi
Vialls John Palmer, flint glass cutter and dealer, 2 George st. Adelphi
Clark John, jewellery case maker, 3 George st. Adelphi
Aitken Charles, bookbinder, 4 George st. Adelphi
Wirgman George, working jeweller, 5 George st. Adelphi
Papps Charles Henry, coal merchant, 6 George st. Adelphi
Jaffray Charles, tailor, 10 George street, Adelphi
Seton, Plomer & Seton, attorneys, 12 George st. Adelphi
Apps & Johnson, coal merchant, 13 George st. Adelphi
Johnson Henry, coal merchant, 13 George st. Adelphi
Seaton Joseph, coal merchant, 13 George st. Adelphi
Topham George, coal merchant, 13 George st. Adelphi
Waller Charles B. coal merchant, 13 George st. Adelphi
Warren Edward, coal merchant, 13 George st. Adelphi
Knox G F, surgeon, 14 George st. Adelphi **[R36]**
Brookbank William, tailor, 19 George st. Adelphi **[R36]**
Bayley William, tailor, 21 George st. Adelphi
Lane Charles, medical agent, 22 George st. Adelphi

GEORGE COURT
Dodrell John, *George, P.H.* 2 George court, Strand
Dovell William, carpenter & undertaker, 4 George court, Strand
Knibbs John, boot & shoe maker, 5 George court, Strand

IVY BRIDGE LANE
Willder George, *Fox, P.H.* Ivy Bridge Lane, Adelphi (entered under Eastern Adelphi Wharf in **[R37]**)

JAMES STREET
M'Inerheny William, accountant, 1 James st. Adelphi
Underwood George, medical agent, 1 James st. Adelphi
Woodhead Joseph, navy agent, 1 James st. Adelphi

JOHN STREET
Aikin Arthur, F.L.S. Secretary to the Society of Arts, John st. Adelphi
Chesswright Richard, secretary to the Equitable gas light Co. John st. Adelphi
Chaplin William, *Osborne's Hotel,* 1,2,3 & 4, John st. Adelphi & *Caledonian Hotel,* 3 Robert st. Adelphi
Cumberledge Charles Nathaniel, architect & surveyor, 5 John st. Adelphi
Bullock Edward T. attorney, 6 John st. Adelphi

Bullock James T. attorney, 6 John st. Adelphi
Savery Frederick, merchant, 6 John st. Adelphi **[R36]**
Cox Edward Homersham, auctioneer, &c. 6 John st. Adelphi
Du Bois Edward, treasurer of the Metropolitan lunacy commissioners, Chambers, Adelphi
COMMISSIONERS OF LUNACY, Du Bois Edward, secretary, 8 John st. Adelphi **[R36]**
Savery Frederick, wine merchant, 6 John st. Adelphi
Banks Robert Olddiss, attorney, 7 John st. Adelphi
Hinrich Andrew, attorney, 9 John st. Adelphi
Pittar & Co. diamond & jewel merchants, 10 John st. Adelphi
Chippendale John, banker and naval and commission agent, 10 John st. Adelphi
Jones Owen, architect, 11 John st. Adelphi
Stutely M J, architect, 11 John st. Adelphi **[R36]**
Rigley Henry Adolphus, attorney, 11 John st. Adelphi
Todd & Bosanquet, wine merchants, 11 John st. Adelphi
Watkins George, attorney, 11 John st. Adelphi
Avern William, tailor, 12 John st. Adelphi
Robinson Christopher, solicitor, 13 John st. Adelphi **[R36]**
Sanford Thomas, attorney, 13 John st. Adelphi
SOCIETY OF ARTS, 19 John st. Adelphi **[R36]** [19 John st. Arthur Aiken, secretary]**[R36]**
Duthie James, attorney, 20 John st. Adelphi
EQUITABLE GAS LIGHT COMPANY, Cheesewright Richard, secretary, 21 John st. Adelphi **[R36]**

ROBERT STREET
Lawrie John, army agent, 1 Robert st. Adelphi
Bocquet Edward, artist, 2 Robert st. Adelphi **[R36]**
Cates George, attorney, 5 Robert st. Adelphi
Guy John, surgeon, 6 Robert st. Adelphi
Clementson Charles, navy agent, 8 Robert st. Adelphi

VILLIERS STREET
Laing Margaret and Son, plumbers, painters, paperhangers and decorators, 2 Villiers st. Strand
Price James, *Green Dragon, P.H.* 3 Villiers st. Strand
Maplestone John, tinman, 4 Villiers st. Strand
Eitel Abraham, coppersmith, 5 Villiers st. Strand
Clemence John, carpenter &c. 6 Villiers st. Strand
Frohock Mark, shopkeeper & tailor, 7 Villiers st. Strand
Williams Ann, *Granby's Head, P.H.* 8 Villiers st. Strand
Laith A.L., secretary to the Hungerford market Company. 9 Villiers st. Strand
HUNGERFORD MARKET COMMITTEE, Leith A L , secretary, 10 Villiers st. Strand **[R36]**
Baily & Roberts, engravers, copperplate and lithographic printers, 13 Villiers st. Strand
Bowler Frances, day school, 15 Villiers st. Strand
Robertson Divie and Son, wine merchants, 17 Villiers st. Strand
Hare John, *Hungerford Arms, P.H.* 19 Villiers st. Strand
Charlwood George, seedsman and florist, 14 Tavistock row, Covent garden, and 20 Villiers st. Strand

Armstrong Thomas, bookbinder, 23 Villiers st. Strand
Moss Sarah, map colourer, 24 Villiers st. Strand
Goodlad and Co. flute &c. makers, 25 Villiers st. Strand
Bennett Solomon, seal engraver, 26 Villiers st. Strand
Ward Henry, tailor, 28 Villiers st. Strand
Goodworth George, bricklayer, 29 Villiers st. Strand
Prescott William, *Griffin, P.H.* 30 Villiers st. Strand, and ale brewer, 29 York st., York road
Clemence William, carpenter, builder, &c. 31 Villiers st. Strand
Gould Thomas, coffee rooms, 32 Villiers st. Strand
Pymm George, bookbinder, 33 Villiers st. Strand
Woods William, plumber, painter &c. 34 Villiers st. Strand
Adlard John, bookbinder, 35 Villiers st. Strand

ADELPHI WHARFS
Western Adelphi Wharf
Apps & Johnstone, coal merchant, Western wharf, Strand **[R36]**
Caruthers J S, coal merchant, Western wharf, Strand **[R36]**
Cook James & Son, coal merchants, Western wharf, Strand **[R36]**
Daniel James, coal merchant, Western wharf, Strand **[R36]**
Hull John, coal merchant, Western wharf, Strand **[R36]**
Johnson and Co, coal merchants, Western wharf, Strand **[R36]**
Jones Henry Robert, coal merchant, Western wharf, Adelphi
Keysell Mrs. coal merchant, Western wharf, Adelphi
Maslin Martin, coal merchant, Western wharf, Adelphi
Morris Thomas, coal merchant, Western wharf, Strand **[R36]**
Powell Walter, coal merchant, Western wharf, Adelphi
Revell Thomas, farrier, Western wharf, Adelphi
Rickman James, coal & bottle merchant, Western wharf, Adelphi
Robinson Robert Graham, coal merchant, Western wharf, Strand **[R36]**
Scott John, coal merchant, Western wharf, Adelphi
Seaton Joseph, coal merchant, Western wharf, Strand **[R36]**
Simons John, coal merchant, Western wharf, Adelphi
Snee J A, coal merchant, Western wharf, Strand **[R36]**
Topham George, coal merchant, Western wharf, Strand **[R36]**
Warren J, coal merchant, Western wharf, Strand **[R36]**
Wilson John, coal merchant, Western wharf, Adelphi
Wilson William, coal merchant, Western wharf, Adelphi
Wilson William, lath render, Western wharf, Adelphi
Middle Adelphi Wharf
Bottomley and Co, coal merchants **[R36]**
Eastern Adelphi Wharf
Christie James B. sack maker, Eastern Wharf, Adelphi
Lees Henry, coal merchant, 219 Simpson pl, Edgware road, and Adelphi wharf, Strand
Paterson William, ale merchant, Adelphi wharf, Strand

Sant, Leslie & Tullock, coal merchants, Adelphi wharf, Strand
Sant William and Co, coal merchants, Eastern Adelphi wharf, Strand [R36]
Thompson Elizabeth, egg merchant, Great Scotland yard, and 7 Adelphi wharf, Strand
Thomson Elizabeth, egg merchant, Eastern Adelphi wharf, Strand [R36]
Tutin Christopher, coal merchant [R36]

Additions to the Robson directory in the following year (1837), shown below, illustrate the accelerating development of larger-scale commercial activity and the growing influx of offices of national organisations

ADAM STREET
ROYAL NAVAL CHARITABLE INSTITUTION, Hancock Samuel, secretary, 18 Adam st. Adelphi [R37]
NEW BRUNSWICK & NOVA SCOTIA LAND COMPANY, Hayne Richard, secretary, 18 Adam st. Adelphi [R37]

ADELPHI TERRACE
UNITED KINGDOM BEET-ROOT CO, Wells Joseph, Secretary, 8 Adelphi terrace, Strand [R37]

JOHN STREET
SOUTH BRITISH COTTON MANUFACTURING CO, 6 John st. Adelphi [R37]

ROBERT STREET
NORTH & SOUTH JUNCTION RAILWAY, 1 Robert st. Adelphi [R37]

VILLIERS STREET
LONDON & WESTMINSTER STEAM BOAT CO. 8 Villiers st. Strand [R37]
HUNGERFORD & LAMBETH SUSPENSION FOOT-BRIDGE CO. 8 Villiers st. Strand [R37]

Directory Extracts 1841 to 1936
The information in this section was extracted from the *Post Office London Street Directory for (year)* (F. Kelly, later Kelly & Co., then Kelly's Directories Ltd.)
Years included in the survey:

1841 1845 1850 1855 1860 1865 1870
1875 1880 1885 1890 1895 1900 1905
1910 1915 1920 1925 1930 1935 1936

The street lists for the major streets are given in alphabetical order at the five year intervals indicated. The lists for the minor streets and the Strand entry to Durham Street, later Durham House Street are given for 1841, 1870, 1900 and 1930. Generally the three Strand properties to each side of the Durham/Durham House Street intersection are included.

ADAM STREET

1841

Adam st. *Adelphi, 72 Strand.*

1	Flight Edward Gill, solicitor
3	Ramsey Miss Ann, lodging house
4	Franklin William, esq
4	Grimshaw George Garnet, stockbroker
4	Julian Richard, architect
4	Nuttall John Parker, esq
5	Black Charles, general agent
6	Brookes W. M'Intosh, architect&surveyor
7	Dommes Mrs Emma, boarding house
8	Wallace Mrs C. M. boarding house
9	Smith Rev. Elijah
10	Reynolds John Hamilton, attorney
11	Pitt Mrs Mary, lodging house
15	Andrews Jonathan, tailor
16	Grainger Charles George, esq
16	Koch Christian, esq
17	Gray Robert, tailor
18	Alexander George, architect
18	Burn John, esq
18	Coppin John Frederick, solicitor
18	Lang Charles Evans, architect
18	Morgan John G. wine & spirit merchant
18	Roberts Henry, architect
18	*Royal Naval Benevolent Society,*
	Commander Dickson, secretary
18	White George, esq
	. . . . *John street* . . . .
19	Bliss William, boarding house
20	Bell John C. esq
20	Bell William, esq
20	Bourne Robert, esq
20	Dyce William, esq
20	Scott Henry, esq
20	*Australasian Steam Navigation Co*
20	*Falkland Islands Association*
20	Locke Joseph, civil engineer
20	Whittington George Thomas, merchant
	. . . . *Adelphi terrace* . . . .

1845

Adam st. *Adelphi, 72 & 73 Strand.*

1	Adams William Bridges, esq
1	Flight Edward Gill, solicitor
1	Walmsley William Elyard, esq
1	Wintle John & Co. wine merchants
3	Hamstede Frederick William, esq
3	Ramsey Miss Ann, lodging house
4	Axford John, esq
4	Butterfield William, architect
4	Day Arthur G. esq
4	Horsburgh James, esq
4	Hyde Charles Tunstall, esq
4	Mackintosh James, esq
4	Moon James, solicitor
4	Scott William, wine merchant
4	Silvester Henry, esq
5	Black Charles, general agent
6	Brookes W. M'Intosh, architect&surveyor
7	Lewis Edward, solicitor&parliamenty agt
8	Wallace Mrs C. M. boarding house
9	Reed John, solicitor
9	Robinson Christian, solicitor
9	Trimen Andrew, architect & surveyor
10	Reynolds John Hamilton, attorney
13	Veale George, esq
15	Andrews Jonathan, tailor
16	Grainger Charles George, esq
16	Koch Christian, esq
16	Oldfield George, esq
17	Billings Mrs. Maria, lodging house
17	Maitland Mrs. Mary, artificial florist
18	Baggs Isham, practical chemist
18	Burn John, esq
18	Lang Charles Evans, architect
18	Morgan John Godfrey, wine merchant
18	*Royal Naval Benevolent Society,*
	Commander Dickson, secretary
18	Yearsley John, esq
	. . . . . . *here John street intersects* . . . .
19	Bliss William, boarding house
19	Wynn Sir William, bart
20	*is now 1A, Adelphi terrace*
	. . . . . *here Adelphi terrace intersects* . . . . .

1850

Adam st. *Adelphi, 72 & 73 Strand.*

1	Adams William Bridges, esq
1	Flight Edward Gill, solicitor
1	Forsyth James, esq
1	Blamire George, esq
1	Marshall James, esq
1	Wintle John & Co. wine merchants
3	Hamstede Frederick William, esq
3	Ramsey Mrs. Ann, lodging house
4	Butterfield William, architect
4	Brasseur Isidore, esq
4	De Vaux Augustus Romaine, esq
4	Mackintosh James, esq
4	Moon James, solicitor
4	Woodyer Henry, architect
5	Black Charles, general agent
6	Brookes W. M'Intosh, architect&surveyor
7	*Evangelical Alliance, British Organisation.*
	Rev. William Bevan, sec
7	Lewis Edward, solicitor
8	Wass Charles Wentworth, engraver
8	Brassey Thomas, railway contractor
9	Braithwaite Frederick, sen. civil engineer
9	Braithwaite Frederick, jun. civil engineer
9	*Irish Land Improvement Society*
9	*Ritterbandt's Patent for preventing*
	Incrustation
9	Trimen Andrew, architect & surveyor
10	White William Gillham, esq
11	ALBION CHAMBERS:—
	Errington John Edward, civil engineer
	Locke Joseph, civil engineer, M.P.
	for Honiton
11	Waring Alexander, wine merchant
13	Veale George, esq
15	Aitchison & Horsbrugh, wine merchants
16	Aitchison Robert, esq
17	Walsh Thomas, tailor
18	Burn John, esq
18	Lang Charles Evans, architect
18	*Royal Naval Benevolent Society,*
	Commander Dickson, R.N. secretary
18	Yarrow Thomas Alfred, civil engineer
	. . . . . . *here John street intersects* . . . .
19	Bliss William, lodging house
20	*is now 1A, Adelphi terrace*

1855

Adam st. *Adelphi, 72 & 73 Strand.*

1	*Tithe Redemption Trust,*
	William T. Young, sec
1	Adams William Bridges, esq
1	Blamire George, esq
1	Flight Edward Gill, solicitor
1	Nalder Frederick, esq
1	Wintle Robert & Co. wine merchants
3	Bryce James, esq
3	Mora Don José Joaquin de
3	Hamstede Frederick William, esq
3	Ramsey Mrs. Ann, lodging house
4	Brasseur Isidore, esq
4	Butterfield William, architect
4	De Vaux Augustus Romaine Grant, esq
4	Mackintosh James, esq
4	Woodyer Henry, architect
6	Nicholson Rev. Hugh, M.A. clerical agent
7	*Alliance Reading Room,*
	Rev. Henry Jones, M.A. sec. pro. tem
7	*Evangelical Alliance (British Organisation)*
	Rev. Joseph Peniel Dobson, sec
7	*Evangelization in Ireland,*
	Rev. Henry Jones, M.A. sec
7	*Religious Liberty Committee,*
	Rev. Edward Steane, D.D. ⎫
	Rev. Thomas Nolan ⎬ secs
7	*Western Asia Missions Society,*
	Rev. Cuthbert G. Young, sec
8	Brassey Thomas, railway contractor
8	Ogilvie Alexander, contractor
9	Allman Fennell H. consulting engineer
9	*Patentees of the Improved Steam Engine*
9	Rufford Francis, esq
9	Trimen Andrew, architect & surveyor
9	Roberts & Roby, auctioneers & land.agts
10	White William Gillam Saunders, esq
11	ALBION CHAMBERS:—
	Smith, Beacock & Tannett, self acting
	machine tool manufacturers,
	George Buchanan, agent
	Anglo-Californian Gold Mining Co.
	George Frederick Goodman, sec
	Church of England Education Society,
	Rev. George E. Tate, M.A. hon. clrical. sec
	Wilbraham Taylor, esq. hon. sec
	Rev. Reginald Gunnery, M.A.
	clerical sec.
	William Kershaw Davies, assistant sec
	Corry Edward, commission agent
	Davies William Kershaw, accountant
	Kinsey Arthur, esq
	Langford George, architect
	Peto Frederick, esq
	Reynolds Edward, esq
	Watson Dr. Joseph, F.G.S
	Welsh & Irish Slate Companies,
	William Prosser, manager
13	Veale George, esq
15 & 16	*Householders' & General Life*
	Assurance Co. Richard Hodson, sec
18	Burn John, esq
18	Gardner John, civil engineer
18	Iles Charles, esq
18	Lamotte John Lagier, solicitor
18	Phelps William, solicitor
18	*London Liturgical Revision Society,*
	Arthur C. Rainey, provisional sec
18	*Royal Naval Benevolent Society*
18	Stewart, Pim, Kincaid & White,
	land agents
18	White George Preston, civil engineer
	. . . . *here John street intersects* . . . .
19	Bliss William, lodging house
20	*is now 1A, Adelphi terrace*

ADAM STREET

1860

Adam st, *Adelphi* (W.C.), 72 & 73 *Strand.*
1 *Tithe Redemption Trust,*
            Henry Radcliffe, sec
1 Adams William Bridges, civil engineer
1 Blamire George, esq
1 Bull & Weale, wine merchants
1 Radcliffe Henry, solicitor
1 Potter William S. esq
3 Bryce James, esq
3 Mora Jose M. de, esq
3 Hamstede Frederick William, esq
3 Ramsey Mrs. Ann, lodging house
4 Butterfield William, architect
4 Clifton Claude Constable, esq
4 Wilkinson Hooper J. esq
4 Mackintosh James, esq
4 *Milford Estate, Dock & Railway*
    Co's Office,
            Frederick Wehnert, architect
4 Salvin Anthony, architect & surveyor
6 Nicholson Rev. Hugh, M.A. clerical agent
7 *Evangelical Alliance (British Organisation),*
            Rev. William Cardall, M.A. &
            Rev. James Davis, secs
7 *Turkish Missions Aid Society,*
            Rev. George Royds Birch, sec
7 *Evangelical Christendom,* Office of the
7 Eardley Sir Culling Eardley, bart
8 Buchanan George, engineer & iron
            merchant
8 Smith, Beacock & Tannett, self acting
    machine tool manufacturers,
            George Buchanan, agent
8 Smith Thomas Roger, architect & surveyor
8 Hayward Charles Forster, architect &
    surveyor
8 Webster Mr. William Bullock
8 Wright Joseph & Sons, railway carriage
    builders,   George Buchanan, agent
9 Stent Frdk. Warburton, architect & surv
9 Trimen Andrew, architect
9 *National Discount Loan Fund &*
    Deposit Bank,
            George Lawrence, manager
10 Field, Wardell & Co. wine merchants
10 Morice Beaumont, esq
11 ALBION CHAMBERS:—
    Church of England Education Society,
            Rev. Reginald Gunnery, M.A.
            clerical sec
            W. H. Brougham, depositary
            Clark Daniel Kinnear, civil engineer
            Carter Robert, esq
            Hornidge Samuel G. solicitor
            Kinsey Arthur, esq
            Lucas Matthew Bernard, solicitor
    Welsh & Irish Slate Companies,
            Samuel Gwinnett Hornidge, manager
11A, Burge & Warren, importers of india
    rubber goods
13 Veale George, esq
15 & 16 *Wine Importers' Association,*
            Robert Edward Barnes, manager
16 *Evans' Patent Fire-Grate & Smoke*
    Consuming Apparatus for Locomotive,
    Marine & other Boilers & Furnaces,
            Richard Hodson, manager
17 Scott Henry, surgeon
18 *Church of England & General Freehold*
    Land & Building Society,
            Henry Osborne Martin, sec
18 *Cottage Improvement Society,*
            Henry Martin, agent
18 Harcourt H. Durant, esq
18 Walton & Robson, architects
18 Lye Charles Frederick, auctioneer, &c
18 Martin Henry Osborne, land agent
18 Beaumont Henry, solicitor
18 *Royal Naval Benevolent Society,*
            James Thomas Riccalton, R.N. sec
18 Gardner John, civil engineer
. . . . *here John street intersects* . . . .
19 Sherwood Thomas, private hotel
20 *is now 1A, Adelphi terrace*

1865

Adam st, *Adelphi* (W.C.), 72 & 73 *Strand.*
1 *Tithe Redemption Trust,*
            Henry Radcliffe, sec
1 *National Association for the Promotion*
    of Social Science,
            George W. Hastings, sec
1 St. Clare Harry Phillip, esq
1 Bull & Weale, wine merchants
1 Radcliffe Henry, solicitor
1 Potter William S. esq
3 Hamstede Frederick William, esq
3 Ramsey Miss Ann, lodging house
4 Downs Thomas Sturges, esq
4 Bromley Capt. Charles, R.N
4 Butterfield William, architect
4 Mackintosh James, esq
4 Salvin Anthony, architect
6 Adams Charles J. architect
6 Friend William, surveyor & estate agent
6 *National Discount Loan Fund,*
            George Lawrence, manager
6 Lee Frederick, general agent
6 *Laguna Silver Mining Co. (limited),*
            Holland Dell, sec
7 *Evangelical Alliance (British Organisation),*
            Rev. James Davis, secretary
            Rev. Hermann Schmettau, PH.D.
            foreign secretary
7 *Christian Vernacular Education Society*
    for India,
            Rev. J. H. Titcomb, M.A. hon.sec
            Francis William L. Gordon, sec
7 *Turkish Missions Aid Society,*
            Rev. Henry Jones, M.A. sec
7 *Systematic Beneficence Society,*
            Rev. Robert G. Cather, LL.D. gen.sec
8 *Avonside Engine Co.(limited),*
            George Buchanan, agent
8 Buchanan George, engineer & iron mer
8 Barker Henry & Samuel, railway
    wheel &c. manufacturers,
            George Buchanan, agent
8 Cooper Samuel T. & Co. ironmasters,
            George Buchanan, agent
8 *Metropolitan Railway Carriage*
    & Wagon Co. (limited),
            George Buchanan, agent
8 Pease, Hutchinson & Ledward, ironmasters,
            George Buchanan, agent
8 Smith, Beacock & Tannett, tool manfrs.
            George Buchanan, agent
8 Vivian H. H. & Co. tube manufacturers,
            George Buchanan, agent
8 Warners, Lucas & Barrett, ironmasters,
            George Buchanan, agent
8 Warner & Co. manufacturers of railway
    chairs & bowl sleepers &c.
            George Buchanan, agent
8 Hayward Charles F. F.R.I.B.A. architect
8 Webster Mr. William Bullock
9 Carrick James Anderson, civil engineer
9 Harvey George & Alexander, manu-
    facturers of engineers' tools &c
9 Musgrave John & Sons, engineers,
    boiler makers & ironfounders
9 Robinson Thomas & Son, engineers
9 Wylie Allan C. engineer
9 Chaplin Alexander & Co. engineers &c
9 Trimen Andrew, architect
9 Trimen Leonard B. architect & surveyor
9 Forester Thomas B. professor of the
    indian law
10 *The British Ice-making Co.*
            Capt. Thomas E. Symonds, R.N. sec
10 Field, Wardell & Co. wine merchants
10 Roberts Richard & Co. consulting engnrs
10 Symonds Capt. Thomas Edward, R.N

11 ALBION CHAMBERS:—
    Church of England Education Society,
            Rev. R. Gunnery, M.A. clerical sec
            W. H. Brougham, depositary
            Martin Louis E.C. professor of chemistry
            Clark Daniel Kinnear, civil engineer
            Hornidge Samuel Gwinnett, solicitor
            Kennedy & Rogers, architects
            Kinsey Arthur, esq
            Finch John, patentee of porcelain baths
            Wakefield Henry, civil engineer
            Owen Henry B. commsn. & genl. agent
11A, Hurter Hubert & Son, wine merchnts
15 Power Edward Rawdon, ceylon agency
15 & 16 *Wine Importers' Association (limited),*
            Robt. Edwd. Barnes, mangr
16 Anderson George, gas engineer
16 Balfour Henry Thomas, mechanical engnr
16 Balfour Henry & Co.engineers & ironfdrs
18 *Church of England & General Freehold*
    Land Allotment Society,
            Henry Osborne Martin, sec
18 Walton John Wilson, architect
18 Martin Hy.Osborne, auctnr & land agent
18 *Land, Building, Investment & Cottage*
    Improvement Co. (limited),
            Henry Osborne Martin, sec
18 *Royal Naval Benevolent Society,*
            James Thomas Riccalton, R.N. sec
18 Gardner John, civil engineer
. . . . *here is John street* . . . .
19 Sherwood Thomas, private hotel
20 *is now 1A, Adelphi terrace*

ADAM STREET

1870

Adam st, *Adelphi* (W.C.), 72 & 73 *Strand.*
1   *National Association for the Promotion*
    of Social Science,
      George W. Hastings, chairman of Council
1   Bull & Weale, wine merchants
1   Potter William S.
1   Watson William Charles, heraldic painter
3   Blythe Capt. John D
3   Hamstede Frederick William, esq
3   Hall Edward, F.S.A. architect
3   Ramsey Miss Ann, lodging house
4   Downs Thomas Sturges
4   Bromley Capt. Charles, R.N
4   Butterfield William, architect
4   Mackintosh Thomas John Devereux
4   Salvin Anthony, architect
6   Radcliffe Henry, solicitor
6   *The Church of England & Ireland*
    Temperance Reformation Society,
      Rev. Thomas Rooke, M.A.
            clerical secretary
6   T*he National Association for Promoting*
    Amendment in the Liquor Traffic,
      Rev. Thomas Rooke, M.A. ⎫
      H. C. Greenwood, esq   ⎬ hon
      Rev. E. White   ⎭ secs
6   Courtenay Thomas W.
7   *Evangelical Alliance (British Organisation)*
    Rev. James Davis,   ⎫
    Rev. H. Schmettau, PH.D. ⎬ secs
7   *Christian Vernacular Education*
    Society for India,
          Rev. J. H. Titcomb, M.A. hon.sec
          Lockhart Gordon, sec
7   *Church of England & General Freehold*
    Land Allotment Society,
          Henry Osborne Martin, sec
7   *Land, Building, Investment & Cottage*
    Improvement Co. (limited),
          Henry Osborne Martin, sec
7   Martin H. O. land agent
8   Sheldrick Arthur, architect
8   Eyton Henry Medgett, architect
8   Freshwater Henry Thomas, architect
8   Henshaw Edmund Simons, whisky agent
8   Mayne William Colburn, agent-general
      for New South Wales
9   Bernard Benjamin & Co. merchants
9   Bremer Albert & Co. exporters to india,
      america & japan
9   Clayton & Clare, importers of
      foreign produce
9   Dollman Francis Thomas, architect
9   Lambert Philipp & Co. merchants
9   Lavers William M. civil engineer
9   Warren Frederick, architect & surveyor
9   Chellingworth Thomas T. civil engineer
9   Shaw Philander, patentee
9   Levinstein Hugo, merchant
9   *Shaw's Patent Hot Air Company,*
      Philander Shaw, managing director
9   *Boston Shoe Stud & Button Co.*
          Sumner Shaw, president
10 Field, Wardell & Co. wine merchants
10 Roberts Frederick Hebberd,civil engineer
10 Symonds Capt. Thomas Edward, R.N
10 Wardell John Lloyd & Co. wine
      & general merchants
10 Hodge Paul Rapsey, civil engineer
10 Schweitzer H. & Co. cocoatina manufactr
10 Perfect Alfred, surgeon dentist
11 ALBION CHAMBERS:—
    Church of England Education Society,
      Rev. R. Gunnery, M.A. hon. sec
      W. H. Brougham, depository
    Middle Class School Fund Society,
      Rev. Reginald Gunnery, M.A. hon.sec
    Clark Daniel Kinnear, civil engineer
    Kennedy & O'Donoghue, architects

11 Dixon William, emigration agent
    Finch John, patentee of porcelain baths
    Wakefield Henry, civil engineer
11 & 11A, Hürter Hubert & Son,
    wine merchants
11 Storry & Smith, civil engineers
18 Charles Thomas, wine importer
18 *Turkish Missions Aid Society,*
    Rev. Henty Jones, M.A. ⎫
    Lieut.-Col Lawford,   ⎬ secs
18 *Royal Naval Benevolent Society,*
          John M. Jefferson, R.N. sec
18 Oppenheimer Ludwig, encaustic
    tile importer
. . . . *here is John street* . . . .
19 Sherwood Thomas, private hotel
20 *is now 1A, Adelphi terrace*

1875

Adam st, *Adelphi* (W.C.), 72 & 73 *Strand.*
1A,   *London Scottish (15th Middlesex)*
    Rifle Volunteer Corps,
          Capt. John Campbell, paymaster
1   *National Association for the Promotion*
    of Social Science,
      George W. Hastings, president of council
    Metropolitan & Provincial Poor Law
    Officers' Association,
          William H. Jordan, sec
    National Indian Association,
      Hodgson Pratt & ⎫
      Miss E. Manning ⎬ secs
    Union Society of London
    Bull & Weale, wine merchants
    Toker Philip Champion, proctor
    Potter William S.
    Christian Book Society,
          Rev. William Gray, M.A. sec
3   Blythe Capt. John D
    Hamstede Frederick William
4   Downs Thomas Sturges
    Bromley Capt. Charles, R.N
    Mackintosh Thomas John Devereux
    Salvin Anthony, architect
4 & 5 Butterfield William, architect
6   Radcliffe Henry, solicitor
    The Church of England Temperance
    Society, (Province of Canterbury)
          Alfred Sargant, gen.sec
    Courtenay Thomas W.
7   *Evangelical Alliance (British Organisation),*
          Rev. James Davis, sec
    Christian Vernacular Education Society
    for India,
      Rev. J. H. Titcomb, M.A.honorary secretary
      Lockhart Gordon, secretary
    Church of England Provident Benefit
    Building Society,
          Henry Osborne Martin, sec
    Land, Building, Investment & Cottage
    Improvement Co. Limited,
          Henry Osborne Martin, sec
    Central Cottage Improvement Society,
          Henry Osborne Martin, sec
    Martin Henry O. land agent
    Lansdown James Chester, surveyor
    Tasman William James, solicitor
    National Union of Elementary Teachers,
          T. E. Heller, sec
8   Marr James, auctioneer & surveyor
    Emden Walter, architect
    Hendriks Herman, agency offices
    Richards Edward Harrinson
9   Price Henry C. & Co. engineers
    Dollman Francis Thomas, architect
    Whelan Bernard, architect
    Roper Frederick William, architect
    Allen William Taprell, architect
    Revans John
10 Field, Wardell & Sich wine merchants
    Wardell John Lloyd & Co. wine
      & general merchants
    Roberts Frederick Hebberd, engineer
    Symonds Capt. Thomas Edward, R.N
    Schweitzer H. & Co. cocoatina manufactr
    Paull & Bickerdike, architects
11 ALBION CHAMBERS:—
    Church of England Education Society,
      Rev.R. Gunnery, M.A. ⎫ hon.
      Rev. W.M. Mungeam, B.A. ⎭ secs
    Henry Wash, depositary
    Stuart William, solicitor
    Finch John, patentee of porcelain baths
    Wakefield Henry, civil engineer
    Withers Robert J. F.R.I.B.A. architect
    Friend William Leopold
    Merry & Co. financial agents
    Tonge Edward, solicitor
11 & 11A, Hürter & Son, wine merchants

18 Charles Thomas, wine importer
    Turkish Missions Aid Society,
      Rev. Henry Jones, M.A. ⎫
      Lieut.-Col Lawford,   ⎬ secs
    Law Henry, civil engineer
    Royal Naval Benevolent Society,
      John St. J. Wagstaffe, R.N. sec
    Meeson Frederick Richard, architect
18 *Freedmen's Missions Aid Society,*
      Rev. L. D. Bevan, LL.D ⎫ hon.
      Rev. H. Jones, M.A   ⎬ secs
      Rev. Arthur Wickson, LL.D. sec
    O'Byrne Brothers, navy agents
    O'Byrne Robert, barrister
    Naval Chronicle Office
    Military Almanac Office
    Wellington Gazette Office
    Johnson & Co. brick & tile manufacturers
    Atkinson Charles, mechanical engineer
. . . . *here is John street* . . . .
19 Piper John Edward, private hotel
20 *is now 1A, Adelphi terrace*

ADAM STREET

1880

Adam st, *Adelphi* (W.C.), 72 & 73 *Strand.*
1A,   *London Scottish (15th Middlesex)*
    Rifle Volunteer Corps,
        Capt. John Campbell, paymaster
1   *National Association for the Promotion*
    of Social Science,
    George W. Hastings, president of council
    National Indian Association,
        Hodgson Pratt &
        Miss E. Manning } secs
    Poor Law Conferences Central Committee
    Society for Promoting Legislation for the
    Control & Care of Habitual Drunkards,
        S. S. Alford, sec
    Gaelic Society of London,
        John Forbes, sec
    Union Society of London
    Needes John C. medical agent
3   Blythe Capt. John D
    Hamstede Frederick William
    Weedon Miss
4   Downs Thomas Sturges
    Hills Gordon Macdonald, architect
    Bromley Capt. Charles, R.N
    Mackintosh Thomas John Devereux
4 & 5   Butterfield William, architect
6   Clarke Edward, architect
    Gribble Charles Risdon, architect
7   *Evangelical Alliance (British Organisation),*
        J. Field, A. J. Arnold, secs
    Christian Vernacular Education Society
    for India,
        Lockhart Gordon, secretary
    Church of England Provident Benefit
    Building Society,
    Land, Building, Investment & Cottage
    Improvement Co. Limited,
        Henry Osborne Martin, sec
    Central Cottage Improvement Society,
        Henry Osborne Martin, sec
    Martin H. & Son, wholesale cricket
    ball makers
    Martin Henry O. land agent
    National Union of Elementary Teachers,
        T. E. Heller, sec
8   Marr James, auctioneer & surveyor
    Spanish & Portuguese Church Missions,
        Rev. L. S. Tugwell, sec
    Turkish Missions Aid Society,
        Rev. Henry Jones, M.A. sec
    Aitken Memorial Mission Fund,
        S. W. D. Fox, M.A. sec
    Smith Frank Town
9   Price, Lea & Co. engineers
    Roper Frederick William, architect
    Lee Sydney H. wine merchant
    Wheeler Frederick W. surgeon
    Silvester Henry S. draughtsman
    Peirce John Sampson, civil engineer
    Raven Henry, surveyor
10   Field, Wardell & Sich, wine merchants
    Wardell J.L.&Co. wine & general merchs
    Schweitzer H. & Co. cocoatina manufactr
    Symonds Capt. Thomas Edward, R.N
    Buckle James George, architect
    Commercial World Office
11   ALBION CHAMBERS:—
    Church of England Education Society
    Christian Book Society,
        John Shrimpton, sec
    Prayer Book & Homily Society,
        John Shrimpton, sec
    Stuart William, solicitor
    Wakefield Henry, civil engineer
    Withers Robert J. F.R.I.B.A. architect
    Prynne George H. Fellows, architect
    Norman D
11 & 11A,   Hürter & Son, wine merchants
    Berlin Brewery Co. "Tivoli"

18   *Wine Importers Association*
    Charles & Co. wine merchants
    Royal Naval Benevolent Society,
        John St. J. Wagstaffe, R.N. sec
    McEvoy Capt. Charles A. electrician
    Freedmen's Missions Aid Society,
      Rev. O. H. White, D.D. & Rev.
      J. Gwynne Jones, secs
    O'Byrne Brothers, navy agents
    O'Byrne Robert, barrister
    Naval Chronicle Office
    Wellington Gazette Office
    Chapman & Clarke, estate agents
    Church of England Temperance Sick
    & Burial Society,
        Mark Knowles, sec
    General Temperance Agency & Registry,
        Miss E. S. Smith, manager
    Radcliffe Henry, solicitor
    Andrews Samuel
    Weekly Samuel, general agent
    .... *here is John street* ....
19   Slack Frederick, private hotel
20   *is now 1A, Adelphi terrace*

1885

Adam st, *Adelphi* (W.C.), 72 & 73 *Strand.*
1A,   *London Scottish (7th Middlesex)*
    Rifle Volunteer Corps,
        Major John Campbell, paymaster
1   *National Association for the Promotion*
    of Social Science,
        J. L. Clifford-Smith, sec
    Gaelic Society of London,
        Malcolm McLeod, sec
    Needes John C. medical agent
    Palestine Exploration Fund,
        Walter Besant, M.A. sec
    Innes & Burton, civil engineers
    London Sanitary Protection Association,
        Cosmo Innes, sec
    Ballamy Edward Vaux
3   Weedon Miss
4   Downs Thomas Sturges
    Hills Gordon Macdonald, architect
    Bromley Capt. Charles, R.N
    Turner Percival, medical agent
4 & 5   Butterfield William, architect
6   Clarke Edward, architect
    Edwardes George, advertising agent
    Chatterton Balsir, dramatic agent
    Wilson Frederick, artist
7   *Evangelical Alliance (British Organisation),*
    Lieut.-Gen. J. Field, C.B. &
        A. J. Arnold, secs
    Christian Vernacular Education
    Society for India,
        Henry Morris, hon. sec
    Church of England Provident Benefit
    Building Society,
    Land, Building, Investment & Cottage
    Improvement Co. Limited,
        Henry Osborne Martin, sec
    Central Cottage Improvement Society,
        Henry O. Martin, sec
    Martin H. & Son, wholesale cricket
    ball makers
    Martin Henry O. land agent
    Turkish Missions Aid Society,
        Rev. T. W. Brown, M.A. sec
8   Marr James, land agent & surveyor
    Actors' Benevolent Fund,
        C. G. Compton, sec
    Spanish, Portuguese & Mexican
    Church Aid Society,
        Rev. L. S. Tugwell, sec
    Smith Frank Town
9   Price, Lea & Co. engineers
    Cobbold Ernest George, solicitor
    Roper Frederick William, architect
    Silvester Henry S. draughtsman
    Dramatic & Musical Sick Fund,
        E. A. Anson, sec
    Browne George Walter, musical directory
    Abercrombie Chester, house agent
10   Field, Wardell & Sich, wine merchants
    Wardell J.L.&Co. wine&general merchs
    Schweitzer H. & Co. cocoatina manufactr
    Symonds Capt. Thomas Edward, R.N
    Buckle James George, architect
    Commercial World Office
11   ALBION CHAMBERS:—
    Church of England Book Society,
        John Shrimpton, sec
    Buckland & Sons, auctioneers
    Stuart William, solicitor
    Wakefield Henry, civil engineer
    Withers Robert J. F.R.I.B.A. architect
    Norman Daniel
11 & 11A,   Hürter & Son, wine merchants
15, 16 & 17   Attenborough George,
    dealer in works of art
18   *Royal Naval Benevolent Society,*
        John St. J. Wagstaffe, R.N. sec
    Foster Harry & Co. auctioneers

18   *Imperial Deposit Bank & Building*
    Society,
        Charles James Knightley, manager
    McEvoy Capt. Charles A. electrician
    Girdwood James, land agent
    Freedmen's Missions Aid Society,
        Rev. J. Gwynne Jones, sec
    Knowles Mark, barrister
    Andrews Samuel
    Weekly Samuel, general agent
    Oldham Clement Hugh, accountant
    .... *here is John street* ....
19   Sherwood Hotel, William Henry Prust
20   *is now 1A, Adelphi terrace*

ADAM STREET

1890

Adam st. *Adelphi* (W.C.), 72 & 73 *Strand.*
1 *Imperial Institute of the United*
   Kingdom, the Colonies & India,
   Sir F. A. Abel, C.B., organizing secretary
1 School for Modern Oriental Studies
1 Vine Sir J. R. Somers, F.S.S.
1 Needes John C. medical agent
1 *Palestine Exploration Fund,*
   George Armstrong, sec
1 *London Sanitary Protection Association,*
   William Smith, sec
3 Colson Mrs. Sarah, private hotel
4 Hills Gordon Macdonald, architect
4 Bromley Capt. Charles, R.N
4 Turner Percival, medical agent
4 Markwith William Elliott
4 Butterworth Frederick George
4 & 5 Butterfield William, architect
6 *Edwardes Menu Co. Lim.* advertising
   agents
6 Harris John Russell, physician
6 *Admiralty & Horse Guards*
   Gazette Editor's Office
6 The *"Mouilla" Liquid Soap Co. Lim*
6 Wilson Frederick, artist
6 Gibbs Joseph Melton, architect
6 Gill & Carpenter, type-writing office
7 *Evangelical Alliance (British Organisation),*
   Lieut.-Gen. J. Field, C.B. &
   A. J. Arnold, secs
   Christian Vernacular Education
   Society for India,
   Rev. James Johnston F.S.S. hon sec
8 Marr James, land agent & surveyor
   Actors' Benevolent Fund,
   Charles John Coltson, sec
8 *Spanish & Portuguese Church Aid Society,*
   Rev. L. S. Tugwell, sec
8 Fletcher Sidney
9 Price (H. C.), Lea & Co. engineers
9 Brown George, surgeon
9 Roper Frederick William, architect
9 *Dramatic & Musical Sick Fund,*
   Richard L. Tizard, sec
9 Swanborough & Tidd, dramatic agents
9 *Selborne Society,*
   A. J. Western, sec
9 Abud Charles J. theatrical agent
9 Burrell William, architect
10 Gordon, Murray & Co. patent
   medicine vendors
10 *Commercial World Office*
11 ALBION CHAMBERS:—
   Church of England Book Society,
   J. Shrimpton, sec
   Hardman, Powell & Co. art metal workers
   Rowbotham Richard & Co. hotel valuers
   Stuart William, solicitor
   Wakefield Henry, civil engineer
   Withers Robert J. F.R.I.B.A. architect
   Withers John B. architect
   Stirling William, architect
   Minleverer Col. B. B
11 & 11A, Hürter & Son, wine merchants
15, 16 & 17 Attenborough George,
   dealer in works of art
18 *Imperial Deposit Bank,*
   Charles James Knightley, man.dir
   Arthur Sedgwick, manager
18 *Royal Naval Benevolent Society,*
   John St. J. Wagstaffe, R.N. sec
18 Norton Maurice, solicitor
18 Girdwood James, land agent
18 *Freedmen's Missions Aid Society,*
   Rev. J. Gwynne Jones, D.D. sec
18 Knowles Mark, barrister
18 *Leaseholds Enfranchisement Association,*
   Howard Evans, hon sec
   James Rowlands M.P. sec
18 *Holmes's Lights Co. Limited,*
   J. R. Holmes, managing director
18 *Holmes' Ozone Co*
.... *here is John street* ....
19 *Sherwood Hotel,* Miss Sarah Townsend
20 *is now 1A, Adelphi terrace*

1895

Adam st. *Adelphi* (W.C.), 72 & 73 *Strand.*
1 Needes John C. medical agent
1 Wheelhouse George, architect
1 Quilter John Salmon, architect
1 *Railway Mission (The),*
   Richard Nixon, B.A. sec
1 *Railway Mission Convalescent Home*
4 Colson Mrs. Sarah, private hotel
4 Hills Gordon Macdonald & Son, architects
4 Turner Percival, medical agent
4 Kemble Frederick, accountant
4 Earle Arthur Westgarth, architect
5 *Mail & Express Newspaper office*
4 & 5 Gregson Harold S. K. solicitor
4 & 5 Chilcott Harry Warden Stanley, surveyor
6 *Edwardes Menu Co. Lim.* advertising
   agents
6 The *"Mouilla" Liquid Soap Co. Lim*
6 *Zohrab & Biggs' English Patents Lim,*
   railway signal manufacturers
6 Harris John Russell, physician
6 Harries Arthur, physician
6 *St. Martin's Electrical Manufacturing*
   Co. Limited, C. E. C. Hancock, sec
6 Gill Miss Rebecca Valeria, typewriting office
7 *Church Parochial Mission Society,*
   Rev. Merbert Muir, sec
7 *National Anti-Gambling League,*
   E. O. Fold, sec
7 *Evangelical Alliance (British Organisation),*
   A. J. Arnold, sec
7 *Christian Literature Society for India,*
   Rev. James Johnston F.S.S., sec
7 *Bible Lands or Turkish Mission*
   Aid Society, Rev. W. A. Essery, hon. sec
8 Marr James, land agent & surveyor
8 *Actors' Benevolent Fund,*
   Charles I. Coltson, sec
8 *Spanish & Portuguese Church*
   Aid Society,
   Rev. H. E. Noyes, D.D. hon financial sec
8 Mackay William
9 Price (H. C.), Lea & Co. engineers
9 Mortimer James, financial agent
9 Roper Frederick William, architect
9 *Dramatic & Musical Sick Fund,*
   J. D. Tidd, sec
9 Burrell William, architect
10 Gordon, Murray & Co. Limited,
   patent medicine vendors
10 Barclay Walter, money lender
10 Long Harry Vince, money lender
10 *Commercial World Office*
10 Bickerdike Alfred, architect
11 ALBION CHAMBERS:—
   Church of England Book Society,
   J. Shrimpton, sec
   Rowbotham Richard & Co. hotel valuers
   Rebman Francis Joseph, publisher
   Open Air Mission,   Frank Cockrem, sec
   Nursing Record Newspaper office
   Stuart William, solicitor
   Wakefield Henry, civil engineer
   Stirling William, architect
   Wakley Horace M. architect
   Minleverer Col. B. B
11 & 11A, Hürter & Son, wine merchants
18 Richmond George Skitt, wine merchant
18 *Imperial Deposit Bank,*
   Charles James Knightley, man.dir
   Dudley Morton, manager
18 *National Land Corporation Lim.,*
   G. H. Dorrell, manager
18 *Royal Naval Benevolent Society,*
   John St. J. Wagstaffe, R.N. sec
18 Girdwood James, land agent
18 Davis Thomas Buffen, solicitor
18 *Freedmen's Missions Aid Society,*
   Rev. D. MacEwan, D.D.
   hon. sec. & William Jenks, sec
18 *Leaseholds Enfranchisement Association,*
   Howard Evans, hon sec
   James Rowlands M.P. sec
.... *here is John street* ....
19 *Sherwood Hotel,* Miss Sarah Townsend
20 *is now 1A, Adelphi terrace*

1900

Adam st. *Adelphi* (W.C.), 72 & 73 *Strand.*
1 Needes John C. medical agent
1 *Railway Mission (The),*
   Richard Nixon, B.A. sec
1 *Railway Mission Convalescent Home*
1 Scott Sir John, K.C.M.G
1 Quilter John Salmon, architect
4 Wheelhouse Mrs
4 Cahn Joseph
4 Colson Mrs. Sarah, private hotel
4 Abbott, Jones & Co. Lim. publishers
4 Allen W. H. & Co. Ltd. publishers
4 Turner Percival, medical agent
4 *Women's Convalescent Home Association,*
   Robert Frewer, sec
4 Hills Gordon Pettigrew Graham, architect
4 Cooksey Arthur William, architect
4 Cox Alfred, architect
4 Watson Paxton Hood, architect
4 & 5 Gregson Harold S. K. solicitor
4 & 5 Chilcott Harry Warden Stanley, survr.
4 Wood & Co. commission agents
4 Kennedy David William, architect
4 Shore William Teignmouth
6 *Edwardes Menu Co. Lim.* advertising
   agents
6 *Pontin's Patent Butter Box Co. Lim*
6 Harris John Russell, physician
6 Harries Arthur, M.D. physician
6 Gill Miss Rebecca Valeria, typewriting
   office
7 *Hotel Cecil Lim.* (publicity dept)
7 *Evangelical Alliance (British Organisation),*
   Edward P. Field, esq. gen. sec
   Rev. H. R. T. Jackson, }
   Rev. Joseph Woodhouse } secs
7 *Christian Literature Society for India,*
   Rev. George Patterson, sec
7 *Bible Lands or Turkish Mission*
   Aid Society, Rev. W. A. Essery, hon. sec
8 Marr James, surveyor
8 *Actors' Benevolent Fund,*
   Charles I. Coltson, sec
8 Boxall Alfred, surveyor
8 Price (H. C.), Lea & Co. engineers
9 Hurley Alfred, commission agent
9 Roper Frederick William, architect
9 *Dramatic & Musical Sick & Benevolent Fund,*
   Walter John Richards, sec
9 Pugh Frank Harris Ernest Richard
9 Richards H. & Co. general agents
9 Steer Henry Edmund, land agent
10 Coyle James, estate agent
10 Gordon, Murray & Co. Limited
   patent medicine vendors
10 *Commercial World Office*
10 Elliston James Henry, theatrical mgr
10 Clinton Arthur, medical agent
11 ALBION CHAMBERS:—
   Church of England Book Society,
   John Shrimpton, hon. sec
   C. R. Ray, sec
   Rowbotham Richard & Co. auctioneers
11 *Willesden & Acton Brick Co. Lim*
11 Knewing Frederick James, provision agt.
   Open Air Mission, Frank Cockrem, sec
11 *Nursing Record Newspaper office*
11 Evans-Vaughan Charles, architect
   Stirling William, architect
   Wakley Horace M. architect
18 *Standard Wine Co.* (The)
18 Long Harry Vince, money lender
18 *National Land Corporation Lim.*
   G. H. Dorrell, manager
18 *Royal Naval Benevolent Society,*
   Richard Henry Clark, R.N. sec
18 Anderson Frank, architect
18 *Music Hall Benevolent Fund,*
   Horace Marriott, sec
18 Raven & Crickmay, surveyors
18 *Freedmen's Missions Aid Society,*
   Rev. D. MacEwan, D.D.
   hon. sec. & John Foster, sec
18 Putley Frederic Meller, architect
.... *here is John street* ....
18A, *Devonian Club,*
   George Wreford, hon. sec
19 *Sherwood Hotel,* Miss Sarah Townsend

1905

Adam st. *Adelphi* (W.C.), 72 & 73 *Strand.*
1 & 2 Needes John C. medical agent
1 & 2 *Railway Mission (The),*
   Richard Nixon, M.A. sec
1 & 2 *Railway Mission Convalescent Homes;*
   offices
   Richard Nixon, M.A. sec
1 & 2 Doctor Rudolf
1 & 2 Cahn Joseph
1 & 2 Quilter John Salmon, architect
1 & 2 Wheelhouse Mrs
3 Kuettner (B.) & MacDonell,
   electrical engineers
4 & 5 Turner Percival, medical agent
4 & 5 Johnson Reginald B. publisher
4 & 5 Foulis T. N. publisher
4 & 5 Lonsdale John Frederick, solicitor
4 & 5 Wood & Co. general agents
4 & 5 Cox Alfred, architect
4 & 5 Watson Paxton Hood, architect
4 & 5 Wills & Anderson, architects
6 *Stage Pictorial Publishing Co. Ltd*
6 *Inland Revenue Office,*
   Paul La Compte Finnigan, supervisor
6 Cooksey Arthur William, architect
6 Gill Miss Rebecca Valeria, typewriting
   office
7 Gimblett Frederick, accountant
7 *Evangelical Alliance (British Organisation),*
   John Wood, hon. sec
   H. Martyn Gooch, gen. sec
7 Brindley & Foster, organ builders
7 Horby W. & Co. decorators
7 *Bible Lands or Turkish Mission*
   Aid Society,
   Rev. S. W. Gentle-Cackett, sec. pro tem
8 Marr James, surveyor
8 *Actors' Benevolent Fund,*
   Charles I. Coltson, sec
8 Wilkinson Bristowe, architect
8 Boxall Alfred, surveyor
9 Price (H. C.), Lea & Co. engineers
9 Roper Frederick William, architect
9 *Dramatic & Musical Sick &*
   Benevolent Fund,
   George Leitch, sec
10 Gordon, Murray & Co. Limited
   patent medicine vendors
10 *Quick Lunch Co. Ld*
10 Taylor Henry, commission agent
11 ALBION CHAMBERS:—
   Rowbotham Richard & Co. auctioneers
   Willesden & Acton Brick Co. Lim
   Open Air Mission,
   Frank Cockrem, sec
   British Journal of Nursing
   Scottish Legal Life Assurance Society,
   James Spence Leslie, C.A.
   London Superintendent
   Martineau Ernest, architect
   Byrne & Rickwood, surveyors
   Hird & Thatcher, solicitors
   Wakley Horace M. architect
15 Hadlow William, postage stamp dealer
16 & 17 Lack & Son, outfitters
18 Shaw Tom & Co. variety agents
18 *National Land Corporation Lim.,*
   G. H. Dorrell, manager
18 *Church Stretton Building Co. Ltd*
18 *Church Stretton Land Co. Ltd*
18 *Church Stretton Waterworks Co*
18 *Horsell Land Co. Ld*
18 *Mitcham Land Co. Ld*
18 *Royal Naval Benevolent Society,*
   Richard Henry Clark, R.N. sec
18 Anderson Frank, architect
18 *Music Hall Benevolent Fund,*
   Horace Marriott, sec
18 Moore Charles H. motor car agent
18 Willey & Co. Ltd. gas apparatus makers
18 Mathews Rev. George D. D.D.
18 Jones John Martin, architect
18 Putley Frederic Meller, architect
18 Brettell John William, electrical engineer
.... *here is John street* ....
19 *Sherwood Hotel,* Miss Sarah Townsend

ADAM STREET

1910

Adam street, *Adelphi* (W.C.),
(WESTMINSTER), 72 & 73 *Strand*.
1 & 2 Needes John C. medical agent
1 & 2 *Railway Mission (The),*
Richard Nixon, M.A. sec
1 & 2 *Railway Mission Convalescent
Homes; offices*
Richard Nixon, M.A. sec
1 & 2 Kerby Henry, solicitor
1 & 2 Lonsdale & Everidge, solicitors
1 & 2 Cahn Joseph
1 & 2 Wheelhouse Mrs
3 Sidgwick & Jackson Ltd. publishers
4 & 5 Turner Percival, medical agent
4 & 5 Grundy John Francis Edwin,
fine art publisher
4 & 5 Wood & Co. general agents
4 & 5 Cox Alfred, architect
4 & 5 Watson Paxton Hood, architect
4 & 5 Johnson R. H. & Co. accountants
4 & 5 Macdonald & Evans, publishers
4 & 5 Keasley John N. architect
6 *Stage Pictorial Publishing Co. Ltd*
6 *Customs & Excise Office (parts of
Westminster & Holborn districts)*
6 Cooksey Arthur William, architect
6 *Legion of Frontiersmen*
7 Gimblett Frederick, accountant
7 *Evangelical Alliance (British Organisation),*
H. Martyn Gooch, gen. sec
7 *Association for Befriending Boys,*
Henry F. New, sec
7 *Bible Lands Missions' Aid Society,*
Rev. S. W. Gentle-Cackett, sec
8 *Actors' Benevolent Fund,*
Charles I. Colston, sec
8 Boxall Alfred & Son, surveyors
9 Price (H. C.), Lea & Co. engineers
9 Gant & Davis, surveyors
9 Fowler & Hugman, architects
10 Gordon, Murray & Co. Limited
patent medicine vendors
10 Garston Freres, marble importers
10 Wickstead & Beardsell, contractors
11 ALBION CHAMBERS:—
Rowbotham Richard & Co.
auctioneers
Willesden & Acton Brick Co. Lim
Telephone Recorder Co
Open Air Mission,
Frank Cockrem, sec
Chubb Frederick & Co. accountants
Curzon Stuart, financier
British Journal of Nursing
Byrne Ernest Corbett, surveyor
Rickwood Henry, surveyor
Rawlinson John, architect
Hird & Thatcher, solicitors
Canary Islands Agency
Wakley Horace M. architect
12 Hadlow William, postage stamp dealer
15 Collins & Brooks, hairdressers
16 & 17 Lack F. & Son Ltd. outfitters
18 Shaw Tom & Co. variety agents
18 *Royal Naval Benevolent Society,*
Richard Henry Clark, R.N. sec
18 Anderson Frank, architect
18 Willey & Co. Ltd. gas apparatus makers
18 *Vulcan Stove Co. Ltd*
18 Mathews Rev. George D. D.D.
18 Jones John Martin, architect
18 *Workers' Educational Association,*
Albert Mansbridge, sec
18 Brettell John William, electrical engineer
. . . . *here is John street* . . . .
19 *Publishers' Circular Ltd. (The)*
19 *Fishing Gazette Ltd*

1915

Adam street, *Adelphi* (W.C.),
(WESTMINSTER), *Strand.*
1 & 2 Needes John C. medical agent
1 & 2 *Railway Mission (The),*
Richard Nixon, M.A. sec
1 & 2 *Railway Mission Convalescent
Homes; offices*
Richard Nixon, M.A. sec
1 & 2 Lonsdale & Everidge, solicitors
1 & 2 Cahn Joseph
3 Sidgwick & Jackson Ltd. publishers
3 *United Suffragists,* Charles Gray, sec
4 & 5 Turner Percival, medical agent
4 & 5 Grundy John Francis Edwin,
fine art publisher
4 & 5 *Printing Craft Ltd.* publishers
4 & 5 Barns Stephen Allen, surveyor
4 & 5 Watson Paxton Hood, architect
4 & 5 Johnson & Co. accountants
4 & 5 Macdonald & Evans, publishers
4 & 5 Anderson John Reid, civil engineer
4 & 5 Hale Harold, consulting engineer
4 & 5 Keasley John N. architect
6 *Stage Pictorial Publishing Co. Ltd*
6 Cooksey Arthur William, architect
6 *Legion of Frontiersmen*
7 Gimblett Frederick, accountant
7 *International Woman Suffrage Alliance,*
Miss Mary Sheepshanks, sec
7 Silvester George, surveyor
7 Zeitlin Joseph & Co. cigar importers
8 *Actors' Benevolent Fund,*
Charles I. Colston, sec
8 Boxall Alfred & Son, surveyors
9 Price, Lea & Co. heating apparatus
makers
9 Fowler & Hugman, architects
9 Borrowman John, architect
10 Gordon, Murray & Co. Limited
patent medicine vendors
10 *Canadian Associated Press*
10 Elliott J. E. & Co. electrical engineers
11 ALBION CHAMBERS:—
Rowbotham Richard & Co. auctioneers
Macpherson Bros. financiers
Aeronautical Society of Great Britain,
B. G. Cooper, sec
*Incorporated Association of
Hotels & Restaurants,*
D. B. Hedderwick, sec
London Publicity Co. Ltd
Byrne Ernest Corbett, surveyor
Rawlinson John, architect
Hird & Thatcher, solicitors
Metal Jointing Co. Ltd. plumbers' merchants
Canary Islands & Madeira Agency
Wakley Horace M. architect
Hope Linton & Co. naval architects
18 *Royal Naval Benevolent Society,*
Edward H. Shearme, R.N. sec
18 Van Blitz & Lerman, wine &
spirit merchants
18 Brettell John William, electrical engineer
. . . . *here is John street* . . . .
19 *Publishers' Circular Ltd. (The)*
19 *Fishing Gazette Ltd*

1920

Adam street, *Adelphi* (W.C.2),
(WESTMINSTER), *Strand.*
1 & 2 *Railway Mission (The),*
Richard Nixon, M.A. sec
1 & 2 *Railway Mission Convalescent
Homes; offices*
Richard Nixon, M.A. sec
1 & 2 Lonsdale & Everidge, solicitors
1 & 2 Ord Hubert, M.A. private tutor
3 Sidgwick & Jackson Ltd. publishers
3 Mortlake Rev. Charles Bernard, M.A
4 & 5 Turner Percival, medical agent
4 & 5 Wood Gamble, manufacturers' agent
4 & 5 *People's League,*
Capt. H. L. Mason, D.S.O., M.C. sec
4 & 5 *Tryad Co. Ltd.* advertisers' novelty
manufacturers
6 *Stage Pictorial Publishing Co. Ltd*
6 Cooksey Arthur William, architect
6 *Legion of Frontiersmen*
7 Main Alfred G. accountant
7 Silvester George, surveyor
8 Westall W. & Co. Ltd. publishers
8 *Actors' Benevolent Fund,*
Charles I. Coltson, sec
8 Boxall Alfred & Son, surveyors
9 Price, Lea & Co. heating apparatus
makers
9 Fowler & Hugman, architects
9 Watson Paxton Hood, architect
10 Gordon, Murray & Co. Limited
patent medicine vendors
10 *Canadian Associated Press*
11 ALBION CHAMBERS:—
Cantrell & Cochrane Ltd.
mineral water manufacturers
Rowbotham Richard & Co. auctioneers
Bates Alfred William, accountant
Stocken Nevile L. philatelist
*Incorporated Association of
Hotels & Restaurants,*
J. C. Tully, sec
Honey Pot (The) (office of)
*Central Association of Welfare
Workers (Industrial)*
International Woman Suffrage Alliance,
Miss Mary Sheepshanks, sec
Byrne Ernest Corbett, surveyor
Rawlinson John, architect
Hird & Thatcher, solicitors
Thompson A. D. nurseryman
Canary Islands & Madeira Agency
18 Dowsons, solicitors
18 Hopgood, Mills & Somerville, solicitors
18 *Royal Naval Benevolent Society,*
Edward H. Shearme, R.N. sec
18 Thurgood, Son & Chidgey, surveyors
. . . . *here is John street* . . . .
19 *Publishers' Circular Ltd.*
19 *Fishing Gazette Ltd*

1925

Adam street, *Adelphi* (W.C.2),
(WESTMINSTER), *Strand.*
1 & 2 *Railway Mission (The)*
1 & 2 *Railway Mission Convalescent
Homes; offices*
1 & 2 Lonsdale & Everidge, solicitors
1 & 2 Cobbett William Vines Holt, solicitor
1 & 2 Shearman Montague, barrister
1 & 2 Ord Hubert, M.A. private tutor
1 & 2 Blanch John Mortimore
3 Sidgwick & Jackson Ltd. publishers
3 *National 'Hands off Russia' Committee*
3 Mortlake Rev. Charles Bernard, M.A
4 & 5 Turner Percival, medical agent
4 & 5 *Premier School of Journalism*
5 Entwistle Major Cyril Fullard, M.C., M.P
4 & 5 Wood Gamble, manufacturers' agent
4 & 5 *Savoy Press & Publicity Agency*
6 *Stage Pictorial Publishing Co. Ltd*
6 Cooksey Arthur W. & Partners, architects
6 *Legion of Frontiersmen*
7 Main Alfred G. accountant
7 Morgan Joseph, director of
public companies
7 Zarchi Serge, M.D. physician
7 Silvester George, surveyor
7 Westwood & Emberton, architects
8 *Actors' Benevolent Fund*
8 Middletons (Aberdeen) Ltd. fine
art publishers
8 Wallington C. & Co. accountants
9 Price, Lea & Co. heating apparatus
makers
9 Fowler & Hugman, quantity surveyors
9 Aitken Mrs
10 Westall W. & Co. Ltd. publishers
10 Gordon, Murray & Co. Limited,
manufacturing chemists
10 *Gaiety Magazine Publishing Co. Ltd*
10 *To-Day* (office of)
11 ALBION CHAMBERS:—
Cantrell & Cochrane Ltd.
mineral water manufacturers
Rowbotham Richard & Co. auctioneers
Bates & Senior, accountants
Claydon B. general agent
Merton Board Mill Ltd
Jobling, Glennie&Co. general merchants
Franklin W. H. Ltd. merchants
International Woman Suffrage Alliance
Byrne Ernest Corbett, surveyor
Rawlinson John, architect
Hird & Thatcher, solicitors
Thompson A. D. nurseryman
Johnstone Garden Contractor Ltd.
landscape gardeners
Canary Islands & Madeira Agency
18 *Royal Naval Benevolent Society*
18 *National Froebel Union*
18 Thurgood, Son & Chidgey, surveyors
18 Ostrom & Fischer Selling Agency Ltd
18 Rempler R. W. merchant
18 *British National Opera Co. Ltd*
. . . . *here is John street* . . . .
19 *Publishers' Circular Ltd.*
19 *Fishing Gazette Ltd*

ADAM STREET

1930

Adam street, *Adelphi* (W.C..2),
(WESTMINSTER), 73 *Strand.*

1	Floorcraft Ltd. parquet flooring importers
1	Stemp, White & Co. Ltd. flooring
	& panelling
2	Institution of Naval Architects
3	Hardisty, Rhodes & Hardisty, solicitors
4 & 5	Ruddock Robert H. Ltd. printers' valuers
4 & 5	Turner Percival, medical agent
4 & 5	*Premier School of Journalism*
4 & 5	Peters Augustus Dudley, literary agt.
6	Tablet Newspaper Office
6	Cooksey Arthur W. & Partners, architects
8	*Actors' Benevolent Fund*
8	Actors' Orphanage
8	Waller, Mager & Cobbett, solicitors
9	Stage Pictorial Publishing Co. Ltd
9	Aitken Mrs
10	Robert & John, refreshment rooms
10	Williamson Robert, publicity journalist
18	*Royal Naval Benevolent Society*
18	*National Froebel Union*
18	Rawlinson John, architect
18	Mondiale, literary agents
. . . .	*here is John street* . . . .
19	Occident & Orient Trading Corporation
19	Eadie Archibald & Co. Ltd
	lubricating oil manufacturers
19	Nigerian Timber & Construction Co. Ltd.
	timber merchants
19	Nigerian Cooperage Co. Ltd
19	Organisation for the Maintenance
	of Supplies Ltd
19	Littlejohn Thomas G. general merchant

1935

Adam street, *Adelphi* (W.C..2),
(WESTMINSTER), 73 *Strand.*
EAST SIDE

1	Heaton Tabb & Co. Ltd. decorators
2	Institution of Naval Architects
2	Cranfield Walter Thomas, journalist
2	Empire News & Features
2	Taverner Miss
3	Hardisty, Rhodes & Lindner, solicitors
3	Hales William Henry, solicitor
4 & 5	Turner Percival, medical agent
4 & 5	Our Cats' Publishing Co. Ltd
4 & 5	Peters Augustus Dudley, literary agent
6	Tablet Newspaper Office
6	Cooksey Arthur W. & Partners, architects
7	*Lancet (The)*
8	*Actors' Benevolent Fund*
8	Actors' Orphanage
8	Waller, Mager & Cobbett, solicitors
9	Aitken Mrs
10	Robert & John, refreshment rooms
10	Williamson Robert, publicity journalist
	WEST SIDE
18	London Circle of Players & Playrights
18	Adelphi Trading Co. Ltd. colliery agents
18	*Royal Naval Benevolent Society*
18	*National Froebel Union*
18	Rawlinson John, architect
18	Mondiale, literary agents
. . . .	*here is John street* . . . .
19	Hall Chemical Co. (The)
19	Courtenay Ashley R. publicity consultant
19	Kentish Express
19	Williams Lincoln & Co. publishers

1936

Adam street, *Adelphi* (W.C..2),
(WESTMINSTER), 73 *Strand.*
EAST SIDE

1	Heaton Tabb & Co. Ltd. decorators
2	Institution of Naval Architects
2	Cranfield Walter Thomas, journalist
2	Empire News & Features
2	Taverner Miss
3	Hardisty, Rhodes & Lindner, solicitors
3	Hales William Henry, solicitor
4 & 5	Turner Percival Ltd. medical agents
4 & 5	Travel & Sports Press Ltd
4 & 5	Our Cats' Publishing Co. Ltd
4 & 5	Peters Augustus Dudley, literary agent
6	Tablet Newspaper Office
6	Cooksey Arthur W. & Partners, architects
7	*Lancet (The)*
8	*Actors' Benevolent Fund*
8	Actors' Orphanage
8	Mead & Dennis, solicitors
9	Yarnall Ltd. photo printers
10	Robert & John, refreshment rooms
10	Williamson Robert, publicity journalist
	WEST SIDE
18	Adelphi Trading Co. Ltd. colliery agents
18	*Royal Naval Benevolent Society*
18	*National Froebel Union*
18	Rawlinson John, architect
18	Mondiale, literary agents
. . . .	*here is John street* . . . .
19	Samuels Thomas Edward, accountant
19	Hall Chemical Co. (The)
19	Courtenay Ashley R. Ltd. publicity
	consultants
20	Russell House (Adelphi) Ltd
20	General Refractories Ltd
20	International Diatomite Co. Ltd

ADELPHI TERRACE

1841

Adelphi terrace, 20 *Adam st.*.
1   Chaplin William, esq
2   Beavan & Anderson, solicitors
2   Sharpe Daniel, esq
3   Gauntlett Miss
4   Cole John, solicitor
5   Latter Henry, surgeon
6   *Western Australian Emigration Co*
7   Hawes William, surgeon
8   Lindley William, civil engineer
9   Sandford Feake, solicitor
10 Hill James, esq

1845

Adelphi terrace,
20 *Adam st. and 3 Robert st.*
1A, Taylor Thomas, artist
1A, Dyce William, esq
1A, Jerdon William, esq
1A, Locke Joseph, civil engineer
1A, States Charles. esq
1A, States George Spencer, esq
1A, States William, esq
1A, Wass Charles W. artist
1   Chaplin William, esq
2   Beavan & Anderson, solicitors
2   Jansen Frederick Halsey, esq
2   Sharpe Daniel, esq
3   Gauntlett Miss
4   Cole John, solicitor
5   Latter Henry, surgeon
6   *Commissioner for the Census,*
        Thomas Vardon, esq. secretary
7   Hawes William sen. esq
8   Lindley William, civil engineer
9   Giles Francis, civil engineer
10 Hill James, esq

1850

Adelphi terrace,
20 *Adam st. and 3 Robert st.*
1A, Reed Anthony & Robert, surveyors
1A, States William, esq
1A, Woodifield Matthew, civil engineer
        (& 4 Ovington square, Brompton)
2   Beavan & Anderson, solicitors
2   Sharpe Daniel, esq
3   Gauntlett Miss
4   Cole John & Charles, solicitors
5   Latter Henry, surgeon
6   *Office of Metropolitan Buildings,*
        William Hosking,   } official
        Ambrose Poynter,   } referees
        John Shaw,   }
        Arthur Symonds, registrar
7   Hawes Mrs
8   Lindley William, civil engineer
9   Giles Alfred, civil engineer
10 Hill James, esq

1855

Adelphi terrace,
19 *Adam street* and 3 *Robert street.*
1A, Clark Edwin, civil engineer
1A, Leaf Frederick Henry, esq
1A, Reed Anthony R. & Francis, surveyors
1   Allan Thomas, civil engineer
1   *United Kingdom Electric Telegraph Co.*
        Thomas Allan, supt. engineer
2   *London Exchange Advance Fund
        & Life Association,*
        Stephen Hutchinson, treasurer
3   *Safety Life Assurance Co.*
        Ralph Coulthard, secretary
4   Cole John & Charles Nicholas, solicitors
5   Latter Henry, surgeon
6   *Office of Metropolitan Buildings,*
        William Hosking,   } official
        Ambrose Poynter,   } referees
        John Shaw,   }
        Arthur Symonds, registrar
7   Hawes Mrs
8   Lindley William, civil engineer
9   *New Zealand Emigration Office &
        Colonists' Rooms,*
        Frederick Young & Co. proprietors
9   Giles Alfred, civil engineer
9   Jervis Major Thomas Besh, esq
10 Hill James, esq

1860

Adelphi terrace (W.C.),
19 Adam street & 3 *Robert street.*
1A, Homersham W. Collett, civil engineer
1A, Reed Anthony Robert, &
        Robert Francis, surveyors
1A, Crosby James, esq
1   Allan Thomas, civil engineer
1   *United Kingdom Electric Telegraph Co.*
        Thomas Allan, supt. engineer
1   *Great Indian Submarine Telegraph
        Company (limited),*
        Thomas Allen, engineer in chief
2   *London Exchange Advance Fund
        & Life Association,*
        James Lea, sec
2   Isaacson Edward Thomas, esq
2   Strutt John, solicitor
3   *Agriculturist Cattle Insurance Co.*
        Richard W. Goold, sec
4   Austin Edmond John, surveyor
4   Kerwell, Son & Co. commission merchts
5   Latter Henry, surgeon
6   *Cambridge & University Commission
        Office,*
        Edward Henry Bunbury, sec
6   *Office of the Agents General for Crown
        Colonies,*
        Edward Barnard & P.G. Julyan, esqrs.
        agents general
7   Hawes Mrs
8   Parson George John, solicitor
9   O'Byrne Brothers, navy agents
9   *Sailors' Home Journal & Naval
        Chronical office*
9   *Wellington Gazette Office*
9   Giles Alfred, civil engineer
9   Silk John Alexander, solicitor
9   Vines Edward, esq
11 Beck, Henderson & Child, seed merchnts

1865

Adelphi terrace (W.C.),
19 *Adam street* and 3 *Robert street.*
1A, Homersham W. Collett, civil engineer
1A, Reed Robert & Robert Francis, surveyors
1A, Guerin & Dell, accountants
1A, *The East Cambrian Gold Mining
        Co. (limited)*
        *Cumsymlog United Silver Lead
        Mines Co. (limited)*
        *East Bronfloyd Silver Lead
        Mining Co. (limited)*
        Havan Silver Mines Co. (limited)
        *Silver Mountain United Mining
        Co. (limited)*
        Welch Silver Lead Mines Co. (limited),
        Guerin & Dell, secs
1A, *East Kent Flour Mill & Bakery
        Co. (limited),*   William Ward, sec
1   Allan Thomas, civil engineer
1   *The National Telegraph Co. (limited)*
1   *The Ocean Telegraph Co. (limited),*
        Thomas Allan, electrician & engineer
1   *London Telegraph Works Co. (limited),*
        Thomas Allan, managing director
2   Bedwell Arthur Benjamin, solicitor
2   *London Exchange Advance Fund
        & Life Association,*   James Lea, sec
2   *Guaranteed Manure Co.*
        R.W. Goold & Co. proprietors
2   Gardner Henry, accountant
2   *British Paper Manufacturing Co.(limited)*
        Henry Gardner, managing director
2   Gardner Henry, esq
2   Strutt John, solicitor
3   Page Thomas, F.R.S., F.R.G.S., F.G.S.
        civil engineer
4   Boys Mrs
4   { Society of Schoolmasters
    { Royal Literary Fund
        Octavian Blewett, F.R.G.S. sec
4   Blewett Octavian, esq. F.R.G.S.
4   Doughney John Henry Hamer, surveyor
5   Latter Henry, surgeon
5   *Sea Fisheries Commission,*
        E.W.H. Holdsworth, esq. sec
7   Hawes Mrs
7   Merest Mrs. (late Maria B. Hawes)
7   *Institution of Naval Architects,*
        David Trice, assistant secretary
8   Blomfield Arthur William M.A. architect
8   Bunker James Alfred, surveyor
8   Fuller Francis, surveyor &c
8   *African Aid Society,*
        Lord Churchill, M.P. chairman
9   *London Agency (home, foreign & colonial),*
        O'Byrne Bros. agents
9   O'Byrne Brothers, navy agents
9   *Naval Biography Office*
9   *Sailors' Home Journal & Naval
        Chronical Office*
9   *Wellington Gazette Office*
9   *Victoria Cross Office*
9   Giles Alfred, civil engineer
9   Silk John Alexander, solicitor
9   Vines Edward, esq
10 *London Scottish (15th Middlesex)
        Rifle Volunteer Corps,*
        Lieut. R. Macnabb, paymaster
10 *Herne Bay, Hampton & Reculver
        Oyster Fishery Company,*
        A. Francis Pennell, sec

1870

Adelphi terrace (W.C.),
19 *Adam street* and 3 *Robert street.*
1A, *Junior Garrick Club,*
        Charles Harcourt, esq. sec
2   Cunningham Charles, solicitor
2   *Guaranteed Manure Co.*
        R.W. Goold & Co. proprietors
2   Strutt John, solicitor
2   *National Cottage Hospital for Consumption,*
        Neale F. Horne, sec
2   Hassall Dr. Arthur Hill
3   Page Thomas, F.R.G.S., F.G.S.
        civil engineer
4   Boys Mrs
4   { Society of Schoolmasters
    { Royal Literary Fund
        Octavian Blewett, F.R.G.S. sec
4   Blewett Octavian, esq. F.R.G.S.
4   Doughney John Henry Hamer, surveyor
9   *Institution of Naval Architects,*
        Adrian Vizetelly, assistant sec
9   Walker Thomas
9   Giles Alfred, civil engineer
10 *London Scottish (15th Middlesex)
        Rifle Volunteer Corps,*
        Lieut. R. Macnabb, paymaster
10 *Herne Bay, Hampton & Reculver
        Oyster Fishery Company,*
        A. Francis Pennell, sec

1875

Adelphi terrace (W.C.),
19 *Adam street*
1A, *Junior Garrick Club,*
        Charles Harcourt, esq. sec
3   *Crichton Club,*
        Henry Massingberd, sec
3   Williams James Rusell
10 *Revision of Lighting H.M. Ships,*
        Commander H.W. Brent, R.N
    Victoria Institute,
        Capt. Francis W.H. Petrie, hon.sec
    Chambers William

ADELPHI TERRACE

1880

Adelphi terrace (W.C.),
19 Adam street, Strand.

1A, *Junior Garrick Club,*

A. Mowbray, sec

2 *London Bible & Domestic Female Mission,*
Rt. Hon. the Earl of Shaftesbury,
K.G. president; Lord Kinnaird,
treasurer; Mrs H. Selfe Leonard,
hon. sec

3 & 4 *Crichton Club,*
William D. Baikie, secretary

5 Cutler, Palmer & Co. wine merchants
(Garrick's house)
Cutler F. Egerton (Garrick's house)
Institution of Naval Architects,
G. Holmes, sec

6 Hawks, Crawshay & Sons, iron
manufacturers
Blanchard Edward Leman

7 Brown Charles Rouse
Victoria Institute,
Capt. Francis W.H. Petrie, hon.sec
Royal Literary Fund,
Octavian Blewett, K.L.,F.R.G.S.
secretary
Society of Schoolmasters,
Octavian Blewett, K.L.,F.R.G.S.
secretary

8 Lee Brothers & Pain, architects
Lee Charles, architect
Welsh Slate Co.
Henry Frederic Phillips, sec
Phillips Henry Frederic, accountant
Reynell John Rigby, accountant
Page Earnest
Page Arnold

9 Bray Joseph
Logan William George

10 *Green Room Club*
Caledonian hotel,
James Russell Williams
New Thames Yacht Club, J. Skinner, sec
Savage Club, Walter Pelham, sec
Nobodies' Club, Charles D. Yates, sec

1885

Adelphi terrace (W.C.),
19 Adam street, Strand.

1A, *Junior Garrick Club,*
Thomas Mowbray, sec

1 *Société Nationale Française Property
Co. Limited,*
Claude Duché, sec

2 *London Bible & Domestic Female Mission,*
Rt. Hon. the Earl of Shaftesbury,
K.G. president; Lord Kinnaird,
treasurer; Mrs H. Selfe Leonard,
hon. sec
*Indian Female Normal School &
Instruction Society,*
Miss Ballard, hon. sec

3 & 4 *Crichton Club,*
William D. Baikie, secretary

5 Cutler, Palmer & Co. wine merchants
(Garrick's house)
Thomas Andrew, yacht agent
Institution of Naval Architects,
G. Holmes, sec

6 Hawks, Crawshay & Sons, iron
manufacturers
Blanchard Edward Leman
Diplomatic Fly Sheets Office,
C.D. Collet, publisher

7 *Victoria Institute,*
Capt. Francis W.H. Petrie, hon.sec
Royal Literary Fund,
Octavian Blewett, K.L.,F.R.G.S.
secretary
Society of Schoolmasters,
Octavian Blewett, K.L.,F.R.G.S.
secretary

8 Lee Brothers & Pain, architects
& surveyors
Welsh Slate Co.
Henry Frederic Phillips, sec
Phillips Henry Frederic, accountant
Reynell John Rigby, accountant
Jameson & Wallis, architects

9 *Statistical Society,*
Sir Rawson W. Rawson, K.C.,
M.G., C.B. president; J. B.
Martin, A.E. Bateman & G.
S. Baden-Powell, hon. secs.;
John B. Martin, foreign sec.;
Joseph Whittall, assistant sec
Institute of Actuaries,
A.J. Finlayson & H.W.
Manly, hon. secs
*Institute of Chemistry of Great
Britain & Ireland,*
Charles E. Groves, F.C.S. sec

10 Eccles Hugh
Caledonian hotel, Hugh Eccles
Read Clare Sewell, M.P
New Thames Yacht Club, J. Senior, sec

1890

Adelphi terrace (W.C.),
19 Adam street, Strand.

1A, *Christian Police Association,*
R. Titheradge, manager

1A, *Victoria Institute,*
Capt. Francis W.H. Petrie, hon.sec

1A, *Improved Martin's Anchor Co.Limited,*
Edward Jose, sec

1A, *Cyclodal Screw Propeller Co. Limited,*
Edward Jose, sec

1 *Arundel Club,* G.S. Williams, hon sec

2 *London Bible & Domestic Female Mission,*
Lord Kinnaird, treasurer
Mrs H. Selfe Leonard, hon. sec

2 *Indian Female Normal School &
Instruction Society,*
Miss Hamilton, hon. sec

3 *London Electric Supply Corporation
Limited,*
Charles B. Waller, manager & sec

4 Carte R. D'Oyly

5 Cutler, Palmer & Co. east india merchts

5 *Institution of Naval Architects,*
G. Holmes, sec

6 & 7 *Savage Club,* E.J. Wade, hon. sec

8 Lee Brothers & Pain, architects
& surveyors

8 *The Sparre Patents Co. Limited,*
A. Stanley Felton, sec

8 Reynell John Rigby, accountant

8 Jameson & Wallis, architects

9 *Royal Statistical Society,*
T. Graham Balfour, M.D.,
F.R.S. president; J. B. Martin,
A.E. Bateman & Major P.G.
Craigie, hon. secs; John B.
Martin, foreign sec.; Joseph
Whittall, assistant sec

9 *Institute of Chemistry of Great
Britain & Ireland,*
Charles E. Groves, F.R.S. sec

9 *Royal Literary Fund,*

9 *Society of Schoolmasters,*
Llewelyn Roberts, sec

10 *Crichton Club,* Thomas Craston, sec

10 *Caledonian hotel,* Eccles & Townsend

1895

Adelphi terrace (W.C.),
19 Adam street, Strand.

1A, *Christian Police Association,*
Miss C. Gurney, hon. sec

1A, Stoney Arbuthnot Butler, barrister

1 *Arundel Club,* G.S. Williams, hon. sec

2 *London Bible & Domestic Female Mission,
(Bible Women & Nurses Mission)*
Rt. Hon. the Earl of Harrowby,
president
Lord Kinnaird, treasurer
Mrs H. Selfe Leonard, hon. supt

2 *Zenana, Bible & Medical Mission or Indian
Female Normal School & Instruction
Society,*
W.T. Paton, hon. finance sec
Rev. A.R. Cavalier, gen. sec

4 Carte R. D'Oyly

5 Cutler, Palmer & Co. wine merchants

5 *Institution of Naval Architects,*
G. Holmes, sec

5 *Improved Martin's Anchor Co.Limited,*
Edward Jose, sec

6 & 7 *Savage Club,* W.H. Denny, hon. sec

6 *Royal Literary Fund,*
Llewelyn Roberts, sec

6 *Society of Schoolmasters,*
Llewelyn Roberts, sec

8 Godfree A.H. & Co. wine merchants

8 *Victoria Institute,*
Capt. Francis W.H. Petrie, hon.sec

8 Lee & Pain, architects & surveyors
(removed to 63 Lincoln's inn fields W.C)

9 Royal Statistical Society,
Right Hon. Lord Farrar, president;
J. B. Martin, M.A., A. E. Bateman,
C.M.G. & Major P.G. Craigie,
hon. secs; John B. Martin, foreign
sec.; Reginald H. Hooker, assistant
sec.; John A.P. Mackenzie, librarian

9 *British Economic Association,*
Rt.Hon. G.J. Goschen, M.P.
president; T.H. Elliott, H.S.
Foxwell, M.A. & L.L. Price,
M.A. hon. secs.; F.Y. Edge-
worth, M.A., D.C.L. editor &
Henry Higgs, LL.B. sec. &
assistant editor

9 Booth Charles

10 *Crichton Club Lim,* P.S. Levi, hon. sec

10 Banks Frederick William

10 *Caledonian hotel,* Miss Fanny Marriott

ADELPHI TERRACE

1900

Adelphi terrace (W.C.),
19 *Adam street, Strand.*

1A, *Police Institute,*
Miss Catherine Gurney,
Miss Vaughan Barber &
Miss E.Z. Johnson, hon. secs
1A, *International Christian Police Association,*
Miss Catherine Gurney, hon. sec
1 Arundel Club,
G.S. Williams, hon. sec
2 *London Bible & Domestic Female Mission,*
(Bible Women & Nurses Mission)
Rt. Hon. the Earl of Harrowby,
president
Lord Kinnaird, treasurer
Mrs H. Selfe Leonard, hon. supt
2 *Zenana, Bible & Medical Mission or Indian*
Female Normal School & Instruction
Society,
J.C. Andrews, esq. hon. finance sec
Rev. A.R. Cavalier, gen. sec
3 *Lifeboat Saturday Fund of the Royal*
National Lifeboat Institution,
A.P. Smith, sec
3 Saunders Francis, private estate office
4 Carte R. D'Oyly
5 Cutler, Palmer & Co. wine merchants
5 *Institution of Naval Architects,*
George Holmes, sec
5 *Improved Martin's Anchor Co. Limited,*
Edward Jose, sec
5 Isaac Leon Joseph
6 & 7 *Savage Club,* E.E. Peacock, hon. sec
6 *Royal Literary Fund,*
Llewelyn Roberts, sec
6 *Society of Schoolmasters,*
Llewelyn Roberts, sec
8 Godfree Arthr. H. & Co. wine merchants
8 *Victoria Institute,*
Capt. Francis W.H. Petrie, F.G.S. hon.sec
8 *Irish Literary Society (The)*
Alfred Perceval Graves, M.A. hon sec
8 Turner Alfred Mayor
9 *Royal Statistical Society,*
Rt. Hon. Sir Henry H. Fowler,
M.P., G.C.S.I. president; Noel
A. Humphreys & J.A. Baines,
C.S.I. hon. secs; Major P.G.
Craigie, hon. foreign sec.;
Benedict W. Ginsburg, M.A.,
LL.D, assistant sec.; John A.P.
Mackenzie, librarian
9 *British Economic Association,*
Right Hon. G.J. Goschen, M.P.
president; Alfred Spalding
Harvey, B.A. treasurer, T.H.
Elliott, H.S. Foxwell, M.A.
& L.L. Price, M.A. hon. secs.;
F.Y. Edgworth, M.A., D.C.L.
editor & Henry Higgs, B.A.,
LL.B. sec. & editor
9 Booth Charles
10 *London School of Economics &*
Political Science (The),
W.A.S. Hewins, M.A. director
10 *British Library of Political Science,*
W.A.S. Hewins, M.A. director
Caledonian hotel, James Tate

1905

Adelphi ter. 19 *Adam st. Strand.* (W.C.)
(WESTMINSTER).

1A, *Police Institute,*
Miss Catherine Gurney,
Miss Vaughan Barber &
Miss E.Z. Johnson, hon. secs
1A, *International Christian Police Association,*
Miss Catherine Gurney, hon. sec
1 *British Electric Traction Co. Ltd*
2 *London Bible Women & Nurses' Mission,*
Lord Kinnaird, treasurer
Miss Andrews, hon. sec.
& general superintendent
2 *Zenana, Bible & Medical Mission or Indian*
Female Normal School & Instruction
Society,
A.H. Habershon, hon.finance sec
Rev. A.R. Cavalier, gen. sec
3 Unwin Thomas Fisher
4 *Montagu Hon John Walter*
Edward Douglas-Scott, M.P
4 Baylor Armistead Keith
5 Cutler, Palmer & Co. wine merchants
5 *Institution of Naval Architects,*
R.W. Dana, sec
5 Isaac Leon Joseph
6 & 7 *Savage Club,* E.E. Peacock, hon. sec
6 *Royal Literary Fund,*
Llewelyn Roberts, sec
6 *Society of Schoolmasters,*
Llewelyn Roberts, sec
8 Godfree Arthr. H. & Co. wine merchants
8 *Victoria Institute or Philosophical Society*
of Great Britain,
E.Hull, LL.D., F.R.S. sec
8 *Booth Steamship Co. Ltd*
8 *Manaos Harbour Limited*
8 *West India Rubber Plantation*
Syndicate Ltd
8 Atlay James Beresford
8 *Royal Statistical Society,*
Sir Francis Sharp Powell, bart.,
M.P. president; Richard Bidulph
Martin, M.A., M.P. treas.;
Noel A. Humphreys, I.S.O., J.A.
Baines, C.S.I. & R. Henry
Rew, hon. secs.; J.A. Baines,
C.S.I. hon. foreign sec.; J.A.
Cable, assistant sec.; John A.
P. Mackenzie, librarian
9 *Royal Economic Society,*
Henry Higgs, B.A., LL.B. sec
9 *Incorporated Society of Medical*
Officers of Health, Herbert
Jones D.P.H. & Joseph
Priestley M.D. hon. secs
10 *New Reform Club,* A.M. Scott, sec
10 Shaw G. Bernard
Caledonian hotel, Mrs. MariaTate

1910

Adelphi ter. 19 *Adam st. Strand.* (W.C.)
(WESTMINSTER).

1A, *Police Institute,*
Miss Catherine Gurney, hon. sec
1A, *International Christian Police Association,*
Miss Catherine Gurney, hon. sec
1 Unwin Thomas Fisher, publisher
2 *Gordon Hotels Ltd. (The)*
2 *Gordons Advertising Agency*
3 Unwin Thomas Fisher
4 Allen-Lodge Albert Robert, architect
4 Roddick, Colvin & Clark, land agents
4 Lawson Allan John, consulting engineer
4 Holman Henry Martin
5 Baylor Armistead Keith
5 *Institution of Naval Architects,*
R.W. Dana, sec
6 & 7 *Savage Club*
8 Godfree Arthr. H. & Co. wine merchants
8 *General Federation of Trade Unions,*
W.A. Appleton, sec
8 Thurgood, Son & Chidgey, surveyors
8 Atlay James Beresford
9 *Royal Statistical Society,*
Sir Jervoise A. Baines, C.S.I.,
president; R. Henry Rew, G.
Udny Yule & W.H. Clark,
C.M.G. hon. secs.; R. Henry
Rew, hon. foreign sec.; C.M.
Kohan B.A. assistant sec.;
John A.P. Mackenzie, librarian
9 *Royal Economic Society,*
Charles J. Hamilton, M.A. sec
10 *New Reform Club,*
Arthur G. Symonds, sec
10 Shaw G. Bernard
11 Booth Steamship Co. Ltd
11 Booth Alfred & Co. merchants
11 *Propaganda Society of Portugal*

1915

Adelphi ter. 19 *Adam st. Strand.* (W.C.)
(WESTMINSTER).

1A, *Police Institute,*
Miss Catherine Gurney, hon. sec
1A, *International Christian Police Association,*
Miss Catherine Gurney, hon. sec
1 Unwin Thomas Fisher, publisher
2 *Gordon Hotels Ltd. (The)*
2 *Gordons Advertising Agency*
3 Unwin Thomas Fisher
3 Hart John, theatrical manager
4 Roddick, Colvin & Clark, land agents
Institution of Naval Architects,
R.W. Dana, M.A. sec
5 Barrow Ernest
6 & 7 *Savage Club,*
Reginald Geard, hon. sec
8 Godfree Arthr. H. & Co. wine merchants
8 Thurgood, Son & Chidgey, surveyors
9 *Royal Statistical Society,*
Right Hon Lord Welby, G.C.B.,
P.C. president; R. Henry
Rew, C.B. (& hon. foreign sec.),
G. Udny Yule, M.A. & A.W.
Flux, M.A. hon. secs.; C.M.
Kohan, B.A. assistant sec.; John
A.P. Mackenzie, librarian
9 *Royal Economic Society,*
J.M. Keynes, M.A. sec
9 *International Statistical Institute,*
R.H. Rew, C.B. hon. treas
10 *Nation Publishing Co. Ltd*
10 Shaw George Bernard
11 *Booth Steamship Co. Ltd*
11 Booth Alfred & Co. merchants
11 *Amazonas Engineering Co Ltd*
11 *Propaganda Society of Portugal*
11 *Amazonian Society,*
A. Fletcher, hon. sec

ADELPHI TERRACE

1920

Adelphi ter. 19 *Adam st. Strand.* (W.C.)
(WESTMINSTER).

1A, *Police Institute,*
    Rev. G. Twentyman, M.A. gen. sec
1A, *International Christian Police Association,*
    Rev. G. Twentyman, M.A. gen. sec
1 Unwin Thomas Fisher, publisher
2 *Gordon Hotels Ltd. (The)*
2 *Gordons Advertising Agency*
3 Unwin Thomas Fisher
3 Weir Lord, P.C
4 Roddick, Colvin & Clark, land agents
4 Simpson Percy
4 Hastie Arthur Hepburn
5 *Institution of Naval Architects,*
    R.W. Dana, O.B.E., M.A. sec
5 McCarthy Miss Lillah
6 & 7 *Savage Club,* David Urquhart, hon. sec
8 Godfree Arthur H. & Co. Ltd.
    wine merchants
8 *National Service League,*
    R. MacLeod, hon. sec
9 *Royal Statistical Society,*
    Rt. Hon Herbert Samuel, pre-
    sident; A.W. Flux, M.A.,
    T.H.C. Stevenson, C.B.E., M.D.
    & Capt. M. Greenwood, M.R.C.S.
    hon. secs.; Sir R. Henry Rew,
    K.C.B. hon. foreign sec.; John
    A.P. Mackenzie, librarian;
    Miss L. Catharine Thorburn,
    chief clerk
9 *Royal Economic Society,*
    J.M. Keynes, M.A. sec
9 *International Statistical Society,*
    Sir R.H. Rew,K.C.B. hon. treas
10 *Nation Publishing Co. Ltd*
10 *Athenæum* (office of)
10 Shaw George Bernard
11 *Booth Steamship Co. Ltd*
11 Booth Alfred & Co. Ltd. merchants
11 *Amazonian Society,*
    A. Fletcher, hon. sec

1925

Adelphi ter. 19 *Adam st. Strand.* (W.C.)
(WESTMINSTER).

1A, *Police Institute*
1A, *International Christian Police Association*
1 Unwin T. Fisher Ltd. publishers
2 *Christian Science Monitor*
3 Unwin Thomas Fisher
3 Weir Lord, P.C
4 Roddick, Colvin & Clark, land agents
4 Lickford Charles
5 *Institution of Naval Architects*
5 Perry William Thomas
6 & 7 *Savage Club*
8 Godfree Arthur H. & Co. Ltd.
    wine merchants
8 Harwood Harold Marsh
9 *Royal Statistical Society*
9 *Royal Economic Society*
9 *International Statistical Institute*
10 Walton Sidney, advertisement consultant
10 *Nation Ltd.* publishers
10 Shaw George Bernard
10A, *European Mail* (office of)
10A, *Monarch Publication & Printing Co. Ltd*
11 *Booth Steamship Co. Ltd*
11 Booth Alfred & Co. Ltd. merchants
11 Booth & Co. (London) Ltd. merchants
11 *Amazonian Society*

1930

Adelphi ter. 19 *Adam st. Strand.* (W.C.)
(WESTMINSTER).

1A, *Police Institute*
1A, *International Christian Police Association*
2 *Christian Science Monitor*
3 Weir Lord, P.C
3 Tumor Christopher
4 Roddick, Colvin & Clark, land agents
4 Trinidad Lake Asphalt (Overseas) Ltd
4 Lickford Charles
6 & 7 *Savage Club*
8 Godfree Arthur H. & Co. Ltd.
    wine merchants
8 *British Drama League*
8 Harwood Harold Marsh
9 *Royal Statistical Society*
9 *Royal Economic Society*
9 *International Statistical Institute*
10 Walton Sidney, publicity consultant
10 International Management
    Corporation Ltd
10 Martinez Michael, research laboratory
10 Norton Edward
11 *Booth Steamship Co. Ltd*
11 Booth Alfred & Co. Ltd. merchants
11 Booth & Co. (London) Ltd merchants

1935

Adelphi ter. 19 *Adam st. Strand.* (W.C.)
(WESTMINSTER).

1A, *Police Institute*
1A, *International Christian Police Association*
2 *Christian Science Monitor*
3 Weir Lord, P.C, G.C.B.
3 Lipscomb William Percy
4 Roddick, Colvin & Clark, land agents
4 Goldman John M
4 Lickford Charles
5 Martin Clifford Ltd. advertising agents
5 National Radium Commission
5 Fairchild Publications of New York
5 Hardy Mrs
6 & 7 *Savage Club*
8 Godfree Arthur H. & Co. Ltd.
    wine merchants
8 *British Drama League*
8 Shakespeare Memorial National
    Theatre Committee
9 *Royal Statistical Society*
9 *Royal Economic Society*
10 Martinez Patents Ltd. photographic
    materials manufacturers
10 Norton Edward
10A, Adelphi Manufacturing Co. Ltd. engineers
10A, Read Bros. builders
11 *Booth Steamship Co. Ltd*
11 Booth Alfred & Co. Ltd. merchants
11 Booth & Co. (London) Ltd merchants

1936

Adelphi ter. 19 *Adam st. Strand.* (W.C.)
(WESTMINSTER).

2 *Christian Science Monitor*
3 Weir Lord, P.C., G.C.B
3 Lipscomb William Percy
4 Goldman John M
5 Martin Clifford Ltd. advertising agents
5 National Radium Commission
5 Fairchild Publications of New York
5 Hardy Mrs
6 & 7 *Savage Club*
8 Godfree Arthur H. & Co. Ltd.
    wine merchants
9 *Royal Statistical Society*
9 *Royal Economic Society*
10 Norton Edward
10A, Adelphi Manufacturing Co.
    Ltd. engineers
10A, Read Bros. builders
11 *Booth Steamship Co. Ltd*
11 Booth Alfred & Co. Ltd. merchants
11 Booth & Co. (London) Ltd merchants

BUCKINGHAM STREET

1841

Buckingham street, 38, *Strand.*
2   *Prince's Head,* George Weaver
3   Clewley Daniel, dairyman
4   Lilly James, fruiterer
5   D'Arcy William, tailor
. . . . *Duke street* . . . .
6   Shand William, patent artifl. leg maker
8   Minister John, lodging house
9   More George, esq
9   Polhill Charles, esq
9   Rogers Mrs
10   Knowles James, solicitor
10   *Westminster Discount, Loan, &c. Soc*
         Chas. K. Nicholls, mang. direct
         Thomas Gibbard, solicitor
         John Simpson, esq
10   Whitaker Francis Augustus, esq
11   Paxton William Gill, esq
12   HANOVER CHAMBERS.
         Carlos & Fitzgerald, surveyors
         Cobb Thomas Wheatly, esq
         Colman Wm. Gooding, archi.&surv
         Dod Chas.solicitor & foreign law agt
         Freeman Charles, architect
         Lang Alfred, architect, &c
         Louch William Stevens, esq
         Perry George, esq
         Withy Robert, attorney
13   Stafford William, solicitor
14   Etty William, artist
14   Hayward Philip, solicitor
14   Moore Capt. Frederick
14   Rawson Thomas Gekel, esq
14   Sheepshanks Thomas, esq
14   Vertue George, esq
14   Warry Thomas, esq
14   Winkworth John Richardson, esq
15   Engleback Charles, esq
15   Peppercorne Francis Stephen, solicitor
15   Powell Robert, solicitor
15   Waylen James, artist
16   Croome Charles James, esq
17   Barton Thomas, solicitor
19   Brooks Robert, esq
19   *Commissioners of Land & Assd. Taxes*
19B   { Cartwright Henry Charles, esq
      { Crace Winfield, esq
19   Fenner Thomas Paris, esq
19   Gargrave Ralph Burnop, attorney
19   Julius & Cameron, solicitors
19   Julius Alfred Alexander, solicitor
19   Lock James, esq
19   Phipps John, esq
19   Walker John, clerical agent
19   Winfield William, esq
20   Beaumont Mrs. Boarding house
21   Dickson Miss Mary J. milliner, &c
22   Power Mrs
. . . . *Duke street* . . . .
25   Clarke James, straw bonnet maker
27 & 28   Stone Richard, tallow chandler

1845

Buckingham street, 38, *Strand.*
1   Dovell William, carpenter & undertaker
2   *Prince's Head,* George Goodwin
3   Clewley Daniel, dairyman
. . . . . . *here Off Alley intersects* . . . .
4   Lilly James, fruiterer
5   D'Arcy William, tailor
. . . . . *here Duke street intersects* . . . . . .
6   Shand William, patent artifl. leg maker
8   Minister John, lodging house
9   Potts Lawrence Holker, physician
10   Knowles James, solicitor
11   Paxton William Gill, esq
12   HANOVER CHAMBERS.
         Braddon Henry, solicitor
         Brickdale Matthew Inglis, esq
         Brown Charles, solicitor
         Croft John, solicitor
         Curry William Samuel, esq
         Derick John Macduff, architect
         Hodge John Watson, esq
         Lang Alfred, architect, &c
         Louch William Stevens, esq
         Neal Cornelius C. esq
         Willy Robert, attorney
13   Stafford William, solicitor
14   Bamford Charles F. esq
14   Bourne John Cooke, artist
14   Coles James, esq
14   Etty William, R.A. artist
14   Gruaz Henry Cuff, esq
14   Hayward Philip, solicitor
14   Jones William, surgeon
14   Wilson James, esq
. . . . *here is the River* . . . .
15   Chaffin James, esq
15   Curling Robert, esq
15   Jermyn George Alfred. survey.&draftsm
15   Powell Robert, solicitor
17   Barton Thomas, solicitor
17   Bittleston Adam, barrister
19   Barclay Robert, esq
19   Brooks Robert, esq
19   Figdor Benjamin, esq
19   *Commissioners of Land & Assd. Taxes*
19B,   Crace Henry Winfield, esq
19   Gargrave Ralph Burnop, attorney
19   Grant Augustus Romain, solicitor
19   Julius & Cameron, solicitors
19   Julius Alfred Alexander, solicitor
19   Lock James, esq
19   Wells Peter, esq
20   Cope Thomas, printer
21   Matthews William, embosser
22   Power Mrs
. . . . . *here Duke street intersects* . . . . . .
24   Burt James, portmanteau maker
. . . . . . *here Off Alley intersects* . . . .
25   Clarke James, straw bonnet maker
27 & 28   Stone Richard,sen.tallow chandler

1850

Buckingham street, 38, *Strand.*
1   Burrell Alfred Thomas, printer
2   *Prince's Head,* James Robert Street
3   Clewley Daniel, dairyman
. . . . . . *here Off Alley intersects* . . . .
4   Lilly James, fruiterer
5   D'Arcy William, tailor
6   Russell William, chandler's shop
. . . . . *here Duke street intersects* . . . . . .
6 & 7   Shand Mrs.Maria, patent artificial leg
        maker
8   Minister John, lodging house
9   Potts Lawrence Holker, physician
10   Hakewill Richard, wine merchant
10   Collins William W. civil engineer
10   Crampton Thos. R. civil engineer
10   Harrison John, builder
10   Markham Samuel S. architect
11   Paxton William Gill, esq
12   HANOVER CHAMBERS.
         Bowen Owen, esq
         Favell Robert, esq
         Chittenden Thomas, artist
         Eivers John, civil engineer
         Garland & Christopher, architects
         Hodge John Watson, esq
         Lang Alfred, architect
         Louch William Stevens, esq
         Thompson & Johnstone, architects
         Eastham Richard, esq
13   Stafford William & Son, solicitors
14   Manby Edward, esq
14   Baly Pritchard Price, civil engineer
14   Bamford Charles F. esq
14   Coles James, esq
14   Etty William, R.A. artist
. . . . *here is the River* . . . .
15   Comrie Alexander, surveyor
15   Hye Thomas Hayman, esq
15   Jermyn George Alfred, civil engineer
15   Johnson Arthur, esq
15   Rodney Frederick, esq
16   Corfield William, solicitor
18   Cunningham Charles, solicitor
18   Strutt John, solicitor
19   Bristoll Thomas, engraver
19   Homersham Saml. Collett,civil engineer
19   Brooks Robert, esq
19   *Commissioners of Land & Assd. Taxes*
19   Crace Henry Winfield, barrister
19   McVeagh John, civil engineer
19   Julius & Cameron, solicitors
19   Lock James, esq
20   *African Civilization Society*
         Robert Stokes, sec
20   Cope Thomas, printer
20   *Mico Trustees Office*
         Robert Stokes, sec
21   Cooper George Binion, brassfounder
22   Power Mrs
. . . . . *here Duke street intersects* . . . . . .
24   Burt James, portmanteau maker
. . . . . . *here Off Alley intersects* . . . .
25   Clarke James, straw bonnet maker
26   Crocker William, bootmaker
27 & 28   Stone Richard,sen.tallow chandler

1855

Buckingham street, 38, *Strand.*
2   *Prince's Head,* Robert Pearce
3   Clewley Daniel, dairyman
3   M'Donald Mrs. Ann, school
4   Lilly James, fruiterer
5   Fisher John Collin, butcher
6   M'Carthy John, tailor
. . . . . *here Duke street intersects* . . . . . .
6 & 7   Shand Mrs.Maria, artificial leg maker
8   Minister John, lodging house
10   Balam Charles, surveyor
10   Maberly Alfred William, architect
10   Markham Samuel S. architect
10   Field & Stanley, general inquiry agents
11   BUCKINGHAM CHAMBERS:-
         Clegg Samuel.jun.F.G.S. civil enginr
         Heald George, civil engineer
         Hodge Paul Rapsey, civil &
         mechanical engineer
         Lyon Charles James, wine mercht
         Mould George, contractor
         Metropolitan & Provincial General
         Agency Offices
         Henry Thornton, manager
         Official & General Building Society
         William Willis, secretary
         TarletonGeo.HawkesGilbert, gn.agt
12   HANOVER CHAMBERS:-
         Committee for Promoting Baths &c.
         George Woolcott, sec
         Woolcott George, esq
         Clarke George Somers, architect
         Farren Edwin James, esq
         FinchJohn,patentee of porcelain bths
         Louch William Stevens, esq
         Mullins Wlloughby, architect
         Renton Amherst H. civil engineer
         Salter & Laforest, architects
         Taylor Mark, esq
13   Gee & Stafford, solicitors
14   Chadwick William Winter, esq
14   Davies Henry, solicitor
14   Elton Captain Henry
14   Frankfort Lord
14   Howard Captain
14   Hunter James, esq
14   Kier Robert, esq
       M'Cormick Wm. contractor for public
       works, Matthew Catcheside, agent
. . . . *here is the River* . . . .
15   Birch Cecil, esq
15   Collins William Whitaker, civil engineer
15   Crampton Thomas R. civil engineer
15   Grantham James, esq
15   Jermyn George Alfred, civil engineer
15   Johnstone James & Co. foreign agents
15   Miller William, esq
16   Walford Mrs. Elizabeth, lodging house
17   *Belgian Eastern Junction Railway,*
        Wm. George Bicknell, sec
17   Walker, Knowles & Co. sheffield wareh.
        Thomas Francis, agent
18   Cunningham Charles, solicitor
18   Strutt John, solicitor
18   Kellock Miss Anna, lodging house
19   Bristoll Thomas & Son, engravers
19   Bonetto Peter Adolphus, watchmaker
19   *Commissioners of Land & Assd. Taxes*
19   Crace Henry Winfield, barrister
19   Emery Williams, collector of poor rates
19   Homersham Saml. Collett,civil engineer
19   Julius & Cameron, solicitors
19   Lock James, esq
19   Magnay Sir William, bart
19   Roebuck George, esq
19   Quilter James, solicitor
20   *African Civilization Society*
        Robert Stokes, sec
20   Cope Thomas, printer
20   *Mico-Trustees Off.*   Robert Stokes, sec
21   Baker William Beckley, insurance agent
. . . . *here Duke street intersects* . . . .
22½   Pullen William Peacock, wine merchant
24   Burt Mrs. Caroline, portmanteau maker
25   Clarke Mrs. Eliza, straw bonnet maker
26   Croker William, bootmaker
27 & 28   Stone Richard,sen.tallow chandler

BUCKINGHAM STREET

1860

Buckingham st. 38 *Strand.* (W.C.)

2   *Prince's Head,* Edward Bunyard
3   Wreathall, Clewley & Co. dairymen
3   M'Donald Mrs. Ann, school
4   Lilly James, fruiterer
5   Fisher John Collin, butcher
6   M'Carthy John, tailor
. . . . *here Duke street intersects* . . . .
7   Renton Mrs. Eliza Louisa, lodg. houses
8   Minister John, lodging house
9   Leighton Henry, general engraver
9   Livock John, architect & surveyor
9   Wilson Joseph William, civil engineer
10   Balam & Lee, surveyors
10   Billing Arthur, architect
10   Desborough William, architect
10   Jeckell Thomas, architect
10   Markham Samuel Stenton, esq
10   Stanley George, general inquiry agent
11   BUCKINGHAM CHAMBERS:—
    Irish Church Missions to the
    Roman Catholics,
        George Maxwell, esq. sec
    Official & General Building Soc.
        Matthew Forster, secretary
    Protestant Association,
        James Lord, esq. chairman
    Pure Literature Society,
        Richard Turner, assist. sec
    Society for Irish Church Missions,
        George Maxwell, esq. sec
    Missions to Seamen,
        Rev. Theodore Augustus Walrond,
        B.A. secretary
    Smith Alfred, architect & surveyor
    Mid Sussex Railway Office
        James Garrard, esq. chairman
        Theodore Morris Walford, sec
12   HANOVER CHAMBERS:—
    Allom Thomas, architect
    Freeman Robert, esq
    Farren Edwin James, esq
    Finch John, patentee of porcelain baths
    Barber William Swinden, architect
    Louch William Stevens, esq
    National Patent Salt Co.
        James P. Anstice, sec
    Renton Amherst H. civil engineer
    Parken Augustus Henry, architect
13   Montresor Thomas, barrister
13   Gee George, solicitor
14   McCormick William, contractor of
    public works,
        Matthew Catcheside, agent
14   Chadwick William Winter, esq
14   Davies Henry, esq
14   Elton Captain Henry
14   Freeman Charles, architect & surveyor
14   Harvey John, esq
14   Hooper George, esq
14   Perrin James, esq
14   Smyth Robert Maclean, brickmaker
. . . . *here is the River* . . . .
15   Boyce George Price, esq
15   Burges William, architect
15   Collins William Whitaker, civil engineer
15   Crampton Thomas R. civil engineer
15   Jermyn George Alfred, civil engineer
15   Johnson James, esq
15   Miller William, esq
16   Bermes Mrs. Sarah, lodging house
17   Walker, Knowles & Co. sheffield wareh
17   Bowen Charles, esq
18   Walsh Mrs. Mary, boarding house
19   Absolon William Henry, esq
19   Bristoll William & Son, engravers
19   Bonetto Peter Adolphus, watchmaker
19   *Income Tax Office for St. Martin's Parish*
19   Crace Henry Winfield, barrister

19   Emery Williams, collector of poor rates
19   Homersham Saml. Collett, civil engineer
19   Julius & Cameron, solicitors
19   Le Comte John, watch manufacturer
19   Lethbridge William, esq
19   Lock James, esq
19   Roebuck George, esq
19   Quilter James, solicitor
20   *African Civilization Society*
        William Stone, sec
20   Cope Thomas, esq.
20   *Mico-Trustees Off.*   Wm. Stone, sec
21   Towell Mrs. Maria, fishmonger
22   CHANDOS CHAMBERS:—
    Connop Jas. Hen. architect&surveyr
    Davies Henry, solicitor
    Hewitt Saml. architect & surveyor
    Investment & Mutual Advance
    Fund Association,
        Bramston C.A. Gilbert, sec
    Johnson John, architect & surveyor
    Sewell Charles, surveyor
    Regazzoli Antonio, civil engineer
. . . . . *here Duke street intersects* . . . . . .
22½   Pullen William Peacock, wine merchnt
24   Burt Mrs. Caroline, portmanteau maker
26   Croker Alfred, bootmaker
27 & 28   Wreathall, Clewley & Co. tallow
    chandlers

1865

Buckingham st. 38 *Strand.* (W.C.)

2   *Princess's Head,* Edward Bunyard
3   Wreathall, Clewley & Co. dairymen
3   M'Donald Mrs. Ann, school
4   Lilly James, fruiterer
5   Fisher John Collin, butcher
6   Clark & Co. oil merchants
. . . . . . *here is Duke street* . . . . . .
7   Renton Mrs. Eliza Louisa, private hotel
8   Minister John, lodging house
9   Leighton & Leighton, wood engravers
9   Livock John, architect & surveyor
9   Wilson Joseph William, civil engineer
10   Arthur Mr. Henry
10   Balam Charles, surveyor
10   Drew Richard William, M.A. architect
10   Preist John, solicitor
11   BUCKINGHAM CHAMBERS:—
    Irish Church Missions to the
    Roman Catholics,
    Society for Irish Church Missions,
        Lieut.-Col. Gabb, sec
    Protestant Association,
        James Lord, esq. chairman
    Pure Literature Society,
        Richard Turner, assist. sec
    Missions to Seamen,
        Rev.T.A. Walrond, B.A. sec
    Register of Evangelists,
        George Gilbert, sec
    Broderick Cuthbert, architect
    Sang Frederick, architect
    Smith Alfred, architect & surveyor
    Fennell John Greville, reporter
12   HANOVER CHAMBERS:—
    Freeman Robert, esq
    BarkerChas.Stuart,land agt. & survr
    Onslow Thomas Frederick, esq
    Barber William Swinden, architect
    Louch William Stevens, esq
    Pain Egerton J. architect & surveyor
    Patent Carriage Company (lim.),
        D.A.L. Durant, sec
    Fullwood Robt. John, comrcl.travler
    Whitelock Thomas William, esq
    Wilson Mr. Henry
13   Kerry Richard, lodging house
14   Austin Edmund John, surveyor
14   Lee Mr. John
14   Duncan Andrew, esq
14   Hodgson Henry Sibley, esq
14   Hooper George, esq
14   Perrin James, esq
14   Reece William Henry, solicitor
14   Rumball Alfred, civil engineer
14   Rumball Thomas, civil engineer
. . . . *here is the River* . . . .
15   Burges William, architect
15   Collins William Whitaker, civil engineer
15   *Caisse des Mines,*   Aime Fouache, sec
15   Birch Arthur, esq
    French Mining Journal Agency,
        Richard Sinclair, agent
15   Jermyn George Alfred, civil engineer
16   Bermes Mrs. Sarah, lodging house
17   Knowles John & Son, sheffield wareho
17   Clemence Mr. George
17   *Association for Promoting a Revision*
    of the Prayer Book,
        Rev. Richard Bingham, M.A. sec
18   Walsh James, family hotel
19   Jousiffe Charles Joseph, importer of
    dantzic spruce
19   Bristoll William & Son, engravers
19   Tissot & Bonetto, watch manufacturers
19   *Income Tax Office for St. Martin's*
19   Crace Henry Winfield, barrister
19   Emery Williams, collector of poor rates
19   Homersham Saml. Collett, civil engineer

19   Julius & Cameron, solicitors
19   Le Comte John, watch manufacturer
19   Lock James, esq
19   Smith Chas. Wm. & Co. commsn. agts
19   Grant J. Wynniatt, translator
19   Quilter James, solicitor
20   Cope Thomas, esq.
20   *Mico-Trustees' Office,*
        Rev. Wm. Stone, sec
22   CHANDOS CHAMBERS:—
    Davis Matthew Boulton, merchant
    Morton Arthur M & Geo.E coal mers
    Wise Francis, civil & consulting
    mechanical engineer
    Howard Henry William, architect
    & surveyor
    Johnson John, architect & surveyor
    Field Edward, civil & consulting
    mechanical engineer
    Sewill Charles, surveyor
    Tyler Robert Emeric, architect
. . . . . . *here Duke street intersects* . . . . . .
22½   Pullen William Peacock, wine merchnt
24   Burt Mrs. Caroline, portmanteau maker
25   Gould John Thomas, fishmonger
26   Croker Alfred, bootmaker
27 & 28   Hemblen Edward Thomas, grocer

BUCKINGHAM STREET

1870

Buckingham st. 38 *Strand.* (W.C.)
2   *Princess's Head,* Henry Burton
3   Wreathall, Clewley & Co. dairy
4   Lilly Mrs. Mary Ann, fruiterer
5   Fisher John Collin, butcher
6   Brown Charles, tailor
   . . . . . . *here is Duke street* . . . . . .
7   Renton Mrs. Eliza L. private hotel
8   Minister John, lodging house
8   Hoard Wm. Hen. ecclesiastical surveyor
8   De Tivoli Serafino, artist
8   Allen James Milner, artist on glass
9   Leighton & Leighton, wood engravers
9   Hook Henry, surveyor
9   *Representative Reform Association,*
          George Howell, esq. sec
10   Dredge James, civil engineer
10   Dredge William, civil engineer
10   Key Aston, civil engineer
10   Preist John, solicitor
10   Gritten Henry Frederick, surveyor
10   Woodifield Matthew, civil engineer
10   Fleet & Newey, boiler works,
    (West Bromwich) James Dredge, agent
11   BUCKINGHAM CHAMBERS:—
    Church of England Sunday
    School Educational Society,
          David Jones, sec
    Irish Church Missions to the Roman
    Catholics, Society for Irish Church
    Missions,
        Lieut.-Col. Gabb, secretary
        William Pasley, assistant sec
    Home for Little Boys,
        Albert O. Charles, hon sec
        Jonariab Finch, assist. sec
    Protestant Association,
        James Lord, chairman
    Pure Literature Society,
        Richard Turner, sec
    The Word on the Waters,
    Missions to Seamen,
        Rev. T.A. Walrond, B.A. sec
    Open-Air Mission,
        Gavin Kirkham, sec
    Swain Robert, surveyor
    Williams Lieut.Col. Henry Headly
    Broderick Cuthbert, architect
    Charles Albert O
12   HANOVER CHAMBERS:—
    Draper Edward Thomson,
        agent to Royal Marines
    Tear Laming Warren, agent to
        royal marines
    Walton John Wilson, architect
        & surveyor
    Logan Thomas & Co. wine &
        spirit merchants
    Ferguson John Mansfield, architect
        & surveyor
    Pinches Charles Frederick
13   Kerry Richard, lodging house
14   Acland James, parliamentary agent
14   Austin Edmund John, surveyor
14   Watson Robert
14   Johnson John, architect & surveyor
14   Cooke John
14   Fowler Charles, jun. architect &c
14   *Church Association,*
        Major F. Ditmas } secs
        Capt. W.C. Palmer
14   Hooper George
    Longcroft Charles Needham
   . . . . *here is the River* . . . .
15   Burges William, architect
15   Collins W. Whitaker, civil engineer
15   Green Joseph T
15   *Natal Government Immigration Office,*
        Dr. Mann, special agent

15   Mann Robert James, M.D., F.R.G.S
16   Day Arthur Geering
16   Cooke Dutton
16   Tate Captain R.T
17   Knowles John & Son, sheffield wareho
17   Clemence George
17   *Church Reform Society,*
        Rev. Harry Carrow, M.A. hon.sec
18   *Evangelization Society,*
        Capt. William E. Smith } hon
        Admiral Fishbourne, C.B. } secs
18   Chaplin William Henry
18   Rumball Alfred, civil engineer
18   Rumball Thomas, civil engineer
18   Utton Charles Philip, solicitor
18   Collings Patrick
19   Parkinson Frederick K. solicitor
19   Search Alfred, land agent
19   Bristoll William & Son, engravers
19   Browne John, architect
19   Butt Richd. agricul. produce office
19   McNulty Bernard John, civil engineer
19   Christie Capt. George Frederick
19   *Income Tax Office for St. Martin's*
19   Crace Henry Winfield, barrister
19   Homersham Saml. C. civil engineer
19   Pain & Clark, surveyors
19   Smith Alfred, architect & surveyor
19   Le Comte John, watch manufacturer
19   Lock James
20   Cope Thomas
22   CHANDOS CHAMBERS:—
    Wise Francis & Co. civil engineers
    Wise William Lloyd, engineer
        & patent agent
    Patent Office,
        William Lloyd Wise, F.R.A.S.,
        M.S.A. principal
    Johnson John, architect & surveyor
    Edwards Edmd. consulting engineer
    Field Edward, engineer
    Sewell Charles, surveyor
    Morton Arthur M. & Co. coal
        merchants
    Morton Edward George, coal mrcht.
    Payne Alexander, architect
    Stuart Henry
  . . . . *here is Duke street* . . . .
22½   Pullen William Peacock, wine merchnt.
24   Seller Michael, portmanteau maker
25   Gould John Thomas, fishmonger
26   Crocker Alfred, bootmaker
27 & 28 Hemblen Edward Thomas, grocer

1875

Buckingham st. 38 *Strand.* (W.C.)
2   *Princess's Head,* William Smith
3   Wreathall, Clewley & Co. dairy
4   Lilly Mrs. Mary Ann, fruiterer
5   Clifford Henry & Son, gasfitters
6   Murray Henry Francis, tailor
  . . . . *here is Duke street* . . . .
7   Phythian & Sons, wine & spirit merchts
7   Renton Mrs. Eliza L. Private hotel
8   Clark Daniel Kinnear, civil engineer
9   *Workman's Peace Association,*
        William Randal Cremer, sec
    Land Tenure Reform Association,
        Humphrey Sandwith, C.B. hon.sec
    Reformer's Union,
        Howard Evans, sec
    Bosson P. wine merchant
    Wren George, builder
    Kent James, window blind maker
    Goodman & Vinall, architects
    Worthington William James, architect
10   Dredge James, civil engineer
10   Dredge William, civil engineer
    Preist John, solicitor
    Gritten Henry Frederick, surveyor
    Woodfield Matthew, civil engineer
11   BUCKINGHAM CHAMBERS:-
    Irish Church Missions to the
        Roman Catholics,
    Society for Irish Church Missions,
        Lieut.-Col. Gabb, secretary
        William Pasley, assistant sec
    Pure Literature Society,
        Richard Turner, sec
    The Word on the Waters Mission
        to Seamen,
        Commander Wm. Dawson, R.N. sec
    Open-Air Mission,   John Kirk, sec
    East London Iron Works Co.
        Joseph H. Riddell, manager
    British Syrian Schools,
        Miss Burghes, sec
    Williams Lieut.Col. Henry Headly
    Broderick Cuthbert, architect
    Barker Arthur R. architect
    Joseph Michael, engraver on wood
    Home Words on the Waters (Monthly)
    Word on the Waters (Quarterly)
12   HANOVER CHAMBERS:-
    Draper Edward Thomas, agent to
        Royal Marines
    Logan Thomas & Co. wine & spirit
        merchants
    Colne Valley Water Co.
        Philip Verini, sec
    Sugden & Hill, architects
    Raven Henry, surveyor
    Cullen R.L.
    Farjeon Benjamin Leopold
    Barber William Henry, surveyor
    Price Robert William, surveyor
    Lacey John Turk, architect
    Booth Arthur Charles, architect
    Mundy Thomas Edward, architect
    James Robert C. architect
    Walton John Wilson, architect
13   Booth & Co. mining engineers
    O'Neill Stephen William, civil engineer
    Broadmoor Anthracite Coal Co.Limited,
        F.A.Cook, sec
    The Cornwall Tin & Copper Mining Co.
    Limited
14   Austin Edmund John, surveyor
    Johnson John, architect & surveyor
    Fowler Charles, architect &c
    Church Association,
        Major F. Ditmas } secs
        Capt. W.C. Palmer
    Longcroft Charles Needham

14   Williams John
    Alexander Henry
    Bellamy Edward Vaux
    Coleridge Charles Edward
15   *Society for Organising Charitable*
    Relief & Repressing Mendicity,
        C.B.P. Bosanquet, secretary
        C.J. Ribton-Turner, organising secretary
    Burges William, architect
    Everett Edward Yates
    Haliburton Richard Grant
    Wolff Henry W
16   Day Arthur Geering
    Cooke Dutton
17   *Naval & Military Gazette Association*
    Limited,
        A. Bishop Culpeper, sec
    Association for Promoting a Revision of
    the Prayer Book,
        Rev. Harry Carrow, M.A. hon.sec
    Metropolitan Gas Referees
        Proctor Thomas
18   *Evangelization Society,*
        Capt. William E. Smith
18   Rumball Thomas, civil engineer
    Alberga Charles, civil engineer
    Wood George Henry, civil engineer
    Jerningham Adolphus F. civil engineer
    Wilson Alexander Farlie
    Christen Armand, quarry owner
    Christen A. & Co. merchants
19   *Spence's Patent Non-conducting*
    Composition Office
    Smith C.W. Son & Co. non-conducting
        composition manufacturers
    Cottman Arthur, solicitor
    Collings Patrick
    Bristoll William & Son, engravers
    Kitchener Arthur
    Christie Capt. George Frederick
    Tissot & Bonetto, watch manufacturers
    Homersham Saml. C. civil engineer
    Pain & Clark, surveyors
    Cox Samuel Herbert, civil engineer
    Wheeler Frederick William
    Le Comte John, watch manufacturer
    Clarke Edward Francis C. architect
    Fullwood & Co. annatto manufacturers
    Clarke Henry J.B
    Britannia Bank Limited
    Thelin & Co. contractors
    Donzel & Co. foreign agents
    Melhado Alfred & Co. financial agents
    Lirie Thermal Baths Co. Limited
20   Cope Thomas
21   Towell Miss
22   CHANDOS CHAMBERS:—
    Wise Francis & Co. civil engineers
    Wise William Lloyd, engineer
        & patent agent
    Patent Office,
        William Lloyd Wise, consulting
        engineer
    Amos Henry Cooper, public accntnt
    Johnson John, architect & surveyor
    Field Edward, engineer
    Sewell Charles, surveyor
    Morton George Edward, accountant
    Streatham Public Hall & Baths
    Co. Limited
        William Henson, sec
    Ingrey Charles, civil engineer
  . . . . *here is Duke street* . . . .
22½   Pullen William Peacock, wine merchnt.
23 & 24 Seller Michael, portmanteau maker
25   Gould John Thomas, fishmonger
27   Crocker William, bootmaker
28   Fincham Albert, grocer

BUCKINGHAM STREET

1880

Buckingham st. 38 *Strand.* (W.C.)

2 *Princess's Head,* William Smith
3 Wreathall, Clewley & Co. dairy
    Ball Mrs. Eliza, dressmaker
4 Lilly Mrs. Mary Ann, fruiterer
.... *here are York place & Duke street* ....
7 Renton Mrs. Eliza L. Private hotel
8 Clark Daniel Kinnear, civil engineer
    Jenkin-Jones Charles, architect
    Anglo-Oriental Society for the Suppression
    of the Opium Trade,
        Rev. Fredk. S. Turner, B.A. sec
    Boxall Alfred, surveyor
9 *Workman's Peace Association*
        William Randal Cremer, sec
    Anti Game Law League,
        James H. Grant, sec
    Finch John & Co. patentees of
    porcelain baths
    Goodman Thomas W. architect
    Worthington William James, architect
    Society for the Protection of
    Ancient Buildings,
        T. Newman Marks, sec
10 Dredge William, civil engineer
    Woodfield Matthew, civil engineer
    Lacey John Turk, architect
    Wildy Alfred Henry
11 BUCKINGHAM CHAMBERS:-
    Irish Church Missions to the
    Roman Catholics,
        Rev. Horace W. Townsend,
        M.A. clerical secretary
        William Pasley, esq. lay sec
    Pure Literature Society,
        Richard Turner, sec
    Royal Canoe Club,
        H. Evans, sec
    The Word on the Waters Missions
    to Seamen,
        Commander Wm. Dawson, R.N. sec
    Word on the Waters
    Parochial Mission Women's Fund,
        William F. O'Brian, secretary
        Miss E.M. Robinson, hon.sec
    Williams Lieut.Col. Henry Headly
    Barker Arthur R. architect
    Joseph Michael, engraver on wood
    Bloxham Geo. Fredk, wine merchant
12 HANOVER CHAMBERS:-
    Draper Edward Thomas, agent to
    Royal Marines
    Logan Thomas & Co. wine & spirit
    merchants
    Colne Valley Water Co.
        Philip Verini, sec
    Morton A. Sidney, cement merchant
    Morton George Edward, accountant
    Byrne Patrick James, architect
    Tyndale Memorial Committee,
        John McGregor, hon.sec
    Craig William Henry
    Farjeon Benjamin Leopold
    Barber William Henry, surveyor
    Price Robert William, surveyor
    Blake Edward Chas. Henry, architect
    Oswell Arthur E. L. architect
    Booth Arthur Chas. B. architect
    Hodgson & Mundy, surveyors
    Walton John Wilson, architect
13 Kerry Richard
    Christian Evidence Society,
        Rev. P. Barker, sec
    Fellowship of Animals' Friends,
        Andrew Marvel Reid, sec
14 Fraser Arthur J
    Church Association,
        Capt. W.G.Palmer, sec
    Williams John

14 Alexander Henry
    Bellamy Edward Vaux
    Myers Joseph
    Leaf George Hooper
    Gosnell Sidney
    Sampson Henry
15 *Society for Organising Charitable*
    Relief & Repressing Mendicity,
        Charles S. Loch, secretary
    Burges William, architect
    Morton John G
    Black William
16 Day Arthur Geering
    Earle James Howard, artist
17 *Association for Promoting a Revision of*
    the Prayer Book,
        Rev. Harry Carrow, M.A. hon.sec
    Archer & Green, architects
    Metropolitan Gas Referees
    Protestant Tract Society,
        J.T. Burt, hon. sec
18 Lammin William Henry, solicitor
    Glass Thomas
    Dutch Club
    Page Richard C. architect
    Kyrle Harold
19 Pilleau Frederick Startin
    Elvoot Arthur
    Collings Patrick
    Bristoll William, engraver
    Trades Union Congress Parliamentary
    Committee,
        H. Broadhurst, sec
    National Liberal League,
        H. Broadhurst, sec
    Pether Samuel, seal engraver
    Tissot & Bonetto, watch manufacturers
    Baxter Herbert Carlyon, architect
    Gascoine John, architect
    Homersham Saml. C. civil engineer
    Pain Egerton James, surveyor
    Clark Edward, architect
    Melhado Alfred
    Walker Robert, civil engineer
    Monier-Williams & Stanley, architects
    Sugden Henry Townley, architect
    Warren Albert Henry, artist
    Williams George & Stanley, architects
20 Cope Thomas
21 Towell Miss
22 CHANDOS CHAMBERS:—
    Hastings Charles Williams, gas engineer
    Salmon, Barnes & Co. shutter mfrs
    Gas & Water Companies Directory
    American Gas Light Journal Office
    Gas Trade Circular & Review Office
    Holroyde William Frederick, solicitor
    Field, Field & Cotton, consulting
    engineers
    Mercer William, civil engineer
    Sewell Charles, surveyor
    Johnson John, architect
    Ward Frederick, confidential agent
    Goode Charles Henry, surveyor
    Johnson Edward William
.... *here is Duke street* ....
22¹/₁ Norris Edward & Co. wine merchants
23 & 24 Seller Michael, portmanteau maker
24 Gould John Thomas, fishmonger
25 Weddle Frederick, coffee rooms
26 Murray Henry Francis, tailor
27 Croker William, boot maker
28 Thomas John Henry, grocer

1885

Buckingham st. 37 *Strand.* (W.C.)

2 *Princess's Head,* William Smith
3 Clewley & Co. dairy
4 Lilly Mrs. Mary Ann, fruiterer
.... *here is Duke street* ....
7 Renton Mrs. Henry
8 Clark Daniel Kinnear, civil engineer
    Sullivan Henry Eden, solicitor
    Peters Philip Hall, architect
    Vining Reginald Vining, solicitor
    Parsons William, wholesale ironmonger
    Collins Lewis Pratt, surveyor
    Brewer Frank J. architect
9 *Workman's Peace Association*
        William Randal Cremer, sec
    Cremer William Randal, publisher
    Lineff & Jones, consulting engineers
    Finch John & Co. patentees of
    porcelain baths
    Goodman Thomas W. architect
    Society for the Protection of
    Ancient Buildings,
        Thackeray Turner, sec
    Turner Thackeray, architect
    Beesley & Williams, architects
    Wilson James Llewellyn, architect
10 Dredge William, civil engineer
    Woodfield Matthew, civil engineer
    Lacy John Turk, architect
    Wildy Alfred Henry
    De Buriatts Frederick, advertising agent
11 BUCKINGHAM CHAMBERS:-
    Irish Church Missions to the
    Roman Catholics,
        Rev. Horace W. Townsend,
        M.A. clerical secretary
        William Pasley, lay sec
    Pure Literature Society,
        Richard Turner, sec
    Royal Canoe Club,
        T.G.F. Winser, sec
    The Word on the Waters Missions
    to Seamen,
        Commander Wm. Dawson, R.N. sec
    Parochial Mission Women's Fund,
        Miss E.M. Robinson, hon.sec
    Williams Lieut.Col. Henry Headly
    Barker Arthur R. architect
    Bloxham Geo. Fredk, wine merchant
    Rosser & Co. engineers
    London Advertising Co.
12 HANOVER CHAMBERS:-
    Barber, Boxall and Boxall, surveyors
    Price Robert William, surveyor
    Blake Edward Chas. Henry, architect
    Munday Thomas Edward, architect
    Bell Herbert James, solicitor
    Nicholl Donald,J.P.parliamnty agent
    Schomburg Carl R
    Baily Harrington
    Murray Arthur C
    Quentin Cecil
    Saul Richard Hay
13 Walker Robert, civil engineer
    Contractors, Engineering & Financial
    Agency, Robert Walker, F.R.G.S
    Christian Evidence Society,
        Rev. C.L. Engstrom, sec
14 *Church Association,*
    Isaac Plant Fleming, M.A., D.C.L. sec
    Williams John
    Hawkes Mervyn L.
    Gosnell Sidney
    Herbert Henry Arthur
    James Davitt
15 *Society for Organising Charitable*
    Relief & Repressing Mendicity,
        Charles B. Loch, secretary
    Pullan Richard P. architect

15 Morton John G
    Black William
16 O'Donnell Frank Hugh, M.P
    Eaton-Iddins Walter Francis
    Martin Arthur P. journalist
17 *Prayer Book Revision Society,*
        J. Butcher, sec
    Metropolitan Gas Referees' Department
    Teachers' Guild of Great Britain
    & Ireland,
        J. A. De Morgan, B.A. sec
    Elliott Major
18 Lammin William Henry, solicitor
    Glass Thomas
    Dutch Club
    Wilson Ernest H
    Hovell Charles James
19 Collings Patrick, solicitor
    Archer & Green, architects
    Homersham Saml. C. civil engineer
    Bristoll William, engraver
    Trades Union Congress Parliamentary
    Committee, H. Broadhurst, sec
    Tissot & Bonetto, watch manufacturers
19 Pain Egerton James, surveyor
    Smith Arthur Morton
    Champneys Basil, architect
    Lea Frederick, surveyor
    Walker-Romaine & Tanner, architects
    Balfour Eustace James A. architect
    Cooper Neville
    Woodrow Ernest A. E. architect
    Hill Henry Awdus, architect
    Dovaston Adolphus, architect
20 Cope Thomas
21 Towell Miss
22 CHANDOS CHAMBERS:—
    Scientific Publishing Co. Limited
    Gas & Water Companies Directory
    American Gas Light Journal Office
    Gas & Water Review
    Hastings Charles Williams, gas engineer
    Johnson Edward William
    Field, Field & Cotton, consulting
    engineers
    Sewell Charles, surveyor
    Johnson John, architect
    Goode Charles Henry, surveyor
    Mountford Edward Wm. architect
    Stoveld Henry, surveyor
.... *here is Duke street* ....
23 & 24 Seller Michael, portmanteau maker
24 Croker William, boot maker
26 Power Sidney, wine merchant
27 Thomas John Henry, grocer

BUCKINGHAM STREET

1890

Buckingham st. 37 *Strand.* (W.C.)
2   *Princess's Head,* William Thomas Richards
3   Clewley & Co. dairy
4   Bartlett Charles, fruiterer
.... *here is Duke street* ....
6 & 7   Vann Philip Harry, private hotel
8   *The Index Publishing Co. Limited*
8   *Index Newspaper Office*
8   *Mariner Newspaper Office*
8   Clark Daniel Kinnear, civil engineer
8   Parsons William, wholesale ironmonger
8   Holt James Madden
8   Salomons Edward, architect
9   Bevan Henry Arthur, valuer & financial agent
9   Burnet Charles & Co. publishers
9   Goodman Thomas W. architect
9   Simpson Harry William, surveyor
9   *Society for the Protection of Ancient Buildings,*
     Thackeray Turner, sec
9   Beesley Alfred Joseph, architect
9   Higgins Joseph Charles, architect
10   Lacey John Turk, architect
10   Balfour & Turner, architects
10   *Childrens' Country Holidays Fund,*
     Hon. Alfred Lyttelton, hon. treasurer
11   BUCKINGHAM CHAMBERS:-
     Irish Church Missions to the Roman Catholics,
      Rev. J.S.S. Shields, D.D. clerical secretary, pro tem
      William Pasley, lay sec
     Pure Literature Society,
      Richard Turner, sec
     Royal Canoe Club,
      T.G.F. Winser, sec
     Missions to Seamen,
      Commander Wm. Dawson, R.N. sec
     Parochial Mission Women's Fund,
      Miss F. Noble, hon.sec
     Barker Arthur R. architect
     Insurance & Finance Leader Office
     Alce George Edward
     Bennett Arthur & Co. advertising agents
12   HANOVER CHAMBERS:-
     Nicholl Donald, J.P. civil engineer
     Booth Robert, surveyor
     National Association for Employment of Reserve & Discharged soldiers,
      Col. W.J. Boyes, sec
     Barber W.H. & Son, surveyors
     Price Robert William, architect
     Munday Thomas Edward, architect
     Tarver Edward John, architect
     Bell Herbert James, solicitor
     Baily Harrington
     Knight William Francis
     Davey Richard
     Eaton-Iddins Walter Francis
     Cornelius W. Theile
     Thornton & Co. mortgage brokers
13   Houghton & Cony, commission agents
13   *Christian Evidence Society,*
     Rev. C.L. Engström, sec
14   *Church Association,*   H. Miller, sec
14   Jackson Thomas Graham, M.A., F.S.A. architect
14   Anderson Robert
14   Anderson Percy
14   Porteous William
14   Moore Mrs
14   Gilsey Charles
14   Boor Leonard Charles
14   Oddy Herbert
15   *Society for Organising Charitable Relief & Repressing Mendicity,*
     Charles B. Loch, secretary

15   *Metropolitan Discharged Prisoners' Aid Society,*   T. Ralph Price, sec
15   *Matron's Aid Society,*   Mrs. Nichol, sec
15   *Denison Club,*   Miss L. Sharpe, hon. sec
15   *Trained Nurses Club,*
     Mrs. Margaret Nichol, sec
15   Black William
15   St. Quintin Perry
16   *Boys' Public Day School Co. Lim*
17   *Prayer Book Revision Society,*
     J. Butcher F.R.G.S. sec
17   *Metropolitan Gas Referees' Department*
     Teachers' Guild of Great Britain & Ireland,
     H.B. Garrod. M.A. sec
17   *Froebel Society*
17   *National Froebel Union*
17   Buckley Michael J. C
18   Lammin William Henry, solicitor
18   Herbert & Co. patent agents
18   Hadden Herbert J., Reginald & Percy, consulting engineers
18   *Metropolitan Association for Befriending Young Servants*
18   *Invalid Children's Aid Association,*
     Allen D. Graham, hon. sec
19   Homersham Sam. C. civil engineer
19   Collings P. & Co. solicitors
19   Irvine & Co. envelope addressers
19   Bristoll William, engraver
19   *Trades Union Congress Parliamentary Committee,*   H. Broadhurst, M.P. sec
19   *Society for Psychical Research,*
     Edward T. Bennett, assist sec
19   Tissot & Bonetto, watch manufacturers
19   Gotz John Rodolphe, optician
19   Pain Egerton James, surveyor
19   Champneys Basil, architect
19   Smith Arthur Morton
19   Lea Frederick, surveyor
19   Walker-Romaine & Tanner, architects
19   Hill Henry Awdus, architect
19   Cresswell Herbert Osborn
20   Cope Thomas
21   Towell Miss
22   CHANDOS CHAMBERS:—
     Hastings Chas. Williams, gas engnr
     Davies George Humphreys, surveyor
     Alleyne Cecil H. Florida bureau
     Field, Field & Co, consulting engineers
     Morris F. Sanders, consulting engineer
     Sewell Charles, architect
     Johnson John, architect
     Goode Charles Henry, surveyor
     Mountford Edward Wm. architect
     Thompson George W. civil engineer
     Reeves Hildebrand & W. architects
     Browne James & Co. accountants
.... *here is Duke street* ....
23 & 24   Seller Michael, portmanteau maker
24   Croker William, boot maker
28   *Charing Cross Vegetarian Hotel & Restaurant Co. Limited,*
     B. Clarke, manager

1895

Buckingham st. 37 *Strand.* (W.C.)
2   *Princess's Head,* Hounslow Brewery Co. Limited (The)
3   Clewley & Co. dairy farmers, &c
4   Bartlett Charles, fruiterer
     Godfree (E.) Felton & Co. wine merchants
.... *here is Duke street* ....
6 & 7   Jones Miss Margaret, private hotel
8   Buckingham Advance Bank, Lim.
     E.J. Peck, sec
8   Parsons William, wholesale ironmonger
8   Selby Edgar Harry, architect
8   Riley Henry, surveyor
8   Clark Daniel Kinnear, civil engineer
9   Bevan Henry Arthur & Co. valuers
9   Allard Jules & Sons, decorators
9   Goodman Thomas W. architect
9   Simpson Harry William, surveyor
9   *Society for the Protection of Ancient Buildings,*
     Thackeray Turner, sec
9   Beesley Alfred Joseph, architect
9   Higgins Joseph Charles, architect
9   Floyd & Hayman, builders
10   Lacey John Turk, architect
10   Balfour & Turner, architects
10   *Childrens' Country Holidays Fund,*
     Hon. Alfred Lyttelton, hon. treasurer
11   BUCKINGHAM CHAMBERS:—
     Pure Literature Society,
     Richard Turner, sec
     Royal Canoe Club,
     T.G.F. Winser, sec
     Irish Church Missions to the Roman Catholics,
      Rev. N,F. Duncan, A.B. clerical secretary
      William Pasley, lay sec
     Missions to Seamen,
      Commander Wm. Dawson, R.N. sec
     Parochial Mission Women's Fund,
      Miss F. Noble, hon.sec
     Barker Arthur R. architect
     THE T.T. FOLDERS CO
     Tomlinson Walter J.N. architect
     Alce George Edward
     Rackham Arthur, artist
12   HANOVER CHAMBERS:—
     National Association for Employment of Reserve Soldiers, &c
      Col. A.M. Handley, sec
     Froebel Society,
      Miss Christobel Massey, sec
     National Froebel Union,
      Miss E.H. Macklean, sec
     Midwives' Institute & Trained Nurses Club,   Mrs. M. Nicol, sec
     Mundy Thomas Edward, architect
     Bell Herbert James, solicitor
     Graham Walter, architect
     Bailey Harrington, theatrical business manager
     Taylor Alfred Ernest, architect
     Harris Edward Swinfen, architect
     National Society for Employment of Epileptics,
      George P. Gaskell, sec
     Davies Percy Alex. D
     Knight William Francis
     Davey Richard
     Jenner Louis
     Stainer Edward
13   Waldram John C.E. & Son, surveyors
13   Newton Wm. Geo. & Co. electrical engrs
13   *Christian Evidence Society,*
     Rev. C.L. Engstrom, sec
14   *Church Association,*   H. Miller, sec
14   Jackson Thomas Graham, A.R.A. architect

14   Townsend Horace
14   Porteous William
14   Moore Mrs
14   Quintin Cecil
14   Pennell Joseph
14   Ellis William Ashton
15   *Society for Organising Charitable Relief & Repressing Mendicity,*
     Charles B. Loch, secretary
15   *Denison Club,*   E.C. Price, hon. sec
15   Black William
15   St. Quintin Perry
16   *Boys' Public Day School Co. Lim*
16   Hawkins Anthony Hope
16   Borman A. & C. scholastic agents
17   *Metropolitan Gas Referees' Department*
17   Pole William, F.R.S. civil engineer
17   Mountford Edwd. Wm. architect
17   Thompson George W. surveyor
17   Earnshaw-Wall Walter E. Stacey, solicitor
18   *Homes for Working Boys in London,*
     William Denham, sec
18   Hadden Herbert & Co. patent agents
18   *Metropolitan Association for Befriending Young Servants*
18   *Invalid Children's Aid Association,*
18   Warren Albert Henry, artist
19   Irvine & Co. envelope addressers
19   Patent Ramoneur Co. Limited
19   Collings P. & Co. solicitors
19   Evans Frederick Henry
19   Pain Egerton James, surveyor
19   Champneys Basil, architect
19   Lea Frederick, surveyor
19   Bristoll William, engraver
19   *Trades Union Congress Parliamentary Committee,*   Samuel Woods, M.P. sec
19   *Society for Psychical Research,*
     Edward T. Bennett, assist sec
20   Cope Thomas
21   Towell William Frederick, architect
21   Towell Miss
22   CHANDOS CHAMBERS:—
     Barber W.H. & Son, surveyors
     Price Robert William, architect
     Brewer Frank J. architect
     Hill, Percival & Co. electric light engineers
     Field Edward, consulting engineer
     Morris F. Sanders, consulting engineer
     Sewell Charles, architect
     Dennis Langton, architect
     Dawber Edward Guy, architect
     Johnson John, architect
     Goode Charles Henry, architect
     Engineering Price List Office (The)
     Buckler John Thos. commission agt.
.... *here is Duke street* ....
23 & 24   Hyde William, portmanteau maker
24   Croker William, bootmaker
28   *Buckingham Temperance Hotel & Vegetarian Restaurant Co. Lim.*
     G.F. Hemmings, sec

BUCKINGHAM STREET

1900

Buckingham st. 37 *Strand.* (W.C.)
2   *Prince's Head*, Mrs Annie Drowley
3 & 4 Clewley & Co.dairy farmers &c
    Godfree (E.), Felton & Co. wine
    merchants
. . . . *here is Duke street* . . . .
6 & 7 Jones Miss Margaret, private hotel
8   Murray & Co. financial agents
8   Collier Major John Thomas, youth
    employment agency
8   Selby Edgar Harry, architect
8   Collard Allen Ovenden, architect
8   Radio Incubator Co
10 Lacey John Turk, architect
10 Balfour & Turner, architects
10 *Society for the Protection of Ancient*
    Buildings,
              Thackeray Turner, sec
10 *Children's Country Holidays Fund*
    Hon. Alfd. Lyttelton, M.P. hon.treasurer
11 BUCKINGHAM CHAMBERS:-
    Leman, Rogers & Co. distillers' agents
    Slatter Alfred & Co. electrical engineers
    Pure Literature Society,
              Richard Turner, sec
    Hillyard & Co. advertising agents
    Burgiss-Brown John, printer
    Irish Church Missions to the
    Roman Catholics
        Rev. N.F.Duncan, M.A.
        clerical secretary
        William Pasley, lay sec
    Missions to Seamen
        Commander Wm. Dawson, R.N. sec
    Parochial Mission Women's Fund
        Miss J.M. Hollis, secretary
    Barker Arthur R. architect
    Simmons William, architect
12 HANOVER CHAMBERS:-
    Midwives' Institute & Trained
    Nurses' Club,
        Miss R.P. Fynes-Clinton, sec
    Society of Trained Masseuses
        Miss L. Grant, hon sec
    National Society for Employment
    of Reserve Soldiers, &c
        Col. A.M. Handley, sec
    Knight William Francis
    Mundy Thomas Edward. architect
    Women's Industrial Council,
        Miss Catherine Webb, sec
    Davies Percy Alexander D
    Waldram John & Son, surveyers
    National Society for Employment
    of Epileptics,
        George P. Gaskell, sec
    Homes for Working Boys in London,
        William Denham,sec
    Davey Richard
    Bell Herbert James, solicitor
13 Comben Miss Adelaide, apartments
14 Porteous William
14 Faulding Alfred Joseph
14 *Church Association,*   H. Miller, sec
14 Moore Mrs
14 Jackson Thomas Graham, architect
14 Sopper Harry
14 Angle Bernard John
14 Wildy Augustus George
14 Pennell Joseph
15 *Society for Organising Charitable*
    Relief & Repressing Mendicity,
        Charles S. Loch, secretary
15 *Library of the Charity Organisation*
    Society,
        Charles S. Loch, secretary
15 Denison Club, E.C. Price, hon.sec
15 St. Quintin Perry
16 Burnet & Isbister, publishers

16 Fulford Henry & Co. accountants
16 *Hotel World*
16 *Hotel & Restaurant Protection Society,*
        Edgar A. Bernales, hon. sec
16 Belden, Hallett & Co. hotel valuers
16 de Bernales C. & Co. merchants
16 Edgar & Co. advertising agents
16 Hawkins Anthony Hope
17 Mellor Herbert Williams, quantity
    surveyor
17 Mountford Edward William, architect
17 Cresswell Herbert O, architect
17 Lewis Charles
18 Herbert, Haddan & Co. patent agents
18 *Metropolitan Association for*
    Befriending Young Servants,
        Miss Poole, sec
18 *Invalid Children's Aid Association*
18 *Strand Liberal & Radical Association*
19 Irvine & Co.Lim. envelope addressers
19 *Ramoneur Co. Limited*
19 *Hotel & Club Staff Supply Association,*
        Capt. W.H. Cooke, man
19 Collings P. & Co. solicitors
19 d'Adhemar Harry G
19 Barker Albert
19 Pain Egerton Jas. & Son, surveyors
19 Champneys Basil, architect
19 Lea Frederick, surveyor
19 Clay Felix, surveyor
19 Bristoll Frank, engraver
19 *Trades Union Congress Parliamentary*
    Committee,
        Sam Woods, M.P. sec
19 *Society for Psychical Research,*
        Edward T. Bennett, assitant sec
21 Towell Wiliam Frederick, architect
21 Towell Miss
22 CHANDOS CHAMBERS:—
    Barber W.H. & Son, surveyors
    Sewell Charles, architect
    Monson Edward, architect
    Dawber (E.Guy) & Whitwell, architects
    Goode Charles Henry, architect
    Engineering Price List Office (The)
    Buckler John Thomas, advt. contractor
    Tucker & Huntley, architects
. . . . *here is Duke street* . . . .
23 Margeit Ernest, hairdresser
23A, General Agenvy Company
24 Shepperd Frederick, butcher
. . . . *here is York place* . . . .
28 *Buckingham Temperance Hotel &*
    Vegetarian Restaunat Co. Lim.
        E. Jones, sec

1905

Buckingham st. 37 *Strand.* (W.C.)
    (WESTMINSTER).
2   *Prince's Head*, Herbert James Cathie
3 & 4 Clewley & Co. dairy farmers &c
4   Wreathall Arthur Clewley
. . . . *here is York place.* . . . .
. . . . *here is Duke street* . . . .
6 & 7 Jones Miss Margaret, private hotel
8   Murray & Co. financial agents
8   Selby Edgar Harry, architect
8   Collard Allen Ovenden, architect
10 *British Bee Journal Office*
10 Balfour & Turner, architects
10 *Society for the Protection of Ancient*
    Buildings,
        Thackeray Turner, sec
11 BUCKINGHAM CHAMBERS:—
    Penrhyn - Forster & Lacy,
    theatrical agents
    Pure Literature Society,
        Richard Turner, sec
    Irish Church Missions to the
    Roman Catholics,
        Rev. R. E. Waters,
        clerical secretary
        William Pasley, lay sec
    Missions to Seamen,
        Stuart C. Knox, sec
    Barker A. R. & Son, architects
12 HANOVER CHAMBERS:-
    Midwives' Institute & Trained
    Nurses' Club
    Incorporated Society of Trained
    Masseuses,
        Miss L. Grant, hon sec
    Bissell John James, surveyor
    Knight William Francis
    Davie & Son, solicitors
    Waldram John & Son, surveyers
    National Society for Employment
    of Epileptics,
        George P. Gaskell, sec
    Homes for Working Boys in London,
        William Denham,sec
    Davey Richard
    Shirley Walter K. architect
13 *Antipon Company*
13 & 14 *Church Association,*
        Henry Miller, sec
14 Porteous William
14 Rollo Hon. Bernard Francis, M.A
14 Huntington Alfred
14 Moore Mrs
14 Jackson Thomas Graham, architect
14 Angle Bernard John
14 Wildy Augustus George
14 Pennell Joseph
15 *Society for Organising Charitable*
    Relief & Repressing Mendicity,
        Charles S. Loch, secretary
15 *Library of the Charity Organisation*
    Society,
        Charles S. Loch, secretary
15 Littlewood-Clarke Herbert Dell, solicitor
16 Munro, Reynolds & Co. business agents
17 Mellor Herbert Williams, quantity
    surveyor
17 Mountford Edward William, architect
17 Cresswell Herbert O, architect
17 Lewis Charles
18 Herbert, Haddan & Co. patent agents
18 *Metropolitan Association for*
    Befriending Young Servants,
        Miss Poole, sec
18 *Children's Country Holidays Fund,*
        The Earl of Arran, hon. treas
18 *Strand Liberal & Radical Association*
19 Irvine & Co. Lim. envelope addressers

19 *Ramoneur Co. Lim.* chimney sweepers
19 *Cabmen's Shelter Fund*
19 *Moral Instruction League,*
        Harrold Johnson, B.A. hon sec
19 *Union of Ethical Societies,*
        Miss F. Winterbottom, sec
19 *Women's Industrial Council,*
        Miss Wyatt Papworth, sec
19 White Mrs. Lydia Emma, hotel
    staff office
19 *Emerson Club,*   Mrs. Stanton Colt, sec
19 Collings P. & Co. solicitors
19 d'Adhemar Harry G
19 Pain Egerton Jas. & Son, surveyors
19 Champneys Basil, architect
19 Goddard Rainald W. Knightley, architect
19 Bristoll F.W. & Co. copperplate
    engravers
19 Simmins Mrs
21 Wright Herbert Alfred, architect
22 CHANDOS CHAMBERS:—
    Barber W.H. & Son, surveyors
    Laurence George E. T. architect
    Monson Edward, architect
    Dawber Edward Guy, architect
    Goode Charles Henry, architect
    Hewitt Walter Ernest, architect
    Huntley Arthur, architect
. . . . *here is Duke street* . . . .
23 Dodson George Robert, dining rooms
23 Ashplant & Devereux, mortgage brokers
23 *Association for Befriending Boys,*
        Mrs. Graham Simmons, sec
23A, Calupka Frank, hairdresser
23B, Mew George Edgar, solicitor
24 Graham Henry, photo dealer
. . . . *here is York place* . . . .
28 *Buckingham Temperance Hotel,*
        Stephen Moor, proprietor

BUCKINGHAM STREET

1910

Buckingham st. 37 *Strand.* (W.C.)
(WESTMINSTER).
2   *Prince's Head,* Herbert James Cathie
3 & 4 Clewley & Co. dairy farmers
4   Bennett Richard James, verger
     of St. Martin-in-the-Fields
. . . . *here is York place.* . . . .
. . . . *here is Duke street* . . . .
6 & 7 Jones Miss Margaret, private hotel
8   Murray & Co. financial agents
8   Selby Edgar Harry, architect
8   Hillyer William Harold, architect
8   Collard Allen Ovenden, architect
8   Seddon Joseph, architect
8   *Association of Shorthand Writers*
     & Typists
11   BUCKINGHAM CHAMBERS:—
     Pure Literature Society,
           Richard Turner, sec
     Irish Church Missions to the
     Roman Catholics,
        Rev. R. E. Waters, M.A.
           clerical secretary
        E.W. Allden, financl. sec
     Missions to Seamen
           Stuart C. Knox,M.A. sec
     Barker & Kirk, architects
     Barker Arthur Rowland,
        diocesan surveyor
     Stone & Colquhoun, architects
     Forster William Penrhyn,
        theatrical manager
     Smale Harry, inquiry agent
     Motor Finance (office of)
12   HANOVER CHAMBERS:-
     Midwives' Institute & Trained
     Nurses' Club
     Incorporated Society of Trained
     Masseuses,
           Miss D. Elliott, sec
     Bissell John James, surveyor
     Stanhope & Co. Ltd. variety agents
     Davie & Son, solicitors
     Incorporated Society of Trained
     Masseuses,   Miss Hall, sec
     Silica Blending Co
     Waldram John & Son, surveyers
     Melville & Co. publishers
     Ruvigny Marquis de
     Moscrop-Young & Glanfield,
        architects
     Homes for Working Boys in London,
           William Denham,sec
     Shirley Walter K. architect
     Devlin William John, architect
     Wallis William Edmund, architect
13   Forest of Dean Stone Firms Ltd
13 & 14 *Church Association,*
           Henry Miller, sec
14   Huntington Alfred
14   Moore Mrs
14   Jackson Thomas Graham, architect
14   Machel-Smith Mrs
14   Holland Hon. Lionel
14   Littlewood-Clarke Herbert Dell, solicitor
15 & 16 *Royal National Pension*
     Fund for Nurses
15 & 16 *Borstal Association*
15 & 16 *Peabody Donation Fund,*
           Lord Dunluce, sec
15 & 16 *Morgan Junius S. Benevolent Fund*
15 & 16 Grant-Wilson George Wemyss,
        barrister
17   White F. V. & Co. Ltd. publishers
17   *Royal Female Orphan Asylum,*
           Brough Maltby, sec
17   Cresswell Herbert O, architect
17   Lewis Charles
18   *Society for Promoting the Due*
     Observance of the Lord's Day

18   *Children's Country Holidays Fund,*
        The Earl of Arran, hon. treas
18   *Royal National Hospital for*
     Consumption & Diseases of the Chest,
           Ernest Morgan, sec
18   *Strand Liberal & Radical Association*
18   *Billiard Association*
19   Irvine & Co. Lim. envelope addressers
19   *Ramoneur Co. Lim.* chimney sweepers
19   *Cabmen's Shelter Fund*
19   *Union of Ethical Societies,*
     H. Snell & Miss F. Winterbottom, secs
19   *Typographical Association,*
           H . Skinner, sec
19   *Emerson Club (Ladies'),*
           Augustus H. Atkinson, hon.sec
19   Greatorex Joseph Edward Alfred,
        architect
19   Fisher Edmund, architect
19   Waller Frank John, architect
19   d'Adhémar Harry G
19   Champneys Basil, architect
19   Anderson Abbot
20   Balfour & Turner, architects
20   *Society for the Protection of*
     Ancient Buildings,
           Thackeray Turner, sec
20   Williams Thomas, employment agency
20   Oddy Josiah
20   Barraclough Arthur
21   Brindley & Foster, organ builders
21   Towell William Frederick, architect
21   *Sociological Society,*
           J.W.Slaughter, sec
22   CHANDOS CHAMBERS:—
     Barber W.H. & Son, quantity surveyors
     Walsh Frederick Morfee, quantity
        surveyor
     Laurence George E. T. architect
     Dawber Edward Guy, architect
     Hewitt Walter Ernest, architect
     Tucker & Huntley, architects
. . . . *here is Duke street* . . . .
23   Brereton Christopher Francis,
        dining rooms
24   Reeder Louis de Ltd. theatrical agents
24   Bailey Edward Rolls, watchmaker
24   Simmons Henry, surveyor
24   Braund Philip Sidney, general agent
24   Bristoll Frank Winstone & Co.
        copperplate engravers
23A, Calupka Frank, hairdresser
27   Shepperd Frederick, butcher
. . . . *here is York place* . . . .
28   *Buckingham Temperance Hotel,*
           Stephen Moor, proprietor

1915

Buckingham st. 37 *Strand.* (W.C.)
(WESTMINSTER).
       WEST SIDE
2   *Prince's Head,* Herbert James Cathie
3   Marshall's Dairies Ltd.
4   Braund Philip Sidney, stationer
4   Bennett Richard James, parish clerk
     of St. Martin-in-the-Fields
. . . . *here is York place.* . . . .
. . . . *here is Duke street* . . . .
6 & 7 Jones Miss Margaret, private hotel
8   Cope & Fenwick, publishers
8   *London Central Window Cleaning Co Ltd*
8   Selby Edgar Harry, architect
8   Hillyer William Harold, architect
8   Collard Allen Ovenden, architect
8   Seddon Joseph, architect
11   BUCKINGHAM CHAMBERS:—
     Pure Literature Society
     Irish Church Missions to the
     Roman Catholics,
        Rev. R. E. Waters, M.A.
           clerical secretary
        E.W. Allden, financl. sec
     Missions to Seamen,
           Stuart C. Knox,M.A. sec
     Barker & Kirk, architects
     Barker Arthur Rowland,
        diocesan surveyor
     Colquhoun & Kershaw, photo printers
     Smale Harry, inquiry agent
     Truelove John Reginald, architect
12   HANOVER CHAMBERS:-
     Midwives' Institute & Trained
     Nurses' Club
     Bissell John James, surveyor
     Aldwinckle Granville James,
        brick agent
     Shaws Glazed Brick Co. Ltd
     Association of Women Clerks &
     Secretaries
     Women Clerks & Secretaries
     Friendly Society
           Miss A.M. Florence, sec
     Waldram John & Son, surveyers
     Melville & Co. publishers
     Ruvigny Marquis de
     Homes for Working Boys in London,
           William Denham,sec
     Shirley Walter K. architect
     Young Vivian Edward, architect
13   *Valite Ltd.* acetylene gas apparatus
     manufacturers
13   *Men's Political Union for Women's*
     Enfranchisement,
        Victor D. Duval, hon. sec
13 & 14 *Church Association,*
        J.W.P. Barron, J.P. sec
14   Huntington Alfred Kirby
14   Jackson Sir Thomas Graham, bart. R.A.
        architect
14   *Argo Co. Ltd.* mathematical instrument
        makers
14   Machel-Smith Mrs
14   Holland Hon. Lionel Raleigh
14   Littlewood-Clarke Herbert Dell, solicitor
       EAST SIDE
15 & 16 *Royal National Pension Fund for Nurses*
15 & 16 *Borstal Association*
15 & 16 *Peabody Donation Fund,*
           Lord Dunluce, sec
15 & 16 *Morgan Junius S. Benevolent Fund*
15 & 16 Grant-Wilson George Wemyss,
        barrister
15 & 16 *Central Association for the*
     Aid of Discharged Convicts,
        W. Grant-Wilson, director
17   White F. V. & Co. Ltd. publishers
17   *Royal Female Orphan Asylum* (office),
        Bouverie Risk, sec

17   Cresswell Herbert O, architect
17   Lewis Charles
18   *Society for Promoting the Due*
     Observance of the Lord's Day
18   *Children's Country Holidays Fund,*
        The Earl of Arran, hon. treas
18   *Royal National Hospital for*
     Consumption & Diseases of the Chest
        Charles W. Cox, sec
18   Queely John Eugene St. George,
        physician
18   *Billiard Association Ltd*
18   Macpherson James Ian, M.A., LL.B.,M.P
19   *Ramoneur Co. Ltd.* chimney sweepers
19   *Union of Ethical Societies,*
           H. Snell, sec
19   *Typographical Association,*
           H . Skinner, sec
19   *Emerson Club,*
           Dudley Winn, hon. sec
19   Greatorex Joseph Edward Alfred,
        architect
19   Fisher Edmund, architect
19   Garcia Mrs
19   d'Adhemar Harry G
19   Champneys Basil, architect
19   Fuller William
19   Anderson Abbot
20   Grant & Co. lubricating oil manfrs
20   Watson, Gow & Co. Ltd. iron founders
20   Balfour & Turner, architects
20   *Society for the Protection of*
     Ancient Buildings,
           A.R. Powys, sec
20   *Motor Cab Owner-Drivers' Association,*
           S.H.D. Faulkner, sec
20   Phillips George Edward, architect
20   Oddy Josiah
21   Brindley & Foster, organ builders
21   *Sociological Society,*
           S.K. Ratcliffe, hon. sec
22   CHANDOS CHAMBERS:—
     Barber W.H. & Son, quantity
        surveyors
     Benger Alfred Horace, insurance
        broker
     Laurence George E. T. architect
     Dawber Edward Guy, architect
     Hewitt Walter Ernest, architect
     Tucker & Huntley, quantity
        surveyors
. . . . *here is Duke street* . . . .
23   Brereton Christopher Francis,
        dining rooms
24   *Amber Trading Co. Ltd.* amber merchants
     (representatives of amber mines)
24   Welman & Co. theatrical agents
24   *Wellington Press Ltd.* publishers
24   *Austral Co. Ltd.* ice machine makers
24   *Army & Navy Pensioners' & Time*
     Expired Men's Employment Society
24   Johnson George, publisher
24   Bailey Edward Rolls, watchmaker
25   Trapp William, hairdresser
27   Shepperd Frederick, butcher
. . . . *here is York place* . . . .
28   *Buckingham Temperance Hotel,*
           Stephen Moor, proprietor

BUCKINGHAM STREET

1920

Buckingham st. 37 *Strand.* (W.C.)
(WESTMINSTER).
WEST SIDE

2 *Prince's Head,* Frederick W. Whithair &
      Thomas John Noble
3 *Marshall's Dairies Ltd.*
. . . . *here is York place.* . . . . . .
. . . . *here is Duke street* . . . . .
6 & 7 Jones Miss Margaret, private hotel
6 & 7 Roberts Rt. Hon. George Henry M.P
8 Cope & Fenwick, publishers
8 *London Central Window Cleaning Co.Ltd*
8 *Trust Houses Ltd.* (surveyor's dept)
8 *Land Law Reform Association,*
      James Rowlands, M.P. hon. sec
11 BUCKINGHAM CHAMBERS:—
      Pure Literature Society
      Irish Church Missions to the
        Roman Catholics,
        Rev. A. E. Hughes, M.A.
        clerical secretary
        E.W. Allden, financl. sec
      Missions to Seamen,
        Stuart C. Knox, M.A. sec
      Barker & Kirk, architects
      Colquhoun Arthur, photo printer
      Smale Harry, inquiry agent
      Palmer-Jones William John, archtct
      Truelove John Reginald, architect
      Bonding Block Constructional
        Co. Ltd
12 HANOVER CHAMBERS:—
      Midwives' Institute & Trained
        Nurses' Club
      Speakman Miss Ruth, typewriting
        office
      Manley Miss Elizabeth Annie,
        teacher of massage
      Bissell John James, surveyor
      Shaws Glazed Brick Co. Ltd
      Association of Women Clerks &
        Secretaries,
        Miss D. Evans, sec
      Women Clerks & Secretaries
        Friendly Society:
        Miss A.M. Florence, sec
      Buckley Miss Joyce, teacher
        of gymnastics
      Homes for Working Boys in London,
        William Denham,sec
13 Weatherley William Samuel, architect
13 *Art Trade Press Ltd. publishers*
13 & 14 *Church Association,*
        Capt. J.W.P. Barron, J.P. sec
13 & 14 *National Protestant League*
14 Coates Walter, company director
14 *Vacant Land Cultivation Society*
14 Huntington Alfred Kirby
14 *Argo Co. Ltd.* mathematical instrument
      makers
14 Machel-Smith Mrs
14 Balsan Lieut.-Col. Jaques
14 Holland Hon. Lionel Raleigh
14 Littlewood-Clarke Herbert Dell, solicitor
      EAST SIDE
15 & 16 *Royal National Pension Fund for*
        Nurses
15 & 16 *Nurses' Insurance Society*
15 & 16 *Medical Research Committee*
        (National Health Insurance)
15 & 16 *Borstal Association*
15 & 16 *Peabody Donation Fund,*
        Lord Dunluce, sec
15 & 16 *Morgan Junius S. Benevolent Fund*
15 & 16 Grant-Wilson George Wemyss,
        barrister
15 & 16 *Central Association for the*
        Aid of Discharged Convicts,
        W. Grant-Wilson, director

17 Secker Martin Ltd. publishers
17 White F. V. & Co. Ltd. publishers
17 *Royal Female Orphan Asylum* (office),
        Bouverie Risk, sec
17 Lewis Charles
17 Stokes Leonard, Drysdale & Aylwyn,
      architects
18 *Society for Promoting the Due*
        Observance of the Lord's Day
18 *Children's Country Holidays Fund,*
        The Earl of Arran, hon. treas
18 *Royal National Hospital for*
        Consumption & Diseases of the Chest
        Charles W. Cox, sec
18 *Billiard Association Ltd*
19 *Irvine's Ltd*
19 *Ramoneur Co. Ltd.* chimney sweepers
19 *Union of Ethical Societies,*
        H. Snell, sec
19 *Typographical Association,*
        H . Skinner, sec
19 *Co-operative Party,*
        S.F. Perry J.P. sec
19 *Emerson Club,*
        Mrs. Boyd Dawson, hon. sec
19 Abrams Herbert J.S. architect
19 Goddard Rainald William Knightley,
      architect
19 Garcia Mrs
19 Pain Henry James, surveyor
19 d'Adhemar Harry G
19 Ellison Harold Kitching
19 Anderson Mrs.Abbot
20 Grant, Hughes & Co. Ltd. lubricating oil
      manufacturers
20 Watson, Gow & Co. Ltd. iron founders
20 Balfour & Turner, architects
20 *Society for the Protection of*
        Ancient Buildings,
        A.R. Powys, sec
20 *Motor Cab Owner-Drivers' Association,*
        L.B. Butler, general manager
20 *Civic Arts Association,*
        Leonard Pomeroy, sec
20 Oddy Josiah
21 Crocker Thomas Edward, solicitor
22 CHANDOS CHAMBERS:—
      Society of the Faith,
        Rev. H.V. Hughes, bursar
      Symbol Publishing Co. ltd
      National Union of Allotment Holders
      Allotment & Garden Press ltd
      Hart John, theatrical manager
      Barber W.H. & Son, quantity
        surveyors
      Laurence George E. T. architect
      Tucker & Huntley, quantity
        surveyors
. . . . *here is Duke street* . . . .
23 Brereton Frederick Charles,
      dining rooms
24 *Amber Trading Co. Ltd*
24 Grundy John Francis Edwin, fine art
      publisher
24 Bailey Edward Rolls, watchmaker
24 Parker Albert Edward James,
      advertising agent
24 Johnson George, publisher
24 *Ludo Press,* printers
25 Webster George, hairdresser
27 Shepperd Frederick, butcher
. . . . *here is York place* . . . .
28 *Buckingham Hotels Ltd.* private hotel

1925

Buckingham st. 37 *Strand.* (W.C.)
(WESTMINSTER).
WEST SIDE

2 *Prince's Head,* Whithair Bros. Ltd
3 *Marshall's Dairies Ltd.*
4 Gaynor William, boot & shoe maker
. . . . *here is York place.* . . . .
. . . . *here is Duke street* . . . .
8 Chapman Guy, publisher
8 Pearson J.R. (Birmingham) Ltd. metal
      workers
8 *London Central Window Cleaning Co .Ltd*
8 Sinclair William Braxton, architect
11 BUCKINGHAM CHAMBERS:—
      Irish Church Missions to the
        Roman Catholics
      Missions to Seamen
      Barker & Kirk, architects
      Colquhoun Arthur, photo printer
      Smale Harry, inquiry agent
      Palmer-Jones William John, archtct
      Grant Thomas Francis Wiltshire,
        architect
12 HANOVER CHAMBERS:—
      Midwives' Institute & Trained
        Nurses' Club
      Speakman Miss Ruth, type writing
        office
      Shaws Glazed Brick Co. Ltd
      Young, Austen & Young, heating
        engineers
      Thorpe William Henry, civil engineer
      Barham Estates Ltd. property owners
      Warre Captain Edmond L. architect
      Homes for Working Boys in
        London (Incorp)
13 *Art Trade Press Ltd.* publishers
13 & 14 *Church Association,*
13 & 14 *National Protestant League*
14 Coates Walter, company director
14 *Vacant Land Cultivation Society*
14 *Argo Co. Ltd.* mathematical instrument
      makers
14 Pickering Edward A
14 Symons Miss
14 Holland Hon. Lionel Raleigh
14 Littlewood-Clarke Herbert Dell, solicitor
      EAST SIDE
15 & 16 Greyfriars Press Ltd
15 & 16 *Royal National Pension Fund for Nurses*
15 & 16 *Nurses' Insurance Society*
15 & 16 *Borstal Association*
15 & 16 *Peabody Donation Fund*
15 & 16 *Morgan Junius S. Benevolent Fund*
15 & 16 Grant-Wilson Sir Wemyss,
        M.A., J.P., LL.M. barrister
15 & 16 *Central Association for the*
        Aid of Discharged Convicts
17 Warenden H.E. & Co. publishers
17 Lewis Charles
17 Stokes Leonard & Drysdale, architects
17 Clarkson Edward S. architect
17 Aylwin Reginald Francis Guy, architect
18 *Society for Promoting the Due*
        Observance of the Lord's Day
18 *Children's Country Holidays Fund*
18 *Royal National Hospital for*
        Consumption & Diseases of the Chest
        Charles W. Cox, sec
19 Chamberlain Harold E. manufacturers'
      agent
19 New Adelphi Club
19 *Ramoneur Co. Ltd.* chimney sweepers
19 *London & Westminster Window*
        Cleaning Association Ltd
19 Abrams Herbert J.S. architect
19 Goddard Rainald William Knightley,
      architect

19 Garcia Mrs
19 Pain Henry James, surveyor
19 d'Adhemar Harry G
19 Anderson Mrs.Abbot
20 Jones & Campbell Ltd. iron founders
20 Bradbury Samuel William & Co.
      civil engineers
20 Economic Stability League
20 Boyd A. & Co. white lead manufacturers
20 *Trade Guilds Ltd.* general merchants
20 Balfour & Turner, architects
20 *Society for the Protection of Ancient*
        Buildings
20 *Motor Cab Owner-Drivers' Association*
20 Willesford's Ltd. company registration
      agents
20 Oddy Josiah
21 Crocker T. E. & Son, solicitors
21 Wrightson, Crocker & Co. solicitors
22 CHANDOS CHAMBERS:—
      Society of the Faith
      Faith Press Ltd
      Faith Craft Studio Ltd. church
        furniture makers
      Wylson & Long, architects
      Hotel Bureau & Supply Co. Ltd
      Hart John, theatrical manager
      Barber W.H. & Son, quantity
        surveyors
      Tucker & Huntley, quantity surveyors
. . . . *here is Duke street* . . . .
23 Brereton Frederick Charles,
      dining rooms
24 *Amber Trading Co. Ltd*
24 Grundy John Francis Edwin,
      fine art publisher
24 Bailey Edward Rolls, watchmaker
24 White Philip, gauger
24 Hodges & Co. stock brokers
24 *Parker's Advertising Agency*
24 Johnson George, publisher
24 *Ludo Press,* printers
25 Frankel Max, hairdresser
27 Shepperd Frederick, butcher
. . . . *here is York place* . . . .
28 *Buckingham Hotel*

BUCKINGHAM STREET

1930

Buckingham st. 37 *Strand.* (W.C.)
(WESTMINSTER).
WEST SIDE

2   *Prince's Head*, Whithair Bros. Ltd
3   *Marshall's Dairies Ltd.*
4   Rivett Charles, restaurant
. . . . *here is York place.* . . . .
. . . . *here is Duke street* . . . .
6 & 7 BUCKINGHAM HOUSE:—
   LeForestier H. & Co. wine mers
   Pritchard F.C. & Partners Ltd
     advertising consultants
   Catholic Touring Association Ltd
   Catholic Association
   Smiths' Systems Ltd. office
     equipment manufacturers
   Gambrell Radio Ltd. wireless
     apparatus manufacturers
   Cherry Harold Griffith, architect
   Lutyens Eadred John T. architect
   Adams Sidney, dental surgeon
8   Pearson J.R. (Birmingham) Ltd.
     metal workers
8   Hird & Thatcher, solicitors
8   *London Central Window Cleaning Co. Ltd*
8   Munday Eric, sign writer
11   BUCKINGHAM CHAMBERS:—
   Irish Church Missions to the
     Roman Catholics
   Missions to Seamen
   Barker & Kirk, architects
   Colquhoun Arthur, photo printer
   Smale Harry, inquiry agent
   Grant Thomas Francis Wiltshire,
     architect
12   HANOVER CHAMBERS:—
   Canary Islands & Madeira Agency
   Byrne Earnest Corbett, surveyor
   Midwives' Institute & Trained
     Nurses' Club
   Laird A.O. Ltd. building contractors
   Young, Austen & Young, heating
     engineers
   Thorpe William Henry, civil engineer
   Moseley George B.O. wine merchant
   Barham Estates Ltd. property owners
   Warre Captain Edmond L. architect
   Homes for Working Boys in
     London (Incorp)
13   Art Trade Press Ltd. publishers
13   Christmas Miss
13 & 14 *Church Association,*
13 & 14 *National Protestant League*
14   Westwood P.J. architect
14   Pyman, Tracey & Co. Ltd. insurance
     brokers
14   Pickering Mrs. E. A
14   Mallinson Alexander B
14   Dewey Rev. Sir Stanley D. bart. M.A
14   Holland Hon. Lionel Raleigh, J.P.,B.A
     EAST SIDE
15 & 16 Greyfriars Ltd
15 & 16 *Royal National Pension Fund for*
     Nurses
15 & 16 *Nurses' Insurance Society*
15 & 16 *Borstal Association*
15 & 16 *Peabody Donation Fund*
15 & 16 *Morgan Junius S. Benevolent Fund*
15 & 16 Grant-Wilson Sir Wemyss,
     M.A., J.P., LL.M. barrister
15 & 16 *Central Association for the*
     Aid of Discharged Convicts
17   Children's Country Holidays Fund
17   British Commonwealth League
17   Performing and Captive Animals'
     Defence League
17   Clarkson Edward S. architect
17   Aylwin Reginald Francis Guy, architect

17   Evans Samuel H. architect
18   *Society for Promoting the Due*
     Observance of the Lord's Day
18   *Children's Country Holidays Fund*
18   *Royal National Hospital for*
     Consumption & Diseases of the Chest
19   Haymarket Club
19   Regent Advertising Club
19   Chamberlain Harold E. manufacturers'
     agent
19   *Ramoneur Co. Ltd.* chimney sweepers
19   *London & Westminster Window Cleaning*
     Association Ltd
19   Wray Cecil James M.B.E. solicitor
19   Wishart & Co. publishers
19   Abrams H.J.S. & Son, architects
19   Garcia Philip R.
19   Anderson Mrs. Abbot
20   Unaphalt (Roads) Ltd
20   Logan Henry, assessor & collector
     of taxes for St. Mary-le-Strand
20   Powys & Macgregor, architects
20   *Society for the Protection of Ancient*
     Buildings
20   Solicitors' Mortgage Society Ltd
20   Oddy Josiah
21   Croker T.E. & Son, solicitors
21   Van, Alexander & Co. advertisement
     agents
22   CHANDOS CHAMBERS:—
   Society of the Faith
   Faith Press Ltd
   Faith Craft Studio Ltd. church
     furniture makers
   Hart John, theatrical manager
   Barber W.H. & Son, quantity surveyors
   Tucker & Huntley, quantity surveyors
. . . . *here is Duke street* . . . .
23   Warren Charles, dining rooms
24   *Amber Trading Co. Ltd*
24   Grundy John Francis Edwin,
     fine art publisher
24   White Phillip, gauger
24   *Parker's Advertising Agency*
24   Johnson George, publisher
24   Ireland J.F. business agent
24   *Ludo Press*, printers
25   Frankel Max, hairdresser
27   Shepperd Frederick, butcher
. . . . *here is York place* . . . .
28   *Buckingham Hotel*

1935

Buckingham st. 37 *Strand.* (W.C.)
(WESTMINSTER).
WEST SIDE

2   *Prince's Head*, Raphael Patrick Defferary
3   *Marshall's Dairies Ltd.*
. . . . *here is York place.* . . . .
. . . . *here is Duke street* . . . .
6 & 7 BUCKINGHAM HOUSE:—
   LeForestier H. & Co. wine mers
   Bradson Ltd. wine merchants
   Smith & Hammond Ltd.
     electrical engineers
   Catholic Association
   Buckingham Advertising Service Ltd
   Lovell Miss Ena G. theatrical agent
   Hill Earnest Ingram Ltd. advertising
     agents
   Pyman, Tracy & Co. Ltd. insurance
     brokers
   O'Hea Lt.-Col. J
   D. & B. Electrical Co. Ltd.
     electric accumulator makers
   Reekes & Mann, quantity surveyors
   Cherry Harold Griffith, architect
   Lutyens Eadred John T. architect
8   Pearson J.R. (Birmingham) Ltd.
     metal workers
8   Hird & Thatcher, solicitors
8   *London Central Window Cleaning Co. Ltd*
11   BUCKINGHAM CHAMBERS:—
   Irish Church Missions to the
     Roman Catholics
   Missions to Seamen (The)
   Barker Raymond T. architect
   Jackson Basil H. architect
   Adelphi Drawing Office Ltd.
     photo printers
   Smale Harry, inquiry agent
   Grant Thomas Francis Wiltshire,
     architect
12   HANOVER CHAMBERS:—
   Chapman James, consulting engineer
   Osborn Claud Roland, building
     contractor
   Laird A.O. Ltd. building contractors
   Bateson James Wrightson, architect
   Cash Rowland, architect
   Young, Austen & Young,
     heating engineers
   Barham Estates Ltd. property owners
   Ellison Robert Kitching, architect
   Kidd H. Douglas, architect
   R. & C. Ltd. concrete waterproofing
   Homes for Working Boys in
     London (Incorp)
13   Virgo Watson Studio, commercial artists
13   *Fortnightly Review* (office of)
13 & 14 *Church Association,*
13 & 14 *National Protestant League*
14   Westwood P.J. & Sons, architects
14   Dewey Rev. Sir Stanley D. bart. M.A
14   Holland Hon. Lionel Raleigh, J.P.,B.A
     EAST SIDE
15 & 16 *Royal National Pension Fund for*
     Nurses
15 & 16 *Nurses' Insurance Society*
15 & 16 *Peabody Donation Fund*
15 & 16 *Morgan Junius S. Benevolent Fund*
16   Iliffe W. Coker
17   Children's Country Holidays Fund Inc
17   British Commonwealth League
17   Performing and Captive Animals'
     Defence League
17   Clarkson Edward S. architect
17   Aylwin Reginald Francis Guy, architect
17   Evans Samuel H. architect
18   Efficiency Drawing Office Co.
     photo printers

18   Tolley C.H., Rowlands & Co. accountants
18   *Children's Country Holidays Fund Inc*
18   *Royal National Hospital for*
     Consumption & Diseases of the Chest
19   Haymarket Club
19   Regent Advertising Club
19   Outpost Club
19   *Ramoneur Co. Ltd.* chimney sweepers
19   L. V. Staff Agency
19   Westminster Window & General
     Cleaners Ltd
19   Wray, Smith & Halford, solicitors
19   Abrams H.J.S. & Son, architects
19   Garcia Philip H
19   Robeson Mrs. Paul
19   Vaughan Capt. John Bowman
19   Anderson Mrs. Abbot
20   Higginson George S. engineer
20   Winkworth (Herbert Edward) & Pearce
     (William George), assessors of taxes
20   Powys & Macgregor, architects
20   *Society for the Protection of*
     Ancient Buildings
20   Solicitors' Mortgage Society Ltd
20   London Landowners Ltd
20   Oddy Josiah
21   Croker T.E. & Son, solicitors
21   Partridge's Models Ltd
22   CHANDOS CHAMBERS:—
   Society of the Faith
   Faith Press Ltd
   Faith Craft Works Ltd. church
     furniture makers
   Hart John, theatrical manager
   Barber W.H. & Son, quantity
     surveyors
   Tucker & Huntley, quantity
     surveyors
. . . . *here is Duke street* . . . .
23   Warren Charles, dining rooms
24   *Amber Trading Co. Ltd*
24   Cotine Products Ltd. fibre growers
24   White Phillip, gauger
24   Johnson George, publisher
24   Shepherd & Hosking Ltd. publishers
24   Dubois Robert, teacher of french
24   Bechervaise Alan M. artists agent
24   *Ludo Press*, printers
25   Frankel Max, hairdresser
27   Shepperd Frederick, butcher
. . . . *here is York place* . . . .
28   Strand Chinese Restaurant

BUCKINGHAM STREET

1936

Buckingham st. 37 *Strand.* (W.C.2) (WESTMINSTER).
WEST SIDE

2	*Prince's Head,* Raphael Patrick Defferary
3	*Marshall's Dairies Ltd.*
4	Weiner David, tailor

. . . . *here is York place.* . . . .

. . . . *here is Duke street* . . . .

6 & 7 BUCKINGHAM HOUSE:—
LeForestier H. & Co. wine mers
Art & Advertising Assistance Ltd
Farrell John & Co. chartered
accountants
Catholic Association
Hill Ernest Ingram Ltd.
advertising agents
Pyman, Tracey & Co. Ltd. insurance
brokers
O'Hea Lt.-Col. J. & Mrs. O.B.E.
D. & B. Electrical Co. Ltd.
electric accumulator makers
Reekes & Mann, quantity surveyors
Cherry Harold Griffith, architect
Lutyens Eadred John T. architect

8	Pearson J.R. (Birmingham) Ltd. metal workers
8	Hird & Thatcher, solicitors
8	*London Central Window Cleaning Co. Ltd*
8	Marble & Granite Trading Co. Ltd
8	Maschwitz Ruth, journalist
11	BUCKINGHAM CHAMBERS:—

*Irish Church Missions to the
Roman Catholics*
Missions to Seamen (The)
Barker Raymond T. architect
Jackson Basil H. architect
Adelphi Drawing Office Ltd.
photo printers
Smale Harry, inquiry agent
Grant Thomas Francis Wiltshire,
architect

12	HANOVER CHAMBERS:—

Chapman James, consulting engineer
Osborn Claud Roland, building
contractor
Laird A.O. Ltd. building contractors
Bateson James Wrightson, architect
Cash Rowland, architect
Young, Austen & Young,
heating engineers
Barham Estates Ltd. property owners
Ellison Robert Kitching, architect
Kidd H. Douglas, architect
R. & C. Ltd. concrete waterproofing
*Homes for Working Boys in
London (Incorp)*

13	Virgo Watson Studio, commercial artists
13	*Fortnightly Review* (office of)
13 & 14	*Church Association,*
13 & 14	*National Protestant League*
14	Westwood P.J. & Sons, architects
14	Rounding Charles Mowbray, commercial artist
14	Dewey Rev. Sir Stanley D. bart. M.A
14	Vallance Aylmer
14	Holland Hon. Lionel Raleigh, J.P.,B.A

EAST SIDE

15 & 16	*Royal National Pension Fund for Nurses*
15 & 16	*Nurses' Insurance Society*
15 & 16	*Peabody Donation Fund*
15 & 16	*Morgan Junius S. Benevolent Fund*
16	Iliffe W. Coker
17	Children's Country Holidays Fund Inc
17	British Commonwealth League
17	Performing and Captive Animals' Defence League
17	Aylwin Reginald Francis Guy, architect
17	Evans Samuel H. architect
18	Efficiency Drawing Office Co. photo printers
18	Tolley C.H., Rowlands & Co. accountants
18	*Children's Country Holidays Fund Inc*
18	*Royal National Hospital for Consumption & Diseases of the Chest*
19	Procea Products Ltd
19	Regent Advertising Club
19	*Ramoneur Co. Ltd.* chimney sweepers
19	L. V. Staff Agency
19	Westminster Window & General Cleaners Ltd
19	Wray, Smith & Halford, solicitors
19	Abrams H.J.S. & Son, architects
19	Garcia Philip H
19	Robeson Mrs. Paul
19	Vaughan Capt. John Bowman
19	Godfrey Peter
20	Higginson George S. engineer
20	Winkworth (Herbert Edward) & Pearce (William George), assessors of taxes
20	Powys & Macgregor, architects
20	*Society for the Protection of Ancient Buildings*
20	Solicitors' Mortgage Society Ltd
20	London Landowners Ltd
20	Oddy Josiah
21	Croker T.E. & Son, solicitors
21	Le Gallienne & Co. accountants
21	Partridge's Models Ltd
22	CHANDOS CHAMBERS:—

Hart John, theatrical manager
Barber W.H. & Son, quantity surveyors
Tucker & Huntley, quantity surveyors

. . . . *here is Duke street* . . . .

23	Warren Charles, dining rooms
24	*Amber Trading Co. Ltd*
24	Cotine Products Ltd. fibre growers
24	White Phillip, gauger
24	Johnson George, publisher
24	Shepherd & Hosking Ltd. publishers
24	Bechervaise Alan M. artists agent
24	*Ludo Press,* printers
25	Frankel Max, hairdresser
27	Shepperd Frederick, butcher

. . . . *here is York place* . . . .

28	Strand Chinese Restaurant

DUKE STREET

1841

Duke street, Adelphi.
1 Appleyard Mrs. Sarah, bookseller
2 *Bolanas Mining Co.* George Fossett, sec
2 *Real del Monte Mining Company,*
J. Phillips, sec
2 Taylor John, civil engineer
3 Mackenzie Stephen, wine merchant
4 Holland Henry, architect
5 Antrobus William, writing master
6 Watts James, green grocer
. . . . . *George street, George court* . . . . .
8 Roberts, Smith & Co. sheffield plate wa
9 Eaton John, tailor
10 Fairbairn Robert, bookbinder
13 *St. Martin,* Evan Jones
14 Great Western Loan Society
14 Whitaker Francis Augustus, esq
14 Nicholls Charles Kerry, esq
14 McDonald James, esq
. . . . *Buckingham street* . . . .
15 Dyke Vincent, bath & lodging house
16 Brown Daniel, butcher
17 Hughes William, tailor
17 Hughes William, undertaker
19 *Griffin,* Henry Todman

1845

Duke street, Adelphi,
29 Villiers street to 14 John street
1 Appleyard Henry, bookseller
2 *Bolano's Mining Co.* John Head, sec
2 *Real del Monte Mining Company,*
J. Phillips, sec
2 *British Ass. for Advance of Science,*
John Taylor, esq. F.R.S. gen. treasurer
2 Taylor John, civil engineer
2 Williams Richard, esq
3 Mackenzie Stephen, wine merchant
. . *here Buckingham street intersects* . .
4 Holland & Saddler, architects
5 Antrobus William, writing master
5 Gimingham William, surveyor
6 Watts James, green grocer
. . *here George st. George ct. intersects* . .
8 Roberts, Smith & Co. sheffield plate wa
9 Eaton John, tailor
10 Fairbairn Robert, bookbinder
13 *St. Martin,* Mrs. Sophia Jones
14 *Boccius light office,*
Gottlieb Boccius, patentee
14 Hogg Edward jun. wine merchant
. . *here Buckingham street intersects* . .
15 Davidson Charles, esq
15 Monaghan Patrick, esq
16 Seabrook William, butcher
17 Hughes William, tailor
18 Early Edward, shell fishmonger
19 *Griffin,* Henry Todman

1850

Duke street, Adelphi,
29 Villiers street to 14 John street
1 Appleyard Henry, bookseller&newsagent
2 *Bolanos Mining Co.* John Head, sec
2 *Real del Monte Mining Company,*
J. Phillips, sec
3 *Carn Brea Mines Co.* George Meagle, sec
3 Smith Dudley, civil engineer
. . *here Buckingham street intersects* . .
7 Jameson William,plumber,painter & glzr
7 Le Comte John, geneva watchmaker
. . *here George st. George ct. intersects* . .
8 Smith, Sissons & Co. sheffield plate wa
9 Cook William Christopher, tailor
10 Ashley James, accountant
10 Huntsman Benj. manufctg stationer
13 *St. Martin,* Mrs. Sophia Jones
14 Shaw Thomas George&Co. wine merchts
14 Emery William, esq
14 Vialls John Palmer, glass manufacturer
15 Davidson Charles, esq
15 Hansler Henry Stephen, solicitor
15 Owen Hugh, esq
15 Godwin Richard A. coal merchant
. . *here Buckingham street intersects* . .
15 Ranger Robert A. engineering surveyor
16 Borthwick Richard, baker
17 Hughes William, tailor
18 Brightman Benjamin, chandler's shop
19 *Griffin,* Henry Todman

1855

Duke street, Adelphi,
29 Villiers street to 14 John street
1 Appleyard Henry,newsagent&bookseller
2 *National Parliamentary & Financial*
Reform Association,
John Revans, hon.sec
2 Smith Dudley, civil engineer
2 Stocking Henry, bookseller
3 Kennard Thomas William, engineer
3 Welch Frederick, surveyor
3 Blake&Co. publishers & advertising agts
. . . . *here Buckingham street intersects* . . . .
5 Morant Augustus, architect
5 Lote Henry, architect & surveyor
5 Walker William Falconar, surveyor
6 Gisborne Lionel, engineer
6 Gordon & Farrell, wine merchants
6 Gordon Alexander Thomas, engineer &c
6 Ralph John Rhodes, civil engineer
6 Normanville William John, civil engineer
6 Parsons Perceval M. civil engineer
6 Cooke Layton, estate agent & surveyor
. . *here York bldngs & George ct. intersect* .
7 Austin Edmund John, civil engineer
7 Collins Thomas Tindale, civil engineer
7 Jameson Wm. plumber, painter & glazier
7 Walenn William Henry, civil engineer
8 Smith, Sissons & Co. sheffield warehouse
10 Crosbie John J. stationer & bookbinder
11 Bailey Walter Henry, machinist
12 *St. Martin,* Richard Matthew Clark
14 Bennett Robert Dewer, architect & survr
14 Vialls John Palmer, glass manufacturer
. . . . *here Buckingham street intersects* . . . .
15 Lansdown James Chester,architect&surv
15 Maxton James Bald, engineer
15 Morris John, architect
15 Scott Uriah, patentee of the elastic
bearings for carriages
16 Charles George, baker
17 Hughes William, tailor
18 Brightman Benjamin, chandler's shop
19 *Griffin,* Edward Symons

1860

Duke street, Adelphi, (W.C.)
29 Villiers street to 14 John street
1 Appleyard Henry,newsagent&bookseller
2 Heine Ernst & Co. scholastic agency
2 *Educational offices for Governesses*
& Teachers (Ernst Heine & Co)
2 Padmore Harrison, solicitor
2 George Mr. Joseph
2 Smith Dudley, civil engineer
3 Edwards William Finch, esq
3 Edwards Passmore, esq
3 Hudson Benedict Wm.&Co.patent agents
3 Maffey William John, esq
3 Britton James, wine spirit & bottled beer
merchant
3 Challinor Thomas, birmingham &
sheffield agent
3 Harwood Thomas, electro plate manu
3 *Universal Society for the Encouragement*
of Arts & Industry,
B. William Hudson, sec
3A, Christie Alexander, wine merchant
. . . . *here is Buckingham street* . . . .
5 SEYMOUR CHAMBERS:—
Bovet Frères & Co. watch manufacturers
& importers, F.S.Notermann, agents
Frost Brothers & Co. commission agents
Notermann Fabian Sebastian, importer
of geneva watches
Morgan Wm. Hen. swimming instructor
5 Fry Francis George, esq
6 Birch James, esq
6 Gisbourne & Forde, civil engineers
6 Forde Henry Charles, civil engineer
6 Sircombe John, esq
here are York buildings & George court
7 Jameson Wm. plumber, painter & glazier
7 Pocock Samuel, brick merchant
8 Sissons Wm.& George, sheffield wareho
10 Crosbie John Jackson, bookbinder
11 Stoddart Charles, solicitor
11 Burden John, foreign & english agent
12 *St. Martin,* James Smith
14 Peters Geo.Edwd.engineering contractor
14 Vialls John Palmer, glass manufacturer
14 Mendham Edward, manufacturer of
aquarium & flower stands
. . . . *here is Buckingham street* . . . .
15 Browne John Henry, surveyor
15 Lowe James, esq
15 Hall Henry, architect
15 Horn Thomas William, architect
15 Maxton James Bald, engineer
15 Arnold Robert Arthur, land agent
15 Gover Richard, architect
16 Cameron John, baker
17 Hughes William, tailor
19 Brightman Benjamin, grocer
19 *Griffin,* John Pullen

1865

Duke street, Adelphi, (W.C.)
29 Villiers street to 14 John street
1 Neate Robert, butcher
2 *Hungerford Market Company,*
R. J. W Leith, sec
2 *London & Westminster Steam Boat*
Co. (lim.) Richard J. W. Leith, sec
2 *Westminster Brewery Co. (limited),*
Richard J. W. Leith, sec
2 Waller & Kirby, solicitors
2 Laing David Gordon, builder
3 Bonvoille & Vuilleaume, champagne
merchants
3 Corbett John M. birmingham agent
3 Ridge Lacey Walter, architect
3 Walter John William, architect
3 *Sailors' Home Society,*
Admiral William H. Hall, C.B.
hon. managing director
Thomas M. I. Tilby, R.N. sec
3 *Acclimatisation Society of Great Britain,*
James Lowe, esq. ⎰hon.
B. Waterhouse Hawkins, esq.⎱ secs
3 Jackman James Tyndale, architect &
surveyor
3 Kinnard James, iron & general merchant
3 Harwood & Son, electro plate manufacturers (John M. Corbett, agent)
4 Gurton John, wine & spirit merchant
. . . . *here is Buckingham street* . . . .
5 SEYMOUR CHAMBERS:—
Heyworth Capt. L
Parson George John, solicitor
MorganWm.Hen.swimming instrctr
Wakley Henry Membury, barrister
6 Deane Alfred Wood, esq
6 Ford & Fleeming Jenkin, civil engineers
6 Gisborne Mr. Francis
. *here are York buildings & George court* .
7 *The London Drawing Association,*
Frederic Young, C.E. manager
7 Young Charles Fred. T. civil engineer
7 Pocock Samuel, brickmaker
8 Jameson & Hobson, plumbers &c
8 Sissons Wm.& George, sheffield wareho
10 Hart & Reeves, vellum binders
10 Scoffield James, dairyman
11 Smith William, bookseller & newsagent
11 Hutcheson Charles, engineer
12 Hutcheson Joseph, civil engineer
12 *St. Martin,* Mrs. Sophia Smith
14 Peters George Edward & Co. contractors
14 Vialls John Palmer, glass manufacturer
14 Fuld F. E. & Co. bankers (Frankfort-
on-the-Maine)
14 Stahl C. Emmanuel, foreign agent
. . . . *here is Buckingham street* . . . .
15 Browne John Henry, surveyor
15 Middleton Henry Samuel, esq
15 Hall Henry, architect
15 Arnold Robert Arthur, civil engineer
16 Cameron Charles, baker
17 Cole George, tobacconist
18 Brightman Benjamin, coffee&chop house
19 *Griffin,* Mrs. Anne Everitt

DUKE STREET

1870

Duke st, *Adelphi,* (W.C.)
29 Villiers street to 14 John street
1 Neate Robert, butcher
2 *East London Mission & Relief Society,*
    Somerset R. Saunderson, } hon
    C. S. Hogg   } secs
2 Waller William Henry, solicitor
2 Laing David Gordon, builder
3 Corbett John M. birmingham agent
3 Wyon Edward Alex. architect
3 Leuchars Edgar, A.R.I.B.A. architect
3 De Ville Louis, architect
3 Coad Richard, architect
3 Harwood & Son, electro plate
    manufactrs,   John M. Corbett, agent
. . . . . . *here is Buckingham street* . . . . . .
5 SEYMOUR CHAMBERS:—
    Morgan William Henry, swimming
    instructor
    Wakley Henry Membury, barrister
6 Goodchild Thomas, architect
6 Forde & Fleeming Jenkin, civil engineers
6 Ogleby Richard Louis, wine merchant
. *here are York buildings & George court* .
7 *The London Drawing Association,*
      Frederic Young, C.E. manager
7 *Daft's Patent Improvements in the*
    Construction of Iron Ships & Vessels &
    in Sheathing the Same,
      Charles F. T. Young, C.E. agent
7 Young Charles Fred. T. civil engineer
7 Pocock Samuel, brickmaker
7 Lavoine Jules A. watch importer
7 Hobson John Dalby, builder
8 Crosskill W. & Sons, wagon builders
      Jenkin Jones Ingram, agent
8 Scott Bros. wine merchants
8 Schaltin Pierry & Cie. liqueur merchts
8 Ingram & Bazeley, auctioneers
8 Karslake & Mortimer, architects
8 Hynam William, architect
8 *Seacombe Forge Rivet & Bolt Co.*
    (Birkenhead).
      Jenkin Jones Ingram, agent
8 Warrington Thomas Alfred, civil engineer
    Mortimer John Camden
10 Reeves Edmund Alfred, vellum binder
10 Hamilton Charles, secondhd. bookseller
11 Lewis Frederick,surgical inst. case maker
11 Smith William B. bookseller&newsagent
12 *St. Martin,* Henry Alexander
14 Peters George Edward & Co. contractors
14 Peters George E. civil engineer
14 Brooks Charles William, architect & surv
14 Stahl C. Emmanuel, foreign
    bankers' agent
. . . . . . *here is Buckingham street* . . . . . .
15 Browne John Henry, surveyor
15 *Charing Cross Hotel Co. (limited) &*
    *City Terminus Hotel Co. (lim.),*offices,
      George S. Haines, sec
15 Dowling Clement, architect
15 Harris Edward Swinfen, architect
15 Smith Thomas, architect
15 Cox John, architect
15 Young Sidney, surveyor
16 Cameron Charles, baker
17 Vodden John, hairdresser
18 Chattey William, coffee rooms
19 *Griffin,* William Charker

1875

Duke st, *Adelphi,* (W.C.)
29 Villiers street to 14 John street
1A, Copland Henry Syed, civil engineer
    Bosson P. wine merchant
1 Neate Robert, butcher
2 *East London Mission & Relief Society,*
    Hon. Henry Noel, hon. sec
    Christian Evidence Society,
    Major-Gen. A. G. Burrows,
      R.A. hon. sec
    Rev. P. Barker, sec
    Waller William Henry & Son, solicitors
    Laing David Gordon, builder
3 Corbett John M. birmingham agent
    Leuchars Edgar, A.R.I.B.A. architect
    Webb Aston, architect
    Coad Richard, architect
    Harwood & Son, electro plate manufactrs,
      John M. Corbett, agent
3A, Phythian & Sons, wine merchants
. . . . . . *here is Buckingham street* . . . . . .
4 Gideon David, lodging house
5 SEYMOUR CHAMBERS:—
    Monk William
    Wakley Henry Membury, barrister
    Price George
    Webber Josuiah
    O'Malley Capt
6 Goodchild Thomas, architect
    Condy Richard
    Forde & Hockin, civil engineers
    Jenkin Fleeming, civil engineer
    Ogleby Richard Louis, wine&spirit agent
    Tilsey Henry J. wne & spirit agent
    Spanish Evangelical Church Mission,
      Rev. L. S. Tugwell, sec
. *here are York buildings & George court* .
7 Lewes Charles Henry Farmer, architect
    Argent Eugene, surveyor
    Pocock Samuel, brickmaker
    Hobson John Dalby, builder
8 Scott Bros. & Rolfe, wine merchants
    Schaltin Pierry & Cie. liqueur merchts
    Official & General Building Society
    Wise Wm. Henry Robert, civil engineer
9 Clemence John, jun
10 Hamilton Charles, secondhd. bookseller
    Livermore Charles Albert, vellum binder
11 Lewis Frederick,surgical inst. case maker
    Smith William B. bookseller&newsagent
12 *St. Martin,* Thomas Smurthwaite
14 Peters George Edward & Co. contractors
    Peters George E. civil engineer
    Brooks Charles William, architect & surv
    Hummel Francis Henry, architect
    Gradwell William, shutter maker
. . . . . . *here is Buckingham street* . . . . . .
15 Browne John Henry, surveyor
    Charing Cross Hotel Co. Limited,
      George S. Haines, sec
    Dowling Clement, surveyor
    Harris Edward Swinfen, architect
    Cox John, architect
    Young Sidney, surveyor
16 Bourhill Thomas, baker
17 Vodden John, hairdresser
18 Chattey William, coffee rooms
19 *Griffin,* William Charker

1880

Duke st, *Adelphi,* (W.C.)
29 Villiers street to 14 John street
1A, Copland Henry Syed, civil engineer
    Richards Frederick, law stationer
    Perry Henry, architect
1 Chattey William, coffee rooms
2 Laing & Son, builders
    Waller William Henry & Son, solicitors
3 Corbett John M. birmingham agent
    Leuchars Edgar, F.R.I.B.A. architect
    Webb Aston, architect
    Coad Richard, architect
    Beckett George
    Beckett Walter
    Price Robert
    Harwood Thomas & Sons, electroplate
    warehouse
    Norris Edward & Co. wine merchants
. . . . . . *here is Buckingham street* . . . . . .
5 SEYMOUR CHAMBERS:—
    Monk William
    Wakley Henry Membury, barrister
6 Goodchild Thomas, architect
    Condy Richard
    Forde & Hockin, civil engineers
    Davis Frederick William, surveyor
    Allen William Taprell, architect
    Hooker John Marshall, architect
    King Alan & Co. private inquiry agents
. . . . . . *here are York buildings* . . . . . .
7 Hobson John Dalby, builder
    Argent Eugene, surveyor
    Saul Alfred, surveyor
    Pocock Samuel, brickmaker
8 Fowler & Hugman, surveyors
    Fox Mathew A. brick & cement agent
    Official & General Building Society
    Wise Wm. Henry Robert, civil engineer
    Austin Edmund John, surveyor
    Evelyn & Co. publishers
9 Clemence John, jun
10 Carr Walter, general engineer
    Carr Frank, engraver on wood
    Joseph David Arthur, vellum binder
11 Lewis Frederick,surgical inst. case maker
    Smith W. B. bookseller & newsagent
12 *St. Martin's tavern,* James Nixon
14 Brooks Charles William, architect & surv
    Open Air Mission,   John Kirk, sec
    Thomson Andrew, Thames yacht agent
    Grant Spencer William, A.R.I.B.A.
    architect
    Northover Arthur George, A.R.I.B.A.
    .architect
. . . . . . *here is Buckingham street* . . . . . .
    CHARING CROSS CHAMBERS:—
    Appleby Chas. Edward, civil engineer
    Tamar Terra Cotta Works
    Balfour E. James Anthony, architect
    Guscotte Thomas, solicitor
    Ullathorne & Co. engineers

1885

Duke st, *Adelphi,* (W.C.)
29 Villiers street to 14 John street
1A Richardson W. F. & Co. stock brokers
    Dickenson Wykeham Corry
2 Laing D. Gordon & Son, builders
    Waller William Henry & Son, solicitors
    Pace Ion, artist in stained glass
3 Coad Richard, architect
    Sladden William, solicitor
    Sladden, Son & Johnson, medical agents
    Rope George Henry, wine&spirit mercht
    Beckett George
    Beckett Walter
    MacLaren James Marjoribanks, architect
    Allen Theophilus, architect
. . . . . . *here is Buckingham street* . . . . . .
4 Owens Mrs. Sophia, private hotel
5 SEYMOUR CHAMBERS:—
    Monk William
    Wakley Henry Membury, barrister
6 Goodchild Thomas, architect
    Condy Richard
    Pratt Hampden William, architect
    Poley & Winn, architects
    Fawn George, stone merchant
. . . . . . *here are York buildings* . . . . . .
7 Hobson John Dalby, builder
    Argent Eugene, surveyor
    Woodward William, architect
    Saul Alfred, surveyor
8 *Official & General Building Society*
    Gwilt Charles, architect
    Homes for Working Boys in London,
      H. Bristow Wallen, sec
    English Land Restoration League,
      Frederick Verinder, sec
9 Clemence John, builder
10 Joseph David Arthur, vellum binder
    Spratt Henry, banjo maker
11 Lewis Frederick,surgical inst. case maker
    Smith William Bryant, news agent
12 & 13 *The St. Martin's,* Richard Burley
14 Pollard Harry Emans, surveyor
    Open Air Mission,   Gawin Kirkham, sec
    Charity Organisation Society,
    Strand Committee,
      H. R. Gifford, hon. sec
    Forman George Melville
    Forman William Scott
. . . . . . *here is Buckingham street* . . . . . .
    CHARING CROSS CHAMBERS:—
    Charing Cross Hotel,   G. S. Haines, sec
    Appleby Chas. Edward, civil engineer
    Tamar Terra Cotta & Fire Brick Works
    Monington & Co. public accountants
    Sharp Lewin, architect
    Deacon C. W. & Co. publishers
    Maritime & Mercantile Compendium
    Office
    Russel & Grant, solicitors
    Food Preserving Syndicate Limited,
      R. Delatorre, sec

DUKE STREET

1890

Duke st, *Adelphi*, (W.C.)
29 Villiers street to 14 *John street*
1 McNeall George, coffee rooms
2 Laing D. Gordon & Son, builders
2 Waller William Henry & Son, solicitors
2 *Light Newspaper Office*
2 *London Spiritualist Alliance,*
Morell Theobald, hon. sec
2 Singer J. W. & Son, art metal workers
3 Allen Theophilus, architect
3 Newland Edward, solicitor
3 Knoop Jacob Sons, wine merchants
3 Sharp (Lewin) & Arpin, architects
3 Towell William, architect
3 Beckett Walter
3A, Roche L. & Co. importers of foreign
produce
. . . . *here is Buckingham street* . . . .
4 Owens Mrs. Sophia E. private hotel
5 SEYMOUR CHAMBERS:—
Trewinnard Arthur Robert,
watchmaker
Lewis & Co. financial agents
5 *Central Press Agency,*
John B. Tanner, manager
5 Merion Charles, press correspondent
6 Loewenthal, Herger & Co. wine growers
6 Herger Otto, wine grower
6 Cudden Bernard, wine grower
6 Hunt Charles, wine grower
6 Johnson William Daniel, medical agent
6 Pratt Hampden William, architect
6 Hale Raymond Henry, surveyor
6 Thompson Arthur Henry, architect
6 Condy Richard
6 Tyack Henry S. architect
6 Allen Henry, surveyor
6 Jonquet Adolphe, artist
6 Norman George Lewis, solicitor
. . . . . . *here are York buildings* . . . . . .
7 Hobson John Dalby, builder
7 *Theosophical Publishing Co. Lim*
7 Argent Eugene, surveyor
7 Woodward William, architect
7 Hobson William Robert, architect
8 *Homes for Working Boys in London,*
H. Bristow Wallen, sec
8 Gwilt Charles, solicitor
8 *English Land Restoration League,*
Frederick Verinder, sec
9 Clemence John, builder
10 Joseph David Arthur, vellum binder
10 Spratt Henry, banjo maker
11 Smith William Bryant, news agent
12 & 13 *The St. Martin's,* Mrs. Fanny Maddick
14 Pollard Harry Emans, surveyor
14 *Open Air Mission,* Gawin Kirkham, sec
. . . . . . *here is Buckingham street* . . . . . .
CHARING CROSS CHAMBERS:—
Charing Cross Hotel, G. S. Haines, sec
Gresham Advance & Discount Co.
S. Henry, sec
Deacon C. W. & Co. publishers
Maritime & Mercantile Compendium
Office
Seawell, Kershaw & Warren, auctioneers
Grant James Edward Roney, surgeon

1895

Duke st, *Adelphi*, (W.C.)
29 Villiers street to 14 *John street*
1 Williams John, coffee rooms
2 Laing D. Gordon & Son, builders
2 Waller William Henry & Son, solicitors
2 *Light Newspaper Office*
2 *London Spiritualist Alliance,*
B. D. Godfrey, sec
2 *Grand Hotel, Clacton-on-Sea, Ltd*
2 Pettit & Hards, electrical engineers
3 Baccigaluppi Bros. wine merchants
3 *Life Newspaper Office*
3 Allen Theophilus, architect
3 Marshall Charles Wooley, assessor
of taxes
3 Evershed George Puttock, collector of
vestry rates
3 Sharp Lewen, architect
3 Arpin John Edward, architect
3 Towell Henry James
3 Beckett Walter
3A, Roche L. importer of foreign produce
. . . . . . *here is Buckingham street* . . . . . .
SEYMOUR CHAMBERS:—
Trewinnard Arthur Richard,
watchmaker
Lewis & Co. financial agents
6 Loewenthal, Herger & Co. wine merchants
6 Herger Otto, wine merchant
6 Cudden Bernard, wine merchant
6 Hunt Charles, wine merchant
6 *Equitable Finance Co.*
Robert P. Hart, sec
6 *Theatrical Choristers' Association,*
Edward Herbert, sec
6 *General Trading Assets & Mortgage Co.*
Limited,
R. J. Jenner, managing director
6 Blakemore William A. auctioneer
6 Taite & Co. toothache tablets
6 Todd Robert, solicitor
. . . . . . *here are York buildings* . . . . . .
7 Hobson John Dalby, builder
7 *Theosophical Publishing Society*
7 Argent Eugene, surveyor
7 Woodward William, architect
7 Hobson William Robert, architect
7 Crickmay Ernest W. architect
8 Foghill & Warner, business agents
8 Gwilt Charles, solicitor
8 Gwilt Charles Evelyn, solicitor
8 *English Land Restoration League,*
Frederick Verinder, sec
9 McLachlan James & Sons, builders
10 Joseph David Arthur, vellum binder
10 Jones John, hairdresser
11 Smith William Bryant, newsagent
12 & 13 *The St. Martin's,* Charles Pullen
14 Pollard Harry Emans, surveyor
. . . *here is Buckingham street* . . . .
CHARING CROSS CHAMBERS:—
1 *Charing Cross Hotel,* G. S. Haines, sec
2 Grant James Edward Roney, surgeon
8 & 9 Godfree (E.), Felton & Co.
wine merchants
10, 11 & 12 Deacon Charles William
& Co. publishers
13 Potts & Cogswell, public house
brokers

1900

Duke st, *Adelphi*, (W.C.)
29 Villiers street to 14 *John street*
1 Williams Mrs. Emma, coffee rooms
2 *London Irish Rifle Volunteers*
(16th Middlesex) (Orderly Room)
Capt. William C. Olpherts, adjt
3 Bristow Essex & Co. solicitors
3 Keppel Frederick, print seller
3 Marshall Charles Wooley, assessor
of taxes
3 Evershed George Puttock, collector
of vestry rates
3 Allen Theophilus & Son, architects
3 Sharp Lewen, architect
3 Marquis Oscar & Co. wine merchants
3A, Roche L. importer of foreign produce
. . . . . . *here is Buckingham street* . . . . . .
4 International Letter Bureau
5 SEYMOUR CHAMBERS:—
Trewinnard Arthur Robert,
watchmaker
5 Cuxson (Pryce, F.S.I.) & Overall,
surveyors
6 Warr Frank & Co. Limited,
refreshment contractors
6 Parsons William, ironmonger
6 Loewenthal, Herger & Co. Lim. wine
merchants
6 Clifford Edward, bill broker
6 Blakemore William A. auctioneer
6 Todd Robert, solicitor
. . . . . . *here are York buildings* . . . . . .
7 Hobson John Dalby, builder
7 Gwilt Charles, solicitor
7 Gwilt Charles Evelyn, solicitor
7 Argent Eugene, surveyor
8 Stanton, Ramsey & Co. general agents
8 Fisher & Co. art decorators
8 Foster Frank, F.S.I. architect
McLachlan J. & Sons, builders
10 Anglo-American General Agency
10 Pheasant Ernest William, solicitor
10 Bell Miss Lillian Jessie, type writer
10 Evans George, quantity surveyor
11 Frodsham Charles & Co. Ltd. (workshops
(late of 84 Strand)
12 & 13 *St. Martin's,* Mrs. H. B. Ashplant
. . . . . . *here is Buckingham street* . . . . . .
CHARING CROSS CHAMBERS:—
1 *Charing Cross Hotel,* G. S. Haines, sec
2 Grant Jas Edward Roney, surgeon
8&9 Godfree (E.), Felton & Co.
wine merchants
10, 11 & 12 Deacon Charles William
& Co. publishers
13 Potts & Co. auctioneers

1905

Duke street, *Adelphi* (W.C.)
(WESTMINSTER),
29 Villiers street to 14 *John street.*
1 Williams Mrs. Emma, coffee rooms
2 *Middlesex (16th) (London Irish)*
Rifle Volunteers; orderly room
Col. Sir Howland Roberts, bart.
V.D. officer commanding
3 Garrad George, carman
3 Perkins Montague Thornton, solicitor
3 Keppel Frederick, print seller
3 Marshall Charles Wooley, assessor
of taxes
3 Allen Theophilus, architect
3 Sharp Lewen, architect
3 Arpin John Edward, architect
3 Beckett Walter
3A, Roche L. importer of foreign produce
. . . . . . *here is Buckingham street* . . . . . .
4 *International Letter Bureau*
4 *Arrowsmith's Press Agency*
4 Ornum George&Co. conjuring trick mas
4 Trewinnard Arthur Richard,
watchmaker
5 Hall B. J. & Co. photo. printers
5 Cuxson (Pryce, F.S.I.) & Overall,
surveyors
6 Warr Frank & Co. Limited,
refreshment contractors
6 Lawrence H. & Co. advert. contractors
6 Head Francis, architect
6 *Metal Casement Co*
6 Loewenthal, Herger & Co. Lim.
wine merchants
6 Blakemore William A. auctioneer
6 Rose H. & Co. variety agents
. . . . . . *here are York buildings* . . . . . .
7 Hobson John Dalby, builder
7 Gwilt Charles Evelyn, solicitor
7 Palmer William Edward King, surveyor
8 Wilson John Alfred, stationer
8 Kingston E. & Co. mortgage brokers
8 Foster Frank, F.S.I. architect
8 Hughes & Howlett, wine mercahnts
9 *Library Press*
9 *Gaelic League (The)*
9 *Christian Literature Society for India,*
Rev. George Patterson, sec
Rev. J. A. Armstrong, association sec
10 Pheasant Ernest William, solicitor
10 Pell, Frye & Co. mill furnishers
10 Bush Lester James, solicitor
11 Hart Mrs. Annie Clemson, shirt maker
11 Frodsham Charles & Co. Ltd. (workshops
removed to 115 New Bond Street W)
12 & 13 *St. Martin's,* Mrs. H. B. Pheasant
. . . . . . *here is Buckingham street* . . . . . .
CHARING CROSS CHAMBERS:—
1 *Charing Cross Hotel & Restaurant*
(office) G. S. Haines, sec
6 to 9 Thurgood, Son & Chidgey,
surveyors
10, 11 & 12 Deacon Charles William
& Co. publishers
13 Potts & Co. auctioneers

DUKE STREET

1910

Duke street, *Adelphi* (W.C.)
(WESTMINSTER),
29 Villiers street to 14 John street.

1   Williams Mrs. Emma, coffee rooms
2   London Regiment 18th (County of London) Battalion (London Irish Rifles). Territorial Force, Lt.-Col. H. A. Pakenham, commanding; Maj. William Griffiths Baines Phibbs, adjutant
3   Linklater & Co. wine merchants
3   Waltham & Hill, metal workers
3   Radclyffe John, estate agent
3   Garrad George, carman
3   Keppel Frederick, print seller
3   Marshall Charles Wooley, assessor of taxes
3   Allen Theophilus, architect
3   Sharp Lewen, architect
3   Beckett Walter
3A,   Roche L. Ltd. importer of foreign produce
    ...... here is Buckingham street ......
4   *International Letter Bureau*
4   Ornum George & Co. conjuring trick makers
4   Aubrey William & Co. business transfer agents
5   Trewinnard Arthur Robert, watchmaker
5   *Cambridge Typewriting Agency*
5   Cuxson (G. A. Pryce, F.S.I.) & Overall, surveyors
5   Speakman Miss Ruth, typist
6   Loewenthal, Herger & Co. Lim. wine merchants
6   *Camping Club (Amateur)*
6   Head Francis, architect
6   Metal Casement Co
6   Davison William Rupert, architect
6   McLachlan & Brock, architects
6   Blakemore William A. surveyor
    .... here are York buildings ....
7   Hobson J. D. Ltd. builders
7   Gwilt Charles Evelyn, solicitor
7   Palmer William Edward King, F.S.I. surveyor
7   Argent Eugene, surveyor
8   Wilson J. A. & Co. stationers
8   Smith Sidney Robert James, architect
8   Davies Robert Cropley, solicitor
8   Foster Frank, F.S.I. architect
8   Harris Douglas, quantity surveyor
8   *Brakfontein Concessions Syndicate Ltd*
8   Pullin Charles B. & Co. company registration agents
10   Pheasant Ernest William, solicitor
10   Bush Lester James, solicitor
10   Whyte H. & Co. medical agents
10   Ward C. & Co. partnership agents
11   Bird Bros. printers
11   Joseph David A. account book manufctr
12 & 13 *St. Martin's*, Mrs. H. B. Pheasant
14   Green Edward, tailor
    .... here is Buckingham street ......
    CHARING CROSS CHAMBERS:
1   *Charing Cross Hotel & Restaurant* (office)   P. E. Fish, sec
2 & 3   Grant Mrs Drew Louis & Co. inquiry agents

1915

Duke street, *Adelphi* (W.C.)
(WESTMINSTER),
29 Villiers street to 14 John street.
    SOUTH SIDE
2   *Command Paymaster's Office (Eastern Command)*
2   *Eastern Command & London District Army Cashier*
3   Poirez J. A. & Co. wine merchants
3   Waltham & Hill, metal workers
3   Radclyffe John, estate agent
3   Garrad George, carman
3   Keppel Frederick, printseller
3   Tabor Frederick Richard, assessor & collector of taxes
3   Sells Robert Edgar, assessor & collector of taxes
3   Raven Henry, surveyor
3A,   Roche Louis Ltd. importers of foreign produce
    .... here is Buckingham street ......
4   *International Letter Bureau*
4   *Western Electric Railway Development Co. Ltd*
4   Wood Robert, surveyor
4   Kenwin George Dickson, model maker
5   *Cambridge Typewriting Agency*
5   Overall, Son & Wells, surveyors
5   Speakman Miss Ruth, typist
6   Speedy, Eynon & Co. electrical engineers
6   Loewenthal, Herger & Co. Lim. wine merchants
6   Hatchard-Smith & Son, architects
6   Bowden James Albert, architect
6   Brock Alan St. Hill, architect
6   *National Sanatorium Association*, F. W. Wareham, hon. sec
    .... here are York buildings ....
    NORTH SIDE
7   Hobson J. D. Ltd. builders
7   Gwilt Charles Evelyn, solicitor
7   Palmer William Edward King, F.S.I. surveyor
8   Wilson John Alfred & Co. drawing office materials
8   Foster Frank, F.S.I. architect
8   Bylander S. consulting engineer
8   Bywaters Percy, quantity surveyor
8   Harris Douglas, quantity surveyor
9   Munro George & Co. conjuring trick makers
10   Aubrey William & Co. business transfer agents
10   *Garrick Entertainment Bureau Ltd*
10   *Madame Ltd.* publishers
10   Bush Lester James, solicitor
11   *Barway Press Co.* printers
11   Bird Bros. printers
11   Joseph David A. account book manufctr
12 & 13 *St. Martin's*, Mrs. Hannah Breach Pheasant
14   Green Mrs. Jane, tailor
    .... here is Buckingham street ......
    CHARING CROSS CHAMBERS:
1   *Charing Cross Hotel & Restaurant* (office)   P. E. Fish, sec
2 & 3   Grant Mrs
8 & 9   Robertson, Sanderson & Co. Ltd. whisky merchants

1920

Duke street, *Adelphi* (W.C. 2)
(WESTMINSTER),
29 Villiers street to 14 John street.
    SOUTH SIDE
3   Hoare, Gothard & Bond Ltd. coal merchants
3   Poirez J. A. & Co. wine merchants
3   Radclyffe John, estate agent
3   Garrad George, carman
3   Tabor Frederick Richard, assessor & collector of taxes
3   Moore & Neild, architects
3   Sells Robert Edgar, assessor & collector of taxes
3   Raven Henry, surveyor
3A,   Roche Louis Ltd. importers of foreign produce
    .... here is Buckingham street ......
4   *Wallace's Letter Bureau*
4   *Somerset Cigarette Agency*
4   Hardingham Henry, publisher
5 & 6   *Iron & Coal Trades Review*
5 & 6   England & Co. Ltd. publishers
5   Overall Edmund & Son, surveyors
5   Bywaters Percy, quantity surveyor
5   Ernest G. D. & Co. publishers
5   *Music Trades Review*
5   *Institution of British Foundrymen*
5   Hatchard-Smith & Son, architects
    .... here are York buildings ....
    NORTH SIDE
7   Hobson J. D. Ltd. builders
7   Saunders William Moore, telegraph cable code compiler
7   Gwilt Charles Evelyn, solicitor
7   Palmer William Edward King, F.S.I. surveyor
7   Cecil Edward, dramatic author
8   Furst Herbert, fine art dealer
8   Park James Elliott, accountant
8   Needes John Calder, medical agent
8   Hinds Robert Allsebrooke, architect
9   Green Mrs. Bertha Frances, typewriting office
10   *Industrial Orthopaedic Society*
11   Bird Bros. printers
11   *Insurance Record* (office of)
11   Francke Frederick & Son, account book manufacturers
12&13   *St. Martin's*, Mrs. Sara Elizabeth Pheasant
14   Green Mrs. Jane, tailor
    .... here is Buckingham street ......
    CHARING CROSS CHAMBERS:—
1   *Charing Cross Hotel & Restaurant* (office)   P. E. Fish, sec
7   Mufarri Asad & Co. general merchants
9   Whatley Clement Henry, A.C.I.S. sec. to public companies
10   *Aviation Transport Internationale Ltd*
11   Davies O. F. Ltd. merchants
12   Fryer Charles H. advertising contractor

1925

Duke street, *Adelphi* (W.C. 2)
(WESTMINSTER),
29 Villiers street to 14 John street.
    SOUTH SIDE
2   *Royal Engineers* (Commandant for South London)
3   Hoare, Gothard & Bond Ltd. coal merchants
3   Hoare, Sykes & Co. Ltd. bunkering agents
3   *Practical Publicity Ltd.* advertising agents
3   Radclyffe John, estate agent
3   Garrad George, carman
3   Tabor Frederick Richard, assessor & collector of taxes
3   Sells Robert Edgar, assessor & collector of taxes
3   *Central & Western Corporation Ltd*
3   Simpson Victor H. surveyor
3A,   Kember & Co. wine merchants
    .... here is Buckingham street ......
4   *Wallace's Letter Bureau*
4   Haywood Cedric T. architect
5 & 6   *Iron & Coal Trades Review*
5 & 6   England & Co. Ltd. publishers
5 & 6   *Grocers' Journal Ltd*
5 & 6   *Horse & Hound Newspaper Office*
5   Griffiths & Rylands Ltd. publishers
5   Overall Edmund & Son, surveyors
5   Bywaters Percy, quantity surveyor
5   Ernest G. D. & Co. publishers
5   *Music Trades Review*
    .... here are York buildings ....
    NORTH SIDE
7   Hobson J. D. Ltd. builders
7   Saunders William Moore, telegraph cable code compiler
7   Gwilt Charles Evelyn, solicitor
7   Palmer William Edward King, F.S.I. surveyor
7   Cecil Edward, dramatic author
8   Furst Herbert, fine art dealer
8   Amalgamated Brokers Ltd. insurance brokers
8   Hinds Robert Allsebrooke, architect
8   Stone Miss Emily, dramatic agent
9   Grein James Thomas, dramatic critic & consul & attaché for the Republic of Liberia
9   Green Mrs. Bertha Frances, typewriting office
9   Lion Leon M. theatrical manager
10   Sims Goss Walter, tobacconist
10   *Post Office Controlling Officers' Association*
10   Peters Alexander, accountant
11   Thomas Walter Joseph, builder
11   Bird Bros. printers
11   Francke Frederick & Son, account book manufacturers
12 & 13   *St. Martin's*, Mrs. Sara Elizabeth Pheasant
14   Green Mrs. Jane, tailor
    .... here is Buckingham street ......
    CHARING CROSS CHAMBERS:—
1   *Charing Cross Hotel & Restaurant* (office)
6 & 7   Whatley Clement H. accntnt
8 & 9   Knowland Bros. wine merchts
10 & 11   Raweson, Hughes Ltd. land & estate agents
12   Ensign Radio Co

DUKE STREET

1930

Duke street, *Adelphi* (W.C. 2)
(WESTMINSTER),
29 Villiers street to 14 John street.
SOUTH SIDE

2   *Royal Engineers* (Commanding Royal
    Engineer, London district)
2   *Royal Engineers* (Inspector of Works,
    London district)
2   *Royal Engineers* (Officer in-Charge of
    R.E. Stores, London district)
3   Sommers H. & Partners Ltd. finance
    brokers
3   Estate Finance & Development Syndicate
3   Radclyffe John, estate agent
3   Garrad George, carman
3   Tabor Frederick Richard, assessor &
    collector of taxes
3   Simpson Victor H. surveyor
3A, Kember & Wait, wine merchants
3A, Gauntlett Leonard, refreshment rooms
. . . . *here is Buckingham street* . . . .
4   *Wallace's Letter Bureau*
4   Keay William C. consulting engineer
4   Television Society
4   Ord Hubert, M.A. private tutor
5 & 6 *Horse & Hound Newspaper Office*
5   Griffiths & Rylands Ltd. property
    owners
5   Building Industry Council of Review
5   Overall Edmund & Son, surveyors
5   Bywaters Percy, quantity surveyor
5   Ernest G. D. & Co. publishers
5   *Music Trades Review*
5 & 6 Ross Stuart Ltd. general merchants
6   Europa Publications Ltd
6   Davis W. E. & Son, quantity surveyors
6   American Associated Magazines
. . . . *here are York buildings* . . . .
NORTH SIDE
7   Hobson J. D. Ltd. builders
7   Saunders William Moore, telegraph cable
    code compiler
7   Pilborough G. A. architect
7   Adelphi Tracing Co. draughtsmen
7   Cox, Smith & Co. accountants
8   Screen Advertising Service Ltd
8   Furst Herbert, fine art dealer
8   Hinds Robert Allsebrooke, architect
8   Brown Ashley, author
9   Cliffe Mrs. Olive, fine art dealer
9   National Mutual Indemnity
    Insurance Co. Ltd
9   Lambie William Herbert, surveyor
9   Lambert Henry S. business consultant
10 Scammell Philip, tobacconist
11 Thomas Walter Joseph, builder
11 Bird Bros. printers
11 Wright Eustace M. journalist
11 Francke Frederick & Son, account book
    manufacturers
12 & 13 *St. Martin's*, Mrs. Sara Elizabeth
    Pheasant
14 Green Mrs. Jane, tailor
. . . . *here is Buckingham street* . . . .
CHARING CROSS CHAMBERS:—
1   Southern Railway Hotels Dept
6 & 7 Whatley Clement H. accntnt
8 & 9 Knowland Bros. wine merchts
10 & 11 Davy & Co. Ltd. wine
    merchants

1935

Duke street, *Adelphi* (W.C.2)
(WESTMINSTER),
29 Villiers street to 14 John street.
SOUTH SIDE

2   Textile Journals Ltd
3   Radclyffe John, estate agent
3   Garrad George, carman
3   Sears Frederick William, advertising
    contractor
3   Mowl F. M. Ltd. publishers
3   Gray Arthur (Books) Ltd. publishers
3   La Gallienne & Co. accountants
3   Nightingale B. E. & Co. accountants
3   Gibb H. Gardiner & Co. accountants
3A, Kember & Wait, wine merchants
3A, Gauntlett Leonard, refreshment rooms
. . . . *here is Buckingham street* . . . . . .
4   *Wallace's Letter Bureau*
4   Keay William C. consulting engineer
4   Du Val D. Victor, commercial artist
4   Irby & Chambers, motor car claims
    assessors
4   Haywood Cedric T. architect
5 & 6 Horse & Hound Publications Ltd
5   Griffiths & Rylands Ltd. property
    owners
5   Building Industries National Council
5   National Joint Council for the Building
    industry
5   Overall Edmund & Son, surveyors
5   Industrial Journals Ltd. publishers
5   *Music Trades Review*
6   Direct French Wine Supply Co. Ltd
6   Boevey Barratt, wine merchant
6   Echoes Topical News Service
6   Art & Advertising Assistance Ltd
6   Europa Publications Ltd
. . . . *here is York buildings* . . . .
NORTH SIDE
7   Hobson J. D. Ltd. builders
7   Micklewright C. N. & Co. accountants
7   Adelphi Products Co. Ltd. manufactng
    chemists
7   Pilborough G. A. architect
7   Adelphi Tracing & Planning Co.
    draughtsmen
7   Octron Ltd. wireless valve makers
8   Bond Walter Ltd. turf commission agents
8   Hinds Robert Allsebrooke, architect
9   Ann Teaks, dealers in antiques
9   Lambie William Herbert, surveyor
9   Lambert Henry S. business consultant
9   Reid Andrew, publicity journalist
10 Stephens Walter, surveyor
10 Wilkerson Harry C. architect
10 Adelphi Studios, photographers
11 Bird Bros. printers
12 & 13 *St. Martin's*, Mrs. Sara Elizabeth
    Pheasant
14 Foxwell Miss Violet, restaurant
14 Edchards (Chemists) Ltd
. . . . *here is Buckingham street* . . . . . .
CHARING CROSS CHAMBERS:—
1   Southern Railway Hotels Dept
6 & 7 Whatley Clement H. accntnt
10 & 11 Davy & Co. Ltd. wine
    merchants

1936

Duke street, *Adelphi* (W.C.2)
(WESTMINSTER),
29 Villiers street to 14 John street.
SOUTH SIDE

2   Textile Journals Ltd
2   Century Press Ltd. publishers
3   Radclyffe John, estate agent
3   Sears Frederick William, advertising
    contractor
3   Gramol Publications Ltd
3   Nightingale B. E. & Co. accountants
3   Gibb H. Gardiner & Co. accountants
3A, Kember & Wait, wine merchants
. . . . *here is Buckingham street* . . . . . .
4   *Wallace's Letter Bureau*
4   Keay William C. consulting engineer
4   Du Val D. Victor, commercial artist
4   Irby & Chambers, motor car claims
    assessors
4   Haywood Cedric T. architect
5 & 6 Horse & Hound Publications Ltd
5   Griffiths & Rylands Ltd. property
    owners
5   Campbell A. B. & Co. publishers
5   Building Industries National Council
5   National Joint Council for the Building
    Industry
5   Overall Edmund & Son, surveyors
5   Industrial Journals Ltd. publishers
5   *Music Trades Review*
6   Direct French Wine Supply Co. Ltd
6   Boevey Barratt, wine merchant
6   James William Henry Clarke, sec to
    public companies
6   "Steelgrip" Fittings Ltd.
    Empire building system
6   Echoes Topical News Service
6   Europa Publications Ltd
. . . . *here are York buildings* . . . .
NORTH SIDE
7   Hobson J. D. Ltd. builders
7   Eastern Shipping Co. general merchants
7   Stephens W. G. & Co. accountants
7   Richardson L. & Co. south african
    merchants
7   Pilborough G. A. architect
7   Adelphi Tracing & Planning Co.
    draughtsmen
7   Octron Ltd. wireless valve makers
8   Bond Walter Ltd. turf commission
    agents
8   Hinds Robert Allsebrooke, architect
9   Ann Teaks, dealers in antiques
9   Lambie William Herbert, surveyor
9   Lambert Henry S. business consultant
9   Reid Andrew, publicity journalist
10 Stephens Walter, surveyor
10 Wilkerson Harry C. architect
11 Bird Bros. printers
12 & 13 *St. Martin's*, Mrs. Sara Elizabeth
    Pheasant
14 Foxwell Miss Violet, restaurant
14 Edchards (Chemists) Ltd
. . . . *here is Buckingham street* . . . . . .
CHARING CROSS CHAMBERS:—
1   Southern Railway Hotels Dept
6 & 7 Whatley Clement H. accntnt
10 & 11 Davy & Co. Ltd. wine
    merchants

GEORGE STREET – YORK BUILDINGS from 1852

1841

George street, *Adelphi,* 14 *John st.*
1 Taylor George, carpenter, &c
2 Vialls John Palmer, glass warehouse
3 Clark John, jewellery case maker
4 Aitken Charles James, bookbinder
5 Wirgman & Fleming, pearl workers, &c
6 Cook Thomas, lighterman
10 Bottomley James, coal merchant
11 Mackenzie Mrs Mary, lodging house
12 Seton & Nicholson, attornies
   YORK CHAMBERS.
   Hardy Thomas John, coal merchant
   Johnson Henry, coal merchant
   Madden Henry, wine merchant
   Moore James S. solicitor
   Renaud Peter Thomas, coal merchant
   Seaton & Piggott, coal merchants
   Stead David, pat. of wood pavement
   Stead David, merchant
   Waller Charles B. coal merchant
   Warren Edward, coal merchant
19 Brookbank William, tailor
21 Bayley William, tailor
   EASTERN WHARF
   Dew William, coal merchant
   Thomson Robert, egg merchant
   Leslie R. Baker, coal merchant
   Tomlinson & Chatley, boat builders
   WESTERN WHARF
   Apps William, coal merchant
   Bottomley, Hensman & Co. coal merch
   Cook Henry, coal merchant
   Daniell James, coal merchant
   Jones Henry Robert, coal merchant
   Morris Thomas, coal merchant
22 Richardson Henry & Co. wine merchants

1845

George street, *Adelphi,*
14 *John st.* & 6 *Duke st.* to the river.
1 Taylor George, carpenter, &c
2 Vialls John Palmer, glass manufacturer
3 Clark John, jewellery case maker
4 Aitken Charles James, bookbinder
5 Fleming Joseph, pearl worker, &c
12 Seton & Nicholson, attorneys
   Watermen's Steam Co. Adelphi pier
13 & 14 YORK CHAMBERS.
   Allway Samuel P. coal merchant
   Allenby Henry, esq
   Armitage Edward, artist
   Edwards George, civil engineer
   Johnson Henry, coal merchant
   Madden Henry, manfr.pat.knife cleanr
   Madden Henry, wine merchant
   Renaud Peter Thomas, coal merchant
   Seaton Joseph, coal merchant
   Trezevant Theodore M. coal merchant
   Warren Edward, coal merchant
19 Brookbank William, sen. tailor
21 Bayley William, tailor
22 Tuck Edmund, improved electro plater
   WESTERN WHARF
   Apps William, coal merchant
   Hensman & Hensman, coal merchants
   Cook Henry, coal merchant
   Daniell James, coal merchant
   Jones Henry Robert, coal merchant
   Morris Thomas, coal merchant
   Rickman James, coal merchant
   Strickland Frederick William, coal mer

1850

George street, *Adelphi,*
14 *John st.* & 6 *Duke st.* to the river.
4 Aitken Charles James, bookbinder
7 Eaton John, tailor
8 Richardson William, tailor
15 Seton & Nicholson, attorneys
   Watermen's Steam Co. Adelphi pier
   John Stephen Newbon, sec
13, 14 & 15 YORK CHAMBERS:—
   Allenby Henry, esq
   Armitage Edward, artist
   Bacot John, inspector of anatomy
   Johnson Henry, coal merchant
   Trezevant Theodore M. coal merchant
   Warren Edward, coal merchant
21 Wood James Richard, lighterman
   WESTERN WHARF:—
   Batt & Rutley, seedsmen
   Clewley William, coal merchant
   Strickland Henry Charles, coal mercht.

1855

York buildings, Adelphi),
14 *John st.* & 6 *Duke st.* to the river.
1 SEYMOUR CHAMBERS:—
   Barber Joseph, esq
   Cobb Rev. Samuel W
   Pinchbeck George, civil engineer
   Yeldham Richard, architect & surveyor
4 Aitken Fred. G. & Thos. Ed. bookbinders
5 Chapman John, lodging house
7 Hewitt Mrs. Mary, lodging house
8 Richardson William, tailor
8 Dance Edward, tailor
12 THAMES CHAMBERS:—
   Barrett James, proprietor of Dr.
      Fox's patent for fireproof buildings
   Garland Robert, architect
   Griffin Rev. Henry
   Public Works Contract Co.
      Raymond Yates, sec
   Seton & Nicholson, attorneys
13, 14 & 15 YORK CHAMBERS:—
   Allenby Henry, esq
   Armitage Edward, artist
   Bacot John, inspector of anatomy
   Farnley Iron Company,
      Henry Allenby, agent
   Johnson William, coal merchant
   Warren Edward, coal merchant
   Grazebrook Michael & Wm. glass ma
16 *Sons of the Thames Packet Co*
16 Cunningham Wm. steam packet owner
17 Elsam Richard, whitesmith
19 Biffen Henry, tailor
21 Gladman George, fruit salesman
22 Russell Henry Heathcote, architect

1860

York buildings, *Adelphi* (W.C.),
14 *John st.* & 6 *Duke st.* to the river.
1 SEYMOUR CHAMBERS:—
   Blackburn Bewick, esq
   Webber Josiah, architect & surveyor
   Rowan Richard Edward & Co. irish
      malt whiskey stores
   Yeldham Richard, architect & surveyor
4 Aitken Thos. Edwards, bookbinder
5 Potter Hen. Jas. parliamentary reporter
7 Hewitt Mrs. Mary, lodging house
8 Richardson William, tailor
8 Dance Edward, tailor
9 Murray Charles Stuart, shorthand writer
10 Walters John, lodging house
12 THAMES CHAMBERS:—
   Barrett Henry, proprietor of Fox&Bar-
      rett's system of fireproof constructn
   Bourne John Cooke, artist
   Griffin Rev. Henry
   Hill Edward, esq
   Seton Nicholson, attorneys
13, 14 & 15 YORK CHAMBERS:—
   Allenby Henry, esq
   Bacot John, inspector of anatomy
   Farnley Iron Co. Henry Allenby, agent
   Hawkins James, metropolitan in-
      spector of anatomy
   Cursham George, M.D. provincial
      inspector of anatomy
   Grazebrook Michael & Wm. glass ma
16 Jaggs John, lodging house

1865

York buildings, Adelphi (W.C.),
14 *John st.* & 6 *Duke st.* to the river.
1 SEYMOUR CHAMBERS:—
   Blackburn Bewick, esq
1 Edwards Edmund, consulting engineer
1 Furniss Frederick, railway contractor
1 Furniss James Robert, civil engineer
1 *Llanerch-y-Caidd Mining Co.(lim)*
      Edmund Edwards, manager
   Railway Lubricating Co. (limited),
      Robert John Lecky, sec
4 Aitken Thomas Edwards, bookbinder
6 Dennison Mrs. Louisa, ladies' school
7 Southwood Chas. Fredk. lodging house
8 Lecoutur Edward, lodging house
9 Dance Edward, tailor
12 THAMES CHAMBERS:—
   Barrett Henry, proprietor of Fox&Bar-
      rett's system of fireproof constructn
   Bourne John Cooke, artist
   Abbott William Henry, esq
   Rose & Rouse, railway contractors
   Rose Frederick D. railway contractor
13, 14 & 15 YORK CHAMBERS:—
   Atcheson Rev. Henry, M.A
   Watson Edward, civil engineer
   Roberts James, timber merchant
   Fry Edmond, civil engineer
   Woodfield Matthew, civil engineer
   Smyth Robert Maclean, contractor
      & brickmaker
   London Irish (28th Middlesex)
      Volunteer Rifle Corps (Orderly Room)
   Hall Capt. Thurle
   Murray Duncan, designer
   Hawkins Charles, metropolitan in-
      spector of anatomy
   Cursham George, M.D. provincial
      inspector of anatomy
20 Donelly Henry William, naval architect
20 Walkley Arthur, advertising contractor
20 Hanbury F. A. esq
— *The Street Rolling Stock Co (limited)*
      J.T.Hall, sec (temporary offices)

1870

York buildings, *Adelphi* (W.C.), 14 *John*
street. & 6 *Duke street* to the river.
1 SEYMOUR CHAMBERS:—
   Blackburn Bewicke
   Paget Frederick Arthur, civil
      & mechanical engineer
4 Aitken Thosmas Edwards, bookbinder
5 Fleming Charles, pearl worker
6 Dennison Mrs. Louisa, ladies' school
9 Dance Edward, tailor
12 THAMES CHAMBERS:—
   Barrett Henry, proprietor of Fox&Bar-
      rett's system of fireproof constructn
   Bourne Walter
   Macintosh Hugh
13 Liddell John, architect
13 Nash Joseph, jun. architectural artist
13 Vizetelly Adrian, artist
13 Vizetelly Montague, artist
13, 14 & 15 YORK CHAMBERS:—
   Smyth Robert Maclean, brickmaker
   Pain Henry Foxton, solicitor
   Hawkins Charles, inspector of
      metropolitan schools of anatomy
   Cursham George, M.D. inspector of
      provincial schools of anatomy
20 Wicker Charles John, scrivenor

1875

York buildings, *Adelphi* (W.C.).
14 *John street.*
1 SEYMOUR CHAMBERS:—
   Blackburn Bewicke
   Paget Frederick Arthur, civil engineer
   Goodwin John
6 Dennison Misses Louisa & Marian,
      ladies' school
9 Dance Edward, tailor
12 THAMES CHAMBERS:—
   Barrett Henry, proprietor of Fox&Bar-
      rett's system of fireproof constructn
   Jones Capt. Mainwaring
   Macintosh Hugh
   Perry&Hanson, architects&surveyors
   Bell Alexander C
   Giles Francis G
   Maxwell Maj.-Gen. George Vaughan
13, 14 & 15 YORK CHAMBERS:—
   Smyth Robert Maclean, brickmaker
   National Protestant Institute,
      George W. Harrison, sec
   Thames Angling Preservation Society,
      William Henry Brougham, sec
   Ogle John William, M.D. inspector of
      provincial schools of anatomy
   Hawkins Charles, inspector of
      metropolitan schools of anatomy
18 Chatley Joseph William, coal merchant
19 Bottomley William
20 Lovegrove Henry, architect
   Maberly Brothers, engineers
   Wood & Wright, accountants
   Wood Charles, brick agent
21 Gardner William, auctioneer
   Fox Thomas, tailor
22 Avern William Henry, tailor

GEORGE STREET – YORK BUILDINGS from 1852

1880

York buildings, *Adelphi* (W.C.),
14 *John st.*
SEYMOUR CHAMBERS:—
  Blackburn Bewicke
  Goodwin John
5 Osborne John S. wine merchant
  Charing Cross Hotel Co. Limited,
           G. S. Haines, sec
  Hanson & Walker, architects
  Bagg William George E. surveyor
8 Vanderspeck Henry, lodging house
9 Chatley Joseph William, coal merchant
10 Parry William George
12 THAMES CHAMBERS:—
  Barrett Henry, Fox & Barrett's
    fireproof construction
  Hansom Henry John, architect & surv
  Jones Capt. Mainwaring
  Macintosh Hugh
  Bell Alexander C
  Giles Francis G
  Maxwell Lt.-Gen. George V. C.B
13, 14 & 15 YORK CHAMBERS:—
  Hallatt George Wilson T. architect
  Farmer Charles, commission agent
  Harrison George Sparrow, architect
14 Benton William, architect
  Fowler Francis, jun. architect
  Fowler Charles
  Wood Walter J. architect
  Cadney Charles Low, architect
15 Room, Peirce & Co. advertising agents
18 Keeves Joseph
19 Bottomley William
20 Thomson Frederick, architect
  Sandilands Charles James L. architect
  National Protestant Institute,
        George W. Harrison, sec
  Constitution Newspaper Office
  Graham R. & M. patent agents
21 Gardner William, auctioneer

1885

York buildings, *Adelphi* (W.C.),
14 *John st.*
SEYMOUR CHAMBERS:—
  Goodwin John
  Guscotte Thomas, solicitor
  Payne Walter
5 Loewenthal Sons, wine growers
  Herger Otto, wine grower
  National Society for Aid to the
    Sick & Wounded in War
  Hanson John Treadway, architect
9 Chatley Joseph William, coal merchant
10 Parry William Griffiths
12 THAMES CHAMBERS:—
  Barrett Henry, Fox & Barrett's
    fireproof construction
  Jones Major Mainwaring
  Macintosh Hugh
  Knox Capt. William B
  Giles Francis G
  Maxwell Gen. Sir George V. K.C.B
  Joyce & Co. advertising agents
13, 14 & 15 YORK CHAMBERS:—
14 *Church Penitentiary Association,*
    Rev. G. C. Campbell,
    Rev. T. Wodehouse, } hon.
    E. L. Birkett, M.D. } secs
  Cadogan Sidney Russell, artist
15 Aggio Henry, pianoforte maker
  Hallatt George W. T. architect
  Gould William, gauger
  Dudman Charles, gauger
  Poole George Thomas
18 Keeves Joseph
19 Bottomley William
20 Thomson Frederick, surveyor
  Swinstead Bernard, surveyor
  Meiklejohn John, private enquiry agent
  Constitution (The) Office
21 Gardner William, house agent
  Allan William Alexander

1890

York buildings, *Adelphi* (W.C.),
14 *John st.*
SEYMOUR CHAMBERS:—
  Guscotte & Fowler, solicitors
  Payne Walter
  Goodwin John
  Talbot T. W
5 Smee William, solicitor
5 *National Society for Aid to the Sick &*
    Wounded in War (BritishRed Cross Society),
        James G. Vokes, sec
5 Gale Ernest Sewell, architect
5 Wainwright Charles Henry, architect
5 Hunt William, architect
6 *Civil Service & Army & Navy*
    Scholastic & Domestic Agency
12 THAMES CHAMBERS:—
  Jones Major Mainwaring
  Macintosh Hugh
  Giles Francis G
  Maxwell Gen. Sir George V. K.C.B
  Adams Robert J
  Shepherd Lieut.-Col. William
13A, Chevasse Justin, private investigator
13, 14 & 15 YORK CHAMBERS:—
13 Bringloe & Son, publishers' agents
13 Gould William, gauger
13 Walmsley H. B
14 Church Penitentiary Association,
    Rev. G. C. Campbell,
    Rev. T. Wodehouse, } hon
    E. L. Birkett, M.D. } secs
14 *Church Mission to the Fallen,*
        J. W. B. Riddle, hon. sec
14 Iles John Arthur, solicitor
14 Cadogan Sidney Russell, artist
14 Farnworth Samuel A. Mason
14 Whates Harry
15 Newbould Williamson, solicitor
15 *Official & General Building Society*
15 *Central Vigilance Society for the*
    Repression of Immorality
         T. F. Myers, sec
15 Smith Sidney R. J. architect
15 Pickford Edmund D. architect
15 Croal David O
18 Keeves Joseph
19 Bottomley William
19 Hawkins Edwin Elton, architect
19 Buckle James George, architect
20 *The Corporation of Australasia*
20 Bryant William Charles
20 Yates Charles & Co. advertising agents
21 Gardner William, house agent

1895

York buildings, *Adelphi* (W.C.),
14 *John st.*
SEYMOUR CHAMBERS:—
  Guscotte & Fowler, solicitors
  Todd Robert, solicitor
  Hare Henry Thomas, architect
  Payne Walter Rogers
5 Smee William, solicitor
5 *National Society for Aid to the Sick &*
    Wounded in War (British Red Cross
    Society),   James G. Vokes, sec
5 Hunt William, architect
  Orchestral Association,
        Charles S. Bradberry, sec
6 Hart John, bill discounter
6 Hunter William & Sons, bookbinders
10 Ashworth Clarke, architect
12 THAMES CHAMBERS:—
  Ward & Downey, Ld. publishers
  Shepherd Lieut.-Col. William
  Rackham Willoughby
  Wolpman Gustav Charles
  Scarth Leveson
13A, Chevasse Justin, private investigator
13, 14 & 15 YORK CHAMBERS:—
13 *Holmes Lights Co*
13 *Holmes Ozone Co*
13 Gould William, gauger & valuer
14 *Church Penitentiary Association,*
    Rev. G. C. Campbell, M.A. hon sec
    C. H. Baker, assistant sec
14 *Church Mission to the Fallen,*
        Rev. V. G. Borradaile, hon. sec
14 Iles John Arthur, solicitor
14 Morrison Alexander Kinnear, M.A.
    journalist
14 Ramsay Bernard M
14 Croal David O
15 Newbold Francis Thomas, solicitor
15 *Official & General Building Society*
15 Smith Sidney R. James, architect
15 Wills Henry Overton, architect
15 Coggin Clarence, architect
15 Reynolds George Astley
19 Bottomley William, builder
19 Hawkins Edwin Elton, architect
19 Tarbolton & Tugwell, architects
19 Buckle James George, architect
20 Warr Frank & Co. Ltd. refreshment
    contractors
20 Blackmore Henry, news agency
21 Gardner William, house agent
. . . . *here are Adelphi arches* . . . .
22 Avern Mrs. Mary Ann, dressmaker

GEORGE STREET – YORK BUILDINGS from 1852

1900

York buildings, *Adelphi* (W.C.),
14 *John st.*

1 SEYMOUR CHAMBERS:—
  Guscotte & Fowler, solicitors
  Todd Robert, solicitor
  Othen John, jun. solicitor
  Payne Walter Rogers
5 Morison Lennox James, solicitor
5 *National Society for Aid to the Sick &*
  Wounded in War (British Red Cross Society),
  James G. Vokes, sec
5 *Rochester Diocesan Board of*
  Education (Incorporated),
  Rev. A. W. Maplesden, sec
5 *Rochester Diocesan Schools Association,*
  Rev. A. W. Maplesden, sec
5 Houston & Houston, architects
6 McCulloch James, papermakers' agent
7 Perry & Angell, architects
6 Pollard Harry Emans, surveyor
6 Hancock William, theatrical architect
6 Angelo & Wooton, typewriters
8 Oldham & Co. insurance brokers
10 *Fireproof Partition Syndicate Lim*
10 Connah-Wright Co. fireproof
  partitions &c
10 Smith James Trant, architect
12 THAMES CHAMBERS:—
  Dey & Dey, accountants
  Colvile Sir Henry
  Shepherd Lieut.-Col. William
  Gordon Andrew James, architect
  Helmsley Charles
  Hall Henry J
12 Scarth Leveson
  Kerr Walter, lime light supplier
13A Chevasse Justin, private investigator
13, 14 & 15 YORK CHAMBERS:—
13 *Holmes Lights Co*
13 *Holmes Ozone Co*
13 Gould William, gauger & valuer
14 Brereton Austin
14 Smith Sidney R. James, architect
14 *Church Penitentiary Association,*
  Rev. G. C. Campbell, M.A. hon sec
  C. H. Baker, sec
14 *Church Mission to the Fallen,*
  Rev. V. G. Borradaile, hon. sec
14 Iles John Arthur, solicitor
14 Fisher Edmund, architect
14 Littlewood Samuel R. journalist
15 *Official & General Building Society*
15 *Association for the Promotion of*
  the Unity of Christendom
15 Wills Henry Overton, architect
15 Coggin Clarence, architect
19 Bottomley William, builder
19 Hawkins Edwin Elton, architect
19 *British Institution Scholarship Fund,*
  Frederick A. Eaton, sec
20 Hawkins Mrs. Elizabeth, apartments
21 Gardner William, house agent
.... *here are Adelphi arches* ....
22 Avern Mrs. Mary Ann, dressmaker

1905

York buildings, *Adelphi* (W.C.)
(WESTMINSTER), 14 *John st.*

1 Guscotte & Fowler, solicitors
1 Todd Robert, solicitor
1 Hudleston Robert William, solicitor
1 Payne Walter Rogers
5 *British Electric Signs Co. Ld*
5 Van, Alexander & Co. advertising agents
5 *National Society for Aid to the Sick &*
  Wounded in War (British Red Cross Society),
  James G. Vokes, sec
5 Doherty Patrick E. theatrical agent
6 Wooton Miss Elizabeth Mary, typewriter
6 Furmage Francis D. solicitor
6 Harris Douglas, quantity surveyor
6 Stone & Colquhoun, architects
7 Perry & Angell, architects
8 Oldham & Co. estate agents
10 *Fireproof Co. Lim*
10 Smith James Trant, architect
10 Fisher Edmund, architect
12 Armitage Stephen
12 Shepherd Lieut.-Col. William
12 Hall Henry J
  Kerr Mrs. Walter, lime light supplier
13A, Chevasse Justin, private investigator
13 *Holmes Lights Co*
13 *Holmes Ozone Co*
13 Gould William & Co. gaugers
13 Brereton Austin
14 Smith Sidney R. James, architect
14 *Church Penitentiary Association,*
  C. H. Baker, sec
14 Iles John Arthur, solicitor
14 Oddy Josiah
15 *Official & General Building Society*
15 *Association for the Promotion of*
  the Unity of Christendom
15 Wallis Thomas, architect
19 Bottomley William, builder
19 Hawkins Edwin Elton, architect
19 *British Institution Scholarship Fund,*
  Frederick A. Eaton, sec
20 Hawkins Miss Amelia, apartments
21 Gardner William, house agent
  Godfree (E.), Felton & Co. wine
  merchants. (7&9 Adelphi arches)
.... *here are Adelphi arches* ....

1910

York buildings, *Adelphi* (W.C.)
(WESTMINSTER), 14 *John st.*

1 Guscotte & Fowler, solicitors
1 Todd Robert, solicitor
1 Payne Walter Rogers
5 Page George Henry, publisher
5 Day Francis Meredith, solicitor
5 Simmons Walter, accountant
5 Parker Albert Edward James,
  advertising agent
5 White Philip, gauger
5 EstlerE.&Kathan, fancy goods importers
6 Acworth William, M.A. architect
6 Wooton Miss Elizabeth Mary, typewriter
6 *Moral Education League,*
  Harrold Johnson, sec
6 Furmage Francis D. solicitor
6 *Eugenics Education Society*
7 Wieland Eugene John, artist
8 *St. Catherine Press Ltd.* printers
10 Osborne Charles & Co. Ltd. gun makers
12 Treherne A. & Co. Ltd. publishers
12 *National Home Reading Union,*
  Miss Read, sec
12 Shepherd Lieut.-Col. William
12 James Thomas David
  Kerr Mrs. Walter, lime light supplier
  WATERGATE HOUSE
  Hoare & Bond Ltd. coal factors
  Gothard Charles & Co. Ltd. coal merchts
15 *Marconi's Wireless Telegraph Co. Ltd.*
15 *Marconi's International Marine*
  Communications Co. Ltd
15 Saunders Henry Spearman, merchant
15 *Clinical Research Association Ltd.*
  C. H. Wells, managing director
15 *Medical Agency,*
  J. A. Reaside, managing director
15 Reaside James Aikman, medical agent
15 Blencowe John Ebenezer, accountant
15 Wells Charles Henry, accountant
19 Bottomley William, builder
19 Buckle James George, architect
19 *British Institution Scholarship Fund,*
  Frederick A. Eaton, sec
20 Hawkins Miss Amelia, apartments
21 Gardner William, house agent
  Godfree (E.), Felton & Co. wine
  merchants. (8,9&10 Adelphi Arches)
.... *here are Adelphi arches* ....

1915

York buildings, *Adelphi* (W.C.)
(WESTMINSTER), 14 *John st.*

1 Guscotte & Fowler, solicitors
1 Todd Robert, solicitor
5 Parker Albert Edward James,
  advertising agent
5 White Philip, gauger
5 EstlerE.&Kathan, fancy goods importers
6 Crisp Jason Grainger, accountant
6 *Moral Education League,*
  Alexander Farquharson, sec
6 Davies O. F. Ltd. publicity contractors
6 *Church League for Women's Suffrage,*
  Miss L. Corben, organising sec
10 Osborne Charles & Co. Ltd. gun makers
12 Finch Henry William, architect
12 Wilkins Victor, architect
12 Holden & Hardingham, publishers
12 *National Home Reading Union,*
  Miss Josephine Gauntlett, sec
12 Shepherd Lieut.-Col. William
12 Radford George, advertising agent
12 *Ashbourne Publishing Co. Ltd*
12 Evans Charles Edward
  Kerr Mrs. Walter, lime light supplier
15 WATERGATE HOUSE:—
15 Hoare, Gothard & Bond Ltd. coal factors
15 Worsfold & Hayward, auctioneers
15 *London Opinion*
15 *Clinical Research Association Ltd.*
  C. H. Wells, managing director
15 Curry William James, accountant
15 *Medical Agency,*
  J. A. Reaside, managing director
15 Reaside James Aikman, medical agent
15 Blencowe John Ebenezer, accountant
15 Wells Charles Henry, accountant
18 Pattern & Pattern Ltd. estate agents
19 Thomas Walter Joseph, builder
19 Buckle James George, architect
19 *British Institution Scholarship Fund,*
  Frederick A. Eaton, sec
19 Melrose Andrew & Co. wholesale
  coffee dealers
  Godfree (E.), Felton & Co. wine
  merchants. (8,9&10 Adelphi arches)
.... *here is Lower Robert street* .....

166

GEORGE STREET – YORK BUILDINGS from 1852

1920

York buildings, *Adelphi* (W.C. 2)
(WESTMINSTER), 14 *John st.*

1	Guscotte & Fowler, solicitors
5	Baxter James, gauger
6	*League of the Church Militant,*
	Miss L. Corben, organising sec
6	*Rural Housing & Sanitation Association*
6	*Women's Industrial Council (Incorporated),*
	Mrs. Boyd Dawson, sec
10	Osborne Charles & Co. Ltd. gun makers
10	Finch Henry William, architect
12	Wilkins Victor, architect
12	Holden & Hardingham, publishers
12	Bowden Henry W. civil engineer
12	*National Home Reading Union,*
	Miss J. Swanson, sec
12	Radford George, advertising agent
12	Evans Charles Edward
12	Andrée Miss Margot, fashion artist
15	WATERGATE HOUSE:—
15	*Clinical Research Association Ltd.*
	C. H. Wells, managing director
15	Curry William James, accountant
15	*Medical Agency,*
	J. A. Reaside, managing director
15	Reaside James Aikman, medical agent
15	Blencowe John Ebenezer, accountant
18	Clermont & Pattern Ltd. property
	owners
19	Thomas Walter Joseph, builder
19	Buckle James George, architect
19	*British Institution Scholarship Fund,*
	J. G. Buckle, sec
19	Rotary Exchange Ltd
21	Selwyn & Blount, publishers
21	Godfree E. & Co. wine merchants.
	(8,9&10 Adelphi arches)

. . . . . . *here is Lower Robert street.* . . . . . .

1925

York buildings, *Adelphi* (W.C. 2)
(WESTMINSTER), 14 *John st.*

1	Guscotte, Fowler & Cox, solicitors
4	Bevir Ernest & Son, solicitors
4	Ellison Robert K. architect
5	Order of Crusaders
6	Allnutt John & Co. Ltd. wine
	& spirit merchants
10	Osborne Charles & Co. Ltd. gun makers
12	Wilkins Victor, architect
12	Holden Robert & Co. Ltd. publishers
12	Bowden Henry W. civil engineer
12	*National Home Reading Union*
12	Radford George, advertising agent
12	Evans Charles Edward
12	Andrée Miss Margot, fashion artist
15	WATERGATE HOUSE:—
15	Royal Sea Bathing Hospital
	(Margate) (offices)
15	*Medical Research Council*
15	*Industrial Fatigue Research Board*
15	*Clinical Research Association Ltd*
15	Curry William James, accountant
15	*Medical Agency*
15	Bunge Julius Henri O. consulting
	engineer
15	*Institution of Automobile Engineers*
15	Reaside James Aikman, medical agent
15	Blencowe John E. accountant
16 & 17	Pitt Sydney
16 & 17	Kitson Thomas
18	Adelphi (The) (editorial office)
19	*British Institution Scholarship Fund*
19	Cooper George S. accountant
19	Crowe Harry Percy, solicitor
21	Selwyn & Blount, publishers
	Godfree (E.), Felton & Co. wine
	merchants.(7,8,9&10 Adelphi arches)

. . . . . . *here is Lower Robert street.* . . . . . .

1930

York buildings, *Adelphi* (W.C. 2)
(WESTMINSTER), 14 *John st.*

1	Guscotte, Fowler & Cox, solicitors
4	Bevir Ernest & Son, solicitors
5	Middletons (Aberdeen) Ltd. fine
	art publishers
6	Allnutt John & Co. Ltd. wine
	& spirit merchants
12	Wilkins Victor, architect
12	Hamilton Mrs. Mary Agnes, M.P
12	Adelphi Publicity Co. Ltd.
	advertising agents
15	WATERGATE HOUSE:—
15	Royal Sea Bathing Hospital
	(Margate) (offices)
15	*Clinical Research Association Ltd*
15	Curry William James, accountant
15	*Medical Agency*
15	Bunge, Henderson & Co. Ltd
	mechanical engineers
15	*Institution of Automobile Engineers*
15	Blencowe John E. accountant
15	Heywood Bros. iron ore importers
18	Alston Rivers Ltd. publishers
18	Bookman's Journal & Print Collector
	Godfree (E.), Felton & Co. wine
	merchants.(7,8,9&10 Adelphi arches)

. . . . . . *here is Lower Robert street* . . . . . .

21	Halcyon Publicity Ltd. advertising agents

1935

York buildings, *Adelphi* (W.C. 2)
(WESTMINSTER), 14 *John st.*

1	Guscotte, Fowler & Cox, solicitors
4	Bevir Ernest & Son, solicitors
5	Our Cats' Publishing Co. Ltd
6	Allnutt John & Co. Ltd. wine
	& spirit merchants
10	Pilgrim Trust
12	Wilkins Victor, architect
12	Scott, Chesterton & Shepherd, architects
12	Arbuthnot Francis S
15	WATERGATE HOUSE:—
15	Royal Sea Bathing Hospital
	(Margate) (offices)
15	Cartwright Ernest George Frederick,
	accountant
15	Heywood Bros. iron ore importers
15	Pumpmobil Ltd. pump manufacturers
15	*Clinical Research Association Ltd*
15	Royal Humane Society
15	National Federation of Retail
	Newsagents, Booksellers & Stationers
15	*Institution of Automobile Engineers*
	CARLTON MANSIONS:—
	Hancock Mrs
	Johnston Miss
	Newbery Frederick
	Stewart Mrs
	Turpin Robert T
	Wolseley Mrs
	Godfree (E.), Felton & Co. wine
	merchants. (10 Adelphi arches)
18, 19 & 20	Wallis G. E. & Sons
	Ltd. builders
18, 19 & 20	Broadmead Products Co
18, 19 & 20	Bernard R.H.F.W. Ltd.
	advertisement agents
18, 19 & 20	Saturday Review Office
18, 19 & 20	National Review Ltd

. . . . . . *here is Lower Robert street.* . . . . . .

1936

York buildings, *Adelphi* (W.C. 2)
(WESTMINSTER), 14 *John st.*

1	Guscotte, Fowler & Cox, solicitors
4	Bevir Ernest & Son, solicitors
5	Adams Lunch Club
5	Bees Club
6	Allnutt John & Co. Ltd. wine
	& spirit merchants
10	Pilgrim Trust
12	Wilkins Victor, architect
12	Scott, Chesterton & Shepherd, architects
12	Arbuthnot Francis S
15	WATERGATE HOUSE:—
15	Royal Sea Bathing Hospital
	(Margate) (offices)
15	Cartwright Ernest George Frederick,
	accountant
15	*Clinical Research Association Ltd*
15	Royal Humane Society
15	National Federation of Retail
	Newsagents, Booksellers & Stationers
15	*Institution of Automobile Engineers*
	CARLTON MANSIONS:—
	Dolman Mrs
	Earl Max
	Johnston Miss
	Marshall Mrs
	Sharman Miss
	Stewart Mrs
	Turpin Robert T
	Wolseley Mrs
	Godfree (E.), Felton & Co. wine
	merchants. (10 Adelphi arches)
18	York Adelphi Club
18, 19 & 20	Wallis G. E. & Sons Ltd.
	builders
18, 19 & 20	Broadmead Products Co
18, 19 & 20	Bernard Advertising Ltd.
	advertisement agents
18, 19 & 20	Saturday Review Office
21	Hudson Ernest W. solicitor

. . . . . . *here is Lower Robert street.* . . . . . .

JOHN STREET

1841

John street, *Adelphi*, 18 *Adam st.*

1 to 4 *Adelphi hotel*, William Chaplin
5 Bramah Fox & Co.engineers&machinists
5 Cumberledge C.N. architect & surveyor
5 Elster Derrick John, esq
5 Lammin William Henry, solicitor
5 Marratt William, solicitor
6 *Commissioners in Lunacy*
6 Cox Edward H. auctioneer & surveyor
6 Du Bois Edward, clerk to com. in lunacy
6 *Newspaper Press Benevolent Association,*
   attendance Monday & Sat. 11 to 3
6 Nicholson Rev. Hugh, clerical agent &c
6 Puddick John Edward, wine merchant
7 Hilton Thomas W. esq
7 Jarvis Thomas, solicitor
7 *Londn & West. Coal Co.* J.Smith, mgr
7 Speer Edward, esq
8 Goolden Richard Henry, physician
9 Heinrich Andrew, attorney
9 Parker Frederick, esq
9 Todd Anthony M. esq
10 Chippendale John, navy agent
10 Pittar & Co. diamond & jewel merchants
. . . . *Robert street* . . . .
11 Garland & Christopher, architects &c
11 Jackson & Johnson, solicitors, &c
11 Jones Owen, architect
11 Todd & Bosanquet, wine merchants
12 Avern William, tailor
13 Harris William John, esq
13 Lane Charles, medical agent
13 Morton David, coal merchant, &c
13 Powell David Wilson, esq
14 Croft Alban, professor of music
14 Jones William, surgeon
. . . . *George street* . . . . *James street* . . . .
19 *Society of Arts*, William A. Graham, sec.
20 *Metropolitan Wood Paving Company,*
   William Prosser, secretary
20 Bloxam Alfred, wine merchant
21 *Equitable Gas Light Company,*
   George Johnson Gregory,
22 Thomson D.C. surgeon & dentist

1845

John street, *Adelphi,*
18 *Adam st.* & 6 *Duke st.*

1 to 4 *Adelphi hotel*, William Chaplin
5 Cumberledge C.N. architect & surveyor
5 Elster Derrick John, esq
5 Hill David, solicitor
5 Lammin William Henry, solicitor
5 Williams Frederick Sims, solicitor
ADELPHI CHAMBERS:—
6 *London Patent Champagne Company,*
   Walter Watts, secretary
6 Nicholson Rev. Hugh, clerical agent &c
6 Rumble & Sadgrove, architects
7 Cook John Douglas, esq
7 Cooke Layton, surveyor & estate agent
7 Hallett William T. esq
7 Grey Thomas William, solicitor
7 *Londn &Westm Coal Co.* J.Shotter, mgr
7 Speer Edward, esq
7 Winter Henry, solicitor
8 Goolden Richard Henry, physician
9 Alexander George, esq
9 Emmett & Chadwick, architects
9 Enright F.J.C. writing & copying office
9 Gale Joseph Waller, civil engineer
9 Johnson John James, architect
10 Chippendale Augustus, solicitor
10 Chippendale John, navy agent
10 Pittar & Co. diamond & jewel merchants
10 Strickland Frederick, esq
. . . . . . *here Robert street intersects* . . . . . .
11 Garland & Christopher, architects &c
11 Holland Henry, architect
11 Jackson & Jenkyn, solicitors, &c
11 James John Kingston, esq
11 Todd & Bosanquet, wine merchants
11 Todd & James, wine merchants
12 Avern William, tailor
12 *Cwmorthin Slate Company,*
   Thomas Arthur Corlett, sec
12 Sankey & Cundy, civil engineers
12 Saward Alfred, accountant
12 Saward Henry, solicitor
13 Lane & Rathbone, medical agents
13 Williams Charles, solicitor
13 Winter Thomas John, solicitor
14 Strutt John, solicitor
. . *here George st. & James st. intersect* . .
15 Blenkinsop John, esq
19 *Society of Arts*, Francis Whishaw, sec
20 Carlisle Septimus E. esq
20 Grimshaw George Garnet, stockbroker
20 Hatchett John, esq
20 Sanford Feake, solicitor
21 *Equitable Gas Light Company,*
   George Johnson Gregory, esq. sec
22 Peacock Thomas Love, esq

1850

John street, *Adelphi,*
18 *Adam st.* & 6 *Duke st.*

1 to 4 *Adelphi hotel*, Elder & Jurdison
5 Cumberledge C.N. architect & surveyor
5 Elster Derrick John, esq
5 Hill David, solicitor
5 Lammin William Henry, solicitor
5 Sanford Feake, solicitor
ADELPHI CHAMBERS:—
   Derbyshire Henry A. architect
   Jee Alfred S. civil engineer
   Nicholson Rev. Hugh, clerical agent &c
   Scott Michael, civil engineer
7 *Ambergate, Nottingham, &c. Railway*
   Company, Thos. Wm. Gray, agt
7 Grey Thomas William, solicitor
7 *Londn &Westm Coal Co.* J. Smith, mgr
7 Sandys, Vivian & Co. engineers, &c
7 Hocking Samuel, engineer
7 Ornsby Robert, esq
7 Rowland Charles, coal merchant
8 Goddard George Henry, architect
8 Hall Edward, architect
8 Prior William Henry, artist on wood
8 Shearman Montague, solicitor
9 Finden & Lewis, architects
9 *General Telegraph Company,*
   Henry Corbett, sec
9 Johnson John James, architect
9 Ordish Frederick, architect
9 Whishaw Francis, engineer
10 Chippendale John, Navy agent
10 Chippendale Augustus, solicitor
10 Pittar (Parke) & Co. east india agents
. . . . . . *here Robert street intersects* . . . . . .
11 James John K. esq
11 Jenkyn James, solicitor &c
11 Jenkyn Osborn, solicitor
11 Pare William, railway traffic statist
11 *Irish Engineering Company,*
   T.E. Weller, agent
11 Finch John & Sons, iron merchants
   (Liverpool)   T.E. Weller, agent
11 Todd & James, wine merchants
11 Russell John Scott, engineer
12 Avern William, tailor
   NEW ADELPHI CHAMBERS:—
   Brown Charles, solicitor
   Gale William Paul, surveyor
   Parsons Percival Moses, civil engineer
   Shanks Andrew & Co. engineers, &c
   Wells John James, wine & spirit mercht
   Winter Henry, solicitor
13 Lane Gore Ousley, architect & surveyor
13 Lane Edward, medical agent
14 Bishop John Drinkwater, esq
14 Hopper George, esq
14 Price Robert Alexander, esq
14 *Polonceau's Bitumen Company,*
   John Pilkington, manager
. . *here George st. & James st. intersect* . .
15 Blenkinsop John, esq
18 & 19 *Society of Arts*, John Scott Russell,
   secretary
20 Child George & Charles, surveyors
20 Hatchett John, esq
21 *Equitable Gas Light Company,*
   George Johnson Gregory, esq. sec
22 Peacock Thomas Love, esq

1855

John street, *Adelphi,*
18 *Adam st.* & 6 *Duke st.*

1 to 4 *Adelphi hotel*, Charles Elder
5 Cumberledge Charles N. architect
5 Elster Derrick John, esq
5 Fogg William, solicitor
5 Hill David, solicitor
5 Lammin William Henry, solicitor
5 Sanford Feake, solicitor
ADELPHI CHAMBERS:—
   Jee Alfred S. civil engineer
   Wakley James Goodchild, esq
   Withers James, esq
   Withers Richard Jewell, esq
   Wolfhagen & Co. merchants
6 Badock John William, esq
7 Evans Morris, surveyor
7 Hocking Samuel, engineer
7 Siemens William Charles, civil engineer
7 Sams Luke, photographic paper preparer
7 Sandys, Vivian & Co. engineers
8 Ancona Joseph S. auctioneer
8 Ordish Frederick Webster, architect
8 Hall Edward, architect
8 Shearman Montague, solicitor
8 Woods Henry N. engraver on wood
9 Finden & Lewis, architects
9 Johnson John, architect
9 Roe William, architect
9 Whishaw Francis, engineer
10 Chippendale Augustus, navy agent &
   solicitor
10 Wheeler & Caistor, solicitors
. . . . . . *here Robert street intersects* . . . . . .
11 *Catholic Poor School Committee,*
   Hon. Charles Langdale, sec
11 Eden William, esq
11 Nichols Robert Cradock, esq
11 Stead Alexander, esq
11 Todd (R.) & James, wine merchants
12 Avern William Henry, tailor
   NEW ADELPHI CHAMBERS:—
   Barlow James, accountant
   Shanks Andrew & Co. engineers, &c
   Watson&Cuthburt,matrimonl.instn.
   Winter Henry, solicitor
   Messenger John William, esq
   Slater William, architect
   Smith William, architect
13 Deacon George, esq
13 Oneal Miss
13 Soulsby Matthew, esq
14 Carpenter William, esq
14 Lane & Lara, medical agents
14 Lara Benjamin Walters, esq
14 Bernard Madame
14 Stuart Samuel, esq
14 Russell Henry Heathcote, architect
. . *here York bldgs. & James st. intersect* . .
15 Blenkinsop John, esq
18 & 19 *Society of Arts,*
   Peter Le Neve Foster, esq. M.A. sec
   Colonial & International Postage Ass.
   George Wagstaff Yapp, acting sec
20 Burgass George, esq
20 Lawford & Heneker, architects
20 Wood Thomas, esq
20 *Royal National Lifeboat Institution for the*
   Preservation of Life from Shipwreck,
   Richard Lewis, sec
20 *Life Boat Institution,*
   Richard Lewis, secretary
21 *Equitable Gas Light Company,*
   Samuel Andrews, esq. sec
22 *Church of England & General Freehold*
   Land Society

JOHN STREET

1860

John street, *Adelphi* (W.C.),
18 *Adam street* & 6 *Duke street.*
1 to 4 *Adelphi hotel*, Charles Elder
5   Cumberledge Charles N. architect
5   Elster Derrick John, esq
5   Lammin William Henry, solicitor
5   Sanford Feake, solicitor
   ADELPHI CHAMBERS:—
     Lamb Lieut. Henry
     Hale William, civil engineer
     Waller William Henry, solicitor
     Scott William Henry, esq
     Pite Alfred Robert, architect
     Wakley James Goodchild, M.D.
     Porter John Thomas Brown & Co.
       London & Lincoln.
       National coal gas apparatus
7   Evans Morris, surveyor
7   Thompson George & Co. Crookhay
       iron works
7   Rewman Bros.importers of foreign goods
8   Ancona Joseph S. surveyor & auctioneer
8   Freeman Richard Marriott, solicitor
8   Hall Edward, F.S.A. architect
8   Lane Albert, esq
8   Shearman Montague, solicitor
8   Swinburn James, ship broker
8   Woods Henry N. engraver on wood
9   Lewis Thomas Hayter, architect
9   Johnson John, architect
9   Pearson Thomas, surveyor
9   Preston William, appraiser
9   Winton Walter de, civil engineer
10   Chippendale Augustus, navy agent
10   Littaur William, professor of languages
. . . . *here is Robert street* . . . .
11   Eden William, esq
11   Nichols Robert Cradock, esq
11   Noble John Gould, esq
11   Bannister Hugh, esq
11   Tod-Heatly & Co. wine merchants
12   Avern William Henry, tailor
   NEW ADELPHI CHAMBERS:—
     Boissonnas & Pilet, watch manufrs
     Napier Hon. William
     Hills Gordon Macdonald, architect
     Smith William, architect
     Shanks Andrew & Co. engineers, &c
     Stuart Capt. Henry Benson
     Winter Henry, solicitor
13   Deacon Philip, esq
13   Codd Frederick, architect
14   *Royal National Lifeboat Institution for the*
     Preservation of Life from Shipwreck,
       Richard Lewis, secretary
14   *Life Boat Institution,*
       Richard Lewis, secretary
14   Stuart Samuel, esq
14   Ward Capt J.R. R.N.
. . . *here are York buildings & James st.* . . .
15   Blenkinsop John, esq
18 & 19 *Society of Arts,*
     Peter Le Neve Foster, esq. M.A. sec
     Charles Critchett, B.A. assistant sec
     Samuel Thomas Davenport, financial off.
20   Burgass George, esq
20   Stuart & Smith, ironfounders,
       Benjamin Barber, agent
20   Wood Thomas, esq
21 & 22   *Equitable Gas Light Company,*
       Samuel Andrews, esq. sec

1865

John street, *Adelphi* (W.C.),
18 *Adam street* & 6 *Duke street.*
1 to 4 *Adelphi hotel*, Charles Elder
5   Baker Henry, esq
5   Lammin William Henry, solicitor
5   Summerlin & Bruce, solicitors
6   ADELPHI CHAMBERS:—
     Puddick John Edward, auctioneer
     Hale William, civil engineer
     GribbleChas.Risdon,architect&surv
7   *Bonelli's Electric Telegraph Co. (limited),*
       James Gutteres, sec
7   Evans Morris, surveyor
7   Moss (J.) & Gamble Bros. steel manuftrs
7   Porter John Thos.Brown&Co.gas engnrs
7   Peirse & Nash, publishers &c
7   Shearman Montague, solicitor
8   Ancona Joseph Supino, surveyor &c
8   Woods Henry N. engraver on wood
9   Lewis Thomas Hayter, architect
9   Johnson John, architect
9   *Kirkstall Forge Co.*   Wm. Craven, agent
10   DRUMMOND CHAMBERS:—
     Burbidge John, artist
     Gale William Paul, civil engineer
     Lepard John Thos. architect & survr
     Church Samuel King, merchant
     King-Church Samuel, merchant
     Muir William & Co. engineers
     Danish Land Co. (limited),
       Saml.King-Church,mang.directr
     River Fergus Navigation & Embankment Co.
       S. King-Church, mang. director
. . . . *here is Robert street* . . . .
11   Hankey Beaumont, esq
11   Bryant George, esq
11   Bannister Hugh, esq
11   Tod-Heatly & Co. wine merchants
12   Avern William Henry, tailor
12   NEW ADELPHI CHAMBERS:—
     Clarke Thomas Viner, esq
     Griffin George F. civil engineer
     The Economic Permanent Way Co
     Hills Gordon Macdonald, architect
     Napier Hon. William
     Powell John Folliott, esq
     PritchettGeo.Jas.engnr. & contractr
     Smith William, architect
     Shanks Andrew & Co. engineers, &c
     Staunton Henry Charlton, esq
     Sone John, esq
     Winter Henry, solicitor
13   Blunt Captain Richard John
13   Travers Henry & Co. merchants
13   Yeldham Richard, architect & surveyor
14   *Royal National Lifeboat Institution for the*
     Preservation of Life from Shipwreck,
       Richard Lewis, secretary
14   Clemence Mr. John, jun
. . *here are York buildings & James st.* . . . .
18 & 19 *Society of Arts*
20   Burgass George, esq
20   Stuart & Smith, ironfounders
20   Wood Thomas, esq
20   *Lord's Day Observance Society,*
       Rev. Henry Stevens, M.A. sec
21 & 22   *Equitable Gas Light Company,*
       Samuel Andrews, esq. sec

1870

John street, *Adelphi* (W.C.),
18 *Adam street* & 6 *Duke st.*
1 to 4 *Adelphi hotel*, Charles Elder
5   Best Hon. Capt. Robert Rainie
5   Lammin William Henry, solicitor
5   Pamphilon Frederick William, solicitor
6   ADELPHI CHAMBERS:—
     Paice William, architect & surveyor
     Shepard Henry, architect
     GribbleChas.Risdon,architect&surv
     Nightingale J.S. architect & surveyor
     Sharpe & Co. wine merchants
7   Hahn John Mellish Kay, architect
7   Evans Morris, surveyor
7   Cooper Wilbye
7   *West End Stock, Share & Investment*
     Agency,   Frank Limmer, sec
7   Porter John Thomas B. & Co. gas engnrs
7   Pierse & Nashes, publishers &c
8   Ancona Joseph Supino, surveyor
8   Heritage Lewis, solicitor
8   Cooper Francis
8   Mitchell Dr. James Carr
8   Montero J. Manuel
9   Davis John & Co. auctioneers
9   Johnstone Andrew Douglas,
     civil engineer
9   Lewis Thomas Hayter, architect
9   Baynham Walter Lewis, solicitor
9   Cumming John, F.G.S. surveyor
9   Blackwell & Hurdman, auctioneers
10   DRUMMOND CHAMBERS:—
     Burbidge John, artist
     Fish John, architect & surveyor
     Lockwood Alfred & William Henry,
       architects
     Harvey George, artist
     Chapman George Edward, merchant
     Smith William, architect
     Brown Sir John & Co. (limited)
     Atlas Steel, Iron & Armourplate Works
     (Sheffield)
       John Clowes Bailey, Lond. mgr
     Bayley John Clowes, engnrg agent
     Edwards Francis, architect
. . . . *here is Robert street* . . . .
11   Brownrigg Henry Moore
11   Hankey Sydney Alers
11   Hankey Beaumont
11   Bryant George
11   Bannister Hugh
11   Tod-Heatly & Co. wine merchants
12   NEW ADELPHI CHAMBERS:—
     Hills Gordon Macdonald, architect
     Lightfoot & Robson, solicitors
     Pritchett Geo. J. engnr. & contractr
     Sone John
     Köhn Ferdinand, civil engineer
13   Bentley John Francis, architect
13   Seymour William, architect & surveyor
13   Seymour Edward, solicitor
14   *Royal National Lifeboat Institution for the*
     Preservation of Life from Shipwreck,
       Richard Lewis, secretary
14   *New Rupia Co. (limited),*
       William Kelk, sec
. . *here are York buildings & James st.* . . .
18 & 19 *Society of Arts*
20   Carter William Adolphus, architect &c
20   Davey Henry, civil engineer
20   Burgass George
20   *Lord's Day Observance Society,*
       Rev. John Gritton, sec
20   Summerlin Thomas Hopkins, solicitor
21 & 22   *Equitable Gas Light Company,*
       Samuel Andrews, sec

1875

John street, *Adelphi* (W.C.),
18 *Adam street* & 6 *Duke st.*
1 to 4 *Adelphi hotel*, Charles Elder
5   Lammin William Henry, solicitor
     Cockerell John
     Pamphilon Frederick William, solicitor
6 & 7   ADELPHI CHAMBERS:—
     Lynam & Ebbetts, architects
     Anti-Adulteration Association Limited,
     for Enforcing & Amending the
     Laws Against Adulteration,
       Thomas Payne, sec
     London Gas Reform Association,
       M.S. Myers, sec
     Brangwyn William C. architect
     Withall Latham Augustus, architect
     Evans Morris, surveyor
     Allen Theophilus, architect
     Harvie Edward C. F.R.G.S.
     Luker George L
     Hammond Philip
     Hunter Leslie
     Bickerdike George, gas engineer
     Gribble Charles Risdon, architect
       & surveyor
     Axmann Riland Winter, architect
     Perrott Edmund Thomas, architect
     Lizard & Poltesco SerpentineMarble
     Works Co.   William Simons, manager
     Cunningham Percy Burdett, solicitor
8   Ancona Joseph Supino, surveyor
     Cook Charles C. contractor
     Chubb & Maclean, civil engineers
     Parkinson George Lovell, solicitor
     Tupp Gerald John, engineer
     Howie & Young, boiler makers
     Vickarys & Robertson, gas engineers
     Montrose Foundry Co
9   Gardiner William, solicitor
     Middlesex Liberal Registration Society,
       C.S. Dear, sec
     Lewis Thomas Hayter, F.S.A. architect
     Baynham Walter Lewis, solicitor
     Douglass James Heger, solicitor
     Wales George Richard, surveyor
     Birch John, architect & surveyor
     Thorpe John, surveyor
     Taylor Peter de Nully, shorthand writer
10   DRUMMOND CHAMBERS:—
     Royal Literary Fund
     Society of Schoolmasters,
       Octavian Blewett, K.L. sec
     Fish John, architect & surveyor
     Lockwood William Henry, architect
     Smith William, architect
     Brown Sir John & Co. Limited
     Atlas Steel, Iron & Armourplate
     Works (Sheffield)
       Edward Huntley, Lond. mgr
     Edwards Francis, architect
     Richards John, mechanical engineer
     Burrow & Butson Mining Co. Limited,
       Henry von Uster, F.G.S. sec
     von Uster Henry, F.G.S. mining engineer
12   NEW ADELPHI CHAMBERS:—
     Hills Gordon Macdonald, architect
     Lightfoot & Robson, solicitors
     Pritchett George James, engineer
     Sone John
     Butler Frederick Richard
     Ringer Nelson Stewart
     Green Everard
. . . . . . here is Robert street . . . .
13   Bentley John Francis, architect
     Seymour William, architect & surveyor
     Gundry Horace, architect

JOHN STREET

1880

14   *Royal National Lifeboat Institution for the Preservation of Life from Shipwreck,*
        Richard Lewis, secretary
     Royal National Hospital for Consumption,
        Ernest Morgan, sec
     Hassall Dr. Arthur Hill
. . . here are York buildings & James st. . . .
18 & 19 Society of Arts,
        Peter Le Neve Foster, M.A. sec
20   *Lord's Day Observance Society,*
        Rev. John Gritton, sec
     Institution of Naval Architects,
        A. Sedgwick Wooley, assist. sec
     Burgass George
21   Peirce John S. civil engineer
     Foster E. & Co. merchants
     Kennaway & Co. wine merchants

John street, *Adelphi* (W.C.),
   18 *Adam street* & 6 *Duke st.*
1 to 4 *Adelphi hotel,* Charles Elder
5   Pamphilon Frederick William, solicitor
     Palmer Ralph C
     Malcolm John
     Dunnage George A. architect
     Foster Henry Parfoot, architect
     Howard Maurice
6 & 7 ADELPHI CHAMBERS:—
    6 Pemberton William, solicitor
       Cobbett William Vines Holt, solicitor
       Purdue William
       Luker George L. artist
       Bigge Matthew R. land agent
    7 Bickerdike George, gas engineer
       Axmann Riland Winter, architect
       Evans Morris, surveyor
       Allen Theophilus, architect
       Willicombe Alfred, commission agent
       Audley Coal & Iron Co.
       Bignall Hill Collieries,
       Stafford Coal & Iron Co.
       Washorough Iron Co. Rochley Collieries,
          Alfred Willicombe, agent
       Masterman William, B.C.L
       Clunn Alfred J. wine merchant
       Codling Charles Henry, accountant
       General Mortgage (Reversions & Annuities)
         Society, C.H. Codling, manager
    8 Ancona Joseph Supino, surveyor
       Birch John, architect & surveyor
       Howell & Brooks, surveyors
       Smith Henry, surveyor
       Kaye John Edward, land agent
       Russell & Co. publishers
       Finance Chronicle Office
       Harnor Edward, architect
       Waters George Alfred, architect
    9 Gardiner, South & Weedon, solicitors
       Perry & Reed, architects
       Baynham Walter Lewis, solicitor
       Douglass James Heger, solicitor
       Wilkin William
       Thorpe John, surveyor
       Colyer Francis J. solicitor
       Taylor Peter de Nully, shorthand writer
10   DRUMMOND CHAMBERS:—
      London Co-operative Wine Association
        Limited, Walter M. Gee, managing dirctr
      Fish John, architect & surveyor
      Lockwood William Henry, architect
      Smith William, architect
      Edwards Francis, architect
      Patrick George, architect
12   NEW ADELPHI CHAMBERS:—
12   Head Robert Garnett, tea dealer
      Robson John, solicitor
      Pritchett George James, engineer
      Sone John
. . . . *here is Robert street* . . . .
13   Pollard Harry E. surveyor
      Bentley John Francis, architect
      Gundry Horace, architect
      Norman George Lewis, solicitor
14   *Royal National Lifeboat Institution for the*
      Preservation of Life from Shipwreck,
        Richard Lewis, esq. sec
      Robins Edward Cookworthy, architect
. . . here are York buildings & James st. . . .
11   Ward Charles J
18 & 19 *Society of Arts,*
        H. Trueman Wood, B.A. sec
        Henry B. Wheatley, assist. sec
        Howard H. Room, accountant
20   *Lord's Day Observance Society,*
        Rev. John Gritton, sec
      Reid Patrick S. mining engineer
     English Spelling Reform Association,
        John Finton, sec
21   Kennaway & Co. wine merchants
      Foster E. & Co. merchants

1885

John street, *Adelphi* (W.C.),
   18 *Adam street* & 6 *Duke st.*
1 to 4 *Adelphi hotel,* Charles Elder
5   Malcolm John
     Palmer Ralph C
     Dunnage George A. architect
     Foster Henry Pafoot, architect
     Pinches Frederick, architect
6 & 7 ADELPHI CHAMBERS:—
    6 Bigge Matthew R. land agent
       Anthony Robert G
       Hulton Reginald E
       Roughton Kirkham Gardner
       Lewis Arthur C. solicitor
       Brown A. & Co. accountants
       Alley John, accountant
    7 Andrew James, architect
       Chapple John Starling, architect
       Bickerdike George, gas engineer
       Evans Morris, surveyor
       Willicombe Alfred, coal agent
       Masterman William, D.C.L
       Wing Vincent, architect
       Burrell Alfred Lloyd
       Clunn Alfred J. wine merchant
8   *Spelling Reform Association,*
       C. B. Arding & D. Pitcairn, hon. secs
     Index Society,
       H. B. Wheatley, F.S.A. director
     St. George's Society, J. Fenton, hon.sec
     Farrar R. Henry, F.R.Hist.Soc
     Fenton John, B.A
     Birch John, architect & surveyor
     Howell & Brooks, surveyors
     Smith Henry, surveyor
     Pennington & Brigden, architects
     Russell & Co. publishers
     Finance Chronicle Office
     Harnor Edward, architect
     Lochhead John, architect
9   Gardiner & Son, solicitors
     Millington Frederick Gray, solicitor
     Colyer Francis J. solicitor
     Perry & Reed, architects
     Baynham Walter Lewis, solicitor
     Wilkin William
     Thorpe John, surveyor
     Taylor Peter de Nully, shorthand writer
10   DRUMMOND CHAMBERS:—
     London Co-operative Wine Association
       Limited,
        Walter M. Gee, managing dirctr
     Bassett-Smith William, architect
     Munt Edwin James, architect
     Edwards Francis, architect
     LendonRichardWilliamPenry,archtct
     Cycloidal Propeller Co
     Ives John, consulting engineer
     Newbould Williamson, solicitor
     Barber William, architect
     Burbridge John, artist
     Union Investment Corporation Lim.
       Alfred Harrison, man.dir
     Harrison Alfred, accountant
12   NEW ADELPHI CHAMBERS:—
     Robson John, solicitor
     Sacred Harmonic Society,
       A. J. Puttick, hon. sec
     Rodriguez Epfanio
     Hale Major
. . . . *here is Robert street* . . . .
13   Bentley John Francis, architect
     Gundry Horace, architect
     Bristow William, solicitor
     Shaft George Thomas, solicitor
     Purdue William, surveyor
     Green Rev. Arthur, M.A
14   *Royal National Lifeboat Institution for the*
      Preservation of Life from Shipwreck,
        Charles Dibdin, esq. sec

14   Robins Edward Cookworthy, architect
. . . here are York buildings & James st. . . .
11   Logan William George
18 & 19 *Society of Arts,*
        H. Trueman Wood, M.A. sec
20   Cobbett William Vines Holt, solicitor
     Upton Robert Philip, solicitor
     Heritage Lewis, solicitor
     Reid Patrick S. mining engineer
     Reid Thomas Boosey, land surveyor
     Reineker Capt. Hermann
21   *St. Stephen's Review Office*
     Foster Edwin & Co. merchants
     Imperial Deposit Bank & Building Society,
       Charles J. Knightley, man.
     Church of England Mission Society,
       Rev. S.W. Darwin Fox, M.A. sec

JOHN STREET

1890

John street, *Adelphi* (W.C.),
18 Adam street & *6 Duke st.*

1 to 4 *Adelphi hotel*, Charles Elder
5   Malcolm John
5   Pinches Frederick, architect
5   *Thompson's Patent Gravity*
      Switchback Railway Co. Lim
5   Applin Vincent Augustin, solicitor
5   Pope Alexander, architect
6 & 7 ADELPHI CHAMBERS:—
      Chubb Arthur Bruce, solicitor
      Roughton Kirkham Gardner
      Francis Leon A. architect
      Dearle William Henry, architect
      Boxall Alfred, surveyor
      Phillips Basil Watts
7   Robinson James Thomas, land agent
      Scurry & Wright, architects
      Chapple John Starling, architect
      Evans Morris & Son, surveyors
      Cornish & Gaymer, builders
      Colling James Kellaway, architect
      Strong Alfred, architect
      Clunn Alfred J. wine merchant
      Bickerdike George, gas engineer
      Cooper William Laurence
8   Peach Charles Stanley, architect
8   Barber Samuel, civil engineer
8   Birch John, architect & surveyor
8   Smith Henry, surveyor
8   Pennington & Bridgen, architects
8   Waller Frederick William, architect
8   Williams Robert, architect
8   Russell & Co. publishers
8   *Finance Chronicle Office*
8   Harnor Edward, architect
8   Lochhead John, architect
9   Gardiner & Son, solicitors
9   Millington Frederick Gray, solicitor
9   Price Henry Herbert, solicitor
9   Perkins William Jackson, solicitor
9   Perry & Reed, architects
9   Baynham Walter Lewis, solicitor
9   Thorpe John, surveyor
10   DRUMMOND CHAMBERS:—
      London Co-operative Wine Association
        Limited, Lewis J. Fleet, man
      Harrison Alfred
      Slade & Monk, solicitors
      Bassett-Smith William, architect
      Bassett-Smith Charles Aubry,
        architect
      Edwards Son & Wilkinson, architects
      Patrick George, architect
      South Harry, electrical engineer
      Houghton Thomas Marcus, architect
      Amateur Athletic Association,
              C. Herbert, hon. sec
12   NEW ADELPHI CHAMBERS:—
      Robson John, solicitor
      Upton Robert Philip, solicitor
      Rodriguez Epfanio
      Hale Major
      Andrews & Co. whisky merchants
. . . . *here is Robert street* . . . .
13   Bentley John Francis, architect
13   Bristow William, solicitor
13   Bristow Henry Essex, solicitor
13   Shaft George Thomas, solicitor
13   Purdue William, architect
14   *Royal National Lifeboat Institution for the*
      Preservation of Life from Shipwreck,
            Charles Dibdin, esq. sec
14   Phipson Wilson Weatherley, consulting
      engineer
. . . *here are York buildings,*
     James st. & *Duke street.* . . . .
11   Sinclair Rosseter Lenton Walker

18 & 19 *Society of Arts,*
         H. Trueman Wood, M.A. sec
20   Cobbett William Vines Holt, solicitor
20   Heritage Lewis, solicitor
20   Day Richard Philip, architect
20   Brown David & Co. builders
20   Reid Patrick S. mining engineer
20   Reid Thomas Boosey, land surveyor
21   *St. Stephen's Review Office*
21   *Modern Truth Office*
21   *Puck Office*
21   Foster E. & Co. merchants
21   *Church Parochial Mission Society,*
        Rev. Herbert Muir, sec
21   *Channel Islands Vineries & Early*
      Produce Co. Limited
21   Shove George Henry

1895

John street, *Adelphi* (W.C.),
18 Adam street & *6 Duke st.*

1 to 4 *Adelphi hotel*, John Max Kempner
5   Malcolm Col. John Wingfield C.B
5   Pinches Frederick, architect
5   Harnor Edward, architect
5   *Thompson's Patent Gravity*
      Switchback Railway Co. Lim
5   Applin Vincent Augustin, solicitor
5   Dickinson Richard, architect
6 & 7 ADELPHI CHAMBERS:—
      Chubb Arthur Bruce, solicitor
      Strouss Carl
      Francis Leon A. architect
      Dearle William Henry, architect
      Boxall Alfred, surveyor
      Salomons Edward, architect
7   Robinson James Thomas, land agent
7   Batting Walter, architect
7   Murray & Foster, architects
      Scurry & Wright, architects
      Barrow Ernest Robert, architect
      Chapple John Starling, architect
      Evans Morris & Son, surveyors
      Cornish & Gaymer, builders
      Colling James Kellaway, architect
      Bickerdike George, gas engineer
8   Peach Charles Stanley, architect
8   Birch John, architect & surveyor
8   Smith Henry, surveyor
8   Heyes Austin, architect
8   Pennington Nath. G. & Son, architects
8   Russell & Co. publishers
8   *Finance Chronicle Office*
9   Gardiner & Son, solicitors
9   Buckmaster Alfred Christopher, solicitor
9   Ellis & Co. surveyors
9   Perry & Reed, architects
9   Harriss Walter Fordham, architect
9   Taperell Frederick, surveyor
9   *Labour Association,*
            Henry Vivian, sec
9   Horton Samuel Hoult, architect
9   Tatlock Robert J. architect
9   Booth & Fox, architects
10   DRUMMOND CHAMBERS:—
      Dawson S. & Co. wine merchants
      Bassett-Smith William, architect
      Bassett-Smith Charles Aubry,
        architect
      Edwards Son & Wilkinson, architects
      Patrick George, architect
      Hogg Richard B. surveyor
      Putley Frederick Meller, architect
      Amateur Athletic Association,
              C. Herbert, hon. sec
12   NEW ADELPHI CHAMBERS:—
      London Co-operative Wine Association
        Limited, Lewis J. Fleet, man
      Upton Robert Philip, solicitor
      Andrews & Co. whisky merchants
      Rodriguez Epfanio
      Hale Col
      Sprigge Samuel Squire, M.B
. . . . *here is Robert street* . . . .
13   Bentley John Francis, architect
13   Bristow William, solicitor
13   Bristow Henry Essex, solicitor
13   Purdue William, architect
13   Burrell Alfred Lloyd
14   *Royal National Lifeboat Institution for the*
      Preservation of Life from Shipwreck,
            Charles Dibdin, esq. sec
14   Ashwell & Nesbit, ventilating engineers
. . . *here are York buildings,*
     James st. & *Duke street.* . . . .
11   Sinclair Rosseter Lenton Walker

18 & 19 *Society of Arts,*
        Sir Henry Trueman Wood, M.A. sec
20   STRAND BANK
20   Cobbett William Vines Holt, solicitor
20   Day Richard Philip, architect
20   Reid Patrick S. mining engineer
20   Reid Thomas Boosey, land surveyor
21   *Hotel Press Limited (The)*
21   Foster E. & Co. merchants
21   Pearce Arthur William, solicitor
21   Pooley & Follett, architects
21   *Channel Islands Vineries & Early*
      Produce Co. Limited
21   Edwards Charles H. shorthand writer

JOHN STREET

1900

John street, *Adelphi* (W.C.),
18 *Adam street & 6 Duke st.*

1 to 4	*Adelphi hotel*, Frank Evans
5	Malcolm of Portalloch Lord, C.B
5	Palmer Ralph Charlton, B.A
5	Pinches Frederick, architect
5	*Thompson's Patent Gravity*
	Switchback Railway Co. Lim
5	Ashford Henry Leonard, designer
5	Dickinson Richard, architect
5	Graham Walter, architect
6	Girdwood James, land agent
6	Chubb Arthur Bruce, solicitor
6	*British Exploration Mining Trust*
	Limited
6	Dudgeon Frederick Sear
6	Harber William Francis, architect
6	Kibblewhite Charles E.B
7	Wright James Cornwall, architect
7	Batting Walter, architect
7	Murray John, architect
7	Evans Morris & Son, surveyors
7	Cornish & Gaymer, builders
7	Chapple John Starling, architect
8	Adams & Parkes, medical agents
8	Portman & Co. commission agents
8	Heyes Austin, architect
8	Francis Leon Albert, architect
8	Francis Leon Alfred John, architect
8	Russell & Co. publishers
9	Hewy Walter Henry P. general agent
9	Perry & Reed, architects
9	Taperell Frederick, surveyor
9	Knightley Charles James, accountant
9	*Climax Chemical Co*
9	Fox George Hamblin, architect
10	DRUMMOND CHAMBERS:—
	Ceres Letter & Card Files Co
	Amateur Athletic Association,
	C. Herbert, hon. sec
	Wilkinson Bristowe, architect
	Bassett-Smith William & Charles
	Aubrey, architects
	Clift Kelly, surveyor
	Hogg Richard B. surveyor
	Rutland Archibald Hart, valuer
	Coyle Alfred H. architect
12	NEW ADELPHI CHAMBERS:—
	London Co-operative Wine Association
	Limited, Lewis J. Fleet, man
	Upton Robert Philip, solicitor
	Rodriguez Epfanio
	Stafford Francis Edward, architect
	Hale Col. Thomas
	Bower Alfred Louis
	Murray Rev. John Oswald, M.A
	. . . . *here is Robert street* . . . .
13	Peters, Hall & Co. wine merchants
13	Bentley John Francis, architect
13	Burrell Alfred Lloyd
13	Davis William Edward, surveyor
14	*Royal National Lifeboat Institution for the*
	Preservation of Life from Shipwreck,
	Charles Dibdin, esq. F.R.G.S. sec
	. . . *here are York buildings,*
	James st. & Duke street. . . . .
11	Sinclair Rosseter Lenton Walker
18 & 19	Society of Arts,
	Sir Henry Trueman Wood, M.A. sec
20	Corney John B. & Co.electrical engineers
20	Waller W.H. & Son, solicitors
20	Cobbett William Vines Holt, solicitor
20	*B. & S. Folding Gate Co.*
20	Fetch Ernest Edward, architect
20	Jellis John, quantity surveyor
21	Foster E. & Co. merchants
21	Pearce Arthur William, solicitor
21	Pooley & Follett, architects
21	Harris H. & A. builders

1905

John street, *Adelphi* (W.C.)
(WESTMINSTER), 18 *Adam street to*
22 *York buildings on South-east side &*
James st. on North-west side.
SOUTH-EAST SIDE.

1 to 4	*Adelphi hotel*, Samuel Thomas Leigh
5	Cooper Eugene, financier
5	Pinches Frederick, architect
5	*Thompson's Patent Gravity*
	Switchback Railway Co. Lim
5	Ashford Henry Leonard, designer
5	Dickinson Richard, architect
5	Graham Walter, architect
6	Didcott Hugh Jay Ld. dramatic agents
6	Hutchins Frederick, solicitor
6	*Empire Syndicate Limited*
6	Hill Edward May, solicitor
6	Kibblewhite Charles E.B
7	Cope Henry James, surveyor
7	Batting Walter, architect
7	Murray John, architect
7	Cornish & Gaymer, ecclesiastical builders
7	Dearle William Walker, quantity
	surveyor
7	Simpson Harry William, surveyor
8	*Siesta Tobacco Co*
8	Griffith & Biliotti, electrical engineers
8	Portman & Co. commission agents
8	Francis Leon Albert, architect
8	Francis Leon Alfred John, architect
8	Adams Henry Robert, quantity surveyor
8	*New Age Press (The)*
8	Russell Richard F. newspaper proprietor
9	Rogers Percy Willben, auctioneer
9	Perry & Reed, architects
9	Assiter Harry George, surveyor
9	Taperell & Haase, architects
9	Cronk Harold Tylee, surveyor
9	Fox George Hamblin, architect
10	*Ceres Depot*
10	*Amateur Athletic Association,*
	C. Herbert, hon. sec
10	Bassett-Smith W. & C. A. architects
10	Chisholm Robert F. architect
10	Rutland Archibald Hart, estate agent
10	Hogg Richard B. surveyor
10	Coyle Alfred H. architect
12	Hicks James B. surveyor
12	Rodriguez Epfanio
12	Bauhof Philip
	. . . . *here is Robert street* . . . . . .
13	Peters, Hall & Co. wine merchants
13	Bentley J. F. & Son, architects
13	Burrell Alfred Lloyd
13	Davis William Edward, surveyor
	. . . . *here are York buildings* . . . .
	NORTH-WEST SIDE.
	. . . . *here is James street* . . . .
11	Sinclair Rosseter Lenton Walker
18 & 19	*Society of Arts,*
	Sir Henry Trueman Wood, M.A. sec
20	Waller W.H. & Son, solicitors
20	Cobbett William Vines Holt, solicitor
22	Hayward & Maynard, architects
22	Hayward Arthur B. architect
20	Fetch Ernest Edward, architect
20	Jellis John, quantity surveyor
21	Foster E. & Co. merchants
21	Pooley & Follett, architects
21	Sheppard & Burkinshaw, architects
21	Kennard Joseph, quantity surveyor

1910

John street, *Adelphi* (W.C.)
(WESTMINSTER), 18 *Adam street to*
22 *York buildings on South-east side &*
James st. on North-west side.
SOUTH-EAST SIDE.

1 to 4	*Adelphi hotel*, Mrs. Marion Burlet
5	Pinches Frederick, architect
5	*Thompson's Patent Gravity*
	Switchback Railway Co. Lim
5	Ashford Henry Leonard, designer
5	Dickinson Richard, architect
5	Graham Walter, architect
5	Cleveland Charles Barry, architect
6	Didcott Hugh Jay Ltd. dramatic agents
6	Buchanan Robert Colburn, theatrical
	director
6	Trentham George, contractor
	for tramways
6	Reynolds & James, solicitors
6	*Central Small Holdings Society,*
	Herbert Carleton, sec
6	Hill Edward May, solicitor
6	Kibblewhite Charles E.B
7	Turner, Son & Clifford, surveyors
7	Melhuish Frederick Herbert, surveyor
7	Cope Henry James, solicitor
7	Furneaux William, architect
7	*Legion of Frontiersmen, offices*
	of London Command
7	Barlow John Bennet, solicitor
7	Pilbeam Wingham, foreign produce agent
7	Dearle William Walker, quantity
	surveyor
7	Bare Robert George, surveyor
7	Smyth John Henry, quantity surveyor
7	*Women's Industrial Council,*
	Miss Wyatt Papworth, sec
8	Griffith Samuel Barnes, electrical
	engineer
8	Portman & Co. commission agents
8	Francis Leon Albert, surveyor
8	Francis Leon Alfred John, architect
8	Quilter J. S. & Son, architects
8	Bain William Whyte, newspaper propr.
8	Walsh John, inquiry office
9	Assiter Harry George, surveyor
9	Taperell F. & Haase, architects
9	Cronk Harold Tylee, surveyor
9	Cowney James A. quantity surveyor
9	Fox George Hamblin, architect
10	*Ceres Depot*
10	*Amateur Athletic Association,*
	P. L. Fisher, hon. sec
10	Bassett-Smith W. & C. A. architects
10	Shiner Christopher Mitchell, architect
10	Tyers & Jago, architects
10	Rutland Archibald Hart, estate agent
10	Ross Septimus R.C.C. architect
10	Simmons William, surveyor
10	Coyle Alfred H. architect
12	Hicks & Lynam, surveyors
12	Bailey Rev. Arthur Wellesley
12	Rodriguez Chevalier Epfano
12	Bauhof Philip
12	Cullen Rev. Cecil Donald, M.A
	. . . . *here is Robert street* . . . .
13	Peters, Hall & Co. wine merchants
13	Bentley J. F., Son & Marshall,
	architects
13	Davis William Edward, surveyor
13	Lamb Percy A. architect
14	Hayward & Maynard, architects
14	Hayward Arthur B. architect
14	Lohr Mrs. Lewis
14	Wareing Alfred, theatrical manager
	. . . . *here are York buildings* . . . .
	NORTH-WEST SIDE.
	. . . . *here is James street* . . . .
16	Saarbach's News Exchange
16	Aldwinkle Granville J. brick agent
16	*Shaw's Glazed Brick Co. Ltd*
18 & 19	*Royal Society of Arts,*
	Sir Henry Trueman Wood, M.A. sec
20	Waller W.H. & Son, solicitors
20	Cobbett William Vines Holt, solicitor
20	Fetch Ernest Edward, architect
20	Jellis John, quantity surveyor
21	Foster E. & Co. merchants
21	*Land Law Reform Association,*
	James Rowlands, M.P. hon.sec

JOHN STREET

1915

John street, *Adelphi* (W.C.)
(WESTMINSTER), 18 *Adam street to
22 York buildings on South-east side &
Durham house st. on North-west side.*
SOUTH-EAST SIDE.
1 to 4 *Adelphi hotel*, Mrs. Marion Burlet
1 to 4 *O. P. Club (The)*, J. Davis Smith
     & E. H. Miers,   joint hon. secs
5   Secker Martin, publisher
5   *Thompson's Patent Gravity
     Switchback Railway Co. Lim*
5   Ashford Henry Leonard, designer
5   Graham Walter, architect
5   *Magpie Publishing Co. Ltd*
5   Squire John, architect
5   Drysdale & Aylwin, architects
6   Reynolds & James, solicitors
6   Craig Herbert Gordon
6   Henry Martin
7   *Laundry Exchange & Register Ltd.*
     laundry surveyors
7   Gordon Arthur, laundry surveyor
7   Parfitt Aldhelm, solicitor
7   *Boys Country Work Society*
7   *London Diocesan Council for the
     Welfare of Lads,*
            F. A. Bloxham, sec
7   *Seaside Camps for London Working Boys,*
            F. A. Bloxham, sec
7   *London Diocesan Church Lads' Brigade,*
            F. A. Bloxham, sec
7   *London Diocesan Boy Scouts Corps,*
            F. A. Bloxham, sec
7   *Women's Industrial Council (Incorporated),*
        Miss Wyatt Papworth, sec
8   Barrett Bridge & Co. Ltd. builders
8   Roberts-Wray Thomas Henry,
     consulting engineer
8   Francis Leon Albert, architect
8   Francis Leon Alfred John, architect
8   Leighton & Leighton, advertisement
     agents
8   Russell & Co. newspaper proprietors
8   Walsh & Stockley, inquiry office
9   Ouseley J. M. & Son, publishers
9   Beswick Hugh, accountant
9   Tomlins E. Frazer, architect
9   Taperell F. & Haase, architects
10 Bryden & Samuel, solicitors
10 *Amateur Athletic Association,*
         P. L. Fisher, hon. sec
10 Bassett-Smith W. & C. A. architects
10 Pownall Walter Osmund, architect
10 Bunn Henry Leeson, quantity surveyor
10 Hoyland Edward Douglas, architect
10 Tyers & Jago, architects
10 Rutland Archibald Hart, estate agent
10 Simmons William, surveyor
10 Clarke John Walter, publisher
10 Bradley Charles Campion, architect
10 Sirr Harry, architect
12 Turnham & Co. electrical engineers
12 Ferguson Alexander & Co. merchants
12 *Anglo-South American Co Ltd.* merchants
12 *Overseas Travel Association Ltd.*
     shipping agents
12 *Graaf-Reinet Ostrich & Lucern
     Farms Ltd*
12 Bailey Rev. Arthur Wellesley
12 Reynolds Hugh
12 Bauhof Philip
12 Shaw Massey
       . . . . *here is Robert street* . . . .
13 Peters, Hall & Co. wine merchants
13 Bentley John F., Son & Marshall,
     architects
13 Davis William Edward, quantity surveyor
13 Lamb Percy A. architect

13 Dearle William W. quantity surveyor
14 Hayward & Maynard, architects
14 Hayward Arthur B. architect
14 Gregsons Messrs. solicitors
14 Lohr Mrs. Lewis
14 Gwenn Edmund
   . . . . *here are York buildings* . . . .
         NORTH-WEST SIDE.
16 *Union of the Four Provinces of
     Ireland Club,*
            M. T. Segrue, sec
16 Lippincott (J. B.) Co. publishers
   . . . . *here is Durham house street* . . . .
16A, Vallentin Hugo
16A, Guest Leslie Haden, physician
16A, Vaughan Louis
17 *Little Theatre*
17 *Camera Club Co. Ltd.*   H. Philp, sec
17 Arthur Paul
17 Dawson Charles
17 Barker Arthur Granville
18 & 19 *Royal Society of Arts,*
     Sir Henry Trueman Wood, M.A. sec
20 Waller & Mager, solicitors
20 Cobbett William Vines Holt, solicitor
20 Sidford Reginald Guy, accountant
20 Meta Miss
21 Foster E. & Co. merchants
21 *Land Law Reform Association,*
     James Rowlands, M.P. hon.sec

1920

John st. *Adelphi* (W.C.2)
(WESTMINSTER), 18 *Adam street to
22 York buildings on South-east side &
Durham house st. on North-west side.*
SOUTH-EAST SIDE.
6   Rumney Howard, solicitor
8   *Imperial Sunday Alliance &
     Sunday Lay Movement,*
        J. Woodford Causer, sec
8   *London Vegetarian Society*
8   Stockley James, inquiry office
8   Nowell & Turner, solicitors
9   Ouseley J. M. & Son Ltd. publishers
9   Beswick & Aulton, accountants
9   Crane Denis, journalist
9   Palser Edwin, architect
10 Boreham & Co. auctioneers
10 *Amateur Athletic Association,*
        Harry J. Barclay, hon. sec
10 Bassett-Smith W. & C. A. architects
10 Bunn Henry Leeson, quantity surveyor
10 Rutland Archibald Hart, estate agent
10 Simmons William, surveyor
10 Clarke John Walter, publisher
10 Bradley Charles Campion, architect
12 Crisp Jason Grainger, accountant
12 Norman John Norman, general agent
    . . . . *here is Robert street* . . . .
13 Peters, Hall & Co. wine merchants
13 Davis William Edward, quantity surveyor
13 Souster Ernest George William,
     architect
13 Lamb Percy A. architect
13 Dearle William W. quantity surveyor
13 Francis Leon Albert, surveyor
14 Hayward & Maynard, architects
14 Gregsons Messrs. solicitors
14 Gwenn Edmund
   . . . . *here are York buildings* . . . .
         NORTH-WEST SIDE.
   . . . . . . *here is Durham house street* . . . . . .
16A, *Valite Ltd.* acetylene engineers
16A, Vallentin Hugo
16A, Sidney-Vernon Arthur, M.B.
     B.S.Lond. physician & surgeon
16A, Vaughan Louis
16B, James Robert, Son & Co. wine merchants
17 *Little Theatre*
17 *Camera Club Co. Ltd.*
        C. S. Lawrence, sec
17 Arthur Paul
17 Morni Madame
18 & 19 *Royal Society of Arts,*
        G. K. Menzies, M.A. sec
20 Waller & Mager, solicitors
20 Cobbett William Vines H. solicitor
20 Sidford Reginald Guy, accountant
21 Foster E. & Co. merchants

1925

John st. *Adelphi* (W.C.2)
(WESTMINSTER), 18 *Adam street to
22 York buildings on South-east side &
Durham house st. on North-west side.*
SOUTH-EAST SIDE.
1 to 4 *Adelphi hotel*
5   Secker Martin, publisher
5   *Nation Ltd. (The)* publishers
5   *Sindix Ltd.* toilet brush manufacturers
5   Carse (Roland) & Hammond
     (Geoffrey), theatrical agents
5   Platt E. Taylor
5   Rumney Howard, solicitor
6   *British Science Guild,*
        Miss A. D. L. Lacey, sec
6   Mansons, translators
7   *Economic Review* (office of)
7   Smith Percy, artist
7   Mansell George, artist
7   Harris & Porter, quantity surveyors
7   "C. B. C." Society
8   *National Review (The)* Office
8   *London Vegetarian Society*
8   Stockley James, detective agency
8   Pierpoint Raymond A.
8   Reynolds Hugh
9   Grubb Arthur Page, journalist
9   Ouseley J. M. & Son Ltd. publishers
9   *Canadian Official Press Bureau*
9   Beswick & Aulton, accountants
9   Crane Denis, journalist
10 Boreham & Co. auctioneers
10 *Amateur Athletic Association*
10 Bassett-Smith W. & C. A. architects
10 Bunn Henry Leeson, quantity surveyor
10 Rutland Archibald Hart, estate agent
10 *Arts & Industries News Service*
10 Fairchild Edward James, quantity
     surveyor
10 Clarke John Walter, publisher
10 Bradley Charles Campion, architect
   . . . . *here is Robert street* . . . .
13 Peters, Hall & Co. wine merchants
13 Davis William Edward & Son,
     quantity surveyors
13 Lamb Percy A. architect
13 Dearle William W. quantity surveyor
14 Hayward & Maynard, architects
14 Gregsons Messrs. solicitors
14 Gwenn Edmund
    . . . . *here are York buildings* . . . .
         NORTH-WEST SIDE.
   . . . . . . *here is Durham house street* . . . . . .
16 Lippincott (J.B.) Co. publishers
16 *Inland Revenue, H.M. Inspector
     of Taxes (Covent garden)*
16 *Inland Revenue, H.M. Inspector
     of Taxes (St. Giles)*
16A, *Valite Ltd.* acetylene engineers
16A, Prinsep Anthony
16A, Sidney-Vernon Arthur, M.B.
     B.S.Lond. physician & surgeon
16A, Lawrence Miss Susan, M.P
16B, James Robert, Son & Co. wine
     merchants
17 *Little Theatre*
17 *Camera Club Co. Ltd.*
17 Weiner Joseph
17 Frith J. Leslie
17 Morni Madame
18 & 19 *Royal Society of Arts*
20 Waller & Mager, solicitors
20 Hopkins Ernest, nerve consultant
21 Foster E. & Co. merchants

JOHN STREET

1930

John st. *Adelphi* (W.C.2) (WESTMINSTER), 18 *Adam street to 22 York buildings on South-east side & Durham house st. on North-west side.*
SOUTH-EAST SIDE.

1 to 4 *Adelphi* hotel
5   Secker Martin, publisher
5   Dean Basil, theatrical manager
5   Restaurant Public Houses Association
5   Carse Roland, theatrical agent
6   Rumney Howard, solicitor
6   *British Science Guild*
6   Mansons (Translators) Ltd
6   Evans Charles Edward
6   Permanent Posters
7   Holding E. A. & Co. naval & military accoutrement makers
7   Silvester George, surveyor
7   Greenwood J. H. architect
7   Smith Percy, artist
7   Mansell George, artist
7   Granger William Fraser, architect
7   Leathart Julian Rudolph, architect
7   Soper Stanley George, architect
8   *National Review (The)* Office
8   *London Vegetarian Society*
8   Lipscomb W. P. author
8   Stockley James, detective agency
8   Cranfield Walter Thomas, journalist
9   Old Royalty Book Publishers (The), publishers
9   Walker Henry, publisher
9   Empire News & Features
9   Beswick & Aulton, accountants
9   Crane Denis, journalist
10   Boreham & Co. auctioneers
10   *Amateur Athletic Association*
10   Ellison Robert Kitching, architect
10   Chandler Ernest Herbert, quantity surveyor
10   Bunn Henry Leeson, quantity surveyor
10   Rutland Archibald Hart, estate agent
10   Fairchild Edward James, quantity surveyor
10   Clarke John Walter, publisher
10   Bradley Charles Campion, architect
. . . . *here is Robert street* . . . .
13   Sichel H. & Sons Ltd. wine merchants
13   Doubleday, Doran & Co. (Inc.) publishers
13   Lamb Percy A. architect
13   Dearle & Henderson, quantity surveyors
14   Hayward & Maynard, architects
14   Knott & Collins, architects
14   Gwenn Edmund
. . . . here is *York buildings* . . . .
NORTH-WEST SIDE.
. . . . . . here is *Durham house street* . . . . . .
16   Lippincott (J.B.) Co. publishers
16   Magnesite Products Ltd
16   Sal-Ferricite & Trading Co. Ltd
16   Baldwin Frederick Langford, engineers' agent
16A, *Valite Ltd.* acetylene gas apparatus engineers
16A, Harris & Porter, quantity surveyors
16A, Bethell, Swannell & Durnford, architects
16A, Berry R. Power
16A, Trew Ronald Arth
16A, Best Miss Edna
16B, James Robert, Son & Co. wine merchants
17   *Little Theatre*
17   *Camera Club Co. Ltd.*
17   Morni Madame
17   Hardwick Cedrick
18 & 19 *Royal Society of Arts*

20   Waller, Mager & Cobbett, solicitors
20   Hopkins Ernest, nerve consultant
21   Foster E. & Co. merchants

1935

John st. *Adelphi* (W.C.2) (WESTMINSTER), 18 *Adam street to 22 York buildings on South-east side & Durham house st. on North-west side.*
SOUTH-EAST SIDE.

1 to 4 *Adelphi Hotel & Restaurant*
5   Secker Martin, publisher
5   Canary Islands & Madeira Agency
5   Restaurant Public Houses Association
5   Carse Roland, theatrical agent
6   *British Science Guild*
6   Mansons (Translators) Ltd
6   Organisation for the Maintenance of Supplies
6   Evans Charles Edward
7   Kenya Tobacco Co. Ltd
7   Smith Percy, artist
7   Mansell George, artist
7   Granger William Fraser, architect
7   Leathart Julian Rudolph, architect
7   Soper Stanley George, architect
7   Lane William, quantity surveyor
8   Orion Booksellers Ltd
8   *London Vegetarian Society*
8   Quill John Ltd. literary agents
8   Joseph Herbert Ltd. publishers
9   Wishart & Co. publishers
9   Beswick & Aulton, accountants
9   City General Advertising Service
10   Boreham & Co. auctioneers
10   *Amateur Athletic Association*
10   Chandler Ernest Herbert, quantity surveyor
10   Rutland Archibald Hart, estate agent
10   Thomas W.K & Co. manufacturers' agents
10   To-Morrow (office of)
10   Fairchild Edward James, quantity surveyor
10   Bradley Charles Campion, architect
12   Canova V. & Co. wine shippers
. . . . *here is Robert street* . . . .
13   Sichel H. & Sons Ltd. wine merchants
13   Lamb Percy A. architect
13   Dearle & Henderson, quantity surveyors
14   Hayward & Maynard, architects
14   Gwenn Edmund
. . . . here is *York buildings* . . . .
NORTH-WEST SIDE.
. . . . . . here is *Durham house street* . . . . . .
16   Lippincott (J.B.) Co. publishers
16A, Thomas Ivor
16A, Harris & Porter, quantity surveyors
16A, Bethell & Swannell, architects
16B, James Robert, Son & Co. wine merchants
17   *Little Theatre*
17   *Camera Club Co. Ltd.*
17   Adshead Neil R
17   Gunn Herbert James
17   Morni Madame
18 & 19 *Royal Society of Arts*
20   Waller, Mager & Cobbett, solicitors
20   Hopkins Ernest, nerve consultant
21   Foster E. & Co. merchants

1936

John st. *Adelphi* (W.C.2) (WESTMINSTER), 18 *Adam street to 22 York buildings on South-east side & Durham house st. on North-west side.*
SOUTH-EAST SIDE.

1 to 4 *Adelphi Hotel & Restaurant*
5   Secker Martin, publisher
5   Canary Islands & Madeira Agency
5   Carse Roland, theatrical agent
6   *British Science Guild*
6   Hackney John, literary agent
6   Mansons (Translators) Ltd
6   Organisation for the Maintenance of Supplies
6   Evans Charles Edward
7   Kenya Tobacco Co. Ltd
7   Smith Percy, artist
7   Granger William Fraser, architect
7   Leathart Julian Rudolph, architect
7   Soper Stanley George, architect
7   Lane William, quantity surveyor
8   Orion Booksellers Ltd
8   *London Vegetarian Society*
8   Chapman & Hall Ltd. publishers
9   Joseph Herbert Ltd. publishers
9   Wishart Books Ltd. publishers
9   Beswick & Aulton, accountants
9   City General Advertising Service
10   Boreham & Co. auctioneers
10   Charles Guy, theatrical manager
10   *Amateur Athletic Association*
10   Chandler Ernest Herbert, quantity surveyor
10   Rutland Archibald Hart, estate agent
10   Thomas W.K & Co. manufacturers' agents
10   To-Morrow (office of)
10   Fairchild Edward James, quantity surveyor
10   Bradley Charles Campion, architect
12   Canova V. & Co. wine shippers
. . . . *here is Robert street* . . . .
13   Sichel H. & Sons Ltd. wine merchants
13   Lamb Percy A. architect
13   Dearle & Henderson, quantity surveyors
14   Hayward & Maynard, architects
14   MacDonald Alister G. architect
14   Allison Peter, architect
14   Gwenn Edmund
. . . . here is *York buildings* . . . .
NORTH-WEST SIDE.
. . . . . . here is *Durham house street* . . . . . .
16   Lippincott (J.B.) Co. publishers
16   London Theatre Guild
16   Tillett Rusell Leslie, chartered accountant
16A, Thomas Ivor
16A, Harris & Porter, quantity surveyors
16A, Bethell & Swannell, architects
16A, Gray Eric, photographer
16B, James Robert, Son & Co. wine merchants
17   *Little Theatre*
17   *Camera Club Co. Ltd.*
17   Adshead Neil R
17   Gunn Herbert James
18 & 19 *Royal Society of Arts*
20   Waller, Mager & Cobbett, solicitors
20   Hopkins Ernest, nerve consultant
21   Foster E. & Co. merchants

ROBERT STREET

1841

Robert st. *Adelphi*, 10 *John street.*
1 Freeth George, esq
1 Betty William H. West, esq
1 Nicholson George Stephen, esq
1 Ryall H. T. historical engraver
2 Boequet Edward, esq
2 Cunnynghame Robert, esq
2 Duthie James, solicitor
3 *Caledonian Hotel*, William Chaplin
4 Weston John, esq
6 Guy John, surgeon

1845

Robert st. *Adelphi*, 10 *John street.*
1 Betty William H. West, esq
1 Ryall H. T. historical engraver
2 Corfield William, solicitor
2 Dalton Charles, esq
2 Roberts William Prowting, solicitor
3 *Caledonian Hotel*, Elder & Jurdison
4 Carver Edward Turst, F.R.S.
4 Gardiner John, esq
5 Roake George, esq
5 Bird Henry, esq
6 Friend Alfred B. architect & surveyor

1850

Robert st. *Adelphi, John street.*
1 De Boos Thomas John, solicitor
1 Betty William H. West, esq
1 Ryall H. T. historical engraver
2 Barnes Thomas, civil engineer
2 Crump Joseph, appraiser & house agent
2 Grantham Richard B. civil engineer
2 Richardson Henry, conveyancer
2 Roberts William Prowting, solicitor
3 *Caledonian hotel*, Elder & Jurdison
4 Roake George, esq
5 Bird Henry H. civil engineer
5 Barber George, esq
5 Oldfield Charles Frederick, esq
5 Tweedale William, esq

1855

Robert st. *Adelphi, John street.*
1 Betty William Henry West, esq
1 Brandon Woodthorpe, esq
1 *Church Protestant Defence Society,*
Wilbraham Taylor, sec
1 *Open Air Mission,*
John Macgregor, esq. hon. sec
2 Grantham Richard B. F.G.S. civil enginr
2 Halliday Michael Frederick, esq
2 Richardson Henry, esq
2 Webber Henry, esq
3 *Caledonian hotel*, Charles Elder
4 Baly Price Prichard, civil engineer
5 Dredge William, civil engineer
5 *Craigmuir Cobalt & Nickel Mine,*
Edmund Pycroft, secretary
5 Platt Edward John, solicitor
5 Smith Henry J. esq

1860

Robert st. *Adelphi* (W.C.), *John st.*
1 Brandon Woodthorpe, barrister
1 Bird Henry Harrington, civil engineer
1 *Church Protestant Defence Society,*
Wilbraham Taylor, sec
1 Elderton, Mr. Henry
1 *Open-Air Mission,*
John Macgregor, esq. hon. sec
1 *Special Services to Working Classes*
(Exeter Hall Office)
Wilbraham Taylor, esq. hon. sec
2 Allom Arthur, architect
2 Macro Mr. Frederick
2 Parry John Arthur, solicitor
2 Philipps Henry, solicitor
2 Richardson Henry, esq
3 *Caledonian hotel*, Charles Elder
Dayman Charles O. M.A. F.R.S
3 *Royal London Yacht Club,*
Thomas J. Gregory, sec
4 Baly Price Prichard, civil engineer
4 Bennett Joseph, civil engineer
5 Lefroy George Bentinck, solicitor
5 Platt Edward John, solicitor
5 *Christian Vernacular Education*
Society for India,
Henry Carre Tucker, esq. hon. sec
Rev. Jonathan Holt Titcomb, sec

1865

Robert st. *Adelphi* (W.C.), *John st.*
1 Bird Henry Harrington, civil engineer
1 *Church Protestant Defence Society,*
Wilbraham Taylor, sec
1 Deane Dennis Wood, artist
1 *Sidmouth Railway & Harbour Co.'s*
Offices, Raymond Yates, sec
1 *St. George's Harbour Co.'s Offices*
1 *Open-Air Mission,*
John Macgregor, esq. hon. sec
Gawin Kirkham, sec
1 *Special Services to Working Classes*
(Exeter Hall Office)
Wilbraham Taylor, esq. hon. sec
2 Parry John Arthur,
2 *The Cae Seys Hæmatite Iron Ore*
Co.(lim.), John Arthur Parry, sec
2 Philipps Henry, solicitor
2 Richardson Henry, esq
2 Tindall Thomas William, esq
2 Scott James John, esq
2 Crump Joseph, furniture dealer
3 *Caledonian hotel*, Charles Elder
3 *Royal London Yacht Club,*
Thomas J. Gregory, sec
4 Baly Price Prichard, civil engineer
5 Brown John & Co. (limited), Atlas
steel, iron & armour plate works
(Sheffield), John Clowes Bailey, agent
5 Lefroy George Bentinck, solicitor
5 Platt Edward John, solicitor
5 Sheppard Frederick Clapton, solicitor

1870

Robert street. *Adelphi* (W.C.), *John street*
1, 2 & 3 *Caledonian Hotel*, Berkeley & Co
New Thames Yacht Club,
F. A. White, esq. sec
Westminster Chess Club,
Thomas Hewitt, esq. hon. sec
5 Lefroy George Bentinck, solicitor
5 Platt Edward John, solicitor
5 Sheppard Frederick Clapton, solicitor
5 Cooke William, civil engineer

1875

Robert street. *Adelphi* (W.C.), *John street*
1, 2 & 3 *Caledonian Hotel*, Berkeley & Co
George States, manager
New Thames Yacht Club,
E. J. Skinner, esq. sec
Westminster Chess Club,
Robert Bianchi, M.R.C.S. sec
5 Lefroy George Bentinck, solicitor
Platt Edward John, solicitor
Sheppard Frederick Clapton, solicitor

1880

Robert street. *Adelphi* (W.C.), *John street*
5 Lefroy George Bentinck, solicitor
Platt Edward John, solicitor
Amateur Mechanical Society,
T. W. Boord, hon. sec

1885

Robert street. *Adelphi* (W.C.), *John street*
5 Lefroy & Sheppard, solicitors
Platt Edward John, solicitor
Soldiers' Daughters' Home,
Lieut. Charles Rathbone Low,
I.N., F.R.G.S. sec
Jarvis & Edwards, advertising agents

1890

Robert street. *Adelphi* (W.C.), *John street*
5 *Civil Service Guardian & County*
Council Courier
5 Lefroy & Sheppard, solicitors
5 Platt Edward John, solicitor
5 *Soldiers' Daughters' Home,*
Lieut. Charles Rathbone Low,
I.N., F.R.G.S. sec
5 Brough Bennett Hooper

1895

Robert street. *Adelphi* (W.C.), *John street*
5 Sheppard Frederick Clapton, solicitor
5 Platt Edward John, solicitor
5 *Soldiers' Daughters' Home,*
Lieut. Charles Rathbone Low,
I.N., F.R.G.S. sec
5 Saunders Cecil George, surveyor
5 Brough Bennett Hooper

1900

Robert street. *Adelphi* (W.C.), *John street*
5 *Soldiers' Daughters' Home,*
Lieut. Charles Rathbone Low,
I.N., F.R.G.S. sec
5 Sheppard Frederick Clapton, solicitor
5 Platt Edward John, solicitor
5 Saunders Cecil George, surveyor
5 Graves Henry George

1905

Robert street. *Adelphi* (W.C.), *John street*
5 *Royal Soldiers' Daughters' Home, (Office)*
5 "Pyrojim" Syndicate Limited, patent fuel
manufacturers
5 *Scenic Artists' Association,*
H. Lawrence Harris, sec
5 Platt Edward John, solicitor
5 Graves Henry George
[For names at No. 6 see 12
John street, Adelphi (W.C.)]

1910

Robert street, *John street*
Adelphi (W.C.) (WESTMINSTER).
1to3 ADELPHI TERRACE HOUSE:—
Victoria Institute or Philosophical Society
of Gt. Britain,
H. C. Turner, M.A. sec
Women's Freedom League
Scottish Legal Life Assurance Soc.,
James Spence Leslie, London supt.
Thurston E. Temple, author
King Norman Carew
Manaos Harbour Ltd
West India Rubber Plantation
Syndicate Ltd
Round Douglas, architect
Knott & Collins, architects
Henniker Frederick S. surveyor
Pennell Joseph
Craig Miss
Goldsmid Miss
Potter Miss
5 *Royal Soldiers' Daughters' Home, (Office)*
5 Fell Frank, land agent
5 Gowans & Gray Ltd. publishers
5 Graves Henry George
5 Platt Edward John, solicitor
5 Sumpter Herbert James Cecil & Co.
solicitors
[For names at No. 6 see 12
John street, Adelphi (W.C.)]

ROBERT STREET

1915

Robert street, 12 *John st*
Adelphi (W.C.) (WESTMINSTER).
1to3   ADELPHI TERRACE HOUSE:—
   Amazonas Engineering Co. Ltd
   Minerva Publishing Co. Ltd
   Women's Freedom League
   Scottish Legal Life Assurance Soc.,
     James Spence Leslie, London supt
   Actresses' Franchise League,
     Miss Nina Boucicault, hon. sec
   Common Cause Publishing Co. Ltd
   Manaos Harbour Ltd
   West India Rubber Plantation
     Syndicate Ltd
   Bland Charles R.
   Anning Miss
   Round Douglas, architect
   Knott & Collins, architects
   Hodgkinson & Son, architects
   Henniker Frederick S. surveyor
   Pennell Joseph
   Barrie Sir James Matthew, bart

5 *Royal Soldiers' Daughters' Home,*
    Hampstead N.W. (Office)
5 Fell Frank, land agent
5 *Ellis T. H. Optical Co*
5 Gowans & Gray Ltd. publishers
5 Sumpter Herbert J. C. & Co. solicitors
5 Johnson Avis & Co. brace makers
    [For names at No. 6 see 12
    John street, Adelphi (W.C.)]

1920

Robert street, 12 *John st*
Adelphi (W.C.2) (WESTMINSTER).
1to3   ADELPHI TERRACE HOUSE:—
   Amazonas Engineering Co. Ltd
   Booth & Co. (London) Ltd.
     merchants
   Fraser Robert Atkin, merchant
   Pavlova Leather Co. Ltd
   Bailey W. B. & Co. fellmongers
   Savernake Glove Co
   Beach J. & Sons Ltd. leather mfrs
   Scottish Legal Life Assurance Soc.,
     James Spence Leslie, London supt
   Actresses' Franchise League,
     Miss Nina Boucicault, hon. sec
   Manaos Harbour Ltd
   West India Plantation Syndicate Ltd
   Pole David Graham, solicitor,
     Supreme Courts of Scotland
   Egoist Ltd. (The), publishers
   Home Rule for India League
   Arts League of Service
   Pole Richard Graham, accountant
   Elder Mrs
   Johnson Claude
   Thomas Moy
   Rowden Miss
   Knott & Collins, architects
   Hodgkinson & Son, architects
   Henniker Frederick S. surveyor
   Villiers Misses
   Bystrom Miss
   Barrie Sir James Matthew, bart

5 *Royal Soldiers' Daughters' Home,*
    Hampstead N.W. (Office)
5 Fell Frank, land agent
5 Ellis T. H. Optical Co
5 Gowans & Gray Ltd. publishers
5 Sumpter Herbert J. C. & co. solicitors
5 Johnson Avis & Co. brace makers
    [For names at No. 6 see 12
    John street, Adelphi (W.C. 2)]

1925

Robert street, 12 *John st*
Adelphi (W.C.) (WESTMINSTER).
1to3   ADELPHI TERRACE HOUSE:—
   Amazonas Engineering Co. Ltd
   Fraser Robert Atkin, merchant
   Savernake Glove Co
   Beach J. & Sons Ltd. leather mfrs
   Scottish Legal Life Assurance Soc.,
   Manaos Harbour Ltd
   West India Plantation Syndicate Ltd
   Rankin Bros. Ltd. printers
   Pole David Graham, solicitor,
     Supreme Courts of Scotland
   Arts League of Service
   Elder Misses
   Johnson Claude
   McPeake James Young
   Bondfield Miss Margaret G. J.P., M.P
   Knott & Collins, architects
   Henniker Frederick S. surveyor
   Catholic Stage Guild
   Bystrom Miss
   Berry Miss
   Barrie Sir James Matthew, bart. O.M

5 *National Reearch Foundation*
5 Fell Frank, land agent
5 *Ellis T. H. Optical Co*
5 Gowans & Gray Ltd. publishers
5 Sumpter Herbert J. C. & Co. solicitors
5 Johnson Avis & Co. brace makers
6 Apollo Magazine (office of)

1930

Robert street, 12 *John st*
Adelphi (W.C.2) (WESTMINSTER).
1to3   ADELPHI TERRACE HOUSE:—
   Amazonas Engineering Co. Ltd
   Scottish Legal Life Assurance Soc.
   Manaos Harbour Ltd
   West India Plantation Syndicate Ltd
   Unit Construction Co. Ltd
   Wells George Philip
   Barton Miss
   Rudkin Brig.-Gen. Charles
     Mark Clement, D.S.O
   Vickers Miss
   Henniker Frederick S. surveyor
   Concrete Houses Ltd
   Catholic Stage Guild
   Baldwin A. H. & Sons Ltd.
     numismatists
   Barrie Sir James Matthew, bart. O.M
   Thoresby James E
   Coley James William Ernest
   Yeates-Brown Major Francis
   Weiner Joseph

5 Fell Frank, land agent
5 *Ellis T. H. Optical Co*
5 Gowans & Gray Ltd. publishers
5 Sumpter Herbert J. C. & Co. solicitors
5 Mortlock Rev. Charles Bernard, M.A
5 Johnson Avis & Co. brace makers
5 Anglo-Russian Parliamentary
    Committee
6 Apollo Press Ltd
6 Canova V. & Co. wine shippers

1935

Robert street, 12 *John st*
Adelphi (W.C.) (WESTMINSTER).
1to3   ADELPHI TERRACE HOUSE:—
   Amazonas Engineering Co. Ltd
   Manaos Harbour Ltd
   West India Plantation Syndicate Ltd
   Hughes Gervase Ltd. theatrical
     managers
   Dias C. & Co. tourist agents
   Unit Construction Co. Ltd
   Barton Miss
   Waters Frank Henry
   Vickers Miss
   Goldman Charles Sydney
   Hamilton Archibald G
   Wallace James H. insurance broker
   Henniker Frederick S. surveyor
   Reinforced Concrete Buildings Ltd
   Baldwin A. H. & Sons Ltd.
     numismatists
   Barrie Sir James Matthew, bart. O.M
   Bazley Sir Thomas S. bart
   Shearman Montague
   Mortlock Rev. Charles Bernard, M.A
   Sykes Sir Charles Bt. K.B.E

5 Fell Frank, land agent
5 *Ellis T. H. Optical Co*
5 Gowans & Gray Ltd. publishers
5 Sumpter Herbert J. C. & Co. solicitors
5 Johnson Avis & Co. brace makers
5 Anglo-Russian Parliamentary Committee
6 Doubleday, Doran & Co. (Inc), publishers
6 D.C. Electric Co. Ltd
6 British Icyball Refrigerator Co
6 Canova V. & Co. wine shippers

1936

Robert street, 12 *John st*
Adelphi (W.C.) (WESTMINSTER).
1to3   ADELPHI TERRACE HOUSE:—
   Amazonas Engineering Co. Ltd
   Manaos Harbour Ltd
   West India Plantation Syndicate Ltd
   Hughes Gervase Ltd. theatrical
     managers
   Officers' Children's Fund
   Dias C. & Co. tourist agents
   Unit Construction Co. Ltd
   Mansell George, artist
   Waters Frank Henry
   Kenton Godfrey
   Cross & Maitland, journalists
   British Improved Motor Spirit
     (Holdings) Ltd
   Vickers Miss
   Goldman Charles Sydney
   Henniker Frederick S. surveyor
   Reinforced Concrete Buildings Ltd
   Baldwin A. H. & Sons Ltd.
     numismatists
   Barrie Sir James Matthew, bart. O.M
   Shearman Montague
   Mortlock Rev. Charles Bernard, M.A

5 Fell Frank, land agent
5 *Ellis T. H. Optical Co*
5 Gowans & Gray Ltd. publishers
5 Sumpter Herbert J. C. & Co. solicitors
5 Johnson Avis & Co. brace makers
5 Anglo-Russian Parliamentary Committee
6 Doubleday, Doran & Co. (Inc), publishers
6 D.C. Electric Co. Ltd
6 British Icyball Refrigerator Co
6 Canova V. & Co. wine shippers

VILLIERS STREET

1841

Villiers street, 31 *Strand.*

2 Laing Margaret & Son, plumbers
3 *Green Dragon,* James Price
4 Maplestone John, tinplate worker
5 Eitel Abraham, coppersmith
6 Clemence John, carpenter & builder
7 Frohock Mark, general dealer
8 *Marquis of Granby's Head,*
    Mrs A. Williams
   . . . . *Hungerford arcade* . . . .
9 *College for Civil Engineers,*
        John Edward Curtis, secretary
9 *Hungerford & Lambeth Suspension*
    Bridge Co.   R. Lawrence, sec
9 *London & Westminster Steam Boat Co*
9 *Hungerford Market Company's office*
       Andrew L. Leith, secretary
12 Bingham Henry, esq
12 Eden Thomas, solicitor
13 Baily & Roberts, engravers & printers
14 Drew Mrs. lodging house
15 Crisp Charles, lodging house
17 Robertson Divie & Son, wine merchants
19 *Hungerford Arms,* William Polden
23 Armstrong Thomas, bookbinder
24 Lee Michael & Co. tailors
25 Wylde Henry, flute maker
26 Bennett Solomon, seal engraver
27 Steward Charles, tailor
28 Burgis Benjamin & William, plumbers
29 Goodworth George, bricklayer
   . . . . *Duke street* . . . .
31 Clemence William, carpenter
32 Gould Thomas, Hope coffee rooms
33 Cole Thomas, teadealer
34 Woods Wm. plumber, painter & glazier
35 Adlard John, bookbinder

1845

Villiers street, 31 *Strand.*

1 Varty Thomas, esq
2 Laing Margaret & Son, painters
3 *Green Dragon,* James Price
4 Maplestone John, tinplate worker
5 Eitel Abraham, coppersmith
6 Clemence John, carpenter & builder
7 Frohock Mark, general dealer
8 *Granby's Head,* Mrs Ann Williams
  . . . . *here Hungerford arcade intersects* . . . .
9 *Hungerford & Lambeth Suspension*
    Bridge Co.   Richard Lawrence, sec
9 *London & Westminster Steam Boat Co*
9 *Hungerford Market Company's office*
       Andrew L. Leith, secretary
9 *Central Building association,*
      Berkley Westropp, esq. manager
12 Bingham Henry, esq
12 Stephens & Ashton, appraisers
12 Falkner & Bancks, pale stout merchants
12 Wells John James, wine merchant
13 Baily & Roberts, engravers & printers
14 Drew Mrs. Mary, lodging house
15 Crisp Charles, lodging house
17 Robertson Divie & Son, wine merchants
19 *Hungerford Arms,* William Fox
22 Pepper James, tobacconist
23 Armstrong Thomas, bookbinder
25 Wylde Henry, flute maker
26 Bedford Samuel, sexton & undertaker
27 Biffen William, tailor
27 Longstaff William, tailor
30 *Griffin,* Henry Todman
  . . . . *here Duke street intersects* . . . .
31 Clemence William, carpenter
32 Brooks Samuel, law stationer
32 Gould Thomas, Hope coffee rooms
32 Stahl Emanuel, leatherseller & importer
32 Fuld Fred. & Co. bankers at Frankfort
33 Cole Thomas, teadealer
34 Woods Wm. plumber, painter & glazier
35 Adlard John, bookbinder

1850

Villiers street, 31 *Strand.*

1 Varty Thomas, esq
2 Laing David Gordon, painter, &c
3 *Green Dragon,* James Price
4 Maplestone John, tinplate worker
5 Eitel Abraham, coppersmith
6 Clemence John, carpenter & builder
8 *Granby's Head,* Mrs Ann Williams
 . . . *here Hungerford arcade intersects* . . .
9 *Charing Cross Suspension Bridge Co.*
       Richard Lawrence, sec
9 *London & Westminster Steam Boat Co.*
       Richard J. W. Leith, sec
9 *Hungerford Market Company's Office*
       Joseph K. Kilpin, sec
12 Knox Miss Sarah A. bookseller
13 Baily & Roberts, engravers & printers
17 Robertson Edward L.& Co. wine merchts
19 *Hungerford Arms,* Mrs. Mary Fox
20 Charlwood George, seedsman
22 Chatley John, coal merchant
23 Armstrong Thomas, bookbinder
24 Weston George Philip, lodging house
25 Collens William, lithographic printer
25 Wylde Henry, flute maker
26 Bedford Samuel, sexton & undertaker
27 Biffen William, tailor
28 Boarder James, lodging house
29 Dawson Thomas, lodging house
  . . . . *here Duke street intersects* . . . . .
30 *Griffin,* Henry Todman
31 Clemence William, carpenter
32 Gould Mrs. Jane, *Hope* coffee rooms
32 Pymm George, bookbinder
33 Uffman Zachariah, coppersmith
34 Cobbett Richard & E. plumbers&glaziers
35 Adlard John, bookbinder

1855

Villiers street, 31 *Strand.*

1 Varty Thomas, esq
2 Laing David Gordon, painter &c
3 *Green Dragon,* James Price
4 Maplestone John, tinplate worker
5 Eitel Abraham, coppersmith
6 & 7 Clemence John, builder
8 *Granby's Head,* Thomas Corfield
 . . . *here Hungerford arcade intersects* . . . .
9 *Charing Cross Suspension Bridge Co.*
       Richard Lawrence, sec
9 *London & Westminster Steam Boat Co.*
       Richard J. W. Leith, sec
9 *Hungerford Market Company's Office*
       Joseph K. Kilpin, sec
12 Sabberton James, tailor
13 Baily & Roberts, engravers & printers
13 Wylde Henry, flute maker
14 Chatley John, coal dealer
14 Knight Charles, esq
14 Trinder William, auctioneer
17 Robertson Edward L.& Co. wine merchts
19 *Hungerford Arms,* Thomas Willey Price
20 Charlwood & Cummins, seedsmen
23 Silani Frederick, bookbinder
24 Brightman Benjamin, lodging house
25 Austin Edward, carman
26 Bedford Samuel, sexton & undertaker
27 Biffen William, sen. tailor
28 Dean James, bookbinder
28 Boarder James, lodging house
29 Kerby Mrs. Mary Elizabeth, lodging ho
  . . . . . . *here Duke street intersects* . . . .
30 *Griffin,* Henry Symons
31 Clemence William, builder
32 Gould Mrs. Jane, *Hope* coffee rooms
32 Fuld Frederick & Co. foreign agents
32 Pymm George, bookbinder
34 Cobbett Edmund, plumber &glazier
35 Adlard John, bookbinder

1860

Villiers street, 31 *Strand.* (W.C.)

2 Laing David Gordon, painter &c
3 *Queen's Arms,* John Green
4 Maplestone John, tinplate worker
5 Eitel Abraham, coppersmith
6 & 7 Clemence John, builder
8 Drake Mrs. Ann Frances, wine merchant
 . . . . . *here is Hungerford Arcade* . . . . . .
9 *Charing Cross Suspension Bridge Co.*
       George Cox, sec
9 *London & Westminster Steam Boat Co.*
       Richard J. W. Leith, sec
9 *Hungerford Market Company's office*
       Joseph K. Kilpin, sec
9 Leith Richard J. W. secretary to the
    London & Westminster Steam Boat Co.
13 Robins James, pianoforte maker
14 Parker John William, esq
15 Herbert Mrs
17 Robertson & Nicholson, wine merchts
19 *Hungerford Arms,* Jacob Street
20 Charlwood & Cummins, seedsmen
24 Lee Mrs. Elizabeth, lodging house
25 Austin Edward, carman
26 Bedford William, lodging house
27 Biffen William, sen. tailor
28 Chatley Joseph William, coal merchant
  . . . . *here is Duke street* . . . .
29 Silani Frederick, bookbinder
30 *Griffin,* John Pullen
31 Clemence William, builder
32 Gould Mrs. Jane, coffee rooms
32 Fuld F. E. & Co. bankers (Frankfort-
    on-the-Maine)
32 Straus & Co. merchants
32 Stahl C. Emmanuel, foreign agent
33 Uffman Mrs. Henrietta, lodging house
34 Cobbett Edmund, plumber & glazier

1865

Villiers street, 31 *Strand.* (W.C.)

 . . . . . . *here is Hungerford Arcade* . . . . . .
19 *Hungerford Arms,* George Gaze
22 Cook James William, tobacconist
23 Williams John, printer & publisher
23 Robinson James & Co. engineers
23 *The International Wine Depôt,*
       Richard Wilkinson, manager
24 Corby Thomas, refreshment rooms
25 Jablowski Emil & Co. general merchants
25 Neufeld George, cap maker
25 Tyerman Thos. Hy & Co. estate agents
26 Bedford William, lodging house
27 Biffen William, sen. tailor
28 Chatley Joseph William, coal merchant
29 Bullions Alfred, bookbinder
29 Moffatt William, architect
  . . . . *here is Duke street* . . . .
30 *Griffin,* Mrs. Annie Everitt
31 Clemence William, builder
31 Clemence John, builder
32A, Amor John, coffee rooms
33 Uffman Mrs. Henrietta, coffee rooms
34 Cobbett Edmund, plumber & glazier
34 Hides Henry, surgeon
34 Rorke James, chemist

1870

Villiers st. 31 *Strand.* (W.C.)

1 *Charing Cross Hotel Shades*
10 Chaplin (W.H.), Timms & Co.
    wine merchants
10 Timms J.F. & Co. ale & stout bottlers
    Minier, Nash & Nash's seed warehouse
21 Hill & Millard, outfitters
22 Stevens Richard & Sons, billiard
    table makers
23 Evans George, surveyor
25 *Princess of Wales,* James Chamberlayne
26 Muer John, refreshment rooms
29 Youngman Owen, tobacconist
  . . . . *here is Duke street* . . . .
30 *Griffin,* William Charker
31 Clemence William, builder
31 Clemence John, builder
32A, Amor John, coffee rooms
33 Uffman Mrs. Henrietta, coffee rooms
34 Cobbett Edmund, plumber & gasfitter
34 Challice William, chemist & druggist
    Gatti Carlo, billiard & refreshment
    rooms (Railway arches)
    Cutler, Palmer & Co. wine merchants
    (Railway arches)

1875

Villiers st. 31 *Strand.* (W.C.)

1 *Charing Cross Hotel Shades*
10 Chaplin W. H. & Co. wine merchants
    Gatti Carlo, billiard & refreshment
    rooms (Railway arches)
    Deacon R. & Co. wine coopers
    (The Arches)
    Minier, Nash & Nash's seed warehouse
21 Hill & Millard, outfitters
22 Stevens & Sons, billiard table makers
23 Pounce James Henry, florist
    Harris & Co. costume makers
24 *Princess of Wales,* Mrs. Lucy Chamberlayne
25 & 27A, Marioni Giovanni D. confectioner
26 Faulkner Jonathan Horne, hairdresser
26 & 27 Murray William, wine & spirit mercht
    CLARENDON CHAMBERS:—
    Nisbet Ralph Patterson, land agent
    Hirschfeld Washington, accountant
    Addressed Envelope Co.
    Arthur Nicholas Temperley, proprietor
    Mackintire James
    Twigg Joseph, architect
    Representative Reform Association,
       George Howell, sec
    Johnson Thomas Charles, artist
    Operative Masons' Society,
       J. E. Dyer, sec
    Barrett A. W
27 Wakelin Mrs. Rosina, tobacconist
27A, & 25 Marioni Giovanni Domenico
    confectioner
28 Samson Aaron, fruiterer
29 Youngman Owen, tobacconist
  . . . . *here is Duke street* . . . .
32 Clemence John, builder
33 Uffman Mrs. Henrietta, coffee rooms
34 Cobbett Edmund, plumber & gasfitter
    Challice William, chemist & druggist

VILLIERS STREET

1880

Villiers st. 31 *Strand.* (W.C.)
1   *Charing Cross Hotel Shades*
10   Chaplin W. H. & Co. wine merchants
     Gatti Carlo, billiard & refreshment
       rooms & *Music hall* (Railway arches)
     Deacon R. & Co. wine coopers
       (The Arches)
22   Stevens & Sons, billiard table makers
23   Clarke Robert, wine stores
     Irvine & Co. envelope addressers
24   *Princess of Wales,* Charles Queneborough
25   Scales Robert Henry, hotel
26 & 27 Faulkner Jonathan Hurn, hairdrsr
     Faulkner's hotel
27   Goad Herbert A. tobacconist
27A, Metali Giovanni, confectioner
28   Harrison Edward, shirt maker
28A, Staunton Frederick, stationer
29   Vollhardt Charles, tobacconist
.... *here is Duke street* ....
31   *Griffin tavern,* William Fman. Thomas
.... *here is York place* ....
31   Clemence John, builder
33   *Charing Cross Larder*
     Cobbett Edmund, plumber & gasfitter
34   Challice William, chemist & druggist

1885

Villiers st. 31 *Strand.* (W.C.)
1   *Charing Cross Hotel Shades*
10   Chaplin W. H. & Co. wine merchants
     Gatti Carlo, billiard & refreshment
       rooms & *Music hall* (Railway arches)
     Deacon R. & Co. wine coopers
       (15 The Arches)
16   Villiers Charles, photographer
19A, Waters William Henry, restaurant
19   Geld Henry, restaurant
     EMBANKMENT CHAMBERS:—
     Colburn's United Service Magazine
     Nutt William Anthony, oculist
     Buchanan James
     Glover Morton
     Ross Alexander
     Strick C
     Max Gregor
     Clarke A
     Tate Gilbert
     Broad Charles
     Oliver Charles
     Lonegan A. C. E
     Morris Edward
     De Soares J
     De Soares M
     Munday William
     Hatry J
19   Munday Miss Ellen, fruiterer
19A, Ullmann Max, oyster merchant
20   Gatti Carlo, confectioner
22   Stevens & Sons, billiard table makers
23   Irvine & Co. envelope addressers
     Gregory William, wine stores
24   *Princess of Wales,* Charles Queneborough
25   Scales Robert Henry, hotel
26 & 27 Faulkner Jonathan Hurn, hairdrsr
     Faulkner's hotel
27A, Metali Giovanni, confectioner
28   Harrison Edward, shirt maker
28A, Staunton Frederick, stationer
29   Vollhardt Mrs. Charlotte, tobacconist
.... *here is Duke street* ....
31   *Griffin* tavern, William Fman. Thomas
.... *here is York place* ....
32   Lee Charles James, tobacconist
     Crowther William Harding, surgeon
     de Baudot Arthur, professor of languages
33   *Charing Cross Larder*
34   Challice William, chemist & druggist
35   Butler William David, hosier

1890

Villiers st. 31 *Strand.* (W.C.)
1   *Charing Cross Hotel Shades*
1   Bird Charles, card printer
10   Chaplin W. H. & Co. wine merchants
     Gatti Carlo, billiard & refreshment
       rooms & *Music hall* (Railway arches)
     Deacon R. & Co. wine coopers
       (15 The Arches)
16   Villiers Charles, photographer
19A, Harris William, restaurant
19 & 29 Hopkins Joseph Alexander,
       tobacconist
     EMBANKMENT CHAMBERS:—
     Carroll Capt. Frederick Harry
     Glover Morton
     Soward H. E
     Turnbull George B
     Sturges Francis William Murray
     Sturges Hugh Murray
     Tubbs Cyril Bazett
     Watkin Henry
     Waters Hubert
     Bernard Morris
19   Serre Achille, dyer &c
19A, Ullmann Max, oyster merchant
20   Gatti Carlo, confectioner
21   Appleyard John F. fishmonger
22   Stevens & Sons, billiard table makers
23   *Marlborough hotel,* Arthur James Dalton
24   *Princess of Wales,* Arthur John Young
25   Macario Peitro, café restaurant
26 & 27 Faulkner Jonathan H. hairdresser
     Faulkner's hotel
27A, Metali Giovanni, confectioner
28   Wood Reginald D. fruiterer
28A, Young & Co. stationers
29 & 19 Hopkins Joseph Alexander,
       tobacconist
.... *here is Duke street* ....
31   *Griffin* tavern, William Fman. Thomas
.... *here is York place* ....
32   Lee Charles James, tobacconist
33   *Charing Cross Larder*
34   Challice William, chemist & druggist
35   Butler William David, hosier

1895

Villiers st. 31 *Strand.* (W.C.)
1   *Charing Cross Hotel Shades*
1   Bird Brothers, card printers
10   Chaplin W. H. & Co. wine merchants
     Gatti Carlo, billiard & refreshment
       rooms & *Music hall* (Railway arches)
     The Facade:—
     Bayley Frederick Charles,
       outfitter,   1 & 2
     Jacklin William, fruiterer,   3 ⎫
     Levitus Bros. tobacconists,   4 ⎪
     Tetley Mrs. Hilda, confectnr,   5 ⎬
     Potter Miss Mabel, florist,   6 ⎪
     Hawes John, newsagent,   7 ⎭
16   Underwood Louis, photographer
19   Gordon Angus Stafford, wine merchant
19   Landaw John, tobacconist
     EMBANKMENT CHAMBERS:—
     Harman Edward George
     Ingram Charles F
     Butcher J. Langton
     Brine R. E.
     Barlow George
     Kekewich H. Hugh
     Gibb William Alfred Boyd
     Pownall George
19   Serre Achille, dyer &c
19A, Ullmann Max, oyster merchant
20   Gatti Carlo, confectioner
20   Gatti (Carlo) & Stevenson Lim.
       ice merchants
21   Bound George Guy, fishmonger
22   Stevens Richard & Sons, billiard
       table makers
23   *Marlborough hotel,* Thomas Knights
24   *Princess of Wales,* Walter Joyce
25   Macario Peitro, café restaurant
26 & 27 Faulkner Jonathan H. hairdresser
     Faulkner's hotel
27A, Metali Giovanni, confectioner
28   Leonard Charles, coffee bar
28A, Campion Charles Henry & Co.
       stationers
29   Hopkins Joseph Alexander, tobacconist
.... *here is Duke street* ....
31   *Griffin tavern,* Henry James Towell
.... *here is York place* ....
32   Thorpe William, tobacconist
32   *Charing Cross Press Agency*
32   De Baudot Arthur, B.A. teacher
       of languages
33   *Charing Cross Larder*
34   Challice William, chemist & druggist
35   Butler William David, hosier

1900

Villiers st. 31 *Strand.* (W.C.)
1   Bird Brothers, card printers
1   *Charing Cross Hotel Shades*
10   Chaplin W. H. & Co. Ld. wine merchants
     Gatti Carlo, billiard & refreshment
       rooms & *Music hall* (Railway arches)
     The Facade:—
     Hobbs C. & Co. fishmongers,
     Bayley Frederick Charles,
       outfitter,   1 & 2 ⎫
     Crawford Mrs. T. tobacconist,   4 ⎪
     Beaurain Thos. James, confctnr, 5 ⎬
     Crawley George, jeweller,   6 & 7 ⎭
16   Underwood Louis, photographer
19   Gordon Angus Stafford, wine merchant
19A, Landaw John, tobacconist
19   EMBANKMENT CHAMBERS:—
     Ashplant&Devereux, mortgage bkrs
     Devereux George
     Chapman David
     Ingram Charles Frederick
     Scott Andrew
     Brine Robert Edward
     Kekewich Hugh H
     Whyte Frederick
     Delbruck Rouel E
     Doughty John Miller
     Miller Charles Doughty
     Baxter Sam Gibbs
     Finch George
     Esser Hans
     Foster John Arnold
     Brouson Percy
     Munro K
19   Serre Achille, dyer &c
19   Roberts L. & E. photo dealers
19   Guderley & Kay, hairdressers
20   Gatti Carlo, confectioner
21   Gatti (Carlo) & Stevenson Lim.
       ice merchants
21   Ullmann Maximilian, oyster rooms
22   Stevens R. & Sons, billiard table makers
23   *Marlborough hotel,* Thomas Knights
24   *Princess of Wales,* Mrs. Maria Cockburn
25   *Buckingham hotel,* Pietro Macario
26 & 27 Faulkner Jonathan H. hairdresser
     Faulkner's hotel
27A, Metali Giovanni, confectioner
28A, Osborn Walter, hosier
29   Salmon & Gluckstein Ltd. tobacconists
.... *here is Duke street* ....
31   *Griffin tavern,* Isaac Smith Manley
.... *here is York place* ....
32   Thorpe William, tobacconist
33   Merritt William, ham & beef dealer
34   Challice William, chemist & druggist

VILLIERS STREET

1905

Villiers street, 31 *Strand.* (W.C.)
(WESTMINSTER).
1 Bird Brothers, card printers
1 *Charing Cross Hotel Shades*
10 Chaplin W. H. & Co. Ltd. wine merchants
 Gatti Carlo, café restaurant
 Gatti Carlo, music hall (Railway arches)
 Farmer & Co. newagents
 THE FACADE:—
 7 Riley Tom, tattooist
 6 *Incandescent Novelty Co*
 5 Beaurain Thos. James, fruiterer
 4 Spiegel George, tobacconist
 3 Infanti Antonio, confectioner
 2A, Durrant Frank, bird dealer
 2 Moore Frank, postage stamp dealer
 1B, Khan Sardar, photo dealer
 1 Howell William & Son, booksellers
 FIRE ALARM & PILLAR
 LETTER BOX
 ———
16 Villiers Edwin, photo dealer
19 Gordon Angus Stafford, wine dealer
19A, Landaw John, tobacconist
19 Serre Achille, dyer
19 Roberts Lewis, photo dealer
19 Guderley & Kay, hairdressers
20 Bennett Richard James, verger
 St. Martin's-in-the-Fields
21 Ullmann Maximilian, oyster rooms
22 Stevens R. & Sons, billiard table makers
23 Atrill Henry Ernest, dining rooms
24 *Princess of Wales*, Mrs. Elizabeth Baker
25 *Buckingham hotel*, Pietro Macario
26 & 27 Faulkner Jonathan H. hairdresser
 Faulkner's hotel
27A, Metali Giovanni, confectioner
28A, Osborn Walter, hosier
29 Salmon & Gluckstein Ltd. tobacconists
 . . . . *here is Duke street* . . . .
31 *Griffin tavern*, Isaac Smith Manley
 . . . . *here is York place* . . . .
32 Lyons J. & Co. Ltd. café
33 Merritt William, ham & beef dealer
34 Challice William, chemist & druggist

1910

Villiers street, 31 *Strand.* (W.C.)
(WESTMINSTER).
London Underground Electric Railways
 (Charing Cross Station)
1 *Charing Cross Hotel Shades*
10 Chaplin W. H. & Co. Ltd. wine merchants
 Gatti Carlo, café restaurant
 Gatti Carlo, billiard saloon
 Arena Ltd
 THE FACADE:—
 8 Barr Henry William, automatic
 machine proprietor
 6 Spurgin Bros. jewellers
 5 Beaurain Thos. James, fruiterer
 4 Spiegel George, tobacconist
 3 Arpino Luigi & Sons, confectioners
 2A, Durrant Frank, bird dealer
 2 Dawson John, bookseller
 1 & 2 Howell William & Son, booksellers
16 Villiers Edwin, photo dealer
19 Gordon Angus Stafford, wine dealer
19A, Landaw John, tobacconist
19 Serre Achille Ltd. dyers
19 Roberts Lewis, photo dealer
20 Wehner Joseph, hairdresser
20 Nathan Samuel, jeweller
21 Ullmann Maximilian, oyster rooms
21 *London County Council, Local
 Pension Committee*
22 Stevens R. & Sons, billiard table makers
23 Atrill Henry Ernest, dining rooms
24 *Princess of Wales*, Mrs. E. Baker
25 *Buckingham hotel*, Pietro Macario
26 & 27 Faulkner Jonathan H. hairdresser
 Faulkner's hotel
27A, Metali Giovanni, confectioner
28 Leonard Charles. coffee rooms
28A, Osborn Walter, hosier
29 Salmon & Gluckstein Ltd. tobacconists
 . . . . *here is Duke street* . . . .
31 *Griffin tavern*, Baker & Co
 . . . . *here is York place* . . . .
32 Lyons J. & Co. Ltd. café
33 Merritt William, ham & beef dealer
34 Challice William, chemist & druggist

1915

Villiers street, 32 *Strand.* (W.C.)
(WESTMINSTER).
 WEST SIDE
Charing Cross, Euston & Hampstead Railway,
 Charing Cross (Strand) station
1 *Charing Cross Hotel Shades*
10 *British Café Co*
 Gatti Carlo, café restaurant
 Gatti Carlo, billiard saloon
 Arena Ltd
 THE FACADE:—
 8 Necchi & Terroni, confectioners
 6 Spurgin Bros. jewellers
 5 Beaurain Thos. James, fruiterer
 4 Spiegel Brothers, tobacconists
 3 Arpino Luigi & Sons, confectioners
 2A, Clements Arthur, fancy goods dealer
 2 Dawson John, bookseller
 1 Howell William & Son, booksellers
 1A, Fuller's Ltd. confectioners
 EAST SIDE
16 Villiers Edwin, bookseller
19 Gordon Angus Stafford, wine retailer
19A, Landaw John, tobacconist
19 Serre Achille Ltd. dyers
19 Roberts Lewis & Co. photo dealers
20 Wehner Joseph, hairdresser
20 Larby John, bookseller
21 Terroni Georgio, confectioner
22 Stevens R. & Sons, billiard table makers
23 Atrill Henry Ernest, dining rooms
24 *Princess of Wales*, Mrs. E. Baker
25 *Buckingham hotel*, August Grissi
26 & 27 Faulkner Jonathan H. hairdresser
 Faulkner's hotel
27A, Metali Giovanni, confectioner
28 Terrfoni Peter, coffee rooms
28A, Osborn Walter, hosier
29 Salmon & Gluckstein Ltd. tobacconists
 . . . . *here is Duke street* . . . .
31 *Griffin tavern*, Baker & Co
 . . . . *here is York place* . . . .
32 Lyons J. & Co. Ltd. café
33 Merritt William, ham & beef dealer
34 Challice William, chemist & druggist

1920

Villiers street, 32 *Strand.* (W.C.2)
(WESTMINSTER).
 WEST SIDE
Charing Cross, Euston & Hampstead Railway,
 Strand station
1 *Charing Cross Hotel Shades*
10 Baker & Co. café
 Baker & Co. café restaurant
 Baker & Co. billiard saloon
 Baker & Co. cinematograph theatre
 THE FACADE:—
 8 Ferrari Luigi, confectioner
 7 Olivers, naval & military
 badge dealers
 6 Spurgin Solomon. jeweller
 5 Beaurain Thos. James, fruiterer
 4 Spiegel Brothers, tobacconists
 2A, Clements Arthur, fancy goods dealer
 2 Dawson John, bookseller
 1 Howell William & Son, booksellers
 1A, Fuller's Ltd. confectioners
 EAST SIDE
16 Villiers Edwin, bookseller
19 Gordon Angus Stafford, wine retailer
19A, Landaw John, tobacconist
19 Serre Achille Ltd. dyers
19 Roberts Lewis & Co. photo dealers
20 Nathan John, hairdresser
20 Larby John, bookseller
21 Terroni Peter, confectioner
22 Stevens R. & Sons, billiard table makers
23 Courtnay Charles, dining rooms
24 *Princess of Wales*, Mrs. E. Baker
25 *Hôtel de France*, Jules Denut
26 & 27 Faulkner Jonathan H. hairdresser
27A, Lazzeri Luigi, confectioner
28 Terroni Peter, coffee rooms
28A, Osborn Walter, hosier
29 Salmon & Gluckstein Ltd. tobacconists
 . . . . *here is Duke street* . . . .
31 *Griffin tavern*, Knowland Bros
 . . . . *here is York place* . . . .
32 Lyons J. & Co. Ltd. café
33 Merritt Ltd. ham & beef dealers
34 Challice William, chemist & druggist

VILLIERS STREET

1925

Villiers street, 32 *Strand.* (W.C.2) (WESTMINSTER).
WEST SIDE
Charing Cross, Euston & Hampstead Railway, Strand station
    Morden George, tobacconist
1 *Charing Cross Hotel Shades*
    Millett J. M. & Sons, government contractors (The Arches)
    Baker & Co. café restaurant
    Baker & Co. billiard saloon
    THE FACADE:—
8 Ferrari & Giovanni, confectioners
    Charing Cross Garage, motor engineers
    Miller Jack, tobacconist
7 Olivers, naval & military badge dealers
6 Spurgin Solomon. jeweller
5 Beaurain Thos. James, fruiterer
4 Field Ronald, postage stamp dealer
4 Spiegel Brothers, tobacconists
2A, Clements Arthur, fancy goods dealer
2 Dawson John, bookseller
1 Howell William & Son, booksellers
1A, Fuller's Ltd. confectioners
    EAST SIDE
16 Villiers Edwin, bookseller
19 Gordon Angus Stafford, wine retailer
19A, Landaw John, tobacconist
19 EMBANKMENT CHAMBERS:—
    Myer Mrs. Helena, restaurant
    Smith Arthur Croxton, journalist
    Davis & Freedman, financiers
    Ward Bros. cigar importers
    Firbrine Sales Ltd. leather preservative manufacturers
    Desmond Mrs. Hannah, general agt
19 Serre Achille Ltd. dyers
19 Roberts Lewis & Co. photo dealers
20 Nathan John, hairdresser
20A, Daniells Mrs. Polly, confectioner
21 James & Co. estate agents
21 *Grey Manufacturing Co. Ltd.* patent medicine proprietors
21 Terroni Georgio, confectioner
22 Stevens R.&Sons, billiard table makers
24 *Princess of Wales,* Edward Balden
25 *Hôtel de France,* Jules Denut
26 & 27 Faulkner Jonathan H. hairdresser
27A, Cenci Anecieto, dining rooms
28 Terroni Peter, coffee rooms
28A, Osborn Walter, hosier
29 Salmon & Gluckstein Ltd. tobacconists
.... *here is Duke street* ....
31 *Griffin tavern,* Knowland Bros
.... *here is York place* ....
32 Lyons J. & Co. Ltd. café
33 Merritt Ltd. ham & beef dealers
34 Challice William, chemist & druggist

1930

Villiers street, 32 *Strand. to Embankment pl.* (W.C.2) (WESTMINSTER).
WEST SIDE
Charing Cross, Euston & Hampstead Railway, Strand station
    Morden George, tobacconist
2 *Charing Cross Hotel Shades*
    Baker & Medcalf, caterers
12 Thomas Transport Co. Ltd
14 Serre Achille Ltd. dyers & cleaners
16 West End Watch Co. (London)
18 Baker & Medcalf, billiard saloon
    Gate Theatre Studio
    Forum (The), cinematograph theatre
32 Ferrari & Giovanni, confectioners
    Charing Cross Garages Ltd motor engineers
34 Miller Jack, tobacconist
38 Olivers, naval & military badge dealers
40 Spurgin Solomon, jeweller
42 Beaurain Thos. James, fruiterer
44 Spiegel Brothers, tobacconists
46 Reynolds Edgar, postage stamp dealer
    EAST SIDE
3 Challice William, chemist & druggist
5 Merritt Ltd. ham & beef dealers
7 Lyons J. & Co. Ltd. café
.... *here is York place* ....
9 & 11 *Griffin tavern,* Knowland Bros
.... *here is Duke street* ....
13 Salmon & Gluckstein Ltd. tobacconists
15 Osborn Walter, hosier
17 Terroni Peter, coffee rooms
19 Cenci Anecieto, dining rooms
21 & 23 Faulkner Jonathan H. hairdresser
25 Mazzina J. restaurant
27 *Princess of Wales,* Baker & Medcalf
31 Stevens R. & Sons, billiard table makers
33 Guildhall Typewriter Co. Ltd
33 Harley Instrument Co. Ltd. electro medical apparatus supplies
33 Walsh Joseph M. electric sign manufctr
33 Terroni Peter, confectioner
35 Thomas Transport Co. Ltd. gramophone dealers
37 Nathan John, hairdresser
39 Hygienic Stores Ltd drug stores
41 Woodfall Rupert, optician
43 EMBANKMENT CHAMBERS:—
    Ennor Mrs. Violet & Ternouth Miss Madge, restaurant
    London & Counties Carriage Co. Ltd
    Smith Arthur Croxton, journalist
    Smith Alex. James, M.I.Struct.E. constructional engineer
    Homan & Rogers, fireproof floors
    Porter John Brooks, constructional engineer
    Pattinson & Sergeant, type-writing office
    Turf Association
45 Baker Albert & Co. (1828) Ltd. tobacconists
47 Gordon Angus Stafford, wine retailer
49 Villiers Edwin, bookseller

1935

Villiers street, 32 *Strand. to Embankment pl.* (W.C.2) (WESTMINSTER).
WEST SIDE
STRAND UNDERGROUND STATION
    Baker Albert & Co. (1828) Ltd. tobacconists
2 *Charing Cross Hotel Shades*
    Baker & Medcalf, caterers
12 Beresford Radio Co. wireless supplies dealers
14 Serre Achille Ltd. dyers & cleaners
16 Samuel Watch Co. (1930) London, jewellers
16B, King, Son & Co. gun makers
18 Baker & Medcalf, billiard saloon
    Gate Theatre Studio
    Forum (The), cinematograph theatre
32 Zucconi Dominico, confectioner
    Charing Cross Garages Ltd motor engineers
34 Miller John Gordon Ltd. tobacconists
38 Olivers, naval & military badge dealers
42 Phillips David, fruiterer
44 Ovens Edgar, tobacconist
46 Reynolds Edgar, postage stamp dealer
    EAST SIDE
3 Challice Wm. Ltd. chemists & druggists
5 Merritt Ltd. ham & beef dealers
.... *here is York place* ....
9 & 11 *Griffin tavern,* Knowland Bros
.... *here is Duke street* ....
13 Salmon & Gluckstein Ltd. tobacconists
15 Osborn Walter, hosier
17 Morelli Domenico, refreshment rooms
19 Ward's Surgical Stores, surgical appliance makers
21 & 23 Faulkner Jonathan H. hairdresser
25 Davis Estates Ltd
27 *Princess of Wales,* Baker & Medcalf
29 Giacopazzi A. S. & E. refreshment rooms
31 Stevens R. & Sons, billiard table makers
33 Giacopazzi Pietro, confectioner
35 Thomas Transport Co. Ltd. motor coach proprietors
37 Nathan John, hairdresser
39 Hygienic Stores Ltd. surgical rubber goods
41 Woodfall Rupert, optician
43 EMBANKMENT CHAMBERS:—
    Punch & Judy bookshop
    Ennor Mrs. Violet & Ternouth Miss Madge, restaurant
    Crafer Studios, commercial artists
    Smith Arthur Croxton, journalist
    Byrne Ernest Corbett, surveyor
    Applanat Albert, import merchant
    Mikhail K. & Co. Ltd. merchants
45 Baker Albert & Co. (1828) Ltd. tobacconists
47 Gordon Angus Stafford, wine retailer
49 Villiers Edwin, bookseller

1936

Villiers street, 32 *Strand. to Embankment pl.* (W.C.2) (WESTMINSTER).
WEST SIDE
STRAND UNDERGROUND STATION
    Baker Albert & Co. (1828) Ltd. tobacconists
2 *Charing Cross Hotel Shades*
    Baker & Medcalf, caterers
12 Premier Shoe Repairing Service Co. Ltd
14 Serre Achille Ltd. dyers & cleaners
16 Samuel Watch Co. (1930) London, jewellers
18 Baker & Medcalf, billiard saloon
    Gate Theatre Studio
    Forum (The), cinematograph theatre
32 Zucconi Dominico, confectioners
    Charing Cross Garages Ltd motor engineers
34 Miller John Gordon Ltd. tobacconists
38 Olivers, naval & military badge dealers
40 Gray Gwen, milliner
42 Carter Walter, fruiterer
44 Ovens Edgar, tobacconist
46 Reynolds Edgar, postage stamp dealer
    EAST SIDE
3 Challice Wm. Ltd. chemists & druggists
5 Merritt Ltd. ham & beef dealers
.... *here is York place* ....
9 & 11 *Griffin tavern,* Knowland Bros
.... *here is Duke street* ....
13 Salmon & Gluckstein Ltd. tobacconists
15 Osborn Walter, hosier
17 Morelli Domenico, refreshment rooms
19 Ward's Surgical Stores, surgical appliance makers
21 & 23 Faulkner Jonathan H. hairdresser
25 Davis Estates Ltd
27 *Princess of Wales,* Baker & Medcalf
29 Giacopazzi A. S. & E. refreshment rooms
31 Stevens R. & Sons, billiard table makers
33 Giacopazzi Pietro, confectioner
35 Thomas Transport Co. Ltd. motor coach proprietors
37 Nathan John, hairdresser
39 Hygienic Stores Ltd. surgical rubber goods
41 Woodfall Rupert, optician
43 EMBANKMENT CHAMBERS:—
    Ennor Mrs. Violet & Ternouth Miss Madge, restaurant
    Crafer Studios, commercial artists
    Smith Arthur Croxton, journalist
    Byrne Ernest Corbett, surveyor
    Applanat Albert, import merchant
47 Gordon Angus Stafford, wine retailer
49 Villiers Edwin, bookseller

MINOR STEETS, ADELPHI WHARVES and the STRAND
at the intersection with Durham St/Durham House St

Some indication of the changing directory treatment of the small streets and of the Adelphi wharves and Arches seemed appropriate. However space limitations precluded the more detailed five-yearly coverage given to the main Adelphi area streets. As a compromise the increased interval of 30 years in the coverage here allows a broad indication of the changes over the period of the survey. Should more information be required the major London reference libraries (e.g., Bishopsgate Institute, Guildhall, London Metropolitan Archives, and the City of Westminster Archives Centre) provide excellent resources.

STRAND

1841

Strand,
SOUTH SIDE.
62 Weiss J. & Son,
    surgeons'inst.makers &c
63 Minier, Adams & Nash, seedsmen
64 Harvey & Co. goldsmiths &
    watchmakers
64 Grayhurst & Co. goldsm. &
    watchmak'rs
. . . . *Durham street.* . . . .
64 EASTERN WHARF
    Dew William, coal merchant
    Thomas Robert, egg merchant
    Leslie R. Baker, coal merchant
    Tomlinson & Chatley,
    boat builders
65 Millidge William, glass & china
    dealer
67 Beck, Henderson & Co. seedsmen

1870

Strand. (W.C.)
SOUTH SIDE.
62 Weiss J. & Son, surgeons' inst.
    makers
63 Browning John, optician
64 Steer William, trunk maker
. . . . . . *here is Durham street* . . . . . .
65 Joy James, shirt maker
66 & 406 Steward James Henry,
    optician
67 Jackson William Walter,
    commission agt.
67 Pelton Frederick, tailor
67 Herbert & Co. patent agents
67 *Englische Correspondenz,*
    Dr. Max Schlesinger, proprietor
67 Hadden Herbert John, civil engineer
67 Harris Edmund, auctioneer & c,
67 Briggs Frederick, solicitor

1900

Strand. (W.C.)
SOUTH SIDE.
62 & 425 *East Riding Bread Co.*
62 *Society for the Abolition of
    Vivisection*
62 Dougal & Co. unclaimed money
    registry
62 Capper Alfred, musical agent
62 Claxton Miss Adelaide, artist
62 Claxton Miss Adelaide, patent ear
    cap & "Claxton" classical corset
62 Heyes, Cotton & Co. Limited,
    carting contractors
63 Browning John, optician
64 Crabb & Parry, tailors
. . . . *here is Durham street
    leading to William Street* . . . .
65 to 70½ Tivoli (The New) Limited
65 to 70½ Tivoli Theatre of Varieties

1930

Strand (W.C. 2) (WESTMINSTER),
*Northumberland avenue &
Trafalgar square to Fleet street*
SOUTH SIDE.
62 Jacobson Albert & Co. trunk
    makers
62 Hays Afred Ltd. music publishers
63 & 64 Burton Montague Ltd. tailors
63 & 64 Gibbs & Cywan, ladies
hairdressers
. . . . *here is Durham house street,
    leading to Adelphi arches* . . . .
P.D.Q. Co. photographic developers
    (Adelphi arches)
Commercial Camera Repairing Co.
    (Adelphi arches)
Read Leonard T. sign writer
    (Adelphi arches)
Hatch, Mansfield & Co. Lim.
    wine merchants (Adelphi arches)
King William & Sons, gas fitters
    (Adelphi arches)
Tivoli, cinematograph theatre
Tivoli Palace Ltd

DURHAM ST

1841

Durham street, 64 *Strand*
1 *Salisbury Arms,* Samuel Searle
2 Pearce William, goldsmith &
   jeweller
   ADELPHI WHARF.
   Thompson Robert, egg merchant

1870

Durham st. 64 *Strand* (W.C.)
1 Brophy John, builder
3 & 4 *Salisbury Arms,* Ellis Dunrich

1900

There is no entry for Durham street in 1900 and 1905. In c.1905 Durham street as far as the vaults, together with William street and James street, was renamed Durham House street

1930

Durham house street, *Adelphi* (W.C. 2)
(WESTMINSTER),
64 *Strand* to 16 *John st.*
Godfree (E.), Felton & Co.
wine merchants

JAMES ST

1841

James street, *Adelphi,* 14 *John st.*
1 Cam William, esq
1 Hill Thomas, esq
1 Loudensack & Case, navy agents
1 Underwood George, medical agent
1 Woodhead Joseph, navy agent
2 Bolton Charles, esq
2 Bryant Alexander, esq
2 Fairfax Captain James
2 Wilkinson John, esq

1870

James st. *Adelphi,* 14 *John st.*(W.C.)
(No thoroughfare)
1 Case & Loudensack, navy agents
1 Granger Benjamin, solicitor
1 *Free Labour Registration Society,*
   John Mallard, sec
2 Potter Henry Johnson, esq
   Gardner & Sons, lamp makers
2 Heale Robert Watkins

1900

James st. Adelphi, (W.C.)
11 *John street to William street*
2 Bradley James John
2 Holmes Charles Edward

Absorbed into Durham House street in
c. 1905

MINOR STEETS, ADELPHI WHARVES and the STRAND
at the intersection with Durham St/Durham House St

WILLIAM ST

A street heading for William street occurs once only, in 1900. There are occasional references to William street in directory headings to other streets and in street intersection information.

1900

William st. entered from 64 Strand **(W.C.)**
Martin P. & Co. advertising contractor

Absorbed into Durham House street in c. 1905

GEORGE CT

1841

George court, 50 *Strand*
George, John Gale

1870

George ct. 50 *Strand.***(W.C.)**
1   Masters Robert, greengrocer
    George, John Augustus Margot
4   Willocks William, carpenter
5   Lawrence John, locksmith

1900

George ct. 50 *Strand.***(W.C.)**
1   Barry Charles, chandler's shop
3   Comben Mrs. Julia, tailoress
    George, James Fergusson
    Symmons James, greengrocer

1930

George ct. 50 *Strand.***(W.C..2)**
    (WESTMINSTER)
1   Faulkner Charles Joseph, chandler's shop
2   Edwards John Walter, greengrocer
    George, William George Simmonds

YORK PLACE

The first occurrence of a directory heading for York Place (within the five-year interval pattern of years adopted for this survey) was found in 1880.

1900

York pl. *Adelphi* **(W.C.),**
    32 Villiers street, Strand.
4   May Stephen Henry, chandler's shop
5   Sayers & Jones, electricians
6   Howes Mrs. Jane, coffee rooms
7   Simpson George William, tailor
7   Doe John, jun. chimney sweeper
12 Dodson George Robert, coffee rooms
13 Bartlett Charles Edward, greengrocer

1930

York place, *Adelphi* **(W.C.2)**
    (WESTMINSTER),
    32 Villiers street, Strand
5   Shepperd Frederick, fishmonger
6   Hampton Henry Daniel, coffee rooms
7   Simpson Frederick, haberdasher
7   Doe John, jun. chimney sweeper
8   Burgess S. lace paper maker
9   Gaynor William, boot & shoe maker
13 *British Central Window Cleaning Co*

ADELPHI WHARVES

The first and last occurrences of a directory heading for the Adelphi wharves (within the five-year interval pattern of years adopted for this survey) are in 1855 and 1890 respectively. Some indications to Adelphi Wharves and to Adelphi Arches and vaults occur under STRAND, DURHAM STREET (later DURHAM HOUSE STREET) and YORK BUILDINGS

1870

Adelphi wharfs (W.C.),
    South side of Strand
    EASTERN WHARF
    MIDDLE WHARF
Jones Joseph, cod liver oil manufacturer
    WESTERN WHARF
Rutley & Silverlock, seed merchants
Hensman Frederick, coal merchant

Commentary

There is, inevitably, some duplication in references to Adelphi area occupants between this commentary and the main text of the book, but it is hoped that this will not seem excessive. The form of specific references to entries in the directory extracts, which it is hoped are self-explanatory, is shown in the following examples:

[John st.1850]   [York bdgs.1860,65]   [Ad.ter. 1935]

Both the main text of the book and the details given in this survey show that there were considerable numbers of distinguished occupants of the Adelphi area throughout its history.

The first ten years or so covered by the survey were remarkable. This was perhaps one of the more significant periods in the transition from the old to the modern world. Rowland Hill, later knighted, appears in the first year of the survey [Ad.ter. 1836]. He was notable for the introduction of the 'penny post', using pre-paid adhesive stamps, in 1840. The firm of Bramah, Fox & Co., engineers and machinists, appears in 1841 [John st.1841]. This was formed by the partnership of the young and exceedingly able Charles Fox with John Joseph Bramah, thought to be a grandson of Joseph Bramah, one of the prominent figures of the Industrial Revolution and a member of the Society of Arts, who died in 1814. When the Bramah connection ended in 1845, Fox, later knighted, continued the firm, which had works in London, Smethwick and Renfrew, in partnership with John Henderson – who had become a partner in 1841, as Fox, Henderson & Co. Under that name it constructed the Crystal Palace for the Great Exhibition in 1851 in which, from the catalogue, a fair sprinkling of Adelphi occupants had exhibits in the machinery or civil engineering sections. The first steel cables were introduced in 1839 – of great value in deep mining. The electric telegraph was coming into use. The first submarine cable was laid across the Straight of Dover in 1845, the year of the maiden voyage across the Atlantic of *Great Britain*, the archetypal 'modern' metal-hulled ship with screw propulsion, and also the year when the first reliable Portland cement was produced. The phenomenon known as the 'Railway Mania' reached its height in 1846 – the 1845 directory entries shown here do not reflect this, but those following shortly might, with some companies having improbable titles. The pre-eminent railway engineers Joseph Locke and J.U. Rastrick were occupants. Locke [Adam st. 1841, 50; Ad.ter. 1845] was the engineer for the Grand Junction Railway connecting the Liverpool and Manchester Railway with Birmingham, and hence with London, and also for the London and Southampton Railway and the line going northwards from the Liverpool and Manchester connection to Carlisle and Scotland – over the famous Shap summit. He was a pupil of George Stephenson and, on his death in 1860, was described by *The Times* as 'completing the Triumvirate of the engineering world' – with I.K. Brunel and Robert Stephenson. John Rastrick – at 1 Robert St. in 1846 – was a leading advocate of steam locomotion and was one of the adjudicators at the Rainhill trials on the Liverpool and Manchester Railway in 1829, won by Robert Stephenson's *Rocket*. Among his achievements was the construction of the London to Brighton railway line which includes the impressive Balcombe Viaduct (1841) over the river Ouse near Haywards Heath. He was also responsible for the equally impressive London Road Viaduct (1846) at Brighton on the later line from Brighton to Lewes. There was also William Bridges Adams [Adam st.1845, 50, 55, 60], co-inventor of the railway line fish-plate joint which has remained of significance into modern times. Francis Whishaw, Secretary of the Society of Arts [John st.1845] deserves mention as author of the authoritative *The Railways of Great Britain and Ireland* published in 1842 and now regarded as a primary source by transport historians. His successor as Secretary of the Society of Arts, John Scott Russell [**John st.1850**], had a major part in the design and construction of Brunel's *Great Eastern*. Other notable people from that early heroic period of the railways include Thomas Brassey [**Adam st.1850**], the railway contractor who was responsible for the construction of one sixth of the British railway network, and John Cooke Bourne [**Buck.st.1845**] [**York bdgs.1860, 65**], the lithographer whose depiction of the construction of the Great Western Railway and of the London and Birmingham Railway is celebrated both as great art and as a valuable engineering record. There is also Thomas Russell Crampton [**Buck.st.1850**] who designed a highly individualistic style of steam locomotive having a large boiler and a low centre of gravity, which had a limited vogue in Great Britain, but which were used much more widely in France, Germany and Belgium, so much so that the colloquial French for "taking the train" was "prendre le Crampton". Crampton was responsible for laying the first international submarine cable to which reference is made above. He was a founder member of the Institution of Mechanical Engineers in 1847, the second Chartered Engineering Institution of which the Institution of Civil Engineers – which received its Royal Charter in 1828 – was the first. D.K. Clark [**Adam st.1860, 65,70; Buck.st.1875, 80, 85, 90**] was author, in 1855, of the celebrated large two-volume *Railway Machinery*, then the most comprehensive treatise on all aspects of railway locomotives, rolling stock and operating equipment. Another distinguished engineer in this period was the German Karl Wilhelm (William Charles) Siemens [**John st.1855**], manager in England of the German-based firm of Siemens Brothers. He became a British citizen, a Fellow of the Royal Society and was knighted. He was responsible for significant advances in electrical engineering and telegraphy, but perhaps his greatest achievement was the development of the open-hearth regenerative steel furnace which became the most widely used in the world.

In the same early period of the survey there were a number of short-distance river transport firms using steam power, as indicated by: *London and Westminster Steam Boat Co.*[**Vill.st.1841, Duke st. 1865**]; *Watermen's Steam Co.* [**Geo.st.,Adelphi pier1845**]; *Ant & Bee Steam Boat Co.* [**Strand , Middle Wharf Adelphi 1850**] and *Sons of the Thames Packet Co.* [**York bdgs.1855**].

This commentary may appear to place undue emphasis on the earlier years of the survey. This is difficult to avoid as there was such vibrant national development at that time. However names of notable individuals, companies and organisations continued to feature throughout the hundred year period. Further investigation of the entries for engineers would be rewarding, though requiring some dedication. The density of occupation by solicitors and architects was noticeably high throughout. Reference material on architects is perhaps the most readily accessible, through the achievements of the late Sir Nikolaus Pevsner and his successors in the *Buildings of England* series. Also, for our period, there are rich pickings in the short dictionary of architects published in: Dixon and Muthesius *Victorian Architecture* in the Thames and Hudson World of Art Library (1978). Some 320 architects were found in the street lists between 1836 and 1900, a number of which were, or became, of national significance. Twenty-three of these appear in the Dixon and Muthesius dictionary and twenty-seven in the 1973 (third edition) of Pevsner's *The Cities of London and Westminster*. No doubt many more references could be found within the country-wide coverage of the Pevsner series. Among the more notable names are: John Francis Bentley [**John st.1870, 75, 80, 85, 90, 95, 1900**] (Westminster Cathedral); (Sir) Arthur Blomfield [**Ad.ter.1865**]; William Burges [**Buck. st.1865, 70, 75, 80,**]; William Butterfield [**Adam st.1865, 70, 75, 80, 85, 90**]; Basil Champneys [**Buck. st.1885, 90, 95. 1900**] (who designed the Fawcett Memorial, in the Victoria Gardens, mentioned in the main text); Owen Jones [John st.1841] and (Sir) Aston Webb [Duke st.1875, 80], then a young man – he later designed the Admiralty Arch and the eastern facade of Buckingham palace.

Some of the more significant organisations found in the directory extracts include: *British Association for the Advancement of Science* [Duke st.1845]; *Royal National Institution for the Preservation of Life from Shipwreck* [John st.1860, 65, 70, 75, 80, 85, 90, 95, 1900]; *Institution of Naval Architects* [Ad.ter.1865, 70, 80, 85, 90, 95, 1900, 05, 10, 15, 20, 25] [Adam st.1935]; *Society for the Protection of Ancient Buildings* [Buck. st.1880, 85, 90, 95, 1900, 05]; *Froebel Society* and *National Froebel Institute* [Buck. st.1890]; *Cabmen's Shelter Fund* [Buck. st.1910] (a very human cause); *Aeronautical Society of Great Britain* [Adam st.1915] (this became the *Royal Aeronautical Society* in 1918 and is the chartered body for aeronautical engineering); *International Woman Suffrage Alliance* [Adam st.1915, 20, 25] and the *National Radium Commission* [Ad.ter.1935] (this eventually became the *International Commission on Radiological Protection* whose task is to keep radiation protection recommendations under review). Also listed are the *Medical Research Council* [York bdgs. 1925], the *Royal Humane Society* [York bdgs. 1935, 36], the *National Society for Aid to the Sick and Wounded in War* (*British Red Cross Society*) [York bdgs. 1885, 90, 95, 1900, 05] and the *Amateur Athletic Association* [John St. 1905, 10, 15, 20, 25, 30, 35, 36].

Exhilarating thoughts about this generally staid and serious quarter could be stirred by *Thompson's Patent Gravity Switchback Railway Co. Ltd* [John St. 1890, 95, 1900, 05, 10, 15]. Co-existent in the Adelphi for a time, and of immense importance, were the ground-breaking *Marconi's Wireless Telegraph Co. Ltd* [York bdgs.1910] and the *Marconi International Marine Communications Co. Ltd* [York bdgs.1910].

The women's suffrage movement had a notable early success in Margaret Bondfield [Rob. st. 1925] who had became chairman of the Trades Union Congress in 1923 and, as Minister of Labour in 1929-31, was the first woman to be a British Cabinet Minister. The street lists include the Strand at the intersection with Durham St./Durham House St. A few properties in the Strand to either side of the intersection are included, thus bringing in the *Tivoli Theatre of Varieties* mentioned in the main text of the book. The proximity of theatre land is reflected in names throughout the survey. Mrs. Paul Robeson was a late occupant [Buck. st.1935, 36]. Artists abounded as the main text indicates: Arthur Rackham, the book illustrator and water colourist [Buck. st.1895], was another.

References

In addition to *Victorian Architecture* by Dixon and Muthesius, the Pevsner series on the *Buildings of England* and the topographical material already listed, the following have been useful:

Atkins P.J. *The Directories of London*, 1677-1977 (1990)

Jackson Peter (ed) *John Tallis's London Street Views (1838 - 1840)* (1969) (London Topographical Society Publication no.110) (illustrating the elevations of the buildings facing the Strand in the earlier part of the survey period)

Marshall John *A Biographical Dictionary of Railway Engineers* (1978)

Parry Melanie (ed) *Chambers Biographical Dictionary* (6th edition, 1997)

Simmons Jack and Biddle Gordon (eds) *The Oxford Companion to British Railway History* (1997)

Weinreb Ben and Hibbert Christopher (ed) *The London Encyclopaedia* (1983)

APPENDIX V

The Adelphi Idler

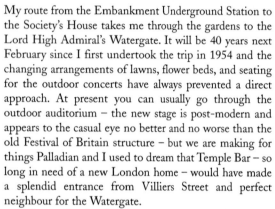

From the RSA Journal CXLII, November 1993, p825
Illustration: Quentin Blake

My route from the Embankment Underground Station to the Society's House takes me through the gardens to the Lord High Admiral's Watergate. It will be 40 years next February since I first undertook the trip in 1954 and the changing arrangements of lawns, flower beds, and seating for the outdoor concerts have always prevented a direct approach. At present you can usually go through the outdoor auditorium – the new stage is post-modern and appears to the casual eye no better and no worse than the old Festival of Britain structure – but we are making for things Palladian and I used to dream that Temple Bar – so long in need of a new London home – would have made a splendid entrance from Villiers Street and perfect neighbour for the Watergate.

The tree lined walk behind the Gate is still much as it appeared when it fronted the river in the 18th century, though it has lost some of its grass to unsightly tarmac in recent years. The eastern end takes you up to York Buildings and there you climb towards John Adam Street, blessing Sichel on your left for preserving one of the old doorways and thinking of Dickens's 'Dark Arches' as you pass the sign to Lower Robert Street on your right. A revived 'Durham House' (not to be confused with the once adjacent medieval Bishop's Palace), early 1900s red brick with a vaguely Queen Anne feeling, faces you as you turn into John Adam Street and the bland lines of the 'Little Adelphi' (post war economy Adam) lead your eyes towards your objective, the Society's house at the angle made familiar in the Malton print – and then suddenly there it is! 'The Large Adelphi', as it ought to be called. 'The huge bully of a building' which to the Society's consternation became its neighbour in the late 1930s and which I used to hope in the 1950s might one day be demolished to make way for a Lincoln Center style Piazza in which the Society's House would have had a river view, has actually grown in height during the past year (rather elegantly one has to admit thanks to C. Hyde's design), so let us get to the Society's front door as quickly as we can.

I always enjoy looking at the porch. Summerson tells us that Adam copied it from the Tower of the Winds at Athens, but I feel anxious when I remember that it is made of wood and am glad to see that it is kept repainted. The neo-classical doorknockers with their heads of Mercury were presented by a member in 1815. I think of Marley's ghost and enter.

Usually there is some function in progress at the Society so one is grateful for Arthur Bolton's imaginative enlargement of the entrance hall in 1922. How did they manage in earlier times? Was it the sort of scramble Rowlandson depicts in his 'Staircase at the Royal Academy?' The four columns with gold capitals and painted scagiola shafts are Bolton not Adam, though they use the same order you can see outside on the porch. Bolton's columns replaced the original dividing walls which had separated the once much smaller central entrance hall from a staircase hall on your left and, to the right, a parlour for a resident officer of the Society known as the Register, who had a special responsibility for the Society's collection of models and machines.

Today we can pass through this parlour with the ease of spectres and enter another, that of the Georgian and early Victorian Secretaries, who had their own front door and used most of No.6 John Adam Street as their private residences. Now, as the old inventories have it, down 'one flight of stairs' and we find ourselves in the Gerard Bar, once I would imagine the Secretary's Breakfast Room, where a fine old iron chimney grate reminds us of things past and the well planned and well stocked servery, occupying the corner of the Register's private kitchen, promises sustenance. A final warning: Samuel More, Secretary 1770-99, was a martyr to gout.

D. G. C. ALLAN
Historical Adviser to the RSA

Index

GORDON'S WINE BAR

47 Villiers Street, Strand, WC2N 6NE
Tel: 020 7930 1408

In a backwater not two minutes from CharingCross, lies a small, unobtrusive Wine bar, which until the present day has traded with Royal Sanctions as a Free Vintner. In the year 1364 King Edward III granted Royal Letters Patent to the Mistery of the Vintners. As a result these worthy merchants were allowed to open premises and sell wine without applying for a licence – this privilege being maintained by the previous owners for the last three generations.

The current owner, Mr Luis Gordon (whose family has spent two hundred years in the Wine Trade) is a fully licensed purveyor of Wine. The bar has been rescued from modern day development and preserved by Mr Gordon in order to sell wine in the manner and surroundings of our forefathers.

The house itself has many interesting associatons in the literary and theatrical field, in the room overhead Rudyard Kipling wrote 'The Light That Failed' and both he and Chesterton wrote some of their works in the little parlour of the Wine Bar. Opposite stands the Player's Theatre and the Bar was patronised by many of the Players (including Vivien Leigh and Sir Laurence Olivier).

One can still sit in the same secluded atmosphere and enjoy the fine wines of France, Spain, Italy and many other Countries of the World. Our food is famous for its flavour, selection and generosity as recommended in all the good food guides, a special feature being the wonderful range of 'Help Yourself' salads.

ROYAL ADELPHI HOTEL

A comfortable, friendly hotel
right in the heart of London

21 Villiers Street
London WC2N 6ND

Tel: 020 7930 8764
Fax: 020 7930 8735
www.royaladelphi.co.uk
email: info@royaladelphi.co uk

RSA

The Royal Society for the encouragement of Arts, Manufactures & Commerce
Founded in 1754

Since its foundation in 1754 the RSA has encouraged new ideas. This has been reflected not only in its programme of work but also in its treatment and use of its house.

The expiry of a long lease on the vaults beneath the Society's house in the 1980's presented the Council with an opportunity to extend the building and bring the space into use as a banqueting and party venue. The skilful conversion by Sam Lloyd of both the subterranean vaults and tunnels and the refurbishment of some of the other large rooms formerly used as repositories, enabled a commercial enterprise to be established as a trading subsidiary.

The RSA now provides facilities and services to Fellows of the Society, its corporate supporters and other charitable and commercial users, With 2 theatres, 3 boardrooms as well as the Vaults the house offers many varied uses as a conference, party and wedding venue.

One of the most significant contributions of this evolution has been the 'opening up' of the house to a much wider audience, including both the public and architectural scholars. More than 50,000 visitors a year are able to enjoy and appreciate the fine Adam architecture along with the history and future development of the Society and its work.

8 JohnAdam Street, London WC2N 6EZ. Telephone 020 7930 5115 Fax 020 7839 5805
e-mail: general@rsa-uk.demon.co.uk www.rsa.org.uk
Charity registration number 212424

BENJAMIN FRANKLIN HOUSE

It is not surprising that Benjamin Franklin has been called 'the most remarkable American ever to live'. He helped shape an Age of Enlightenment celebrating reason, respect for humanity, and the ideals of political and economic liberalism, freedom, and democracy. He was the first US Ambassador; the father of electricity and America's first fire insurance company; subscription library, and modern postal system; and creator of one of the country's earliest hospitals (the Pennsylvania Hospital) and institutions of higher learning (the University of Pennsylvania).

Among the richest periods of his life, though least known, were his years in London when he made significant contributions to diplomacy, science, medicine, letters, music and more. The House on Craven Street in which he lived for nearly sixteen years between 1757 and 1775 still stands. Exciting plans are underway to create a dynamic museum and educational facility in the long-neglected , Grade I listed building. It is the most important Anglo-American heritage project on either side of the Atlantic, and was designated one of 'America's Treasures' by the Presidential Administration and the US National Trust for Historic Preservation.

To discover how you can help, please contact:

The Director, Benjamin Franklin House, 36 Craven Street, London WC2N 5NF
Telephone: 44 020 7930 9121 Facsimile: 44 020 7930 9124
BenjmainFranklinHouse@msn.com www.rsa.org.uk/franklin
The Friends of Benjamin Franklin House (UK), register charity no.276066
The Friends of Benjamin Franklin House (US), US non-profit tax free 50© (3) organization

A. H. BALDWIN & SONS LTD.

NUMISMATISTS

Established 1872

David Garrick in 1772
by L. Pingo and I. Kirk

Ancient, mediæval & modern coins, medals & numismatic books bought & sold

BALDWIN'S
AUCTIONS Limited

Catalogues available on request
Tel: 020 7930 9808
Auctions in London, New York, Hong Kong & Singapore

11 Adelphi Terrace, London WC2N 6BJ
Tel: 020 7930 6879 Fax: 020 7930 9450 E-Mail: coins@baldwin.sh